Another Country

Another Country

German Intellectuals, Unification and National Identity

Jan-Werner Müller

Yale University Press
New Haven and London

Designed by Adam Freudenheim
Set by Best-set Typesetter Ltd., Hong Kong
Printed in Great Britain

Library of Congress Cataloging-in-Publication Data
Müller, Jan-Werner, 1970–
    Another country : German intellectuals, unification and national identity /
Jan-Werner Müller.
        p.   cm.
    Includes bibliographical references and index.
    ISBN 0-300-08388-2 (alk. paper)
        1. Germany – Cultural policy.   2. Intellectuals – Germany – Political activity.
    3. Nationalism – Germany – History – 20th century.   4. Political culture –
Germany – History – 20th century.   I. Title.

    DD256.6 M85   2000
    943.087   dc21   00-031054

A catalogue record for this book is available from the British Library
10 9 8 7 6 5 4 3 2 1

ja wären's leute wie andere leute,
wär es ein ganz gewöhnliches, ein andres
als dieses nacht-und nebelland,
Von abwesenden überfüllt,
die wer sie sind nicht wissen noch wissen wollen,
die in dieses land geraten sind
auf der flucht vor diesem land
und werden flüchtig sein bis zur grube:

wärs anders, wär ihm zu helfen,
wäre rat und genugtuung hier,
wäre es nicht dieses brache, mundtote feindesland!

    Hans Magnus Enzensberger, *Landessprache*, 1960

yes, if they were people like other people,
were it a completely normal, a different
country than this one shrouded in fog and night,
overcrowded with absentees
who neither know who they are, nor want to know,
who happen to be in this country
fleeing from this country
and who will be on flight until their grave:

if it were different, one could help it,
there would be advice and satisfaction,
were it not this fallow, silenced country of enemies!

Contents

Acknowledgements

For helpful advice and occasions to engage in *über Deutschland reden*, I wish to thank Erica Benner, Ralf Dahrendorf, Mary Fulbrook, Sudhir Hazareesingh, Andreas Huyssen, Tony Judt, Richard Kämmerlings, Karen Leeder, Charles S. Maier, Jeff Olick and Peter Schneider. G. A. Cohen, Michael Freeden, Patrick Gavigan, Roger Griffin, Imke Valentien and Cecelia Walsh read all or parts of the manuscript and made highly useful suggestions. Patrick Cohrs kindly read it several times and provided incisive criticism throughout. Special thanks to Andy Rabinbach, and to Hans Mommsen for making a forceful intervention at a crucial stage to give the argument a more historical twist. For an education, intellectual and sentimental, I am deeply grateful to Giuliana Lund. And thanks again for invaluable help to Imke Valentien who has been with this project throughout the years.

I am grateful to the ESRC as well as the *Studienstiftung des Deutschen Volkes* for financial support, and to the Warden and Fellows of All Souls for financial support as well as for providing a place to work during the last two years of this project. Material in chapters six, seven and eight has previously appeared in articles in the *German Studies Review* (May 2000), *German Politics* (December 1999) and *New German Critique* (Winter 1997) respectively. I am grateful to the editors of each journal for allowing me to use the material here. My thanks also to Adam Freudenheim and John Nicoll at Yale University Press, who proved to be supportive and encouraging throughout.

I feel privileged to acknowledge my doctoral advisor Peter Pulzer, a member of a very different 'sceptical generation', as much for what he said about this book as the sensibility for which he stands. I shall always be grateful to my grandmother for financial and, above all, emotional support. And finally, I am grateful to my mother who enabled me to escape German academia (though not questions about German identity) and to write about Germany from another country – for better or for worse.

This book is dedicated to her.

Note on Translations and Terminology

Except where indicated otherwise, all translations from the German are mine. Sometimes, when certain concepts have assumed a particular importance in German discourse, I have left them in the original, and provided as accurate (and contextualized) a translation as possible.

I refer to 'reunification' as a political goal before 1989, since official West German policies were still based on the 'theory of identity' with the Reich of 1937. It is then accurate to refer to the 3rd October 1990 as 'unification', a usage which has become preponderant in Germany itself.

I use 'East Germany' and 'GDR' interchangeably, but refer to West Germany only as the 'Federal Republic', since the expression 'FRG' was part of official GDR language (and used among certain sectors of the West German Left) and still tends to have pejorative overtones.

Finally, to avoid confusion, I have capitalized 'the Left' and 'the Right', when they refer to intellectual groupings.

Introduction

This book analyzes the response of West German intellectuals to unification and the debates about national identity which they have been engaged in since 1989. Unification is widely held to have precipitated a period of crisis and confusion for German intellectuals which has yet to be overcome. 'Four years after the great quake in Europe ... there is still storm and roaring in the minds' is how the Green politician Antje Vollmer described the situation in 1993, and the statement remains true even after the first post-unification decade.[1] The Left has found it difficult to adjust to what is generally thought of as 'the return of the nation state' and to formulate convincing conceptions of nationhood and citizenship in the wake of 1989. Some intellectuals have taken new, supposedly nationalist paths and have been ostracized by those remaining faithful to a post-War West German left-liberal consensus.[2] Conservative historians, on the other hand, proclaim prescriptions based on the past for the 'new' Germany and call for national assertiveness, while a group of younger intellectuals seized on unification as an opportunity to establish a 'New Democratic Right'. While disputes among intellectuals about the meanings of 1989 and the nature of the unified country continue, almost everyone seems at least able to agree that the role of the intellectual is itself in question.

Which conceptions of nationhood have German intellectuals marshalled during and after the debates on unification? How have they envisaged the relationship between nation, state and democracy? And how in turn, are these entities related to the German past, and to the ominous concept of *Vergangenheitsbewältigung* [coming to terms with the past]?[3] Have there been genuinely new intellectual developments in response to unification? And, finally, what lies behind the shared rhetoric about what seems like a thoroughly reified concept of 'national identity', i.e. the kind

---

[1] Antje Vollmer, 'Woher kommt diese Wut?', in *Der Spiegel*, 15 September 1993.

[2] Examples of these supposed 'new nationalists' are Botho Strauß ('Anschwellender Bocksgesang', in *Der Spiegel*, 8 February 1993), Hans Magnus Enzensberger ('Ausblicke auf den Bürgerkrieg', in *Der Spiegel*, 21 June 1993) and Martin Walser ('Deutsche Sorgen', in *Der Spiegel*, 28 June 1993).

[3] The concept of *Vergangenheitsbewältigung*, with its managerial overtones and its implied desire for closure, was itself bound up with the West German approach to the Nazi past in the 1950s. Nevertheless, I shall use it here as a shorthand for the German idea of 'dealing with the past', and return at greater length to the problem of a routinization and professionalization of 'dealing with the past' in the penultimate chapter.

of 'national psychologizing' which many foreign observers find so bewildering? Have new conceptions of 'national identity' actually led to new formulations of 'national interests'? As Marc Fisher, former foreign correspondent in Germany for the *Washington Post*, has pointed out, 'it's slippery stuff, this talk of identity and purpose. The debate tends toward morose, piercingly rational discussion about matters so abstract that solutions are hard to imagine'.[4] Ralf Dahrendorf has expressed exasperation both with a 'pseudo-debate, which does not get people anywhere' and a 'psycho-social analysis of identity searches and identity crises'.[5] Even Jürgen Habermas, one of the foremost participants in the intellectual battle over the nature of unified Germany, has described these 'identity debates' as 'ghostly'.[6] And Hans Magnus Enzensberger has claimed that the 'collective soul deserves no attention whatever' and that 'the microscopic inspection to which the national character is subjected' made him 'increasingly impatient'. Only that Enzensberger expressed this desire to move beyond the vexed identity questions a quarter of a century before the fall of the Wall, in a 1964 article entitled 'Am I a German?' – which suggested both a persistently problematic 'national identity' and the continued inability of German intellectuals precisely to move beyond such national questions.[7] Nevertheless, then as now, foreign and domestic observers agree that 'at bottom festers a real problem, one that begins with shame and guilt and ends in a political and social paralysis that endangers Europe's future'.[8] And, so German intellectuals and their public seem to believe, what German intellectuals have to say will be of real consequence for these real problems.

A study analyzing the response of West German intellectuals to unification and the changes in public discourse which unification has precipitated, immediately has to face a number of pitfalls: how is one to deal with a discourse which is still so much in progress and proliferating? How is some distance to be gained from a debate in which the participants are highly self-conscious about their strategic attempts to acquire intellectual influence and what is often referred to as 'cultural hegemony'? The marked self-referentiality of the debates is both a characteristic in need of

[4] Marc Fisher, *After the Wall: Germany, Germans and the Burdens of History* (New York: Simon and Schuster, 1995), 71.

[5] Interview with Lord Dahrendorf for the *Woodstock Road Editorial*, St Antony's College, November 1994 [unpublished] and Ralf Dahrendorf, ' "Eine deutsche Identität" ', in *Merkur*, Vol. 44 (1990), 231–5.

[6] Jürgen Habermas, 'Die zweite Lebenslüge der Bundesrepublik: Wir sind wieder "normal" geworden', in *Die Zeit*, 11 December 1992.

[7] Hans Magnus Enzensberger, 'Am I a German?', in *Encounter*, No. 4 (1964), 16–18.

[8] Fisher, *After the Wall*, 71.

explanation and a challenge to the observer. Drawn-out, often acrimonious arguments have been waged about 'what is left' and 'what is right', where it is always an unspecified 'Right' and, in particular, 'Left' which is 'ideological' and constrained by 'taboos'. In such intellectual interventions, it is usually the intellectual-cum-political opponent who possesses the worst traits of what is referred to as 'typically German': Protestant inwardness, a tendency to lurch from one extreme to the other, *machtgeschützte Innerlichkeit* [inwardness protected by the power of state, a phrase coined by Thomas Mann], an addiction to political *Lebenslügen* [lifelong political self-deception] and other cliches.

Any scholarly analysis has to go beyond such polemical (and personal) name-calling, which seems strangely characteristic of German debates and itself needs explanation. Even when some of the attacks on the Left, for instance, were fully justified, they hardly ever *explained* why the Left reacted in the way it did. Curiously, however, none of the German observers of the unification debates has undertaken what seems the most prevalent approach in German studies of political argument, namely its *historicization*. In other words, no serious attempt has been made to examine the development of intellectuals' positions prior to unification, and to understand how past positions relate to their stance after the Wall came down. And yet, it is here that the real intellectual puzzles are to be found. For instance, why did the very writers and thinkers who opposed Adenauer and his policies of integrating the Federal Republic into the West during the early 1960s in the name of reunification, also oppose Adenauer's self-declared grandson Helmut Kohl when he actually promised to carry out unification in 1990? Surely, the first and fundamental step in explaining the response of intellectuals is to give a proper, contextualized account of what intellectuals were saying at certain points, whether they changed their views – and if so, why. So far, a number of studies have remained mired in the debates themselves, producing projections, and failing even to provide accurate descriptions of the debates. A nuanced historical analysis must be the basis for all evaluation. But what, then, should be the criteria for evaluation?

Most studies of German intellectuals and unification have in one way or another advanced the thesis of the 'failure of the intellectuals'.[9] Intellectuals have been admonished either for being too critical of developments in 1990, for being out of step with 'the people', or for not being self-critical enough in general. However, it is pointless and in fact part of the polemical battle simply to chide intellectuals for being 'too critical'.

[9] For the most cogent and sophisticated diagnosis of failure, see Andreas Huyssen, 'After the Wall: The Failure of German Intellectuals', in *New German Critique*, No. 52 (1991), 109–43. For a polemical and superficial account, see Paul Noack, *Deutschland, deine Intellektuellen* (Berlin: Ullstein, 1991).

After all, keeping a distance and adopting a principled and responsible critical stance is precisely the (self-appointed) task of the intellectual.[10] But 'being critical' is, of course, not a straightforward matter. In response to the often unjustified right-wing charge of 'failure', the *bien-pensant* Left has put forward self-pitying theories about systematic campaigns to silence any critical voice, in the process advancing defences of 'being critical' which, as I shall argue below, were themselves often uncritical, and, in some cases, indefensible. There has been much lamenting among and about German intellectuals recently, as well as lamenting about the lamenting, and I do not wish to add to either.

The question remains, then, how intellectual responses should be analyzed and judged as in some sense adequate or inadequate. Stuart Parkes, an acute observer of the political interventions of West German writers, is clearly aware of the problem when he asks 'if there are any objective criteria by which to judge the often bitter debate', only to continue by saying that 'the most promising approach would be to relate it to the social role of intellectuals and to ask how far this role has been fulfilled. The trouble is that there is no consensus on this point . . .'[11] And, one might add, for all the theories about intellectuals, even the ones not driven by a desire to settle old scores with the 'clercs',[12] a general consensus on their proper role is unlikely to emerge. In fact, during and after unification the role of the intellectual in the public sphere has itself been contested, and the borders between art, academia and politics constantly embattled.

I propose that the most fruitful way to analyze the unification debate is by first closely examining the intellectual resources which German writers and academics marshalled in response to unification. What has been missing so far is a historically informed effort to trace back to earlier periods the patterns of thought and concepts used by intellectuals.[13] Only through such a 'tracing back' can the changing parameters of German debates about political identity become clear. In addition to analyzing the trajectories of individual intellectuals, I seek to examine how the mean-

---

[10] For some insightful perspectives on the concept of 'responsibility', see Ian Maclean *et al.* (eds), *The Political Responsibility of Intellectuals* (Cambridge: Cambridge University Press, 1990). I hope that my own notion of intellectuals' responsibility will become clear in the course of this study – and that this will prove more fruitful than presenting the reader with yet another abstract model of intellectuals' task at the beginning.

[11] Stuart Parkes, 'Introduction', in Arthur Williams *et al.* (eds), *German Literature at a Time of Change 1989–1991* (Bern: Peter Lang, 1991), 1–20; here 9.

[12] Julien Benda, *La Trahison des Clercs* (Paris: Grasset, 1927). English translation: *The Treason of the Intellectuals*, trans. Richard Aldington (New York: W. W. Norton, 1969).

[13] Most works on the topic remain entirely focused on the present, with no historical references whatsoever. See for instance Wolfgang Jäger and Ingeborg Villinger, *Die Intellektuellen und die deutsche Einheit* (Freiburg: Rombach, 1997).

ings of central concepts which almost all intellectuals feel compelled to contest, in particular the idea of the nation, have changed over time. Concepts, to be politically useful, have to be vague and open to multiple meanings. They acquire determinate meaning only by being placed in a context of other concepts,[14] and intellectuals attempt to redefine their meaning precisely by situating them in new contexts. I want to examine these redefinitions as well as the conceptual language which intellectuals share in debating German identity. In the conclusion, I shall offer an analysis of the concepts and categories which are both central and 'essentially contested' in the German debates – but which also limit them and which, I argue, contribute to the frequent fruitlessness and futility of these debates.[15]

Avoiding the pitfall of repeating the accusations levelled by the Right about the 'failure of the intellectuals', then, should not mean that one cannot offer an evaluation of the arguments and concepts which intellectuals employed. After all, these intellectuals were making *arguments* and wanted them to be understood as such – and it would be a mistake not to argue with them, not least because there are first-order theoretical issues here which transcend the German context: questions about national identity and alternative forms of belonging in supposedly 'post-national times', ways of reconciling nationalism and republicanism, the nature and quality of citizenship and the necessity of 'foundations' for republics. And of course, there is the role of intellectuals themselves – can they really provide a model of 'democratic citizenship', as they often claimed, or are there inherent paradoxes in the intellectuals' role in a democratic, post-totalitarian society? In that sense, the challenge of unification, and intellectuals' responses to it, also has to be a study in applied political theory.

Arguments, then, have to be scrutinized in terms of their coherence, their consistency as well as their real moral and political implications. Consistency refers to internal consistency as well as consistency over time, i.e. claims prior to and after unification. Consistency over time, however, will not be elevated into a moral hurdle to be taken by intellectuals, as, after all, the Federal Republic of the late 1980s was likely to elicit different comments from that of the 1960s. Even then, however, revealing internal contradictions can be found, as well as inconsistencies with what some intellectuals proclaimed shortly before the Wall came down. Most importantly, intellectuals' behaviour can be measured against their own self-conceptions. After all, intellectuals tend to make their own role into one of their favourite concerns, and every figure under consideration here has at

[14] Michael Freeden, *Ideologies and Political Theory: A Conceptual Approach* (Oxford: Oxford University Press, 1996).

[15] W. B. Gallie, 'Essentially Contested Concepts', in *Proceedings of the Aristotelian Society*, Vol. 56 (1955–6), 167–98.

one point or another put forward claims about their ideal role – as suspicious citizen, critic in the public sphere, as a mere individual exhibiting one's feelings, or as an intellectual partisan fighting for 'cultural hegemony'. More importantly, intellectuals' critics often measured them not only against these self-conceptions, but also against an archetypal West German role of the intellectual as democratic citizen which they had supposedly played in the past, and which they had supposedly abandoned. Was such a past role, often located in the late 1960s and early 1970s, an idealized, even imaginary one? Again, a careful *historical* account of the actual role intellectuals played during the course of the Federal Republic is crucial in order to judge these claims.

German Intellectual Generations: From Aristocrats of the Spirit to Democratic Citizens?

An exclusive focus on individual arguments and concepts would neglect another aspect which, particularly in the German context, sheds light on the debates and is crucial for their historical explanation. This aspect is generational conflict. In general, the fashionable focus on so-called generations often explains both too much and too little by homogenizing generational experiences and directly reducing political attitudes to the particular experiences of an age cohort. There can be little doubt, however, that generational conflict has played an unusually large role in German politics, from the Youth Movement early in the century to the 'sceptical generation' of the 1950s, the 'generation of 1968', a newly formed group of '1989ers' and, most recently, a 'Berlin Generation' which sociologists claim to have identified.[16] In particular, the protagonists of these generational conflicts have time and again pointed to the centrality of defining political events in their cohort's experience and noticed their commonalities even across political differences – and there is no reason simply to dismiss these self-descriptions.[17] Generations are here understood as defined by the experience of (and participation in) particularly powerful political events; in short, they are marked as 'political generations'.[18] In the

---

[16] Heinz Bude, 'Generation Berlin: In Vorbereitung auf die neue Republik', in *Frankfurter Allgemeine Zeitung*, 18 June 1998.

[17] Arguably, the single most important reason why generations have been so significant in Germany is the fact that class and status, in a society characterized by continuous political upheavals and high social mobility, has been of little importance in comparison to other countries, which, unlike Germany, retain an aristocracy or a *haute bourgeoisie*. Of course, my claim is not that class or status do not matter in Germany.

[18] Karl Mannheim, 'The Problem of Generations', in *From Karl Mannheim*, ed. Kurt H. Wolff (New Brunswick: Transaction, 1993), 351–98. I shall leave out the more complex relationship between 'generation status', 'generation as actuality' and 'generation unit'.

context of the unification debate, the formative intellectual experiences of the so-called *Flakhelfergeneration* [the teenagers drafted out of school at the end of the Second World War to assist in operating anti-aircraft batteries] and the generational cohorts surrounding them are central.[19] But it would be simplistic to label this entire group the 'Hitler Youth generation', as has sometimes been suggested. Within this generational cohort, one needs further to distinguish between three groups: those born before or in 1927, who still could become soldiers, even lieutenants in the Wehrmacht; those born during 1927 and 1928 who were not drafted into the army properly, but still participated in the War by operating the flak batteries; and those born in 1929 who were not drafted into the anti-aircraft units, but still performed other duties for the defence of the Reich.[20] Those born in or after 1930 then became the *weiße Jahrgänge* [white generation], who were largely deemed to be entirely innocent.[21] Among the first group are, for instance, Günter Grass (born in 1927), Martin Walser (1927) and Kurt Sontheimer (1928); while among the second one finds Jürgen Habermas (1929), Ralf Dahrendorf (1929) and Hans Magnus Enzensberger (1929). Then there is a slightly younger group of intellectuals born in 1932 and after, who also still have deep memories of the War and a childhood under the Nazi regime. As has often been pointed out, the fact that only a few months could separate innocence and guilt, led to an acute consciousness of contingency, even of the fatality of chance among those born in the late 1920s and early 1930s.[22]

Of course, not everyone born between the early 1920s and the mid-1930s thought the same way, or adopted similar political stances – and certainly not all intellectuals, as any cursory glance at the names mentioned above should make clear. Nevertheless, as many members of this generation themselves have recognized, there was significant generational cohesion – and, politically, often a 'narcissism of minor difference', especially in comparison to the range of ideological alliances during the Weimar Republic.[23] More specifically, they frequently claimed that the sociologist

---

[19] Heinz Bude, *Deutsche Karrieren: Lebenskonstruktionen sozialer Aufsteiger aus der Flakhelfer-Generation* (Frankfurt/Main: Suhrkamp, 1987) and *Bilanz der Nachfolge: Die Bundesrepublik und der Nationalsozialismus* (Frankfurt/Main: Suhrkamp, 1992).

[20] Rolf Schörken, *Jugend 1945: Politisches Denken und Lebensgeschichte* (Frankfurt/Main: Fischer, 1994). For a moving account by a political scientist, see Martin Greiffenhagen, *Jahrgang 1928: Aus einem unruhigen Leben* (Munich: Piper, 1988).

[21] Viggo Graf Blücher, *Die Generation der Unbefangenen* (Düsseldorf: Diederich, 1967).

[22] Bude, *Bilanz der Nachfolge*, 81.

[23] Peter Rühmkorf, for instance, once claimed only half-facetiously that 'somehow and among themselves' members of the generation of 1929 were always 'comrades'. See Peter Rühmkorf, *Tabu I: Tagebücher 1989–1991* (Reinbek: Rowohlt, 1995), 108.

Helmut Schelsky's diagnosis from the 1950s that theirs was a 'sceptical generation' had captured an important truth.[24] Schelsky had argued that a generation that had been subject to intense indoctrination in the Hitler Youth, and then experienced the total 'collapse' of 1945, was prone to resisting absolute claims, whether made in the name of identity or ideologies. He had also claimed that the sceptical generation, after the excessive early politicization in the Nazi regime, was particularly oriented towards material security, and was consumerist and profoundly 'apolitical'. As will become clear in the course of this study, at least the latter part of the analysis was untrue in the case of intellectuals – in fact, the sceptical generation was maybe the first successfully to overcome the traditional German chasm between *Geist* [intellect] and *Macht* [power], which had pitted a realm of pure culture against the sordid and shallow world of politics – although, as I shall argue, certain conspicuous blindspots in intellectuals' perceptions of politics persisted long after 1945. Arguably, a generation on which politics had intruded so forcefully so early, could not be truly 'apolitical' ever again. The personal was always the political, as much as present politics always seemed to involve the personal past, a fact which also contributed to the development of what I call a 'culture of suspicion', in which political argument was often reduced to personal motives.[25]

Those born during the late 1920s and early 1930s were of course not the 'founding generation' of the Federal Republic; these were politicians and intellectuals whose formative experience had been the actual experience of living through the failure of the Weimar Republic.[26] But those born around 1930 first burst onto the intellectual scene in the late 1950s, and have wielded particular influence in the Federal Republic to this day. Intellectuals like Habermas, Walser, Dahrendorf, Grass and Enzensberger participated in almost every major debate touching on the political self-understanding of West Germany, and especially questions of 'national

[24] Helmut Schelsky, *Die skeptische Generation: Eine Soziologie der deutschen Jugend* (Düsseldorf: Eugen Diederichs, 1957). Schelsky's study was not about intellectuals and was the subject of major controversies at the time of its publication and after. My point is not to vindicate his views of youth culture in the 1950s, but to recognize the accuracy of his diagnosis of 'scepticism', which many observers, past and present, seem to have denied simply because it was associated with a right-wing, anti-intellectual social scientist. 'Sceptisicm' did not have to translate into apolitical consumerism and career-oriented pragmatism, as both Schelsky and his critics assumed, but could also become the basis of a certain kind of anti-tragic and anti-heroic post-war liberalism that dared not speak its name. See also Odo Marquard, *Skepsis und Zustimmung: Philosophische Studien* (Stuttgart: Reclam, 1994).

[25] It is worth noting how adamantly and persistently personal accounts were demanded of intellectuals, such as Habermas, who were reluctant to talk about their own experience.

[26] For this 'founding generation' and the historical lessons from Weimar which they relied on after 1945, see Jeffrey Herf, *Divided Memory: The Nazi Past in the Two Germanys* (Cambridge, Mass.: Harvard University Press, 1997).

identity'. In particular, they often felt that, despite the establishment of democratic institutions after 1945, Germany was still suffering from what has often been called a 'post-fascist democratic deficit' – consequently, their interventions were above all aimed at preventing the resurgence of nationalism and authoritarianism. They sought to complement – and strengthen – the democratic institutions established in 1949 by promoting a democratic political culture – and, in particular, the formation of a democratic public sphere.[27] At the same time, they themselves often felt what the psychoanalysts Alexander and Margarete Mitscherlich – in another context – called *Identifikationsscheu* [a reluctance to identify], and to some extent distrusted their own people.[28] As Enzensberger, for instance, pointed out, 'one must not forget that I have experienced the catastrophe at first hand. I was sitting in the basements and as we re-emerged, the houses were gone. After that a certain type of *Weltvertrauen* [trust in the world] will not be rebuilt'.[29] Instead of the appeal to 'substantial' entities such as the nation, the sceptical generation favoured formalism and proceduralism, as well as what Klaus Wagenbach labelled 'pragmatism from a moral point of view'.[30] But they also wanted to draw the right lessons from the failure of the Weimar Republic, and provide a model of democratic citizenship, lest another German republic foundered for a lack of democrats. As Grass put it, 'What did Tucholsky say, when in the mid-1920s he poured his scorn over the Social Democratic flag: "This Republic is not my Republic". And even during the emigration the self-destruction of the German left would not stop. I have drawn my lessons'.[31] In the unification debate, they often repeated stances from earlier decades, since with the addition of East Germany, a seemingly 'more German Germany' steeped in authoritarianism, and with the supposed return of the nation-state, they feared a resurgence of nationalism and even authoritarianism. However, apart from this repetition of stances, which was also due to what they perceived as the similarities between the Kohl government and Adenauer's rather autocratic 'Chancellor Democracy' in the 1950s, there were also

---

[27] Wilfried van der Will, 'From the 1940s to the 1990s: The critical intelligentsia's changing role in the political culture of the Federal Republic', in *Debatte*, Vol. 5 (1997), 25–48.

[28] Alexander and Margarete Mitscherlich, *Die Unfähigkeit zu trauern: Grundlagen kollektiven Verhaltens* (Munich: Piper, 1967), 262. English translation: *The Inability to Mourn: Principles of Collective Behavior*, trans. Beverly R. Placzell (New York: Grove Press, 1975).

[29] Quoted in 'Der Fahrplaner der Lüfte', in *Der Spiegel*, 14 December 1998.

[30] Klaus Wagenbach, 'Intellektuelle an der Wahlfront', in *Die Weltwoche*, 17 September 1965.

[31] Günter Grass, 'Über das Ja und Nein (1968)', in Günter Grass, *Essays, Reden, Briefe, Kommentare* [*Werkausgabe in zehn Bänden*, Vol. 9], ed. Daniela Hermes (Neuwied: Luchterhand, 1987), 320–6; here 326.

some notable (and sometimes subtle) changes in the opinions of thinkers like Habermas and Grass. I shall pay careful attention to these shifts in the individual analyses.

Discrimination and Distrust

Two points, then, are central about the experience of the sceptical generation: one is the shock that most of them experienced in and after 1945. Overnight, or, much more often, in delayed reactions and drawn-out processes, they realized that despite having lived a seemingly 'normal life' in the 1930s, they had in fact participated in a totalitarian regime.[32] As Enzensberger recognized in his poem 'Führer', 'during the time of fascism I did not know that I was living during the time of fascism'.[33] Their situation, however, was an altogether ambivalent one and could not simply be reduced to uncritical complicity in the Third Reich and subsequent guilt. They often, in a gesture of youthful rebellion, distanced themselves from the Hitler Youth, they were not part of the Wehrmacht proper and they frequently had a thoroughly positive experience of the Western Occupiers, the Americans in particular. In the last phase and after the War, they often felt liberated in more than one sense: traditional authorities, parents, schools and the military, collapsed in front of their eyes – and, after 1945, they could in many cases feel superior to their morally compromised elders. And yet, despite the supposed 'grace of late birth', which Helmut Kohl pointed to forty years later, guilt was never far from the surface. In the words of Grass, who had been part of the Wehrmacht proper, members of his generation felt that they had been 'too young to have been a Nazi, but old enough to have been formed' by the Nazi regime.[34] But they then suddenly – or, more typically, in a gradual and tortured manner – realized 'what amount of guilt our people had knowingly and unknowingly accumulated, what burden and responsibility mine and the following generation would have to carry'.[35] The self-consciously sceptical attitude induced by this shock also seemed warranted by the fact that the very mentalities and some of the social structures which had made National Socialism possible, persisted after the War. Distrust, then,

---

[32] Although there were notable exceptions, too: Ralf Dahrendorf, for instance, participated in the resistance as a teenager. See his *Reisen nach innen und außen: Aspekte der Zeit* (Munich: Deutscher Taschenbuch Verlag, 1986).

[33] Hans Magnus Enzensberger, *Die Furie des Verschwindens* (Frankfurt/Main: Suhrkamp, 1980), 63.

[34] Günter Grass, 'Rede von der Gewöhnung (1967)', in Grass, *Essays*, 199–212; here 205.

[35] Günter Grass, 'Rede an einen jungen Wähler, der sich versucht fühlt, die NPD zu wählen (1966)', in *ibid.*, 162–7; here 163.

remained a basic outlook of these post-war intellectuals, even though there were also some who sought to salvage the innocence and authenticity of their childhood experience. Some tried to defend their primary experience against retrospective knowledge, and insist on the point that 'to know is better than to know better', as the historian Reinhart Koselleck (born in 1923) put it.[36] This attitude was most notably adopted by the writer Martin Walser, whose intellectual trajectory I shall analyze in chapter five.

Second, the sceptical generation after the War consciously constituted itself against a certain image of Weimar intellectuals as either radical nationalists or as anti-Weimar leftists, but, above all, as antidemocratic 'mandarins', a supposedly apolitical *Geistesaristokratie* [intellectual aristocracy] founded on a mixture of nineteenth-century German *Bildung*–humanism and Nietzscheanism.[37] The nationalists of the so-called Conservative Revolution and the mandarin professors who opposed the notion of the intellectual – denounced as modern, Western, rootless and, of course, Jewish – with an emphatic concept of German culture and German *Geist*, played into each other's hands in undermining the Weimar Republic. Whether the dominance of the mandarin professorate is an accurate picture of Weimar intellectual life is very much open to question – what is not, is that post-war intellectuals took such an image as a negative foil. Jürgen Habermas, for instance, claimed in retrospect, that 'the negative example of the radical Weimar intelligentsia and the corruption of the German mandarins during the time of National Socialism were an incentive for my generation for political engagement'.[38] But it was also an incentive to recognize the democratic achievements of the Federal Republic, despite all its faults, and, this time, to support a liberal 'bourgeois' Constitution, rather than dismiss it as a sorry shell for capitalist interests, as so many on the Weimar Left had done. In that sense, the fundamental feeling of scepticism rooted in the shock of 1945 was combined with a liberal effort to see the Federal Republic realistically; distrust went hand in hand with a willingness among intellectuals to be more discriminating in their political judgements than their Weimar predecessors. As I seek to show in this study, this generation always used the Constitution as

[36] Reinhart Koselleck, 'Glühende Lava, zur Erinnerung geronnen', in *Frankfurter Allgemeine Zeitung*, 6 May 1995.

[37] Fritz K. Ringer, *The German Mandarins: The German Academic Community, 1890–1933* (Cambridge, Mass.: Harvard University Press, 1969) and the revealing review by Jürgen Habermas, reprinted in *Philosophisch-politische Profile* (Frankfurt/Main: Suhrkamp, 1973), 239–51. See also Dietz Bering, *Die Intellektuellen: Geschichte eines Schimpfwortes* (Stuttgart: Klett-Cotta, 1978) and Dirk Hoeges, *Kontroverse am Abgrund: Ernst Robert Curtius und Karl Mannheim: Intellektuelle und 'freischwebende Intelligenz' in der Weimarer Republik* (Frankfurt/Main: Fischer, 1994).

[38] Jürgen Habermas, 'Ein politisch zivilisiertes Land', in *Focus*, 28 August 1995.

a powerful argumentative and rhetorical weapon, rather than opposing it altogether in a stance of Marxist *Totalkritik* [total critique], as was common among members of the generation of 1968. In that sense, these intellectuals are exemplary for the development of a liberal democratic political culture in Germany, reflected and carried forward by intellectuals traumatized through the experience of National Socialism. At the same time, these intellectuals had particular blind spots, and the culture of suspicion they fostered – as well as political culture in West Germany more generally – suffered from peculiar weaknesses which are becoming increasingly apparent in retrospect.

In addition, however, members of the 'generation of 1968' will feature prominently in the chapter dealing with the response of the West German Left to unification. '68ers had a much more ambivalent, if not sometimes outright hostile relationship with West Germany. Their formative experience had been the stale anti-communism and the silence about the Nazi past during the 1950s and 1960s, which they opposed with a version of anti-anti-communism, as well as ideological fragments of anti-fascism and anti-capitalism. While members of the sceptical generation disapproved of what seemed like an indiscriminate attack on the institutions of the Federal Republic, the '68ers in fact only radicalized many of the positions which their predecessors held, in particular the culture of suspicion inaugurated by the sceptical generation. When the Wall came down, these intellectuals saw unification as a threat to these 'anti-attitudes' and to any utopian thinking, but a significant number of them also suddenly adopted a much more positive stance vis-à-vis the Federal Republic.

The most prominent attempt at changing the intellectual landscape and political culture of the larger Germany also has had a significant generational dimension. The self-declared right-wing 'generation of 1989' sided with the 'discredited grandfathers', figures tarnished by National Socialism such as Martin Heidegger, Carl Schmitt and Ernst Jünger, against the supposedly ideologically hegemonic generation of 1968. Mostly, members of the New Right were part of the generation of *Zaungäste* [the generation in-between], i.e. those who were too young to participate in the '68 student protests, but old enough to have their formative intellectual experiences with the 1980s *Historikerstreit* [the historians' dispute, a term I shall explain in chapter one] – which they saw as indicative of the moralization of politics by a self-serving Left.[59] However, apart from generational conflict, there are further peculiarities of German intellectual life which are crucial for understanding the often acrimonious conversations which intellectuals conduct. Discussing these is more than an exercise in scene-setting – as will, I hope, become clear in the course of

---

[59] Reinhard Mohr, *Zaungäste: Die Generation, die nach der Revolte kam* (Frankfurt/Main: S. Fischer, 1992).

this study, these peculiarities have direct consequences for the outcomes of German debates.

Contestants on the 'Intellectual Field'

Intellectuals make their own choices, but not in a context of their own choosing. In particular, they always face a context of pre-existing intellectual opinions, orthodoxies and heterodoxies, in which they somehow have to position themselves, and, of course the particular institutions of intellectual life in a given national context. This study envisages the debate between intellectuals as taking place on an 'intellectual field', a concept borrowed from Pierre Bourdieu to capture the antagonistic nature of intellectual exchange.[40]

An intellectual field is a systematic and historically specific structure of intellectual orthodoxies and heterodoxies, so that positions on a field come to be defined in terms of each other. As John McCole has argued, 'the structure of orthodoxies and heterodoxies objectively constrains the discourse it supports by giving doctrines, concepts and images a positional value'.[41] The intuition here is simple: the notion of the field makes the observer sensitive to the 'pull' which is exerted by an ideational context on specific claims and concepts. But the notion also draws one's attention to the antagonistic nature of intellectual debate and the basis of the field in institutionalized power. Intellectuals possess a certain amount of 'intellectual capital' through their reputation in a specific area of intellectual endeavour and because of past interventions. The notion of the field then also helps to solve the vexing question of whom to choose as intellectual protagonists: dominant intellectuals are those whose claims exert most power and lead others to define themselves through or against their positions. In this sense, the intellectuals to be studied here have 'selected themselves' through their previous positions and the prominence of their interventions in 1989 and beyond.

The intellectual field is populated by a number of writers, academics and, to some extent, prominent journalists who in the German context would best be described as *Meinungsführer* [opinion leaders]. *Meinungsführer* self-consciously aim at influencing public discourse – and contest

[40] Pierre Bourdieu, *The Field of Cultural Production* (Cambridge: Polity, 1993) and *In Other Words* (Cambridge: Polity, 1994); David Swartz, *Culture and Power: The Sociology of Pierre Bourdieu* (Chicago: University of Chicago Press, 1997), 218–46. In this study, I am reducing Bourdieu's socio-analysis of 'fields' as structured arenas of conflict to its 'interactionist' dimension, leaving out his emphasis on domination (and reproduction). I am not necessarily denying the importance of this dimension – even though Bourdieu, in my opinion, has far too determinist a view of it.

[41] John McCole, *Walter Benjamin and the Antinomies of Tradition* (Ithaca: Cornell University Press, 1993), 24.

each other – through addressing a *Meinungselite* [an opinion elite]. They stage their public interventions in what are usually called the *Intelligenzblätter*, i.e. highbrow newspapers, but they are not, for the most part, journalists themselves. While their stances are often idiosyncratic, they tend to set the terms of debates both in more specialized highbrow journals such as *Merkur* and *Kursbuch* and in more popular dailies such as the *Frankfurter Allgemeine Zeitung* and the *Süddeutsche Zeitung*, influential weeklies such as *Die Zeit* and magazines such as *Der Spiegel*, *Stern* and *Focus*. There is a peculiar German tradition of *Publizistik* [intellectual journalism] with the *Publizist* writing in newspapers and magazines, while often not being a professional journalist, and publishing scholarly books, while not being an academic. This tradition, with the exception of France, has no equivalent in Europe or the United States. In Germany, public opinion still often equals published opinion.[42]

Only in Germany does one find intellectuals such as Jürgen Habermas occupying the first two pages of a weekly such as *Die Zeit*; only in Germany could a critic literally tearing apart the latest book by Günter Grass make the cover of the country's most important magazine, *Der Spiegel*; only in Germany does one find political scientists regularly publishing popular books on the state of the nation, often with pictures of themselves looking diffident and angst-ridden on the front cover; and only in Germany would a random flicking through TV channels inevitably lead the viewer to one of the numerous 'talk shows' in which a small group of intellectuals earnestly debate political-cum-philosophical topics on an almost daily basis. In short, in Germany, unlike in Britain and the United States, it is almost self-evidently legitimate that men and women who have distinguished themselves in cultural and academic matters, should comment on affairs of state.[43] None of this is to say that intellectuals actually 'lead opinion' or necessarily achieve their aim of setting the terms of political discourse – in fact, as I show in the course of this study, more often than not, intellectuals were 'belated' and best at reacting against firmly entrenched, but morally compromised, authority, rather than acting as 'seismographers' during new developments, as their self-images frequently suggested. So just as an overly deterministic account à la Bourdieu, which is seductive because it tends to explain too much, is to be resisted, the

---

[42] For a striking example of the influence of the *Intelligenzblätter* on public opinion as well as on the perceptions of the political elite, one only need think of the *Publizistik* power wielded by the *Frankfurter Allgemeine Zeitung* journalist Johann Georg Reißmüller in advancing the cause of the recognition of Slovenia and Croatia in 1991.

[43] There is, unfortunately, no single account which explains Germany's 'literary (and philosophical) culture' as well as Priscilla Parkhurst Clark's *Literary France: The Making of a Culture* (Berkeley: University of California Press, 1987) does for France.

exaggerated claims for intellectual autonomy and moral-cum-political leadership are to be treated with caution.

The boundaries of the intellectual field themselves are constantly contested, as questions of who is allowed to speak on political matters, to what extent intellectual life ought to be compartmentalized and whether literature should embody political convictions are renegotiated. The field also depends on an institutional base of newspapers, magazines and broadcasts. It could be shown that in Germany there have been not only regroupings on the intellectual field, but also important changes in the institutional base.[44] However, these changes, as well as the rules of exclusion and inclusion more generally, are beyond the scope of this book.

The intellectual field, then, is not populated by isolated figures; German intellectuals constantly write to and about each other, and, as will become clearer in the course of this study, have a tendency to separate themselves neatly into camps of ideological allegiance. Above all, intellectuals tend to be highly aware of their own 'positionality'. A study on such a self-conscious discourse should be sensitive to this fact by looking for 'elective affinities' as well as influences. This is particularly important for the New Right, which faced the problem of salvaging conservative patterns of thought from across the gap of twelve years of Nazi dictatorship. As ideological newcomers – or latecomers, depending on one's perspective – New Right intellectuals needed to be extremely careful in constructing a conservative genealogy, if they wanted to avoid the charge of 'neo-fascism'.[45] But they also needed to situate themselves vis-à-vis positions already prominent on the intellectual field, especially the real or perceived orthodoxies of the '68ers. Their highly self-conscious project of overcoming the perceived cultural hegemony of the Left and establishing a new nationalism after 1989, I shall argue, is highly instructive about the nature of the intellectual field in Germany, but also about political culture more broadly. In sum, I shall take into account individual actors, a shared language of concepts, generational experiences and the notion of the intellectual field. Only such a pluralist approach can do justice to – and explain – a situation in which 'ideological, generational, political and aesthetic arguments criss-cross to form an ever denser web'.[46]

---

[44] Examples of these institutional changes would be the emergence of the magazine *Focus*, the loss of readership and prestige of a newspaper such as *Die Zeit*, and, above all, the proliferation of private TV channels.

[45] For the problems faced by ideological latecomers, see Juan Linz, 'Some Notes Towards a Comparative Study of Fascism in Sociological Historical Perspective', in: Walter Laqueur (ed.), *Fascism: A Reader's Guide* (Aldershot: Scolar, 1979), 3–121.

[46] Huyssen, 'After the Wall', 114.

An Overview

This study begins with an account of national identity and the quest for legitimacy in West Germany since 1945. I will place special emphasis on the public uses of history as a base for legitimacy, and the fact that German intellectuals feel compelled to change perceptions of the past if they seek to alter Germany's self-perception in the present. Subsequently, the responses to unification of two major West German intellectuals, Günter Grass and Jürgen Habermas, will be analyzed in detail. Grass and Habermas powerfully projected themselves into the public sphere and brought the most intellectual capital to bear on their interventions. After the death of Heinrich Böll, Grass was arguably the most eminent of all German writers, while Habermas could claim to be an all-round intellectual giant in the old Federal Republic. Moreover, their critiques of the unification process were at once the most fundamental, the most prominent and, one might add, the most passionate.[47] They were not 'representative' in any narrow sense, since their stance was often highly idiosyncratic, but their claims on the intellectual field were most powerful in exerting a 'pull' on other positions.

Then follows a more general categorization of responses by West German left-wingers and liberals. Left-wing intellectuals identified the fall of the Wall with a loss of utopianism and predicted the return of an ethnic nationalism in the larger Germany. But they also suddenly discovered a new attachment to West Germany, which they had long resented, as a post-national, post-materialist polity. Generally, however, the Left was trapped in debates of the past, and arguably lacked the political and moral criteria for judging and reacting to a radically changed situation. By rejecting the concept and language of nationhood altogether they arguably missed yet another opportunity in German history to link the 'new' Germany with the ideas of civil society and popular sovereignty, which had played crucial roles in the East German and East European revolutions. This argument is different from saying that the Left 'failed' because it failed to support unification; rather, it is about a loss of constructive engagement with the future. The Left, by turning in on itself and debating 'what was left', created a vacuum of ideas which came to be filled with proposals by older conservatives and a New Right of young academics.[48] The prominent political-cum-aesthetic positions of the *Publizist* and professor Karl Heinz Bohrer influenced both groups, and, accordingly, his

---

[47] There is a consensus on this point among observers of the unification debate. See for instance Peter Graf Kielmannsegg, 'Vereinigung ohne Legitimität?', in *Merkur*, Vol. 46 (1992), 561–75.

[48] There was actually a serialized debate in the *Frankfurter Allgemeine Zeitung* under the heading 'what's left' and subsequently on 'what's right' between 1992 and 1994. The 'left' half was published as *What's Left: Prognosen zur Linken* (Berlin: Rotbuch, 1993).

critique of the Federal Republic and his response to unification are examined. Before turning to Bohrer, I shall analyze the public interventions of the writer Martin Walser who had supported unification long before 1989 and who specifically claimed to represent the 'people' and the petty bourgeoisie in particular.

Subsequently, I offer an intellectual anatomy of the New Right itself. In contrast to the idiosyncratic responses by Grass and Habermas and unlike a Left in disarray, the Right formed a much more cohesive group. Its members had similar objectives, constantly referred to each other's works and shared a language of concepts. Consequently, the section on the New Right considers a number of intellectuals as its subject. Analyzing the New Right also affords an opportunity to paint a more nuanced picture of right-wing and conservative thought both in the old Federal Republic and in unified Germany which goes beyond alarmism and apology. Too often, observers both inside and outside the country have homogenized conservative thought, and missed what is distinctive about the German Right as well as its diverse strands – and especially what its limits in finding an effective political language are. Finally, in the last chapter which takes me away from unification, but not from German identity debates, I analyze the debate on the nature of 'the political' as such, which was a direct result of the rupture of 1989, and normative visions for the so-called 'Berlin Republic', i.e. post-unification Germany, which were explicitly linked to a re-examination of the political. I also briefly discuss the debate about German post-unification 'normality' sparked off by a highly controversial speech given by Martin Walser in October 1998. While there are obvious dangers in discussing such recent events, an analysis of this debate is the logical conclusion for a study which takes as one of its starting points the *Historikerstreit*, not least because the debate demonstrated what had and what had *not* changed since the historians' dispute.

For a number of pragmatic as well as substantive reasons, the response of East German intellectuals to unification and their subsequent contributions to debates about German identity are not included in this study. This is not yet again to deny the East Germans a voice in all-German debates. I have chosen this approach because any account doing justice to East German intellectuals would have to discuss the 'patterns of domination, complicity and dissent' in the GDR, the debates about the *Stasi* involvement of various writers and the 1990 German *Literaturstreit* [dispute about literature].[49] All three issues are so complex – and polemically contested – that they would require a larger framework to be dealt with adequately. Also, there can be no straightforward comparisons

---

[49] Mary Fulbrook, *Anatomy of a Dictatorship: Inside the GDR* (Oxford: Oxford University Press, 1995), 16.

between the pronouncements on Germany by West and East German intellectuals before and after unification, as the latter were subject to censorship, most often enforced by the regime, sometimes self-imposed.[50] After the fall of the Wall, they came under pressure to justify their actions in a way that West German intellectuals never did. Finally, East German intellectuals had to deal with socio-economic changes on an unprecedented scale. A state was disappearing around them and with it a whole framework of cultural institutions and, to a certain extent, privileges.[51] In that sense, East German intellectuals were faced not only with a thinking crisis, but also an existence-threatening crisis, as they adjusted to a Western-type media society dominated by market forces.[52] Moreover, to the extent that in the GDR literature functioned as a substitute for the public sphere when the media was state-controlled, the reconstitution of that sphere in the context of a liberal democracy robbed them of a rather elevated, though often involuntary position of importance. For all these reasons, East German intellectuals could be dealt with only in a larger framework. Having said that, there was of course significant interaction, even, one might say, a 'dialectic' between West and East German intellectuals before, during and after 1989, and peculiar distortions of intellectual positions which can only be explained by the Cold War and the peculiar mutual mirroring of intellectuals in 'another Germany'. To the extent that coalitions between Easterners and Westerners are relevant to the argument, I shall take this Eastern dimension into account.

Finally, a note on terminology: intellectuals here are grouped into chapters and 'camps' according to their ideological self-descriptions as 'left' and 'right'. In that sense, the approach is purely 'nominalist', though part of the argument is about discovering the hidden assumptions – about German nationhood, democracy and the Nazi past – which the Left and the Right might actually share. But the distinction between left and right has of course itself come under criticism after 1989, with some intellectuals claiming that it has dissolved altogether. Of course the obsolescence of the distinction has been declared many times before, most notably in the 1890s and the 1920s – and also immediately after 1945. As Norberto Bobbio has pointed out, when ideologies are evenly balanced, few question the value

[50] John Torpey, *Intellectuals, Socialism and Dissent: The East German Opposition and its Legacy* (Minneapolis: University of Minnesota Press, 1995).

[51] Robert von Hallberg (ed.), *Literary Intellectuals and the Dissolution of the State: Professionalism and Conformity in the GDR*, trans. Kenneth J. Northcott (Chicago: University of Chicago Press, 1996), David Bathrick, *The Powers of Speech: The Politics of Culture in the GDR* (Lincoln: University of Nebraska Press, 1995), and Wolfgang Bialas, *Vom unfreien Schweben zum freien Fall: Ostdeutsche Intellektuelle im gesellschaftlichen Umbruch* (Frankfurt/Main: Fischer, 1996).

[52] Huyssen, 'After the Wall', 115.

of the distinction.[53] But in times of ideological instability, the weaker side has an interest in denying it. In particular, as in the 1920s, leftists might have wanted to blur the left–right distinction to divert attention from the fact that they were moving to the right.[54] In that sense, only (former) members of the Left claimed that left and right no longer referred to stable, identifiable entities. But I conclude that left and right remain very much in existence, especially with reference to their respective views of the nation-state and German national identity.

[53] Norberto Bobbio, *Left and Right: The Significance of a Political Distinction* (Cambridge: Polity, 1996).

[54] Zeev Sternhell, *Neither Right nor Left: Fascist Ideology in France*, trans. David Maisel (Princeton: Princeton University Press, 1996).

1   Nation, State and Intellectuals in West Germany since 1945: The Public Uses of History

In the light of past difficulties in defining a German national identity, it seemed all the more unlikely after 1945 that the Germans would be able to identify with – and invest any legitimacy in – states which were built on the ideals of Anglo-American-style democracy and Soviet Communism respectively.[1] While the Western state was not imposed in the way the GDR was and, arguably, reflected the will of the majority of its citizens, democracy was suffered, rather than welcomed.[2] Both systems were born of defeat and contrary to the 'ideas' and 'the spirit of 1914,' which had championed deep German 'culture' against shallow Western 'civilization', and which had directed the German national project for more than thirty years.[3] Intellectuals, in particular historians, had played a primary role in legitimating these nationalist ideas which were opposed to the Western, democratic ideals associated with the French Revolution.

The founding of two separate states seemed to give a definitive answer to the 'German question', i.e. the question of how to contain the German nation-state in the middle of Europe, since both states were soon to be firmly integrated into their respective alliances. At the same time it reopened the old – and original – pre-1871 German question of whether Germany might one day be unified. But the division also tied the German question to a range of other questions. Due to the confrontation of the two ideological systems, which implied radically different socio-economic

---

[1] On past difficulties, see Harold James, *A German Identity: 1770 to the Present Day* (London: Phoenix, 1994) and the chapter 'Volk, Nation, Nationalismus, Masse' in Otto Brunner, Werner Conze and Reinhart Koselleck (eds), *Geschichtliche Grundbegriffe*, Vol. 7 (Stuttgart: Klett-Cotta, 1992), 141–432, in particular Koselleck's 'Lexikalischer Rückblick', 380–431.

[2] Wolfgang Benz, *Zwischen Hitler und Adenauer: Studien zur deutschen Nachkriegsgesellschaft* (Frankfurt/Main: Fischer, 1991), 211.

[3] The best study of the 'spirit of 1914' – and of 1933 – in the making remains Fritz Stern, *The Politics of Cultural Despair: A Study in the Rise of the Germanic Ideology* (Berkeley: University of California Press, 1961).

arrangements, the national was inextricably linked with the social question, and both questions were in turn reflected in a wider European question. The overarching question of Yalta meant that the problems of a divided Germany and a divided Europe had parallel structures, and potentially parallel solutions, although it was far from certain whether German politicians – and intellectuals – would necessarily give the same answers to both the German and the European questions. Freedom, peace and unity seemed imperative and yet incompatible goals when the two Germanies were founded in 1949. Was a nation to survive in two states, or could the new states mould new and separate forms of national consciousness? Were intellectuals going to cling to a nationalist project, as they overwhelmingly had done after the First World War, or would they finally accept seemingly 'un-German' political systems and support the Allies' goal of Re-education? How were they to deal with Germany's 'post-fascist condition', and the fact that the Germans, even when they were disillusioned with Nazism, remained suspicious of liberalism and democracy? In other words, what was an appropriate response to the on-going 'democratic deficit' characteristic of German political culture? And was the Holocaust, what was later to be called a fundamental *Zivilisationsbruch* [rupture with civilization], to be forgotten, or could its memory be incorporated into a new post-war identity?[4] Could such memory even become a source of legitimacy? Thus, apart from the intra-German and the European dimension, there was also a 'Jewish question' hidden in the German question. Consequently, after 1945 every change in the state of German sovereignty would in some way, at least symbolically, be linked to a particular image of the Nazi past – and towards Jews both in the past and the present.[5]

Foundations and the Two Cultures

In both East and West – though of course much more so in the East – the initial German answer to National Socialism was an étatiste one. In the West, the founding fathers of the Federal Republic took up the ideas of a number of emigrants about a 'militant democracy', i.e. a democracy capable of defending itself against its enemies, and sought strong institutional safeguards against antidemocratic movements, which had been

---

[4] Dan Diner (ed.), *Zivilisationsbruch: Denken nach Auschwitz* (Frankfurt/Main: Fischer, 1988). The concept of *Zivilisationsbruch* is of course ambiguous: for many intellectuals, the problem was precisely that after 1945 the civilization which had produced the Holocaust *continued* in so many respects.

[5] Anson Rabinbach, 'The Jewish Question in the German question', in *New German Critique*, No. 44 (1988), 159–92. On Jewish life in post-war Germany, see Michael Brenner, *After the Holocaust: Rebuilding Jewish Lives in Postwar Germany*, trans. Barbara Harshav (Princeton: Princeton University Press, 1997).

missing in the Weimar Republic.[6] In other words, West Germany dealt with the fascist past by 'internalizing' the possibility of a new fascist threat, and by guarding against it through a democratic and, in theory, indestructible Constitution.[7] A concrete consequence was the prohibition of a neo-Nazi party as well as the German Communist Party as an 'internal enemy' – a measure unique in Western Europe.[8] The GDR, on the other hand, in line with traditional anti-fascist doctrine, sought the remedy for fascism in the complete transformation of social structures – and in particular, the destruction of feudal and capitalist elites. Precisely because of this total transformation, the leadership could uphold the fiction that fascism was historically impossible in the GDR, and that any remaining fascists had been exported to the Federal Republic – in fact, it seemed that Hitler himself had been a West German. Fascism had effectively been 'universalized', as the latent possibility inherent in advanced capitalism anywhere, but also 'externalized' to the extent that a fascist threat could now only emanate from outside the GDR, and West Germany in particular. Thus, both Eastern and Western foundations were explicit negations of the National Socialist past, both were characterized by varying degrees of antidemocratic wariness vis-à-vis their own populations – and both were directed against the 'other German state' which was seen in each case as a continuation of the past. While West Germans viewed the GDR as another instance of totalitarianism, GDR propaganda portrayed the Federal Republic as essentially fascist. In that sense, the foundations of the two states were doubly negative.

Against the background of this double foundation, intellectuals were soon to make their voices heard. Even immediately after the War, historians in particular were offering ready-made explanations of the Nazi period, which was almost universally described in a language of 'catastrophe', 'tragedy', 'fate' and the 'demonic'. Sweeping narratives of German history gone wrong focused on the failed revolutions from the peasants' revolt onwards, on the 'Prussianization' of Germany after 1871 and on the evils of 'massification'. The latter pattern of explanation proved especially popular, since it allowed for blaming an amorphous entity, 'the masses', which seemed to universalize and therefore under-specify responsibility,

---

[6] Alfons Söllner, *Deutsche Politikwissenschaftler in der Emigration: Studien zu ihrer Akkulturation und Wirkungsgeschichte* (Opladen: Westdeutscher Verlag, 1996).

[7] M. Rainer Lepsius, 'Das Erbe des Nationalsozialismus und die politischen Kulturen der Nachfolgestaaten des "Großdeutschen Reiches"', in Michael Haller *et al.* (eds), *Kultur und Gesellschaft: Verhandlungen des 24. Deutschen Soziologentages* (Frankfurt/Main: Campus), 247–64. Austria, on the other hand, externalized fascism by claiming to have been the first victim of the Nazis' foreign aggression.

[8] Patrick Major, *The Death of the KPD: Communism and Anti-communism in West Germany, 1945–1956* (Oxford: Oxford University Press, 1997).

while at the same time opening the path to re-asserting traditional values of the individual and the unique 'personality'.[9] The doyens of German historical studies, Friedrich Meinecke and Gerhard Ritter, saw massification, which had begun with the French Revolution, at the root of the 'totalitarian dictatorships' and what Meinecke called 'democratization, Bolshevization, fascisization'.[10] Not least, the discourse of massification expressed an underlying distrust of democracy.

Meinecke and Ritter also called for a revision of the German *Geschichtsbild* [image of history]. However, this revision never extended further than shifting some of the concepts and categories inherited from before 1933. Meinecke, clinging to a traditional dichotomy of power and culture, criticized German militarism and the overemphasis of the *Machtstaat* [state based on power], which had to be redressed in favour of 'culture'. Ritter also condemned the 'cult of power', but sought to isolate the Third Reich from previous German traditions by explaining National Socialism through a history centred on the pathological aspects of modernity *per se*. For such intellectuals, National Socialism was not a specifically German phenomenon, but part of wider developments – in particular the decline of religion, nineteenth-century liberalism and humanist values. The appropriate response was a return to humanism and the idea of the Christian *Abendland* [Occident] in particular. Meinecke advocated the formation of 'Goethe communities' and a renewed devotion to the 'German spirit'. While such recommendations are easy to ridicule in retrospect, they also corresponded to a very real hunger for culture among the soldiers returning from the War and the younger generation in particular. The immediate post-war period saw a flowering of high culture, which even prompted Theodor W. Adorno, upon his return from the United States, to claim in 1950 that 'the relationship with *geistige* [spiritual] issues, in the widest sense', was 'strong' and 'even greater than in the years before the National Socialist seizure of power'.[11]

For Meinecke and Ritter, the nation-state remained the seemingly self-evident framework of historical analysis. However, as much as later historians were to criticize the continued emphasis on the nation-state, the tendency to adopt a more European perspective was also problematic: it often seemed to serve as a means of escaping political and moral

---

[9] For a liberal 'total anti-fascism' which opposed the individual personality to 'massification', see Wilhelm Röpke, *Die deutsche Frage* (Erlenbach-Zurich: Eugen-Rentsch, 1945). Like many others, Röpcke envisaged a central role for the intellectual in bringing about a 'moral revolution', which would then 'trickle down' to the population at large. *Ibid.*, 225.

[10] Friedrich Meinecke, *Die deutsche Katastrophe* (Zurich: Aero, 1946) and Gerhard Ritter, *Europa und die deutsche Frage* (Munich: Bruckmann, 1948).

[11] Theodor W. Adorno, 'Auferstehung der Kultur in Deutschland?', in *Frankfurter Hefte*, Vol. 5 (1950), 469–77; here 469.

responsibility for the immediate past.[12] Many intellectuals were in fact in favour of a European federation, animated by a 'European patriotism', including a united Germany, which was to act as a counterweight to both East and West. But this very position seemed to contain a moral ambiguity: would the dissolution of Germany into Europe not have to be preceded by a national coming-to-terms with the post-fascist condition? And would a form of univeralism, as evident for instance in the historians' devotion to humanism, not also constitute an escape from the German question? There was not necessarily a contradiction between the universal and the particular here. One could start from the universal, such as the claim about the general decline of Western values, and see the German case as a particular instantiation of this decline. Or one could claim that Germany's case was unique, and still link it with wider theories so as to argue that other countries might learn something from the German experience, just as Germany supposedly had. But the starting point made a difference. And the question of whether the past, which was necessarily particular, and a universalist stance could be combined in a coherent manner proved vexing for German intellectuals, even when they were not driven by a desire for apologetics. In particular, the question of whether the national framework of past crimes also mandated a continued national community of responsibility was inscribed in debates about German identity from the beginning and was to appear in various forms over the next forty years.

While many historians sought more or less exculpatory explanations, emigré writers immediately seized on the role of 'conscience of the nation', claiming to be accountable for the past and building a better, democratic and socialist, future. Anna Seghers, for instance, returning from her Mexican exile in 1947, wrote on her first journey through Germany that 'this was the moment when German writers had to enter the picture to be as clearly accountable as possible. Through the means of their vocation, they had to help their people in grasping its self-caused situation and in evoking its energy for a different, a better, peaceful new life'.[13]

Like the country itself, however, writers were deeply divided, most importantly between those who had to leave Germany and those who tried to survive in the Third Reich. Among the latter, there was a further divide between those, like Walter von Molo, who had remained silent in the German provinces and refused to publish, and those who had experienced actual conflicts with the regime and ended up in court or even in

---

[12] Bernd Faulenbach, 'Historistische Tradition und politische Neuorientierung: Zur Geschichtswissenschaft nach der "deutschen Katastrophe"', in Walter H. Pehle and Peter Sillem (eds), *Wissenschaft im geteilten Deutschland: Restauration oder Neubeginn nach 1945?* (Frankfurt/Main: Fischer, 1992), 191–204; here 198–9.

[13] Seghers quoted in Lerke von Saalfeld *et al.*, *Geschichte der Deutschen Literatur: Von den Anfängen bis zur Gegenwart* (Munich: Droemer Knaur, 1989), 645.

concentration camps. Moreover, a significant generational divide emerged between those authors who entered the War as adults and those who entered the War as adolescents, and who vigorously called for a renewal of the corrupted German language. Soon a fierce debate ensued between aggressive defenders of the experience of 'inner emigration', most notably Frank Thiess, and the exiles, primarily Thomas Mann, who condemned the literature written in Germany between 1933 and 1945. At the heart of this controversy was the question of the proper relation between aesthetics and politics, as well as the necessity of a political role for the writer – questions which were to be central to many intellectual debates in the Federal Republic, including the debate on unification.

However, these divides were in turn to be crosscut by the Cold War divide between East and West. The exiles were welcomed in the GDR and had many opportunities to publish, but were regarded with diffidence or even as traitors in the West. At the same time, many Western writers resorted to concepts of Western culture such as the normatively charged notion of the *Abendland* which they marshalled against Communism. The fact that the East–West divide had become almost impossible to transcend was made painfully obvious at the first – and last – all-German writers' congress in Berlin in October 1947.

From early on, however, some writers tried to bridge the gap between East and West. Thomas Mann was the first to make the argument that German writers needed to remain united by means of their primary *Heimat* [home], the German language. In a speech which he deliberately gave both in the Frankfurt Paulskirche and in the Weimar National Theatre on the occasion of Goethe's 200th birthday in the summer of 1949, Mann claimed: 'I do not know any zones. My visit is to Germany itself, Germany as a whole, and not to an occupation zone. Who should guarantee and represent [German] unity, if not an independent writer, whose true *Heimat* is the free German language, which is untouched by occupations.'[14] He marshalled the traditional German concept of the *Kulturnation* – a nation defined by a common culture transcending state borders, rather than a political community – which had already served nationalist poets in the eighteenth and nineteenth centuries, when Germany remained divided into numerous states and principalities. In that sense, rather than weakening the role of intellectuals in public, the Cold War and the national division seemed to strengthen it. Writers like Mann could play off culture against politics, and claim a representativeness which transcended the narrowness of ideological divides. Tending to – rather than healing – what was often referred to as the 'wound' of a divided Germany, while remaining above the direct political interests of either the East or

[14] Thomas Mann, 'Ansprache im Goethejahr 1949', in *Gesammelte Werke*, Vol. 11 (Frankfurt/Main: S. Fischer, 1960), 481–97; here 488.

West German government, became a public occupation which writers in particular consciously fashioned for themselves.

Immediately after the War, most intellectuals subscribed to a humanism which could take liberal, socialist or religious forms. These types of humanism shared a language of 'new beginnings', 'youth' and 'choice', which betrayed many remnants of the earlier interwar discourse of existentialist resoluteness.[15] The young intelligentisa which had returned from the battlefields adopted an attitude of disillusioned toughness and realism: already during the *Endkampf* [the final battles fought in defence of the Reich], they had acquired a thoroughgoing scepticism and distrust of grand political rhetoric.[16] This was most clearly pronounced in the journal *Der Ruf* [The Call], which found its intellectual core in a mixture of anti-fascism and democratic socialism.[17] Hans Werner Richter and Alfred Andersch, both of whom had been members of the KPD before 1933, had started working on a first version of *Der Ruf* in an American POW camp, attempting to make it an organ of the 'homeless', i.e. anti-Communist Left, a term which they adopted from Arthur Koestler. The *Ruf* authors directed their 'calls', which were often fatefully reminiscent of the Nazi language of heroic resoluteness, against both the older generation and, to a much lesser extent, the emigrants. While the emigrants were invited to unite with 'Germany's young generation', the emphasis on youth and the centrality of the experience of the front in the thought of the *Ruf* intellectuals effectively precluded such a coalition. *Der Ruf* reached an astonishing circulation of 70,000, but was banned by the Allies in 1947.

The group surrounding *Der Ruf*, however, was only the most prominent among a large web of intellectual circles and proto-parties which called for a 'third way' between capitalism and Communism, and which sought to construct an anti-fascist 'popular front'-style movement for Germany as a whole.[18] Their new humanism was to return to 'man as such', but it was also to bring about the unlikely union of 'allied soldiers, the men of European resistance and the German soldiers of the front, between political prisoners of the concentration camps and the former "Hitler boys"'.[19] The fact that the basis for this union was to be the 'existential' quality of their experience, which Hitler Youth and concentration camp survivors sup-

---

[15] Alfred Andersch, 'Das junge Europa formt sein Gesicht', in Hans Schwab-Felisch (ed.), *Der Ruf: Eine deutsche Nachkriegszeitschrift* (Munich: Deutscher Taschenbuch Verlag, 1962), 21–6.

[16] Bude, *Bilanz der Nachfolge*, 82.

[17] Jost Hermand, *Kultur im Wiederaufbau: Die Bundesrepublik Deutschland 1945–1965* (Munich: Nymphenburger, 1986), 138–40.

[18] Rainer Dohse, *Der Dritte Weg: Neutralitätsbestrebungen in Westdeutschland zwischen 1945 und 1955* (Hamburg: Holsten, 1974).

[19] Andersch, 'Das junge Europa', 23.

posedly shared, only demonstrated how even left-wing intellectuals were prone to collapse moral distinctions and turn a blind eye to the criminal complicity of many Germans. Within a united Europe pursuing a socialist third way both anti-capitalist and anti-Stalinist, Germany would also remain one, neutral country, acting, in Richter's conception, as a 'bridge' between East and West. After the Allies had banned *Der Ruf*, its protagonists formed the *Gruppe 47*, a loose association of writers chosen by Richter who met annually to discuss their work – and became an enormously influential cultural and political institution in the early Federal Republic.

By contrast, conservative intellectuals mostly advanced humanism, and the *Abendland* and its European Christian values in particular, as a rallying point against the Communist threat from the East, against the immediate past, and, later and less obviously, against the increasing Americanization and liberalization of German daily life in the 1950s.[20] This stance was most prominent in the 'Journal for European Thought', *Merkur*, which disavowed all ideologies and became the platform for traditional literary criticism, publishing international exponents of the *Abendland* ideology, most prominently Ortega y Gasset and T. S. Eliot.

At the universities only a minority called for a reckoning with the immediate past. In philosophy, only Theodor Litt, Julius Ebbinghaus and, most prominently, Karl Jaspers, engaged with the question of guilt. Litt, in a deeply ambivalent, but highly influential argument, claimed that the horrors of the Nazi period had, on one level, constituted an 'unmasking of man' and yielded a 'clarity of knowledge of ourselves'. The 'truth which makes us free' by recognizing the universal evil of which man was capable proved to be the insight which the Germans had learned from their time in the 'abyss of error, pain and guilt'[21]. Ebbinghaus called for a revival of traditional Kantianism and a thorough 'self-enlightenment' of the Germans about their behaviour during the past twelve years.[22] Most importantly, however, after a long silence imposed by the Nazis, Karl Jaspers published *The Question of German Guilt* in 1946. The book established the fundamental parameters for post-war discussions of German guilt and its connection to the German nation – to such an extent, in fact, that left-liberal intellectuals like Grass and Habermas continued to return to Jaspers's categories, in the unification debate in particular.

Jaspers drew a seminal distinction between criminal, political, moral

---

[20] Axel Schildt, *Zwischen Abendland und Amerika: Studien zur westdeutschen Ideenlandschaft der 50er Jahre* (Munich: R. Oldenbourg, 1999).

[21] Theodor Litt, *Von der Sendung der Philosophie* (Wiesbaden: Dieterich'sche Verlagsbuchhandlung, 1946), 24–5.

[22] Helmut Fahrenbach, 'Nationalsozialismus und der Neuanfang "westdeutscher Philosophie" 1945–1950', in Pehle and Sillem (eds), *Wissenschaft*, 99–112.

and metaphysical guilt.[23] Criminal guilt resulted from having broken positive laws; political guilt was due to being implicated as a citizen in the crimes of a murderous regime; moral guilt was incurred by failing to live up to one's moral duties; and, finally, metaphysical guilt referred to the rupture of a fabric of basic solidarity between all human beings. Criminal guilt could be dealt with by the courts, evaluating political guilt was in the hands of the War's victors, but every German individually had to work through moral guilt. Finally, metaphysical guilt could only be judged by God. Jaspers rejected the thesis of 'collective guilt', arguing for the concept of 'collective responsibility' instead. He linked the question of guilt with the question of German unity, claiming that both a democratic political identity and a German *Gemeinsamkeit* [togetherness], i.e. social integration, could only be achieved if the Germans shouldered collective responsibility.

But Jaspers's account of the institutional expression of this imperative to assume guilt – lest it be imposed – remained ambiguous: had the Germans once and for all squandered their nation-state, allowing what he called the 'true German as world citizen' to emerge, and, in some sense, even making the Germans take the place of the Jews as a 'pariah' nation – or was the German nation to be a pariah for a limited time only, potentially regaining its statehood after a period of purification?[24] The first option was suggested by Jaspers's remark in a letter to Hannah Arendt that 'Germany is the first nation that, as a nation, has gone to ruin', and by his admission – which horrified Arendt – that 'now that Germany is destroyed, I feel at ease for the first time'.[25] Jaspers rejected his previous nationalism, which he had adopted from his teacher Max Weber, denying that a liberal political identity and a nation-state framework could go together for the Germans. Yet he still identified with German high culture, which supposedly could be rescued from the Third Reich, and clung to the notion of the *Kulturnation* as an untainted source of social cohesion. Moreover, he was primarily occupied with the meaning of being German after the War, which made the debate on German guilt more of a dispute about national identity than an engagement with the past as such. As Dagmar Barnouw has pointed out, Jaspers's psychological and personal approach to the Germans' 'political victimization and moral responsibility' was largely

---

[25] Karl Jaspers, *Die Schuldfrage: Ein Beitrag zur deutschen Frage* (Zurich: Artemis, 1946), 10–14. Trans., E. B. Ashton (New York: Dial Press, 1947).

[24] Anson Rabinbach, 'The German as Pariah: Karl Jaspers' *The Question of German Guilt*', in *In the Shadow of Catastrophe: German Intellectuals between Enlightenment and Apocalypse* (Berkeley: University of California Press, 1997), 129–65; here 138.

[25] *Hannah Arendt–KarlJaspers–Briefwechsel 1926–1969*, eds. Lotte Köhler and Hans Saner (Munich: Piper, 1985), 82 and 93.

'informed by a diagnostic and therapeutic empathy'.[26] Not only did this approach obscure the more socio-political reasons for the rise of Nazism; it also betrayed a certain German self-centredness, including the nucleus of the argument that Germans, after their historical 'catastrophe', were in fact more than other peoples in a position to contribute to the renewal of human existence 'from its origins' for which Jaspers called.

And yet, Jaspers's stance, supported by licensed journals such as Dolf Sternberger's *Die Wandlung*, stood in significant contrast to many intellectuals' pronouncements which simply dissolved German guilt in universal narratives of the decline of the West. Jaspers also insisted that, as much as moral guilt was a question for one's individual conscience, the only way to deal with German guilt as a whole was through free public communication and what he called the 'solidarity of charitable struggle', instead of mutual moral condemnation.[27] This claim, rooted in Jaspers's philosophy of free communication between equals, was taken up by numerous intellectuals who established a link between remembrance and a democratic political culture, most importantly by Habermas who drew on Jaspers's thought during both the historians' dispute and the unification debate. Moreover, Jaspers had also wished for free and equal communication about the democratic foundations of the West German Constitution – even if he himself, still driven by a 'fear of the masses', envisaged rather 'authoritarian liberal' foundations.[28] Nevertheless, like many intellectuals, he felt that the opportunity for a proper foundation had been missed and might have to be compensated for at some point in the future.

Not surprisingly, some of the intellectuals most discredited by their involvement with National Socialism opposed this trend towards humanism, internationalism, and, most importantly, an open discussion about the past in the public sphere. Where many writers, even Ernst Jünger, called for a revival of faith, Carl Schmitt, the 'Crown Jurist of the Third Reich', blamed theology (and technology) for the corruption of justice.[29] Where most intellectuals demanded a form of humanism, Martin

---

[26] Dagmar Barnouw, *Germany 1945: Views of War and Destruction* (Bloomington: Indiana University Press, 1996), 146.

[27] Jaspers, *Die Schuldfrage*, 17.

[28] Kurt Salamun, *Karl Jaspers* (Munich: C. H. Beck, 1985), 105. See also Hans Mommsen, 'Von Weimar nach Bonn: Zum Demokratieverständnis der Deutschen', in Axel Schildt and Arnold Sywottek (eds), *Modernisierung im Wiederaufbau: Die westdeutsche Gesellschaft der 50er Jahre* (Bonn: Dietz, 1993), 745–58.

[29] Jünger called for a 'European fatherland' united by one Church and a liberal–authoritarian state in 'Der Friede', in *Gesammelte Werke*, Vol. 7: Essays I (Stuttgart: Klett-Cotta, 1980), 193–236. Schmitt disingenuously defended jurists against theologians in *Ex Captivitate Salus: Erfahrungen der Zeit 1945/47* (Cologne: Greven, 1950).

Heidegger blamed Western humanism (and its philosophical tradition of 'metaphysical subjectivism') for the atrocities of the twentieth century.[30] Arguably, they were laying the seeds of the nationalist postmodernism of post-unification Germany, or, rather, sending out a proto-postmodernist message in a bottle, which was found by ideological movements forming themselves in the late 1980s and early 1990s. These movements opposed the later democratic humanism advanced, for instance, by Habermas, but were eager to take up the message left to them by their intellectual great-grandfathers.

More importantly, these intellectuals formed what one might call a 'conservative counterculture'. Rather than wanting to debate guilt in public, right-wing intellectuals preferred a stance of 'shame' and silence. They were highly indignant about what they perceived as the outside world charging the German people with 'collective guilt' – although the Allies had been careful not to give this impression – and they were eager to portray themselves as, above all, victims.[31] As Ernst Jünger put it, 'after the War, one bangs on the seismographers. One cannot, however, let the barometer be punished for the typhoon, unless one wants to be counted among the primitives'.[32] They also strongly resented the returned emigrants, whom Schmitt denounced as the post-war era's democratic 'pin-ups' and whose call for confronting the past they saw as merely a means to consolidate the personal power they had acquired with the Allies' help.[33] Personal dignity and integrity, or so these intellectuals thought, could only be preserved through an aristocratic ethos of tact and distance – whereby a veil of knowing silence was drawn over the past and the intrusions of public pedagogy and psychology were fiercely resisted. A rigid demarcation was kept vis-à-vis any demands to 'confess', 'convert' or reveal one's feelings directly. In that sense, these intellectuals revived the cult of 'cold conduct' and the ethos of distance which had already helped many of the 'free-floating' intellectuals of the 1920s to remain afloat during a time of rapid change as well as widespread moral and political disorientation.[34]

[30] Martin Heidegger, 'Brief über den "Humanismus" (1946)', in *Wegmarken* [Collected Works, Vol. 9] (Frankfurt/Main: Vittorio Klostermann, 1976), 313–64. See also Anson Rabinbach, 'Heidegger's Letter on Humanism as Text and Event', in *In the Shadow of Catastrophe*, 97–128.

[31] Dirk van Laak, 'Trotz und Nachurteil: Rechtsintellektuelle im Anschluß an das "Dritte Reich"', in Wilfried Loth and Bernd-A. Rusinek (eds), *Verwandlungspolitik: NS-Eliten in der westdeutschen Nachkriegsgesellschaft* (Frankfurt/Main: Campus, 1998), 55–77.

[32] Jünger quoted by Elliot Y. Neaman, *A Dubious Past: Ernst Jünger and the Politics of Literature after Nazism* (Berkeley: University of California Press, 1999), 155.

[33] Carl Schmitt, *Glossarium: Aufzeichnungen der Jahre 1947–1951* (Berlin: Duncker & Humblot, 1991), 256.

[34] Helmut Lethen, *Verhaltenslehren der Kälte: Lebensversuche zwischen den Kriegen* (Frankfurt/Main: Suhrkamp, 1994).

Two cultures, then, opposed each other in early post-war Germany. On one side, there was an official public culture of guilt and democratic humanism, sanctioned by the Allies through the licensed journals, and centred on emigrants and liberals such as Jaspers. On the other side stood an obstinate culture of silence, in which honour was preserved through taboos. The culture of guilt and communication, not surprisingly, dominated in public, but the counterculture of silence became more characteristic for the private and semi-private life of the young Republic.[35]

Legitimation Projects and Cultural Pessimism

In 1950s Germany, feelings of social cohesion centred on a fierce anti-communism which Konrad Adenauer encouraged to forge a new political consensus. Anti-communism was subsumed under a general anti-totalitariansm, so that opposition to the Soviet Union could also be presented as *ex-post* resistance to National Socialism. In opposition to Adenauer's project of integrating the state into the Western Alliance – all the while claiming that reunification was compatible with the policy of Western integration – the Social Democratic Party and most left-wing intellectuals clung to the goal of national unity, which they thought the 'Chancellor of the Allies' was cynically betraying. At the same time, Adenauer seemed to carry out Jaspers's conceptions in the realm of *Realpolitik*, since he effectively made the GDR into a pariah, denying it – and any state maintaining diplomatic relations with East Germany – recognition.

The GDR also started its first consolidation with an ideological definition *ex negativo*. The leaders of the SED [Socialist Unity Party of Germany, the GDR's ruling party] constructed a legitimation narrative of anti-fascist Communist heroes and fascist villains, from which all victims who could not be transformed into heroes disappeared. Thus Jews and homosexuals did not feature in the anti-fascist canon of interpretation, and the GDR saw a return of public antisemitism in the early 1950s with the 'anti-cosmopolitan purges'.[36] Anti-fascism, based on anti-capitalism, remained dangerously close to antisemitism, and later contributed to a pronounced stance of anti-Zionism on the part of the GDR.

Thus, a division of memory was established by the two states, as they parcelled out the heritage of the National Socialist 'catastrophe'. The Federal Republic took on the legacy of the Third Reich, both by claiming to be its official heir in international law, and by claiming that legally the

---

[35] Aleida Assmann and Ute Frevert, *Geschichtsvergessenheit/Geschichstversessenheit: Vom Umgang mit deutschen Vergangenheiten nach 1945* (Stuttgart: Deutsche Verlags-Anstalt, 1999), 112.

[36] Herf, *Divided Memory*, 106–61.

Reich continued to exist in its borders of 31 December 1937. West Germany also claimed to be the only representative of the German nation, not recognizing the East German state and East German citizenship, thereby paradoxically making the East Germans virtual citizens of a country to which they had no access. The GDR, on the other hand, monopolized anti-fascism *and* universalized fascism by arguing that the fascism latent in capitalism could break out again anywhere in the West. The SED also confiscated its Communist share of the resistance, while the West Germans expunged the Communist resistance from the historical canon altogether (and only reluctantly exonerated the conservative resistance from a lingering suspicion of treason). The West also from early on decided to deal with *Vergangenheitsbewältigung* in a procedural manner, paying 'restitution' to the victims, and, after many delays, holding trials in the late 1950s and early 1960s. A stale philosemitism in the public sphere, however, was complemented by a retrospective attempt to exclude the Jews from the history of Germany proper.[37] While 'Auschwitz', as a shorthand for the Holocaust as a whole, was condemned, Adenauer no less than prominent historians insisted that the German people had not known of the Judeocide, which had been instigated by Hitler and his small band of political gangsters. Isolating Auschwitz from the structures of the Nazi 'racial state' and patterns of everyday complicity, remaking National Socialism into Hitlerism and thereby exculpating traditional German elites and the Wehrmacht, were the main strategies of coping with what increasingly seemed like a demonic, even unreal twelve-year interlude.[38] At the same time, the government complemented procedural *Vergangen-heitsbewältigung* with what retrospectively has been called *Vergangenheits-politik* [politics of dealing with the past]: amnesty and integration were offered to Nazis and even War criminals in exchange for accepting the political order of the Federal Republic and refraining from extreme right-wing agitation. This policy found broad support among the population, and was clothed in a language of 'honour' which allowed the smooth transition of former Nazis into the Federal Republic and which was perfectly compatible with the counter-culture of silence discussed above.[39] *Vergangenheitspolitik* was not an aberration from democracy, but its consequence.

The process of coming to terms with the past, then, was fundamentally warped by the East–West conflict from the very start. While the GDR had

---

[37] Frank Stern, *The Whitewashing of the Yellow Badge: Antisemitism and Philosemitism in Postwar Germany* (Oxford: Pergamon, 1992).

[38] Michael Burleigh and Wolfgang Wippermann, *The Racial State: Germany 1933–1945* (Cambridge: Cambridge University Press, 1991).

[39] Norbert Frei, *Vergangenheitspolitik: Die Anfänge der Bundesrepublik und die NS-Vergangenheit* (Munich: C. H. Beck, 1996).

begun *Vergangenheitsbewältigung* with a state-directed, anti-fascist social transformation, which allowed for individual exoneration and amnesia, the Federal Republic initially had considerable difficulty in going beyond a procedural approach to the past. Nevertheless, the past was not simply repressed *tout court*, as the generation of 1968 in particular later asserted. Rather, as always, memory was highly selective, often conflated as well as conflicted, and operated through multiple media such as cheap novels, journals and, increasingly, television. In general, the Third Reich, which remained associated with 'good times', was separated from the Holocaust, which was peripheral to a larger collective memory of the War itself, and the Wehrmacht was separated from the SS. The period of 1933 to 1941 continued to be remembered positively, while 1941 to 1948 retained negative, even traumatic associations, and explained the seeming 'numbness' among the population which so many critics remarked upon.[40] These dissociations and traumas accounted for the sense foreign observers had of what Hannah Arendt in 1950 described as a 'flight from reality'.[41]

Left-liberal intellectuals were fiercely critical of what they saw as the early Federal Republic's 'restorative tendencies', economic reconstruction and rearmament, making themselves into specialists for the detection of continuities with pre-1945 Germany.[42] This critique was based on the notion that West Germany had missed crucial opportunities in the immediate post-war period, as anti-fascism and democratic socialism, supposedly widespread among the population, could have been the foundations for a genuinely new beginning. Instead, there seemed to be continuities everywhere: in the bureaucracy, in the 'culture industry', in business, where former SS members now taught management techniques, and, above all, in the government itself, where Adenauer symbolized his willingness to integrate former Nazis through his state secretary Hans Globke, who had written the commentary on the Nuremberg racial laws.[43] What left-liberal intellectuals could not — or did not want to — see was that 1950s were not a simple 'restoration', but a much more paradoxical modernization under 'conservative auspices'.[44] Since the focus was so firmly on continuities, and

---

[40] Axel Schildt, 'Der Umgang mit der NS-Vergangenheit in der Öffentlichkeit der Nachkriegszeit', in Loth and Rusinek (eds), *Verwandlungspolitik*, 19–54.

[41] Hannah Arendt, 'Besuch in Deutschland 1950: Die Nachwirkungen des Naziregimes', in *Zur Zeit: Politische Essays*, ed. Marie Luise Knott (Munich: Deutsche Taschenbuch Verlag, 1989), 43–70.

[42] The foundational text for the critique of the restoration was Walter Dirks's 'Der restaurative Charakter der Epoche', in *Frankfurter Hefte*, Vol. 5 (1950), 942–5; here 954.

[43] Ulrich Herbert, *Best: Biographische Studien über Radikalismus, Weltanschauung und Vernunft, 1903–1989* (Bonn: J. H. W. Dietz, 1996).

[44] Christoph Kleßmann quoted in Axel Schildt, *Konservatismus in Deutschland: Von den Anfängen im 18. Jahrhundert bis zur Gegenwart* (Munich: C. H. Beck, 1998), 229.

since the standard for a successful break with the past was nothing less than an all-German anti-fascist revolution, these critics often failed to see that even the 'conservative democracy' of Adenauer was in fact promoting a revolution. Only that this was more a revolution in patterns of everyday life, and consumption habits in particular, on the one hand, and in foreign policy on the other, which integrated Germany, or parts of it at least, into the West for the first time.

At the same time, reunification became an issue frequently raised by the Left. This was not only because the Left felt that Adenauer was betraying the East Germans, but also because a united Germany might be an altogether different country, in which the ossified structures in both East and West Germany could be shaken up again — or so Walter Dirks, who had first diagnosed a 'restoration', claimed in a radio speech in 1957. Significantly, however, Dirks also sought to differentiate between 'restoration' and 'reaction', and argued that the response to the former had to be a sober 'working on public opinion', an attitude of 'telling it as it is', rather than violent or even revolutionary politics. Unlike in the aftermath of the First World War, political violence was discredited, as were many of the cultural traditions which had been the foundation of antidemocratic politics before 1945 — even if its remnants survived as the basis for both left- and right-wing cultural critiques in the 1950s.

Intellectually, the 1950s were above all characterized by cultural pessimism — which could be found on the Left and well as the Right. Many intellectuals rather defensively advocated 'culture' as an antidote to the threats of massification and technology. A consciousness of crisis and catastrophe, particularly the pre-war fear of 'the masses' and a tendency to build whole philosophical systems on the basis of bourgeois anxieties, continued well into the 1950s. The most widely read philosophical book in Germany from the 1930s to the 1950s was Ortega y Gasset's *Revolt of the Masses*.[45]

Another kind of pessimism was propagated most effectively by thinkers who had put their faith in a collective and total political self-transformation earlier in the century. They had subscribed to the movement loosely known as the 'Conservative Revolution' in the 1920s, when radical nationalist intellectuals had abandoned the idea of 'conservatism' in the sense of resisting modernity — instead, they sought to actively reshape present conditions, especially through a rebirth of the national collective, and create conditions which were then worth preserving again. After the War and the discrediting of any kind of radical activism, they resigned themselves to a so-called state of *posthistoire*: an 'end of history' in the sense that technology would continue its victorious march of

[45] Axel Schildt, *Moderne Zeiten: Freizeit, Massenmedien und 'Zeitgeist' in der Bundesrepublik der 50er Jahre* (Hamburg: Christians, 1995), 327.

rationalization, while all ideological and cultural options had been effectively exhausted.[46] In other words, the gesture of existential resoluteness, so typical of the 1920s, was replaced by a gesture of resignation. In a spirit of *tristesse oblige*, this supposed disavowal of all ideologies was accompanied by an affirmation of modern, technocratic government, guided by the supposedly inevitable imperatives associated with the dominance of 'secondary systems' (Hans Freyer), 'superstructures' (Arnold Gehlen) and the 'technical state' (Helmut Schelsky). Like narratives about the decline of the West, the theory of *posthistoire* was a reaction to the excesses of nationalism, which allowed such a thoroughgoing historical scepticism, that any specific engagement with the failure of intellectuals during and after Weimar could be avoided. This in fact enabled right-wing intellectuals to re-adopt the aura of antidemocratic detachment which had already been prevalent during the Weimar Republic, and which fitted with the counter-culture of silence. One of the side effects of *posthistoire* was simply that the most recent history did not matter. Nevertheless, while the advocacy of technocratic government hardly constituted a real reconciliation between conservatives and liberal democracy, it also did mark a decisive 'deradicalization' of German conservatism.[47] Like the Marxist Weimar Left, radical conservative nationalism did not find a home in the Federal Republic.

The apologia for a modernity both ceaselessly racing forward *and* philosophically frozen at the same time, as well as culturally pessimistic attitudes also tended to downplay the importance of the East–West division. For thinkers like Schmitt and Heidegger, East and West followed the same 'progressivist' philosophies of history, and both succumbed to the pervasive spirit of what Schmitt had earlier called 'technicity', i.e. a faith in technology linked to a hedonist promise of complete human happiness.[48] Such views did not prescribe a particular attitude to reunification, since the entire East–West confrontation was subsumed under a general disenchantment with what seemed to be an age of unfettered instrumental rationality.

The tendency to close off history among conservative intellectuals was mirrored by a widespread distrust of politics among the population as a whole. After many years characterized by an excessive 'primacy of the political' and mass mobilization, democracy was expected to be

---

[46] Lutz Niethammer, *Posthistoire: Has History Come to an End?*, trans. Patrick Camiller (London: Verso, 1992).

[47] Jerry Z. Muller, *The Other God That Failed: Hans Freyer and the Deradicalization of German Conservatism* (Princeton: Princeton University Press, 1987).

[48] See Carl Schmitt, *Römischer Katholizismus und politische Form* (1923; Stuttgart: Klett-Cotta, 1984) for Schmitt's initial critique of instrumental rationality.

administered 'from above', with little participation and the persistence of authoritarian attitudes. Institutionally, the Federal Republic of the 1950s was a liberal-democratic state, but in terms of political culture, it was still characterized by remnants of a patriarchal authoritarianism best embodied in the figure of Adenauer himself. In short, Germany still suffered from a post-fascist democratic deficit.

Unlike in the fields of philosophy or the social sciences, almost no exiles returned to redirect the course of German historiography. Political scientists, on the other hand, consciously sought to carve out a space for 'contemporary history' in opposition to the traditional historians, and aimed to newly constitute their subject as a 'science of democracy' and Re-education, with the double task of research and public pedagogy. Operating mainly with the concept of totalitarianism, they sought to contribute to an 'antitotalitarian consensus', and also to draw the appropriate lessons from Weimar. Taught by older liberal intellectuals and emigrants who had returned from exile, they came to subscribe to what one might call 'liberal institutionalism'. This stance consisted primarily in a defence of the integrity and dignity of liberal-democratic institutions, especially the parliament and the parties which had been treated with such contempt during Weimar. It also involved an attempt to overcome a traditional German view of the state as standing completely above society and determining society's general interest. A pluralism of organized interests was explicitly recognized, and the state was seen as the instrument of society and private interests, rather than reigning supreme above them.[49] Liberal institutionalists like Theodor Eschenburg and Wilhelm Hennis also had a noticeable influence on politics, as they regularly commented on institutional questions in German newspapers, and often discreetly advised members of the government. Moreover, these intellectuals engaged in a kind of intellectual *Vergangenheitsbewältigung* through writing a critical history which sought to explain why bourgeois intellectuals had succumbed to National Socialism.[50] Such explorations into recent intellectual history were also to provide normative guidelines for intellectuals in the present, by enabling them to draw historically accurate lessons from Weimar failures.

More radical exiled scholars who had returned to the Federal Republic also consciously 'deradicalized' their theories. In particular, Horkheimer

[49] Christian Graf von Krockow, 'Staatsideologie oder demokratisches Bewußtsein: Die deutsche Alternative', in: *Politische Vierteljahresschrift*, Vol. 9 (1965), 118–31.

[50] For instance Cristian Graf von Krockow, *Die Entscheidung: Eine Untersuchung über Ernst Jünger, Carl Schmitt, Martin Heidegger* (Stuttgart: F. Enke, 1958) and Kurt Sontheimer, *Antidemokratisches Denken in der Weimarer Republik: Die politischen Ideen des deutschen Nationalismus zwischen 1918 und 1933* (Munich: Nymphenburger, 1962).

and Adorno, who came to exert an unprecedented intellectual influence in the 1950s and 1960s, sought to expunge overt references to Marxism from the Frankfurt School's literature, and adapted to the *bürgerliche* climate of the Federal Republic. But Adorno in particular also sought to remind the West Germans that, even if everyday 'normal life' seemed to have been re-established, the thought of 'normality' after the 'catastrophe' of the Holocaust was 'idiotic'.[51] While his philosophical writings were characterized by increasing cultural pessimism about a world dominated by instrumental reason and bureaucracy in particular, Adorno also adopted the public role of a democratic adult educator, thereby contributing significantly to the intellectual foundations of West Germany.

Intellectual Foundations: In Search of Another Country

The end of the 1950s and the early 1960s have rightly been called the period of the 'intellectual foundation' of the Federal Republic. It is no accident that Jürgen Habermas once called himself a member of the 'generation of 1958', rather than adopting the label of the 'sceptical generation'.[52] During this time, the members of his generation, who were to dominate public life in the Federal Republic up to the present day, first burst onto the public scene. Grass for instance caused a sensation (and a scandal on account of its supposed pornography) with the *Tin Drum* in 1959, while Habermas, having started his publishing career with an attack on Heidegger in 1953, wrote an increasing number of articles pointing out the continuities between Nazi and West German intellectuals. It was at this time that the building blocks for the peculiar role of the left-liberal intellectual in West Germany were put into place.

Most importantly, in the late 1950s, the attitude to dealing with the past slowly began to change. The public was stirred up by a succession of scandals, in particular a number of antisemitic attacks such as the desecration of the Cologne synagogue on Christmas day 1959, and the now apparent failings of the judiciary which were revealed in a number of trials. It was in 1959 that Adorno delivered an influential radio talk on 'What does working through the past mean?' In the same year the philosopher and sociologist Helmuth Plessner republished *Die verspätete Nation* (The Belated Nation), which he had written in his Dutch exile in the

---

[51] Theodor W. Adorno, *Minima Moralia: Reflexionen aus dem beschädigten Leben* (Frankfurt/Main: Suhrkamp, 1951), 91.

[52] Clemens Albrecht *et al.*, *Die intellektuelle Gründung der Bundesrepublik: Eine Wirkungsgeschichte der Frankfurter Schule* (Frankfurt/M.: Campus, 1999).

mid-1930s.[53] The former argued for a democratic 'vaccination' through enlightenment and knowledge about the past, and pointed to the particular dangers of fascist continuities within democracy, rather than of anti-democratic neo-Nazis. Plessner, in turn, contrasted the healthy democratic developments of the states of Western Europe with the pathological course of German history. Germany had been a 'belated nation' since it had 'missed' the seventeenth century crucial for the development of a strong bourgeoisie and a modern, liberal democracy. Its desperate efforts to catch up and compensate for deficiencies in state building and national consciousness had contributed to the fact that it had been led down a 'special path' – a so-called *Sonderweg* – the end point of which was the Third Reich.

The advocacy both of an active engagement with the past and of the Westernization of Germany became central to the role of left-wing and liberal intellectuals in the Federal Republic. The intellectual was to be watchful about continuities with the pre-1945 past, and re-orient Germany towards the political and cultural traditions of the West. This did not exclude the possibility of German intellectuals sometimes criticizing the West themselves *de haute en bas*, which, however, stood in marked contrast to the fact that political leaders – in both East and West – were over-eager to please their respective superpowers with their ideological zeal. Moreover, in contrast to the academic doyens and their cultural pessimism which had still dominated the early and mid-1950s, younger scholars tried to consciously define themselves in opposition to the tradition of the 'German mandarins' and to the illiberal inter-war intellectuals in particular. But the role of the critical intellectual was also defined in contrast to the 'party intellectual' co-opted by the state in the GDR, a point Grass insisted on at a number of meetings between East and West German writers. Finally, this 'liberal reconstitution' of the intellectuals was also opposed to the 'restoration' under Adenauer – and in particular his increasingly autocratic behaviour in the late 1950s and early 1960s, when he attempted to become president and establish a government-directed television station. In that sense, the role of the intellectual was based on a triple negative – against the mandarins of the past, the party intellectuals to the East and the technocratic specialists which the 'economic miracle' seemed to require.

Often themselves of petty bourgeois origins, left-liberal intellectuals were horrified by the crass materialism of the 1950s, and revolted by the petty bourgeois nature of West Germany – and their criticism was in fact not entirely free from the cultural pessimism and anti-modernism

[53] Theodor W. Adorno, 'Was bedeutet: Aufarbeitung der Vergangenheit?', in Theodor W. Adorno, *Gesammelte Schriften*, ed. Rolf Tiedemann, Vol. 10, (Frankfurt/Main: Suhrkamp, 1977), 555–72. Helmuth Plessner, *Die verspätete Nation: Über die Verführbarkeit bürgerlichen Geistes* (1935; Stuttgart: W. Kohlhammer, 1959).

pervasive among figures on the Right. Jürgen Habermas, for instance, analyzed the 'illusions on the marriage market' in terms of the commodification of emotional life during the 'economic miracle', while Hans Magnus Enzensberger and Martin Walser wrote satirical novels and hostile poems about the philistinism of the late 1950s.[54]

Opposing Adenauer's anti-communism, the intellectuals often opted for a vaguely defined anti-anti-communism. But while they were sometimes quicker in denouncing the supposed oppression of French intellectuals under de Gaulle than mobilizing support for their imprisoned East German counterparts, they had few illusions about the true nature of the GDR – in fact, some saw the GDR as worse in certain respects than the Third Reich. For them, East Germany was hardly the 'better', anti-fascist Germany – if anything, the existence of the GDR did as much damage to the West German Left, as the Third Reich had done to the Right.[55] Rather than the GDR, it was the vaguely defined anti-fascist, democratic-cum-socialist Germany, which Richter, Andersch and Dirks had advocated immediately after the War that became the implicit standard of critique. Not least, however, this stance was an ex-post facto resistance to National Socialism – which also explained the curious hostility of some post-war intellectuals to the emigrants. After all, an imaginary democratic socialist German *Résistance* would have worked from within the country, rather than constituting another intellectual and moral possibility outside Germany, as the emigrants supposedly did.[56] On the other hand, it was noticeable how many left-liberal intellectual themselves actually chose to live in another country, especially in the neutral states of Scandinavia and Switzerland, while fully participating in the *Gruppe 47* and making frequent political interventions. Hans Magnus Enzensberger, for instance, drafted his polemics and his tortured answer to 'Am I a German?' on a Norwegian island, while a whole 'colony' of writers, including Grass, resided in the Ticino.

Intellectuals, however, were in fact not as alienated from the politics of the Federal Republic as Andersch's slogan of the 'homeless Left' or Hans Magnus Enzensberger's longing for 'another country' and his notion of the Federal Republic as a *feindesland* [a country of enemies] would suggest. While they attempted to foster a culture of suspicion vis-à-vis the new state, they *did*, by and large, subscribe to the liberal values of the West

[54] Jürgen Habermas, 'Illusionen auf dem Heiratsmarkt', in *Merkur*, Vol. 10 (1956), 996–1004.

[55] Hans Werner Richter, 'In einem zweigeteilten Land', in Horst Krüger (ed.), *Was ist heute links? Thesen und Theorien zu einer politischen Position* (Munich: Paul List, 1963), 94–100; here 96.

[56] Frank Trommler, 'Die nachgeholte Résistance: Politik und Gruppenethos im historischen Zusammenhang', in Justus Fetscher *et al.* (eds), *Die Gruppe 47 in der Geschichte der Bundesrepublik* (Würzburg: Königshausen & Neumann, 1991), 9–22.

German Constitution, and supported its democratic institutions – even if it was sometimes a logic of the lesser evil that led them to this stance. They were reformers, not revolutionaries. In particular, they sought to provide a model of 'critical' and 'democratic citizenship' as an antidote to Germany's continuing democratic deficit.[57] They were eager to complement the establishment of democratic institutions with a change in political culture and the development of genuinely democratic attitudes among the population, an aim which was bound to be frustrated in the short run.[58] Consequently, as much as Heinrich Böll was a critic of and a cultural 'counter-figure' to Adenauer, he also came to complement the Chancellor in the project of democratization 'from above' – an irony which many intellectuals could only see (and admit) in retrospect, just as much as they could only later see that critique and consumerism were ultimately *both* part of the Westernization of the Federal Republic.

The *Gruppe 47*, while rejecting any explicit political programme, also understood itself as a 'democratic fire brigade' (Hans Werner Richter), and, de facto, came to play the role of a central, institutionalized antiestablishment, which would instruct the people on how to be democratic citizens. As Richter pointed out, the intellectuals aimed at 'the formation of democratic elites, preceding the Re-education of the masses' – an idea which had also been at the heart of American Re-education policies and which Richter probably had first picked up in a POW camp.[59] Richter, the uncontested chief of this democratic fire brigade, however, consciously rejected the direct politicization of literature as well as the acquisition of direct power, instead working through a method of 'indirect influence'. The gunpowder of literature as such was to be kept dry – and, so the theory went, through their independent cultural standing, intellectuals would have all the more political influence.

More or less consciously, the writers of the *Gruppe 47* came to re-enact the very process which Jürgen Habermas was to describe in his famous 1962 book *Structural Transformation of the Public Sphere* about the eighteenth century: the formation of a public sphere, in which intellectuals reasonably discussed literary matters, before beginning to make moral and political claims in the name of public reason on the government, thereby

[57] van der Will, 'From the 1940s to the 1990s'.

[58] For a useful distinction between 'institutional' and 'cultural' strategies in democratization, see Anne Sa'adah, *Germany's Second Chance: Trust, Justice, and Democratization* (Cambridge, Mass.: Harvard University Press, 1998), who makes a convincing case why institutions as part of an essentially 'Hobbesian' strategy have to come first. It is nevertheless crucial to recognize that institutions have a moral content and are subject to demands for legitimacy – lest one succumbs to the adulation of institutions put forward by Arnold Gehlen and his followers.

[59] Hans Werner Richter, 'Fünfzehn Jahre', in *Almanach der Gruppe 47 1947–1963* (Reinbek: Rowohlt, 1962), 7–16; here 10.

providing a model for civic deliberation among the population more gen-erally.[60] Only that intellectuals did not debate political matters in salons and coffee houses, as they had done two hundred years earlier, but in the popular late-night radio programmes and highbrow journals, as well as the increasingly publicized meetings of the *Gruppe 47*. At these meetings, writers had fifteen minutes to sit on the 'electric chair' and read from their works, which were then ruthlessly judged by fellow writers and critics. While their criteria might have differed from those prevalent in the culture of intrigue and intimacy of the eighteenth-century salon, there was nevertheless a premium put on non-polemical and non-personal exchange based on what Richter saw as an 'Anglo-Saxon model' of debate.[61] Richter's generation was traumatized by the disunity and polemical self-destruction of the Left during the 1920s and especially the early 1930s. 'Anglo-Saxon debating' was thought a barrier to such polemical self-destruction.

While proclaiming that there was no 'group ideology', Richter was in fact eager to present a united front to the outside world through an *esprit de corps*, express a general will in petitions and pursue his own left-liberal 'policy of strength'.[62] In the same vein, while writers were quick to deny that they saw their role as that of the 'conscience of the nation', the circles and groups which Richter and his allies initiated in fact sought to fulfil precisely this function.[63] Nevertheless, the only official common denomi-nator they could agree on was democratic socialism, although it was never entirely clear what was either socialist or especially democratic about it.[64] Or, as Enzensberger admitted in retrospect, they had been 'latter-day lib-erals, good Social Democrats, moralists and socialists without clearly defined aims, anti-fascists without a programme for the future'.[65] Still, for all their programmatic vagueness, the intellectuals were able to do what was indispensable for intellectuals in order to have any effect at all, namely to define one general interest, in this case 'democratization', to which criticisms of particular issues could be related.

As 'democratic elites', they were also slowly to move into the media, or

---

[60] Jürgen Habermas, *The Structural Transformation of the Public Sphere: An Inquiry into a Category of Bourgeois Society* trans. Thomas Burger and Frederick Lawrence (1962; Cambridge, Mass.: MIT Press, 1989).

[61] Hans Werner Richter to Fritz J. Raddatz, 3 August 1966, in Hans Werner Richter, *Briefe*, ed. Sabine Cofalla (Munich: Hanser, 1997), 622–6; here 623.

[62] *Ibid.*

[63] Hans Werner Richter to Ernst Nolte, 10 March 1957, in Richter, *Briefe*, 245–7.

[64] The notion of democratic socialism also explained the enthusiasm of these intellectuals for the 'other '68', namely the Prague spring, which seemed to come closest to realizing some of their political ideals.

[65] Hans Magnus Enzensberger, 'The Writer and Politics', in *Times Literary Supplement*, 28 September 1967.

found their own medium, as Rudolf Augstein had done when he started the left-wing magazine *Der Spiegel* in 1947. Moreover, left-liberal intellectuals began to approach the SPD, especially through a number of meetings with Willy Brandt in the early 1960s. Richter encouraged direct cooperation, urging Grass, for instance, to lend Brandt some of his ' "German humour" '.[66] The 'boring and mediocre' Social Democrats, however, were hardly ever satisfied with what they saw as rather lukewarm and possibly counterproductive endorsements by intellectuals, and by writers in particular.

Apart from the formation of 'democratic elites', the late 1950s also saw the beginning of a peculiar 'protest culture' which the sociologist Niklas Luhmann has identified as one of the defining features of the Federal Republic.[67] The campaigns against atomic weapons for the West German army mobilized large crowds, far larger in fact than any demonstrations connected with the student movement of the 1960s. The intellectuals of the sceptical generation consciously established points of contact with this protest culture. Habermas, for instance, delivered a speech in front of almost 30,000 students in Frankfurt in May 1958, arguing against a 'policy of strength' and making 'speaking up' a 'citizen's first duty'.[68] In his rhetoric, he combined an explicit condemnation of German continuities with the appeal for students to become genuinely democratic citizens.

There was also from the very beginning, however, a paradox inherent in the role of the democratic intellectual, i.e. of the elitist opinion-leader and defender of cultural distinctions in a politically egalitarian society. In theory, this paradox could only be solved over time through the thorough democratization of society – or through ending the role of the intellectual as national preceptor.[69] Moreover, there seems to be a second paradox for liberal-democratic intellectuals. Often, in order to make the substance of their interventions count, they might have to exaggerate and adopt a rhetoric which is contrary to the procedures of civilized deliberation which they claim to be committed to at the same time – a paradox I shall return to when discussing Grass and Habermas.

'Angry young men' like Martin Walser and Enzensberger were inducted

---

[66] Richter, *Briefe*, 345.

[67] Niklas Luhmann, 'Immer noch Bundesrepublik? – Das Erbe und die Zukunft', in Otthein Rammstedt and Gert Schmidt (eds), *BRD Ade! Vierzig Jahre in Rück-Ansichten* (Frankfurt/Main: Suhrkamp, 1992), 95–100.

[68] Jürgen Habermas, 'Unruhe erste Bürgerpflicht', reprinted in Wolfgang Kraushaar, *Die Protestchronik 1949–1959*, Vol. 3 (Hamburg: Rogner and Bernhard, 1996), 1999.

[69] Jeffrey Goldfarb, *Civility and Subversion: The Intellectual in Democratic Society* (Cambridge: Cambridge University Press, 1998).

into this democratic anti-establishment and what I call its 'culture of suspicion'. Given their own experience as part of the sceptical generation, they at least initially came to share the distrust of ideology, and the categorical democratic imperative to learn the lessons of Weimar. In retrospect, Enzensberger described their task as 'the sanitary chore of the intellectuals after the end of fascism, the whole ideological waste disposal, a very wearisome and protracted job'.[70] But not surprisingly, involuntary democratic representatives like Böll were later criticized by younger writers for having been complicit in the 'bourgeois character' of the Adenauer regime.

Intellectuals, then, came to gain particular importance because of the past and because of a democratically deficient present, which implied the danger that the safest way to reject the past was to reject the present. They saw themselves as 'representative' both in the sense that they kept alive the memory of missed opportunities after the War, and in that they were the representatives of a future Germany, another, more democratic country-yet-to-come, in which the role of the critical citizen would become universal. Criticism was couched in the language of continuities, and had the purpose of substituting for a broader critical public sphere which had yet to develop. Germany's present problems came to be debated mainly through the grammar of the past. Consequently, a culture of suspicion vis-à-vis the new polity and a catalogue of categorical, negative imperatives to avoid the mistakes of Weimar intellectuals guided the intellectuals' interventions. The advantage of this culture of suspicion was its essentially egalitarian and democratic nature – after all, nobody was to be 'above suspicion', and democratic citizens should be citizens suspicious of their governments and demand their accountability. The downside of this culture was that it could lead – and often did lead – to a primary concern, even an obsession, with unmasking politicians and other intellectuals, and with ascertaining their true moral and personal motivations. Suspicion is of course typical of almost any post-totalitarian as well as post-authoritarian society, as well as exile and expatriate cultures. Suspicion could also prove indispensable for proving one's democratic credentials – and every generation, or so it might have seemed, had to prove its ex-post facto resistance to National Socialism through its discovery of continuities with the past. Every generation, it also seemed, had to question the previous generation's *Vergangenheitsbewältigung*, and there was a danger that automatic dissent would be the result of automatic distrust. Already in the late 1950s, observers like Manès Sperber were struck by how freely serious young intellectuals labelled anybody whom they politically disliked as 'fascist' – and how much this label seemed to serve their

---

[70] 'Die Gesellschaft ist keine Hammelherde', in *Der Spiegel*, 19 January 1987.

self-image more than any discernible political agenda.[71] Finally, the culture of suspicion also had its peculiar dialectical twists and turns: following Adorno's lead, who argued that the danger was less neo-Nazis outside a democratic political system than the fascist potential within a liberal democratic order, many intellectuals often came to suspect what was least suspicious.

It has often been claimed that in addition to their task of 'ideological waste disposal', intellectuals of the sceptical generation, while generally suffering from *Identifikationsscheu*, attempted to construct what a German sociologist has called a German 'Holocaust identity', based on the genocide as a unique distinguishing characteristic of German history.[72] Reminding the Germans of their past was indeed a frequent claim to shake up the complacent 'economic miracle identity' of the middle class based on material wealth and allowing for an escape from the past. Moreover, in the attack on this economic miracle identity a desire to remember the past and a culturally pessimistic anti-materialism often coalesced. It is less clear, however, whether intellectuals at the time really saw the Holocaust *per se* as a unique feature of German history, and therefore sought to foster what observers have called a 'negative national identity'. Often, Hiroshima and Auschwitz were mentioned in the same breath, alongside an impending Third World War, while fascism was 'universalized', for instance by Enzensberger in 1964 when he claimed that 'fascism is abominable, not because the Germans practised it, but because it could be practised any-where'.[73] Intellectuals raised the alarm about catastrophes such as the civil War in Biafra by warning of 'another Auschwitz', thereby suggesting that the latter was in fact not uniquely revelatory of the 'Holocaust nation', but of human nature as such. At the same time, there was little focus on the Holocaust itself, either in historical research, among writers or philosophers. Intellectuals seemed to draw attention to the Holocaust, while at the same time subtly distancing themselves from it – which amounted to a complex and sometimes contradictory process of communication and simultaneous dissociation, as observers as different as Martin Walser and Peter Rühmkorf noted in the 1960s.[74] An ambiguity persisted between on the one hand universalizing the Holocaust, for instance by claiming that it had ruptured some deep layer of human solidarity, as, to some extent,

---

[71] Manès Sperber, 'Vom Mißgeschick deutscher Intellektueller in der Politik: Erwägungen eines aufmerksamen Zeitgenossen', in *Süddeutsche Zeitung*, 31 December 1977.

[72] Bernhard Giesen, *Intellectuals and the German Nation: Collective Identity in an Axial Age*, trans. Nicholas Levis and Amos Weisz (Cambridge: Cambridge University Press, 1998), 145–63.

[73] Enzensberger, 'Am I a German?', 18.

[74] For instance, Peter Rühmkorf, *Die Jahre die Ihr kennt: Anfälle und Erinnerungen* (1972; Reinbek: Rowohlt, 1999), 161.

Jaspers and later Habermas did, and on the other hand 'nationalizing' it, i.e. particularizing it as German — with many intellectuals often sliding between the two choices or in fact, attempting to have it both ways. At the same time, making *Vergangenheitsbewältigung* indispensable for the role of the intellectual could still mean that the Holocaust as such remained a blind spot.

Consolidation and the Great Refusal: Revolutionary Uses of the Past

The 1960s marked the beginning of a phase of consolidation for both Germanies. As the division was increasingly viewed as permanent, West and East Germans were coming to terms with their respective states. In the East, the erection of the Wall provided a fleeting sense of stability and allowed for some economic experiments. In the West, the Cold War foreign policy of the Adenauer government, which held that only a policy of strength and opposition, rather than détente could lead to reunification, was increasingly seen as unrealistic. Immobilism in the government was accompanied by economic difficulties, culminating in the mini-recession of 1966. At the beginning of the decade, there had been talk of a corporatist, so-called *formierte Gesellschaft* [aligned society], even of a 'new nationalism' to provide social cohesion.[75] Instead, *Vergangenheitsbewältigung* became an even more public and acute issue in the early 1960s, with the parliamentary debates on extending the statute of limitations for Nazi crimes and the unmasking of public figures as former Nazis, the Auschwitz trials in Frankfurt, and, in particular, the Eichmann trial in Jerusalem.[76]

Meanwhile, intellectuals of the sceptical generation noticeably intensi-fied their democratic engagement in the face of the declining Adenauer regime. 1961 saw the publication of the book *The Alternative*, in which intellectuals like Grass and Walser, albeit reluctantly, advocated the election of Willy Brandt. What was noteworthy about the volume was not only that it sold 75,000 copies within eight weeks, but the awkward mixture of panic about any power and contempt for party politics in many of the contributions — a mixture very much reminiscent of the Weimar mandarins. As Martin Walser pointed out, writers in particular lacked a 'political vocabulary' — but since other institutions, such as the Churches, intervened in politics, they felt they should take part in election campaigns,

[75] Rüdiger Altmann, 'Die formierte Gesellschaft (1965)', reprinted in: *Abschied vom Staat: Politische Essays* (Frankfurt/Main: Campus, 1998), 61–70.

[76] Hermann Langbein, *Der Auschwitz-Prozeß: Eine Dokumentation*, 2 Vols. (1965; Frankfurt/Main: Büchergilde Gutenberg, 1995).

too.[77] Subsequently, in a collection imaginatively entitled *I live in the Federal Republic*, many intellectuals reflected on their reluctant identification with West Germany — although this uneasy identification was also polemically directed against the government's increasingly fictitious insistence on the existence of one country shortly to be reunified.[78]

In the run-up to the 1965 federal elections, even more intellectuals entered the public sphere as self-declared 'democratic citizens', adopting a stance of a democratic 'pragmatism from a moral point of view'.[79] The preferred mode of their interventions, apart from petitions and polemical essays in newspapers and magazines, was the hastily put together, edited paperback, which, like *The Alternative*, continued to sell in astonishing numbers. The government and CDU officials in turn became increasingly irritated by the intellectuals, dignifying their engagement with angry outbursts and insults, comparing the *Gruppe 47* to a Nazi institution which had controlled literature during the Third Reich and writers to 'Doberman pinschers'. This polarization or, rather, division of labour between sceptical intellectuals and politicians who acted more like Wilheminian notables viewing all criticism not offered by experts as illegitimate, also furnished the intellectuals with a sense of their own importance. The state which supposedly had not become their 'home' in fact gave them unprecedented prominence in the media, a fact which increasingly made talk of the 'homeless Left' seem like 'whining' even to a figure like Böll.[80] Intellectuals also provoked unprecedented impotent anger by public officials whose first impulse always seemed to be the moral expatriation of the intellectuals, painting them as representatives or secret agents of another country, in particular one immediately to the east of the Federal Republic.

A decisive clash came with the so-called *Spiegel* Affair in 1962: the editor of the magazine and a number of journalists had been arrested and accused by Adenauer of 'treason' for reporting critically on military capabilities. An immediate protest by a number of intellectuals backfired, as they issued an ambiguously worded declaration which seemed to make it a duty to betray secrets. Overall, however, the affair proved that a critical public sphere was slowly coming of age, as the minister responsible for the arrest had to resign. In fact, in many ways the early 1960s were the 'halcyon days' (Enzensberger) for intellectuals of the sceptical generation. The *Gruppe 47*

---

[77] Dieter Schmidt, 'Wird die "Gruppe 47" überschätzt? WdA-Interview mit dem Schriftsteller Martin Walser', in *Welt der Arbeit*, 10 May 1963.

[78] Wolfgang Weyrauch (ed.), *Ich lebe in der Bundesrepublik: Fünfzehn Deutsche über Deutschland* (Munich: List, 1961).

[79] Klaus Wagenbach, 'Intellektuelle an der Wahlfront'.

[80] Heinrich Böll, 'Polemik eines Verärgerten', in Krüger (ed.), *Was ist heute links?*, 43–6; here 44.

was a highly influential, moveable cultural centre in a country without a clear political or economic centre, whose writers became celebrated as representatives of another, democratic Germany with state receptions and awards abroad. Even for those outside Germany who had never heard of the Auschwitz trials or the *Spiegel* Affair, the worldwide best-seller *The Tin Drum* was a clear sign that the Germans were engaging with the past and capable of effective – and humorous – self-criticism. Böll and Grass came to be among the most widely read authors in Eastern Europe. Rather than criticism being viewed as detrimental to the country's honour, the intellectuals began to represent and gain respect for the Federal Republic. Paradoxically, however, this only proved possible because they in fact rejected the function of 'conscience of the nation' – which Böll called a 'mad idea', since parliament and the laws should be the conscience of the nation. 'But in this way', Adorno observed, 'he really has become the intellectual representative of the people, in whose language he writes'.[81] Not surprisingly, even CDU politicians eventually came to court the intellectuals, inviting them to engage in dialogue and 'productive conflict' – as, for instance, Helmut Kohl did in 1973.[82]

The building of the Wall in 1961, to which intellectuals reacted with a moral outcry, finally exposed the illusion of the compatibility of integration into the Western alliance, democracy and unification – at least for the time being. Younger intellectuals still saw unification and nationality as 'oppositional topics' with which the supposedly hypocritical Adenauer policies on the German question could be countered.[83] And as with Thomas Mann's earlier speech given in the two Germanies, culture was seen as a prime antidote to the deepening division. Richter, for instance, suggested in late 1961 that all intellectuals should move to Berlin to underline the cultural unity of the nation, while later in the decade, Grass was suggested as a potential mayor for the city.[84] At the same time, Karl Jaspers, by now very much a *praeceptor Germaniae*, caused a scandal by suggesting publicly what many politicians tacitly assumed, namely that freedom for East Germans had absolute priority over unification. His claim that the causes of the division could ultimately be rooted in the 'moral evil' of the

---

[81] Adorno quoted in Michael Serres, 'Das Sakrament des Büffels: Zum Umgang mit dem Nationalsozialismus im Frühwerk Heinrich Bölls', in Stephan Braese et al. (eds), *Deutsche Nachkriegsliteratur und der Holocaust* (Frankfurt/Main: Campus, 1998), 213–27; here 214.

[82] Helmut Kohl, 'Für einen produktiven Konflikt', in *Die Zeit*, 4 May 1973.

[83] For instance Hans Magnus Enzensberger's acceptance speech for the 1963 Büchner Prize, 'Darmstadt, am 19. Oktober 1963', in *Deutschland, Deutschland unter anderm: Äußerungen zur Politik* (Frankfurt/Main: 1967), 14–26.

[84] Hans Werner Richter to Georg Ramseger, 4 December 1961, in Richter, *Briefe*, 385–6; here 385 and Margret Boveri, 'Variationen des Selbstverständlichen', in *Merkur*, Vol. 22 (1968), 765–71.

Bismarck Reich, also made a lasting impression on younger intellectuals like Habermas.[85]

While by now established intellectuals like Grass saw themselves as undertaking the painstaking work of reform and democratic reconstruction, their efforts were soon overtaken by the student movement. The central theme of the student revolt of 1968 was the 'repression of the past' and the universal 'suspicion of fascism', which radicalized the suspicion which the sceptical generation had cultivated. 'Fascism' became a blanket term not only for a particular political system, but also a particular mind-set. The explanation for National Socialism was no longer a general decline of the West, as for Meinecke, or historical, as for Plessner and a number of younger historians of the sceptical generation: it was psychological, and centred on the 'weak egos' and 'authoritarian personalities' of the Germans. This diagnosis extended into the present, and made it imperative to oppose all kinds of inherited social constraints and patterns of life which persisted in the Federal Republic, and which, or so the students alleged, contained latent fascism. In that sense, anti-fascism was not only psychologically internalized, but also universalized in West Germany. Directed against what they saw as 'helpless', i.e. liberal, anti-fascism, the students sought a complete socio-economic transformation – and a profound change in family structures, sexual behaviour and mentalities – as the only bulwark against a resurgence of fascism.[86] Institutional safeguards were simply not sufficient, and the strategies pursued by the sceptical generation to democratize German political culture had ostensibly failed. Student leaders accused the *Scheißliberale* ['shitty liberals'] of the 1950s of having remained fixated on reactionary ideologies as the only danger, rather than questioning the proto-fascist features of the actually existing, supposedly liberal state. The students were not alone in the perception that the sceptical generation had not lived up to its standards of acting as democratic citizens and detectors of continuity. Hannah Arendt complained to Jaspers in 1965 that 'the so-called left-wing opposition in Germany, the *Gruppe 47* and all these oppositional intellectuals have really left their government in peace in this respect [i.e. National Socialism]. They waffled about capitalism and exploitation and God knows what – all completely harmless . . .'.[87]

It was essential for the students to draw on theories which, unlike liberalism, the supposed prelude to fascism, had not been discredited by

[85] Karl Jaspers, *Freiheit und Wiedervereinigung: Über Aufgaben deutscher Politik* (Munich: Piper, 1960).

[86] Wolfgang Fritz Haug, *Der hilflose Antifaschismus: Zur Kritik der Vorlesungsreihen über Wissenschaft und NS an deutschen Universitäten* (Frankfurt/Main: Suhrkamp, 1967).

[87] Hannah Arendt to Karl Jaspers, 15 May 1965, in: *Hannah-Arendt–Karl Jaspers Briefwechsel*, 621–4; here 622.

National Socialism, particularly Marxism and psychoanalysis. The sceptical generation thus seemed doubly delegitimized in the eyes of the students: not only were their accounts of their actual experience during National Socialism not to be trusted, but their own efforts at *Vergangenheitsbewältigung* had also clearly failed. The sharp disagreement between students and the sceptical generation on the success of dealing with the past in the 1950s was due most of all to a difference of perspectives: where members of the sceptical generation focused on public life, which, despite all shortcomings, had seen the success of liberal-democratic institutions, the students saw their experiences of private life as primary.[88] And in families, a markedly authoritarian culture had indeed survived, which reinforced the students' suspicion of the Republic as a whole. Nevertheless, in retrospect, there seemed to be more continuity than either side would have admitted at the time: in particular, the student movement radicalized and broadened the culture of suspicion, which had been central for the sceptical generation. More importantly, both sides debated each other using a language of the past, as the charge of fascism stood against the counter-charge of 'left fascism'.

For some members of the sceptical generation, reflective distrust also turned to despair, as the SPD yet again lost the elections in 1965. Writers like Walser and Enzensberger, no longer content with the 'the Anglo-Saxon model of a democracy of the privileged', now sought to radicalize the project of democratic Re-education and flirted with Communism.[89] In light of the new Emergency Laws, which were supposed to grant the executive extensive power in cases of internal crisis and which seemed to establish a legal path to dictatorship, and the formation of the Grand Coalition, which included the CDU and the SPD and therefore seemed to leave no effective parliamentary opposition, Enzensberger claimed that

> the political system in the Federal Republic is quite beyond repair. We can agree with it, or we must replace it with a new system. *Tertium non dabitur.* It was not the writers who narrowed the alternative down to such an extreme; on the contrary, for twenty years they have been trying to avoid it. It is the power of the state itself which is ensuring that the revolution is becoming not only necessary (it would have been necessary in 1945) but also conceivable – even if, for the foreseeable future, it remains impossible.[90]

[88] A. D. Moses, 'The 'The Forty-Fivers: A Generation Between Fascism and Democracy', in *German Politics and Society*, Vol. 17 (1999), 94–126.

[89] Martin Walser in 'Ist die Revolution unvermeidlich: Schriftsteller antworten auf eine Spiegel-Umfrage', in *Der Spiegel*, 8 April 1968.

[90] Enzensberger, 'The Writer and Politics'.

Enzensberger made good on his words, and, with much fanfare, resigned a fellowship at Wesleyan University, and resettled in Cuba to help the revolution by teaching socialist diplomats to see through the imperialist intellectuals' techniques – while unable to see how the Cubans were using him.[91] He eventually returned to the Federal Republic, disillusioned, but failed to report on his experiences and destroy some of the New Left's illusions.[92]

'Affirmative culture' and 'repressive tolerance' became the targets of the student movement, which understood itself as much more 'political' than older intellectuals – and which practised the 'great refusal', rather than the distrustful engagement of the sceptical generation. However, their positions also often exhausted themselves in a stance *ex negativo*, a thorough 'anti-stance' consisting of anti-imperialism, anti-capitalism, and, most importantly, anti-fascism. On the other side of the opposition stood a utopian anarchism and an aversion to pragmatism and proceduralism – in other words, precisely those values to which the sceptical generation had subscribed. The student leaders uncovered the bleakest diagnoses of the Frankfurt School, which Horkheimer had tried to keep safely locked away, and distributed them widely in a flourishing 'literary underground' of pirate copies, in which Wilhelm Reich, Horkheimer and Stalin became the three most pirated authors.[93] Drawing on Horkheimer' s writings in particular, they saw the Federal Republic as an instance of 'integral étatisme' – a concept describing a state in which manipulation was so pervasive that open violence was no longer necessary. According to student leader Rudi Dutschke, only an urban guerilla, modelled on South American terrorists, might disrupt such an all-pervasive social control.[94] Eventually, this aversion to parliamentary procedures and the romantic-cum-surrealist emphasis on spontaneity would tie in with a call to direct action, which in turn seemed guided by the maxim *l'idée vient en parlant*.[95] Such direct action then led many members of the sceptical generation to disown the radicals, most prominently Grass and Habermas who charged the students with 'left fascism'.[96] For the sceptical generation, the students themselves

---

[91] Hans Magnus Enzensberger, 'On leaving America', in *New York Review of Books*, 29 February 1968. See also Jörg Lau, *Hans Magnus Enzensberger: Ein öffentliches Leben* (Berlin: Fest, 1999).

[92] Lau, *Hans Magnus Enzensberger*, 264.

[93] Günter C. Behrmann, 'Kulturrevolution: Zwei Monate im Sommer 1967', in Albrecht et al., *Die intellektuelle Gründung*, 312–86; here 378.

[94] Wolfgang Kraushaar, 'Autoritärer Staat und Antiautoritäre Bewegung: Zum Organisationsreferat von Rudi Dutschke und Hans-Jürgen Krahl auf der 22. Delegiertenkonferenz des SDS in Frankfurt (4.–8. Sept. 1967)', in Wolfgang Kraushaar (ed.), *Frankfurter Schule und Studentenbewegung: Von der Flaschenpost zum Molotowcocktail 1946–1995*, Vol. 3 (Hamburg: Rogner and Bernhard, 1998), 15–33.

[95] *Ibid.*

[96] Jürgen Habermas, *Protestbewegung und Hochschulreform* (Frankfurt/Main: Suhrkamp, 1969), 148.

(and the behaviour of their opponents) now became further evidence for what they had long suspected, namely the continuing 'political immaturity' of 'the Germans'.

Meanwhile, historiography also broke away from the consensus of the 1950s. Starting with Fritz Fischer's extremely controversial *Germany's Aims in the First World War*, historians no longer treated the Third Reich as an aberration or exception, but linked it with the Wilhelmine Empire, thereby imploding the idea of preserving a commitment to an untainted pre-1933 nation-state.[97] At the same time, a generation of younger historians, trained in the social sciences and familiar with the way historical research was conducted in Britain and the United States, entered the scene. They shifted the discipline of history from an implicit affirmation of the nation-state to the goal of social emancipation. Employing social scientific methods rather than the flowing narrative associated with historicism, young scholars such as Hans-Ulrich Wehler repudiated the paradigms of nationalism and historicism, instead advancing the idea of a German *Sonderweg*, which had already been hinted at by Plessner and which was now grounded in social history. The 'West', meaning essentially the rest of Western Europe, had become the historiographical and political standard for a new generation of historians. These historians had actually experienced the West through a number of scholarly exchanges and had often been taught by those who had returned from their exile in the West. In retrospect, their lives and intellectual careers seemed to become synonymous with the Westernization of West Germany itself. By the 1970s, their teleological reading of German history based on Marxism, modernization theory and positivist social science, had become dominant. Still, traditional historiography, though with less of an emphasis on the apologetics of the nation-state, continued to be practiced, most prominently in the works of Thomas Nipperdey. Moreover, Ernst Nolte almost single-handedly replaced the theory of totalitarianism with his theory of fascist dictatorships.[98] Later, critics were to charge Nolte with having assisted the anti-fascist student movement by means of his rehabilitation of the concept of fascism.[99]

The late 1960s then saw the partial disintegration of a consensus among

[97] Fritz Fischer, *Griff nach der Weltmacht: Die Kriegszielpolitik des Kaiserlichen Deutschland* (Düsseldorf: Droste, 1991), English translation: *Germany's Aims in the First World War* (London: Chatto and Windus, 1967).

[98] Ernst Nolte, *Der Faschismus in seiner Epoche: Die Action française, der italienische Faschismus, der Nationalsozialismus* (Munich: Piper, 1963), English translation: *Three Faces of Fascism*, trans. Leila Vennewitz (London: Weidenfeld and Nicolson, 1965).

[99] See for instance Bracher's intervention in the *Historikerstreit*, when he charged that both Nolte and Habermas had been responsible for an 'inflationary use' of the 'formula of fascism'. Karl Dietrich Bracher, 'Leserbrief an die "Frankfurter Allgemeine Zeitung", 6. September 1986', in *'Historikerstreit': Die Dokumentation der Kontroverse um die Einzigartigekeit der nationalsozialistischen Judenvernichtung* (Munich: Piper, 1987), 113–14.

left-wing intellectuals which had centred on reformism and the vague notion of democratic socialism. Initially dismayed by the Grand Coalition and the Emergency Laws, the student movement drifted from calls for democratic reform to a form of anti-fascism and anti-capitalism, which ended in a totalizing critique of the Federal Republic and sought redemption in a complete transformation of political structures. Drawing on anti-fascist theory which connected monopoly capitalism and fascism, the students also tended to blur the specificity of National Socialism and considered antisemitism peripheral.[100] Paradoxically, then, the great reproach of fascism was also a generous offer of exculpation to the parents – since there was nothing specifically German about a National Socialism which seemed rather like a necessary stage in the terrible unfolding of monopoly capitalism. Moreover, anti-fascism, coupled with a desire, often inspired by the writings of the New Left icon Walter Benjamin, to identify with history's victims, turned into anti-Zionism – which, paradoxically, allowed both for an attack on Zionism as a kind of Nazism, and for an import of antisemitic images into left-wing discourse. Finally, anti-fascism was linked to an anti-Americanism, which was grounded in opposition to the Vietnam War, but also facilitated the adoption of older anti-Western clichés rooted in romantic anti-capitalism and the apolitical critique of modernity prefigured in the Youth Movement. Most importantly, however, it seemed, in the eyes of many observers, to have been a massive *ex post facto* resistance to National Socialism – a resistance in which the fathers and grandfathers had failed to engage.

Intellectual institutions like the Frankfurt School came under attack both from the students for being too bourgeois and from conservative critics who blamed the excesses of the student revolt on its supposed academic godfathers. The *Gruppe 47*'s balancing act of being both critical and in favour of the democratic institutions of the Federal Republic, was effectively destroyed, as some members, primarily in opposition to the Vietnam War, sought to radicalize it politically. It was also perceived as part of the status quo; students famously shouted the ultimate insult – 'poets, poets!' – outside the Group's last meeting in Franconia in 1967. Moreover, the cultural landscape was reconfigured with the emergence of new left-wing journals such as Enzensberger's *Kursbuch*, a generation of critical theorists who were much less reluctant than Horkheimer and Adorno to carry forward the theoretical legacies of Marxism, and, finally, a new politics of street riots and terrorism.

The *Kursbuch* in particular quickly assumed the role of an intellectual vanguard, even though most of its cultural diagnoses turned out to be mistaken. In 1968, its contributors famously declared the end of literature and,

---

[100] Anson Rabinbach and Jack Zipes (eds), *Germans and Jews since the Holocaust: The Changing Situation in West Germany* (New York: Holmes & Meier, 1986).

in a classically modernist avant-garde move, called for a complete politicization of art. In fact, the 1960s saw the last stand of an avant-garde in the style of High Modernism, only to be followed by a 'New Inwardness' and retreat of writers from political engagement in the 1970s. Under the spirited leadership of Enzensberger, however, *Kursbuch* writers also engaged with the German question, calling for more realistic policies centred on the concept of 'active co-existence', which effectively anticipated Brandt's *Ostpolitik*.[101] National unity was still perceived as an extremely provocative and, above all, progressive topic, which could be polemically played off against the supposed hypocrisy of a regime holding steadfastly to the 'policy of strength'. In general, however, the students and activists cared little about the GDR. Unlike the sceptical generation in the 1950s, they were not interested in marshalling national solidarity against official reunification policies. If anything, they subscribed to the view that Germany's post-fascist condition – in which fascism was still latent – called for transcending national identity altogether, and increasingly justified the division as a punishment for Hitler.

Tendenzwende and Terrorism: The State in Question

For all the internal upheaval, the late 1960s and early 1970s meant a time of 'normalization' in German foreign relations. The theory of West Germany's legal 'identity' with the Reich of 1937 had slowly given way to the conception of 'two states in one nation'. With the treaties between West Germany and the GDR, Poland and the Soviet Union respectively, the Federal Republic came to subscribe to a view of its Eastern borders as 'inviolable' and accepted the GDR as an equal partner without according it the status of a sovereign state or recognizing a separate GDR citizenship. Both the GDR and the Federal Republic sought a form of normalization through treaties, although normality meant very different things on each side of the Iron Curtain. In the West, normality, or so politicians at least officially still claimed, could only mean reunification, while in the East, the concrete meaning of 'normalization' was made painfully obvious by the Soviet crushing of the Prague Spring in 1968. The West German Constitutional Court reaffirmed the 'identity theory' in its landmark verdict of 1974, while also holding that the Basic Treaty between the two Germanies conformed to the Constitution.

The mid-1970s saw a severe backlash against the reforms of the Brandt government, which had promised 'more democracy' in 1969, and against the Left more generally, which was quickly labelled a *Tendenzwende* [shift

---

[101] 'Katechismus zur deutschen Frage', in *Kursbuch* No. 4 (1966), 1–55.

in intellectual climate to the right]. This shift, above all, caused a fateful split between some of the 'liberal institutionalists', who felt that the student revolution had gone too far and that reforms were overburdening the state, and some of the left-liberal members of the sceptical generation, most notably Böll and Habermas. When Böll, for instance, suggested 'mercy' for Ulrike Meinhof, Dolf Sternberger shot back that 'the democratic state is also a state . . . render onto the state what is the state's, Böll!'[102] While older left-liberal intellectuals sought to defend the foundations of the Federal Republic against the illiberal excesses of the state response to terrorism, which seemed to put raison d'état above democracy, many younger writers became disillusioned with politics and at least partially retreated into what became known as the 'new subjectivity'.[103]

Once again, terrorists and state representatives tended to view each other through the lens of the past: 'fascism' stood against the charge of 'Hitler's children'. Anti-intellectual feelings ran high not only among the population in general, but also among liberal conservative thinkers who, in their attacks on the Left, tended to run legal and illegal oppositions together, and castigated intellectuals in general for being the 'new priests'.[104] They charged that the constitutional consensus had been eroded, and that since a language of 'cultural revolution' and 're-ideologization' had extended political discourse far to the Left, a Weimar-style political polarization might tear the Republic apart. While such polarization remained a rhetorical threat, the 1970s certainly were an era of political, intellectual and economic retrenchment. In particular, there was widespread anxiety about a 'legitimation crisis', even the 'ungovernability' of an overburdened welfare state – rather than the nation, the state itself now seemed to be in question. The oil crisis of 1974 was compared to the Lisbon Earthquake in having shattered rationalist optimism, and there was a sense that the *dix glorieuses* of intellectuals in politics had lasted exactly until 1973, when Böll received the Nobel Prize and when Grass and Böll were closely associated with Brandt and the policies of détente. Instead, by the end of the decade, there were lengthy debates about the 'silence of the intellectuals', although intellectuals were still denounced as 'rats and blow flies' by conservative politicians.

The politics of history intensified, too. The *Sonderweg* had not only

---

[102] Dolf Sternberger, 'Böll, der Staat und die Gnade', in *Frankfurter Allgemeine Zeitung*, 2 February 1972.

[103] The best example of this disillusionment is Peter Schneider, *Lenz* (Berlin: Rotbuch, 1973).

[104] See for instance, Kurt Sontheimer, *Das Elend unserer Intellektuellen: Linke Theorie in der Bundesrepublik Deutschland* (Hamburg: Hoffmann und Campe, 1976), and the response by Jürgen Habermas, 'Stumpf gewordene Waffen aus dem Arsenal der Gegenaufklärung: An Prof. Kurt Sontheimer', in Freimut Duve et al. (eds), *Briefe zur Verteidigung der Republik* (Reinbek: Rowohlt, 1977), 54–72.

become a historiographical orthodoxy; left-wing intellectuals also argued that the axiom of the *Sonderweg* had evolved into a necessary pillar of the democratic consciousness of the Federal Republic, thereby predicating the present order on a historical hypothesis.[105] Consequently, any attempt at reclaiming a supposedly untainted past could be seen as putting the democratic present into question. Nevertheless, conservative historians increasingly asked to what extent an explicitly national identity could – and should – be constructed for the West German state, and to what extent history might be used to invest it with legitimacy. One of the ironies, however, was that while West Germany remained the legal representative of a unified Germany, it was in the GDR, which had adopted an explicit policy of demarcation and of constructing a separate 'socialist national identity', that national consciousness remained alive much more than in the Federal Republic – even prompting the later Federal President Richard von Weizsäcker to observe that there was 'a more stable, serious and despite all attempts at ideologization more truthful consciousness of German history' developing in East Germany than in the free, but also sometimes 'insecure' and 'unstable' West Germany.[106]

As the 1970s drew to a close, two contrary developments were discernible. On the one hand, there was little question that, on the thirtieth anniversary of the Federal Republic, West Germans had come genuinely to identify with a political order which was supposed to be transitional but had by then proven to be the most successful democratic experiment in German history.[107] Dolf Sternberger accordingly coined the term *Verfassungspatriotismus* [constitutional patriotism], to delineate a new form of patriotism in 'half a nation' which could build on Germany's liberal traditions and take pride in a functioning constitutional framework. On the other hand, the enormously emotional public reaction to the American TV series *Holocaust* seemed to indicate continued psychological repression of the past, particularly of the actual victims of the Nazis.[108] Moreover, with the end of 'daring more democracy' under Brandt, there was a sense of failure, and a return to more traditional sources of meaning and morality was advocated by intellectuals whom the Left quickly labelled as 'neoconservatives'. Both the question of what kind of national identity was appropriate for what, constitutionally, remained a provisional state, and of the

---

[105] Kurt Sontheimer, *Von Deutschlands Republik* (Stuttgart: Deutsche Verlags-Anstalt, 1991), 62.

[106] v. Weizsäcker quoted by Bruno Schoch, 'Renaissance der Mitte – Ein fragwürdiger Bestandteil deutscher Ideologie kehrt wieder', in *Deutschlands Einheit und Europas Zukunft*, ed. Bruno Schoch (Frankfurt/Main: Suhrkamp, 1992), 120–49; here 136.

[107] Martin and Sylvia Greiffenhagen, *Ein schwieriges Vaterland: Zur politischen Kultur Deutschlands* (Munich: List, 1979).

[108] Peter Märthesheimer and Ivo Frenzel (eds), *Im Kreuzfeuer: Der Fernsehfilm Holocaust: Eine Nation ist betroffen* (Frankfurt/Main: Fischer, 1979).

nature of German memory became central concerns in the 1980s, despite
– or maybe because of – the fact that the decade was to be a politically less
turbulent one than the 1970s. The very fact that the state itself had been
in crisis in the Seventies, it seemed, left little room for an engagement with
the nation. The calmer 1980s refocused attention on issues of identity, but
critics also charged that national feeling was mobilized as a form of compensation for the end of reformist hopes.

The *Wende* and the Historians' Dispute: Normalization in Half a Nation?

The early 1980s saw the return of a CDU–FDP government, which
announced an intellectual-moral *Wende* [turn]. Apart from a general
renewal of tradition, the intellectual leaders of the *Wende* also sought a
more national, reunification-oriented foreign policy. However, while
the rhetoric changed to include frequent references to reunification
and the claim that the German question remained open, de facto
policies changed little. Moreover, the *Wende* owed less to the *Tendenzwende*
of the 1970s than to economic dislocation and the fact that the SPD was
torn apart between its left and right wings. The Left, fiercely fighting
against the stationing of new American missiles on German soil, built an
alliance between the West German and East German peace movements,
glued together to some extent by anti-American sentiments and a desire
to escape the deadly logic of Cold-War confrontations for good. Apocalyptical visions of nuclear War led to the revival of the idea of German
neutrality and national feelings among the Left.[109] Not for the last
time, the Left claimed that the German question could not be left to the
Right exclusively, and sought to recover its own 'national traditions'. A
number of right-wing historians also began to advocate reunification in a
rather aggressive manner. While their historical work was largely dismissed by the mainstream, they were still able to cause a number of major
controversies and push the issue of national identity onto the public
agenda.[110]

German writers, in particular Grass and Peter Schneider, also once again
took up national themes, and once again found themselves in opposition
to what they saw as a hypocritical official stance by a conservative government vis-à-vis the GDR. However, writers were deeply split over how
to deal with the GDR's official 'culture creators' and its dissidents. Could

---

[109] See for instance Peter Brandt and Herbert Ammon (eds), *Die Linke und die nationale Frage:
Dokumente zur deutschen Einheit seit 1945* (Reinbek: Rowohlt, 1981).

[110] The first major controversy centred on Hellmut Diwald's *Geschichte der Deutschen* (Frankfurt:
Ullstein, 1978). See also chapter eight, below.

human rights violations and the voices of ex-GDR dissidents who had been expelled to the West be ignored for the sake of peace? The fierce controversies over these dilemmas culminated in the most acrimonious meeting of West German writers in the post-war period, the 1984 meeting of the West German Writers' Association in Saarbrücken. There a group centred around the writers Bernt Engelmann and Dieter Lattmann who favoured contacts with high-ranking GDR functionaries was opposed by Grass and Böll who rejected silence in the face of human rights violations which this policy necessarily seemed to demand.[111]

In general, however, the 1980s saw a diminished role for intellectuals. In contrast with the 1950s, West Germany was arguably no longer suffering from a democratic deficit, and the always contradictory role of intellectual elites instructing the population in democratic citizenship was itself becoming democratized or at least more widespread with the arrival of the Greens and the citizens' movements. Böll and others were literally submerged in the hundreds of activists sitting outside and blocking American nuclear bases. The critical task of preserving a 'Holocaust identity' and reminding the Germans about the past, had been widely taken up by the media, rather than a few towering intellectuals, with an increasing number of television series on the War in particular. Heinrich Böll's death in 1985 was widely perceived to mark the end of an era.

At the same time, despite the emergence of the Green movement as a major political force, there was a pervasive sense of an 'exhaustion of utopian energies', as Habermas put it in 1984. While most older left-wing intellectuals felt uneasy about the crisis of the welfare state and what they perceived as the ascendancy of 'neoconservatives', a younger generation sought to take on board postmodern thought. Philosophically, a playful revelling in the end of the rationalist promises of the Enlightenment and an 'enlightened false consciousness' found their major theoretical expression in Peter Sloterdijk's *Critique of Cynical Reason*.[112] This not altogether joyless resignation in the wake of failed reforms was complemented by a renewed fascination with history and memory. Attempts to recover the past fitted into a conservative programme of offering comforting historical narratives for the 'unstable' Federal Republic, but were also condemned as simple nostalgia, even an uncritical longing for fascist symbols, as was supposedly the case in the work of Anselm Kiefer.[113]

---

[111] Renate Chotjewitz-Häfner and Carsten Gansel (eds), *Verfeindete Einzelgänger: Schriftsteller streiten über Moral und Politik* (Berlin: Aufbau, 1997)

[112] Peter Sloterdijk, *Critique of Cynical Reason*, trans. Michael Eldred (1983; Minneapolis: University of Minnesota Press, 1987).

[113] For a suitably complex exploration of these issues, see Andreas Huyssen, *Twilight Memories: Marking Time in a Culture of Amnesia* (London: Routledge, 1995).

Conflicts over the past, rather than becoming more attenuated over time, intensified during the 1980s. The philosopher Hermann Lübbe caused an important controversy when he claimed at the fiftieth anniversary of the Nazis' seizure of power in 1983 that collective *kommunikatives Beschweigen* [communicative silence] about the past in the early Federal Republic had in fact enabled West Germany to evolve into a functioning democracy. Stability had been predicated on an 'asymmetrical discretion' between perpetrators and victims willing not to challenge them in the 1950s.[114] Apart from the string of anniversaries of National Socialist rule and the War, there were a number of other controversies which, in retrospect, seem to have prepared the polemical ground for the most acrimonious dispute of the 1980s: the call by Franz Josef Strauß, by then the second-most powerful politician in West Germany, that Germany 'should become a normal nation again', so that Germans might feel 'proud' once more; the botched Bitburg visit of President Reagan; a clearly expressed desire on the part of Chancellor Kohl to see the Germans as victims and to establish a moral equivalence of German soldiers and Jews; and President Weizsäcker's implicit rebuke in his 1985 speech on the fortieth anniversary of the War's end, which he called above all a 'liberation', rather than 'defeat' or 'collapse'; the highly acclaimed television series *Heimat*, which was a direct response to *Holocaust*, and the projects of building museums commemorating the past of the Federal Republic and Germany as a whole.[115] Moreover, compared to debates among historians in the early 1960s, the intellectual field of mid-1980s Germany had become structured by new orthodoxies and heterodoxies. Social history no longer reigned supreme. It had come under attack from oral historians and historians of everyday life on the one side, and on the other from historians reasserting the importance of political and diplomatic history as well as geopolitics, in particular Germany's *Mittellage* [position in the middle of Europe]. Moreover, the *Sonderweg* thesis had been effectively put into question, not accidentally by two young British historians who claimed that the German bourgeoisie had not been nearly as submissive and 'feudalized' as the *Sonderweg* adherents had made them out to be.[116] Finally, Martin Broszat had challenged German historians to finally 'historicize' the Nazi past, calling especially for a more nuanced view of everyday experience in the Third Reich, instead of what often seemed to amount to perfunctory moral condemnation.

---

[114] Herman Lübbe, 'Es ist nichts vergessen, aber einiges ausgeheilt: Der Nationalsozialismus im Bewußtsein der deutschen Gegenwart', in *Frankfurter Allgemeine Zeitung*, 24 January 1983.

[115] On *Heimat* and other post-war films dealing with National Socialism, see Anton Kaes, *From Hitler to Heimat: The Return of History as Film* (Cambridge, Mass.: Harvard University Press, 1989).

[116] Geoff Ely and David Blackbourn, *The Peculiarities of German History* (Oxford: Oxford University Press, 1984).

The 'official' beginning of the *Historikerstreit* was marked by Ernst Nolte's June 1986 article published in the *Frankfurter Allgemeine* 'Vergangenheit, die nicht vergehen will', [The Past that Will not Pass Away] where Nolte asked the central rhetorical question: 'Was not the "class murder" of the Bolsheviks logically and factually prior to the "race murder" of the National Socialists?'[117] However, the *Streit* in *Historikerstreit* was only sparked off with Jürgen Habermas's polemical 'Eine Art Schadensabwicklung' [A Kind of Settling of Damages] in *Die Zeit*. There Habermas charged 'neoconservative' historians, i.e. Nolte, Michael Stürmer and Andreas Hillgruber, with attempting to resurrect a 'conventional' national identity as a kind of substitute religion for the sake of national cohesion, which was to be directed at Communist states.[118]

Subsequently, almost all post-war historians of the sceptical generation took sides in what became an ever more vituperative debate with a decidedly personal subtext which touched directly on the experiences of the sceptical generation. The coalitions which faced each other over the 'past which will not go away' were heterogeneous. Nevertheless, four central questions which effectively grouped friends and enemies could be discerned: the central question, which was seen as most salient for present politics and state legitimation, was the singularity of the Holocaust, or its possible relativization through a comparison with other genocides. Methodologically speaking, the question of singularity was incoherent, or led back to the 'discourse of demonization' inherited from Meinecke and Ritter. But singularity came to be a kind of conceptual shorthand for the quality of memory, political responsibility, and guilt which could be legitimately expected of Germans forty years after the end of the War. A second and related question, which, however, was less necessary for drawing a *Schlußstrich* [a thick line under the past] was the question of causality: had what Nolte called the 'Asiatic deeds' of Stalinist Communism not just preceded, but effectively 'caused' Hitler's atrocities, making Auschwitz into a 'copy crime' of the Gulag? Or was it at least the case, as Stürmer implied, that the German special path had been 'caused' by Germany's geographic position in the middle of Europe?

Then there was the question to what extent Germans could legitimately cast themselves as victims, and whether any equivalence of suffering, particularly of the German Army fighting the Red Army in the East,

---

[117] Ernst Nolte, 'Vergangenheit, die nicht vergehen will: Eine Rede, die geschrieben, aber nicht gehalten werden konnte', in *Historikerstreit*, 39–47; here 45.

[118] Jürgen Habermas, 'Eine Art Schadensabwicklung: Die apologetischen Tendenzen in der deutschen Geschichtsschreibung', in *ibid.*, 62–76. Trans. as 'Apologetic Tendencies' in Jürgen Habermas, *The New Conservatism: Cultural Criticism and the Historians' Debate*, ed. and trans. Shierry Weber Nicholsen (Cambridge, Mass.: MIT Press, 1989), 212–28.

could be construed with other victims of the period 1933–45. This raised the additional question whether it was necessary or even permissible to identify with German historical actors such as the German Army, as Hillgruber's study *Zweierlei Untergang* [Two Sorts of Demise] suggested.[119] Finally, there was the question of the supposedly 'modernizing' features of the Third Reich. None of these historiographical and theoretical issues was entirely new. The applicability of the theory of totalitarianism already entailed the issue of singularity; the question of the *Sonderweg* had so far given a firm answer to the question of causality, and the thesis about the modernizing effects of the Third Reich had already been advanced in the 1960s. However, the question how Germans could or even should treat their own victimization, and whether a positive view of the past was necessary for a 'healthy' present-day identity had never been discussed so intensely.

All participants in the debate agreed that what was at stake was not so much historical knowledge as the Federal Republic's present self-conceptualization. While almost all participants condemned a simple instrumentalization of history, everyone also agreed that, positively or negatively, history could and should play a role in a present *Sinngebung* [provision of meaning] and in contributing to social cohesion – whether in the form of fostering national consciousness or with the aim of deepening the democratic consciousness of 'constitutional patriots'. Ironically, conservative historians seemed to have come to share a version of the Mitscherlichs' diagnosis of the West Germans having 'weak egos' in a 'wounded nation'.[120] They argued that a 'normal' attitude towards the past was vital in constructing a firm sense of national identity, which in turn was a precondition for domestic stability and Germany's successful role as an outpost of the West under the renewed Cold War conditions of the 1980s. Habermas opposed this project by arguing in favour of a 'post-conventional identity', which would make West German patriots adhere to the principles of the Constitution and universalist values, rather than invest emotions in a national past. Having presented the opening of the Federal Republic to the political culture of the West as the historical, but also moral achievement of which his generation 'could be proud', he went on to claim that the 'only patriotism which does not alienate us from the West is constitutional patriotism'.[121]

The *Historikerstreit*, however, also proved curiously ahistorical: the

---

[119] Andreas Hillgruber, *Zweierlei Untergang: Die Zerschlagung des Deutschen Reiches und das Ende des europäischen Judentums* (Berlin: Siedler, 1986)

[120] Elisabeth Noelle-Neumann and Renate Köcher, *Die verletzte Nation: Über den Versuch der Deutschen, ihren Charakter zu ändern* (Stuttgart: Deutsche Verlags-Anstalt, 1987).

[121] Habermas, 'Eine Art Schadensabwicklung', 75.

conservative claim about the necessity of constructing a national identity mostly referred to the present Federal Republic and, with the important exception of Hillgruber, left the question of national unity to one side. Intellectuals on the Right and the Left were in step with a broad consensus among politicians, journalists and the population as a whole who accepted the status quo. The government even unrolled the red carpet for Erich Honecker in 1987 on his first (and last) visit to the Federal Republic.

The *Historikerstreit*, was *the* major national self-interrogation about historical responsibility and national consciousness of the 1970s and 1980s.[122] It had more public repercussions than any other intellectual debate during that time, but, ironically, also proved that any effort to 'normalize' the past only reinforced its claims on the present.[123] It disproved the Right's frequent prediction that with the passage of time and the fading of memory, a conservative project would be more likely to succeed. In fact, the contentiousness of these historical-cum-moral issues seemed to be disconnected from any 'normal' temporality, and depended more on present-day political concerns. While the dispute, unlike the Fischer controversy, yielded few scholarly insights, it also confirmed that at that time most intellectuals rejected a 'conventional national identity', and called for a continuation of 'working through the past'. In particular, still clinging to *Identifikationsscheu*, they rejected an emotional identification with German soldiers as victims as well as a substantial relativizing of the Holocaust and the thesis of the German special path, which, paradoxically, would only have come to an end as long the Germans remained conscious of it.[124] But the dispute was also governed by the seeming logic of mutual suspicion and unmasking, which was the darker side of the culture of suspicion which the sceptical generation had developed and which the generation of 1968 had radicalized further. In the eyes of Habermas and his allies, there was a systematic attempt to 'normalize' the Nazi past and promote nationalism – which had to be opposed by left-liberal intellectuals, whose own role, according to Habermas in 1986, had finally become 'normalized' – which seemed to mean that it conformed to French standards. For conservatives, on the other hand, Habermas and the Left were 'moralizing' politics and erecting taboos to further their own power. 'Hypocrisy', then, had to be the ultimate, mutual charge. Both sides, however, seemed implicitly to agree that intellectuals remained crucial as national or post-national preceptors in a 'wounded nation'.

---

[122] Charles S. Maier. *The Unmasterable Past: History, Holocaust, and German National Identity* (Cambridge, Mass.: Harvard University Press, 1988), 2.

[123] Anson Rabinbach, 'Editor's Introduction', in *New German Critique*, No. 2 (1988), 3–4; here 4.

[124] Sontheimer, *Von Deutschlands Republik*, 63.

While the dispute ended with a victory for the advocates of the *Son-derweg* theory and constitutional patriotism, it also left a discourse about a somewhat reified 'national identity' firmly entrenched and fostered the 'often unreflective belief that identity is reducible to history'.[125] It resulted in a fruitless stalemate between a right-wing discourse which operated with convoluted rhetorical questions and insinuations, and what appeared as a polemical, overly defensive response of the Left which told a teleological narrative from *Sonderweg* to 'post-national identity'. Most importantly, it taught intellectuals the point made by Stürmer that 'in a country without history, he who fills the memory, defines the concepts and interprets the past, wins the future'.[126] In other words, redefining German national identity was mostly a matter of recasting the past. It meant that all intellectuals had to situate themselves vis-à-vis the past and confront the thesis of German exceptionalism both in the sense of the uniqueness of the Holocaust and the special path of German development. Moreover, the notion that historians were in a position to draw an authoritative *Schlußstrich* and determine the future through their readings of the past, betrayed a certain hubris. Only a minority of scholars asked whether in the pluralist society of the 1980s Federal Republic, one homogeneous reading of history, whether left or right, was desirable or even possible – and whether in a more pluralist public sphere and an increasingly visual culture, which had seen the arrival of private television channels in 1984, intellectuals could still perform the role of defining national identity in quite the same way historians in the nineteenth century had done.

Finally, the polemical tone of the dispute left scars for a number of historians, and in the end there were no intellectuals who had not in some way been tarnished by it. Habermas, the theorist of the 'ideal speech situation', was often criticized for patrolling the boundaries of public discourse. The scholarly reputations of Stürmer and Hillgruber were damaged, while Nolte was discredited among many scholars as an obscurantist right-winger and, in what seemed like a defiant reaction, he subsequently radicalized his theses further. If one is to believe the biographical accounts of New Right intellectuals, the *Historikerstreit* also marked a key experience for young conservative historians: they saw the dispute as a witch-hunt unleashed by an intolerant Left, which ultimately resulted in Nolte's car being fire-bombed.

Implicitly, the political lessons from the *Historikerstreit* were reinforced when the President of the Bundestag had to resign after delivering a historicist, or at least overly 'phenomenological' speech on the occasion of the

---

[125] Maier, *The Unmasterable Past*, 149.

[126] Michael Stürmer, 'Geschichte in geschichtslosem Land', in *Frankfurter Allgemeine Zeitung*, 25 April 1986.

fiftieth anniversary of *Kristallnacht*, in which he seemed to have identified with the perspective of 'ordinary Germans' during the Third Reich. However, for all its significance, the importance of the *Historikerstreit* can be exaggerated. After all, the major ideological success story of the 1980s with any impact on party politics, i.e. the Greens, was a decidedly 'postnational' phenomenon. Moreover, for all the intellectual resistance to 'normalizing the past', by 1989 most observers agreed that this was now, after all, a normal, even a *stinknormal* [disgustingly normal], state – in fact, a decade in which 'identity' and 'stability' seemed to be more in question than ever before among intellectuals, had proved to be the most stable in West German history.[127] Moreover, the Federal Republic, for all its faults, had long ceased to lack legitimacy in the eyes of its citizens. It had reduced the democratic deficit which intellectuals had attempted to remedy in the 1950s. It had also ceased to be negatively fixated on its ideological opponent, the GDR. And while the *Modell Deutschland* had been somewhat tarnished after the economic crisis of the 1970s, domestic and foreign observers still viewed the country not only as an economic, but also as a political success. Finally, the role of the intellectual had to some extent been democratized by the Greens, with the consequence that the intellectuals of the sceptical generation had retreated somewhat from the public sphere.

And then the Wall came down.

---

[127] Wilhelm Bleek and Hanns Maull (eds), *Ein ganz normaler Staat? Perspektiven nach 40 Jahren Bundesrepublik* (Munich: Piper, 1989).

2 Günter Grass and his Critics: The Metaphysics of Auschwitz

Das edelste Vorrecht und das heiligste Amt des Schriftstellers ist dies, seine Nation zu versammeln, und mit ihr über ihre wichtigsten Angelegenheiten zu berathschlagen ganz besonders aber ist dies von jeher das ausschliessende Amt des Schriftstellers gewesen in Deutschland...

The most noble prerogative and holiest office of the writer is to gather his nation, to consult with it about its most important affairs, but, in particular, this has always been the exclusive office of the writer in Germany...

Johann Gottlieb Fichte, *Reden an die deutsche Nation*

It was not surprising that, after the fall of the Wall, Günter Grass came to be one of the major intellectuals commenting on the dramatic events unfolding. From the early 1960s onwards Grass had immersed himself in politics and supported the Social Democrats in elections, in the process redefining the public role of the German writer.[1] He had posited this role as that of the responsible and well-informed citizen who takes a stand on current affairs, urging his fellow citizens to act in a similarly reasonable way. In the same vein, he had rejected the traditional German division between *Geist* [intellect] and *Macht* [power], instead placing the writer in 'the middle of society'.[2] Sober, anti-utopian scepticism and a pragmatism which was not itself to become an 'ideology', were to characterize this type of citizen.[3] Increasing the number of such citizens, Grass thought, would finally move Germany closer to the traditions of the Enlightenment, which he had always explicitly supported.

---

[1] Grass came from a lower-middle-class family and was not a 'born Social Democrat', but had identified the SPD as the prime carrier of humanism and Enlightenment values. See 'Ich klage an: Rede im Bundestagswahlkampf (1965)', in Grass, *Essays*, 126–35. But significantly, the SPD and its leaders Kurt Schumacher, Ernst Reuter and Willy Brandt, had initially also been the voice of national unity. *Ibid.*, 133.

[2] K. Stuart Parkes, *Writers and Politics in West Germany* (London: Croom Helm, 1987), 137. Grass, 'Des Kaisers neue Kleider: Rede im Bundestagswahlkampf (1965)', in *Essays*, 110–25; here 113.

[3] Grass, 'Der Schriftsteller als Bürger – eine Siebenjahresbilanz (1973)', in *Essays*, 577–93; here 584.

At least until the early 1980s, his thinking centred on notions of compromise and piecemeal progress, which led him to endorse the revisionist tradition in Social Democratic thought and to declare categorically in 1969, 'I am an opponent of the revolution'.[4] It was his scepticism which made Grass reject the claims of the student movement in the 1960s, which he saw as another instantiation of German idealism in the vein of Fichte, rather than as Marxism in practice; while his revisionism made him support the reform course of the SPD, which he caustically, yet compassionately portrayed as the slowly progressing snail in *From the Diary of a Snail*.[5] When election time came around, he was always willing to 'throw aside his writing table' and engage in 'democratic *Kleinkram* [nitty-gritty]', which meant above all the hard work of arriving at political compromise but also resolving difficult aesthetic dilemmas, such as choosing the colour scheme for SPD election posters.[6] He involved himself in the rather unexciting details of policy-making such as the coal industry laws of the late 1960s, combining this realism with a punchy, polemical style. Nevertheless, in his election speeches he cautioned that he did not aim at whipping up 'political enthusiasm', which he saw as dangerous and discredited by the German past.[7] While his polemics left no doubt who the political opponent was, he insisted that politics was not a matter of black and white, but shades of grey. He would steadfastly support the SPD, however flawed the party might have been, and refuse to play the role of Cassandra or doomsayer, i.e. the negative role which he thought had been performed by left-wing Weimar intellectuals such as Tucholsky and Carl von Ossietzky who had turned their back on the SPD.[8] Rejecting a stance of resignation even after political failures, Grass had adopted Sisyphus as a 'private saint', and George Orwell and Albert Camus as his intellectual models.

Throughout, however, he had seen his role as a modest one, frequently ridiculing a *littérature engagée* and the claim that the writer could act as the conscience of the nation. Such a representative conscience, Grass

---

[4] Grass, 'Literatur und Revolution oder des Idyllikers schnaubendes Steckenpferd (1969)', in *Essays*, 411–17; here 417.

[5] Parkes, *Writers and Politics*, 140–1.

[6] Grass, 'Vom mangelnden Selbstvertrauen der schreibenden Hofnarren unter Berücksichtigung nicht vorhandener Höfe (1966)', in *Essays*, 153–8; here 158. Günter Grass, *Aus dem Tagebuch einer Schnecke* [*Werkausgabe im zehn Bänden*, Vol. 4], ed. Volker Neuhaus (Neuwied: Luchterhand, 1987), 265–567; here 418–19. English translation: *From the Diary of a Snail*, trans. Ralph Manheim (London: Minerva, 1997).

[7] Grass, 'Es steht zur Wahl: Rede im Bundeswahlkampf (1965)', in *Essays*, 76–87; here 79.

[8] *Ibid.*, 83. Grass also stressed that he regarded those who politically disagreed with him as 'opponents, not as enemies'. Laudable as the sentiment might have been, even his rhetoric in the 1960s was not always compatible with this claim. See Grass, 'Konflikte (1969)', in *Essays*: 327–33; here 331–2.

thought, would have relieved ordinary citizens from examining their own conscience. He often emphasized that he firmly subscribed to the basic tenets of the West German Constitution and opposed radicals who took a 'typically German' attitude of 'all-or-nothing'.[9] Despite his supposedly anarchist temperament, his criticisms centred not on the Constitution itself, but on what he construed at various points – such as the deployment of Pershing missiles in the early 1980s – as breaches of the Constitution.[10] Thus, Grass could claim to have been a 'constitutional patriot' long before Dolf Sternberger coined the term in the late 1970s, having argued that 'the most beautiful thing about our state . . . is our Basic Law' and that only democracy could be his *Heimat*.[11]

By the early 1980s, however, his stance had become somewhat more radical – even apocalyptical – in the face of what he considered an impending ecological or nuclear catastrophe.[12] Moreover, aesthetic considerations came to play a larger role in his political thought, leading to rather crude attacks on Chancellor Kohl's lack of style in comparison to Brandt. He also for the first time dismissed parliamentary majorities as irrelevant in the face of apocalyptical dangers, and called for passive resistance in what he described as a situation of constitutional emergency.[13] What had once been constitutional patriotism *avant la lettre*, seemed to have turned into a kind of apocalyptical anti-parliamentarism more reminiscent of the '68ers Grass had once opposed.

For almost three decades before the fall of the Wall, Grass had also commented frequently on the German question, claiming that 'thinking about Germany is part of my literary work'.[14] He often explained that the 17 June 1953, which he had witnessed on the Potsdamer Platz in Berlin, had been his first consciously formative political experience.[15] Before that, Grass, as a young sculptor – his other, and original, creative pursuit – had only experienced the early Federal Republic in a 'passive' and 'traumatic-sceptical' manner.[16] But the 17 June had also been a key experience in another respect: Grass always claimed that Adenauer had falsely portrayed the

---

[9] Grass, 'Über das Ja und Nein', 325.

[10] Rühmkorf, *Die Jahre*, 196.

[11] Grass, 'Loblied auf Willy: Rede im Bundestagswahlkampf (1965)', in *Essays*, 88–98; here 88 and see 'Ich klage an', 135.

[12] Grass 'Jungbürgerrede: Über Erwachsene und Verwachsene (1970)', in *Essays*, 429–39; here 437.

[13] Volker Neuhaus, *Schreiben gegen die verstreichende Zeit: Zu Leben und Werk von Günter Grass* (Munich: Deutscher Taschenbuch Verlag, 1997), 182.

[14] Günter Grass, *Gegen die verstreichende Zeit* (Hamburg: Luchterhand, 1991), 73.

[15] Grass, 'Der Schriftsteller als Bürger – eine Siebenjahresbilanz (1973)', in *Essays*, 577–93; here 581.

[16] *Ibid.*

uprising as a popular one, when in fact it had been purely a workers' revolt, with the bourgeoisie and the intellectuals in particular keeping their distance. In 1961 he wrote his famous open letter to Anna Seghers, fiercely criticizing the building of the Wall and calling upon East German writers to speak out against it.[17] At the same time, he was highly suspicious of the West German government's position, arguing that Adenauer and Ulbricht effectively mirrored each other in their nationalist 'separatism'. The West Germans, he charged, having been seduced by capitalist prosperity and a facile anti-communism, had abandoned their fellow nationals in the East.[18]

Against this 'separatism', Grass, from the mid-1960s onwards, became an advocate of a confederation between the two German states, and, as he himself used to point out, of 'unity, but not unification' in the sphere of the German *Kulturnation*. He also effectively acted as the 'bad conscience' of the West Germans in the name of East Germans, urging his fellow citizens to vote as those who were denied the vote, i.e. the East Germans, would have done.[19] In 1980, at a time when most politicians – and most Germans – had reconciled themselves to the prospect of an indefinite continuation of the division, he published *Headbirths, or, the Germans are Dying Out*, in which he elaborated his conception of the two Germanies as still being united through the *Kulturnation*.[20] He also called upon the two Germanies to cease being satellites of their respective super powers, live up to their special historical responsibility and initiate a common peace initiative.

Given this long and increasingly radical record as a politically active writer, how would Grass react to the sudden prospect of unification? Would he welcome the re-establishment of national unity, which he had demanded in the 1950s? Or would he see 'reunification' as a hollow CDU slogan, which he thought it had been since the mid-1960s? Grass had never veiled what seemed like an almost visceral hatred of Helmut Kohl and the Christian Democrats – in fact, Grass only formally joined the SPD on the day that Kohl was elected Chancellor. He had also increasingly rejected simple parliamentary procedure, if fundamental questions of human survival were at stake. Would the stakes of unification justify such a radical stance? And which intellectual resources would be deployed by Germany's

---

[17] Grass, 'Und was können die Schriftsteller tun? (1961)', in *Essays*, 33–4.

[18] Grass, 'Was ist des Deutschen Vaterland? Rede im Bundestagswahlkampf (1965)', in *Essays*, 99–109; here 105.

[19] Grass, 'Loblied auf Willy', 97.

[20] Günter Grass, *Kopfgeburten oder die Deutschen sterben aus* [*Werkausgabe in zehn Bänden*, Vol. 6], ed. Christoph Sieger (Neuwied: Luchterhand, 1980), trans. Ralph Manheim (London: Secker and Warburg, 1982).

most famous and most politically engaged writer, who could draw on an enormous amount of accumulated cultural capital?

Kulturnation or Einheitsstaat?

When the Wall came down, Grass immediately lived up to his chosen role as *Zeitgenosse*. He powerfully projected himself into the public sphere, using *Die Zeit* and *Der Spiegel* as platforms, thereby not least disproving the thesis of the 'silence of the opinion-leaders' in the face of unification advanced by conservative journalists such as Joachim Fest.[21] After November 1989, he wrote essays, gave interviews and spoke passionately at the SPD party congress in Berlin in December 1989. From the start, he reiterated his 1960s idea of a confederation encompassing the German *Kulturnation*. With a confederation, he argued, there would be sufficient time for intra-German *Einigung* [unification, but, significantly, also agreement], which would entail cultural unification, personal reconciliation and, most of all, mutual understanding. One day, such a confederation might usher in a Federation of German States. Grass claimed that this gradual solution would be most likely to avoid arousing any fears among Germany's European partners. Moreover, a federal structure of two German states would foreshadow and tie in with the project of a European federation. It would create a truly novel political entity, rather than an enlarged Federal Republic, and, if accomplished through Article 146 of the Basic Law, would help the East Germans to identify with this new polity and develop their own constitutional patriotism. In the first half of 1990, the constitutional options were Article 23, which allowed individual German states to accede to the federation whenever they chose, and Article 146, according to which the Basic Law lost its validity when the Germans reunified and consequently had to ratify a new constitution. The former Article was mainly intended for the Saarland, which acceded to the Federal Republic in 1957, while the latter was to underline the provisional nature of the Basic Law, which made the pursuit of reunification imperative in its preamble. In short, for Grass the German *Kulturnation* could unite the two states, while a confederation would ensure diversity and preserve a particular 'GDR identity'.

Grass's wish to preserve GDR identity did not stem from any secret love for East Germany. Quite to the contrary, Grass had always been an outspoken critic of the SED regime: he had openly attacked East German censorship at the 1961 Writers' Congress in East Berlin, compared Ulbricht to the commander of a concentration camp and generally saw the GDR as a monstrous reincarnation of Prussia, in certain respects even of the Third

---

[21] Joachim Fest, 'Schweigende Wortführer', in *Frankfurter Allgemeine Zeitung*, 30 December 1989.

Reich.[22] Nevertheless, he thought there was something to conserve in East German identity for a number of reasons. Grass saw this identity as constituted not only by the experience of forty years of oppression, but also by the bloodless revolution in 1989. The uprising had suddenly revealed a fighting spirit among the East Germans, and, as the first successful revolution in German history, had been an achievement for Germany as a whole. Grass directly referred back to Karl Jaspers's dictum from the 1960s that freedom had priority over unification, claiming that the freedom achieved by the East German revolutionaries had to be the key element in unification.[23] Mostly, however, Grass referred to GDR identity as 'damaged', implying that it had to be handled with care and protected in a separate state – at least for a certain period. For Grass, the mentalities which had evolved in forty years of GDR history were worth preserving, even if they had been either directly caused by suffering under the state or evolved as defensive responses to suffering. Implicitly, this suffering was contrasted with the hedonism and consumerism in West German society. However, there was a second component of GDR identity worth protecting: in Grass's view, the 'niche society' of the GDR had preserved what he described as 'a slower pace of life, accordingly more time for conversations . . . something of the *Biedermeier*-type as in the times of Metternich'. He claimed that this was something of which he was not sure whether it had not already disappeared again with 'the opening towards the streets and towards democracy'.[24]

Apart from that, Grass perceived a recurring pattern of West Germans, as the lucky 'victors of history', riding roughshod over the wishes of the East Germans and exploiting them for short-term advantage. This pattern had been established with rearmament and Adenauer's signing of the Germany Treaty in 1955, which had effectively meant the 'sell-out' of the East, to some extent for the party-political reason of avoiding a Social Democratic majority in a united Germany.[25] Consequently, East Germans had had to continue carrying most of the burden of the lost War. In 1965, Grass had still called for the election of the Social Democrats so that Germany might embark on the road to reunification, which in turn would require significant sacrifices.[26] However, he thought that with the election

---

[22] Grass, 'Wer könnte uns das Wasser reichen? Rede auf dem V. Schriftstellerkongreß in Ostberlin (1961)', in *Essays*, 27–9; 'Und was können die Schriftsteller tun?', 33.

[23] *Ibid.*, 74. Karl Jaspers, 'Freiheit und Wiedervereinigung', in *Lebensfragen der deutschen Politik* (Munich: Deutscher Taschenbuch Verlag, 1963), 171–281; here 198.

[24] *Ibid.*, 17–18. The concept of the 'niche society', into which east Germans supposedly retreated from the claims of the overpowering SED state, was first used by Günter Gaus in *Wo Deutschland liegt* (Hamburg: Hoffmann und Campe, 1983).

[25] 'Loblied auf Willy', 102 and 105.

[26] Grass, 'Ich klage an', 134.

of Ludwig Erhard in 1965, the West Germans had implicitly renounced reunification. Only then had Grass begun to advocate a confederation. In that sense, it was the East Germans who had had to carry an economic burden, but it was the West Germans who carried a moral responsibility for having betrayed the East Germans. Not surprisingly, Grass had come to identify the concept of 'reunification' with political hypocrisy, an option for capitalist consumerism and the betrayal of East Germans.

Apart from gently incorporating a separate GDR identity, there were other reasons why Grass preferred a confederation to a unified state, some of which he had also first formulated more than twenty-five years earlier. In 1967, at the same time that Enzensberger's *Catechism on the German question* appeared, he had elaborated his vision of 'national self-understanding' as the precondition of any change in the political relations between the Federal Republic and the GDR.[27] Against the CDU's 'separatism', he set what was then a critical, oppositional concept of confederation.[28] At the same time, he insisted that 'separatism' could not simply be blamed on the government, but had been a tradition deeply ingrained in German history. The Germans had been both unwilling and unable to form a nation.[29] Germany had sometimes been forced into a 'nationally united bloc', but more frequently fallen victim to separatism, and, in general, oscillated between both extremes. But, Grass suggested, between nationalism and separatism lay a 'third way': Germany's 'only and rarely used possibility, the confederation', which could be a real 'patria' – a concept he used to avoid the discredited notion of 'fatherland'.[30] Only federalism would serve the Germans (and the world) well in the long run.[31] And, importantly, federalism was already part of the structure of both German states: nominally in the GDR Constitution, and as a lived reality in the West. Speaking to an Israeli audience in 1967, he claimed

> that my compatriots do not like to be *einig* [in agreement and unified]. Even if they talk about it loudly and frequently, they are afraid of an *Einigkeit* [unity and agreement] which has already cost them dearly once. Thus taught, they engage in the detailed business of *Uneinigkeit* [disunity] with such bitter consistency, that soon a reversal into nationalist hubris has to be feared. The fathers of the Basic Law were well-advised to think of preventing this tendency to fall into either extreme. Since only when organized in a federation, but responsible for the

[27] Grass, 'Die kommunizierende Mehrzahl (1967)', in *Essays*, 222–35.

[28] *Ibid.*, 225.

[29] *Ibid.*, 230.

[30] *Ibid.*

[31] Grass, 'Politisches Tagebuch: In Ermangelung (1971)', in *Essays*, 493–5; here 494 and 495.

general welfare of both German states, but without coercion to be a nation against their own capacity and inclination, are the Germans, as Swabians and Saxons, Westphalian and Mecklenburgers, *verträglich und erträglich* [do they get along and are bearable], even amiable and of use to the world. That is how I like them and that is the way I belong to them.[32]

Grass held that the striving for unity had always been 'vulgar' and 'abstract', with the Germans only capable of forming a nation 'in the negative', and unleashing Wars because they were unable to comprehend themselves.[33] The Germans, it seemed, would always need a great number of opponents to be truly *einig*. In any political constellation other than a confederation, the Germans were likely to cause problems for their neighbours again.[34] Without a reasonable *nationales Selbstverständnis* [national self-understanding], which at points he termed *Nationalbewußtsein* [national consciousness], the Germans would always be prone to move between political extremes and substitute a complex-laden *Selbstbewußtsein* [here in the sense of overblown self-confidence] for their lack of self-understanding.[35] In a sense, he was simply taking up Jaspers's call to replace a political national consciousness with a common consciousness of what Jaspers called 'the other, greater, deeper Germany', i.e. the *Kulturnation*. He was also in line with numerous suggestions for a 'confederation' made at the time by intellectuals, politicians and journalists, who saw such a structure as the only conceivable way out of an increasingly immobile official West German position.[36]

Grass complemented his call for national consciousness with the demand that Germany finally accept the consequences of the lost War and learn that *Einigkeit* did not require *Einheit*.[37] Introspective realism (as well as the concrete political recognition of the Oder–Neisse border, i.e. the border between the GDR and Poland) and an acceptance of the historical lesson that nation-statehood was not a stable political arrangement for the Germans thus were meant to be the core components of a reasonable national self-understanding. Should such a self-understanding not be

---

[32] Grass, 'Rede von der Gewöhnung (1967)', in *Essays*, 199–212; here 201.

[33] Grass, 'Politisches Tagebuch: In Ermangelung', 494.

[34] *Ibid.*, 212.

[35] Grass, 'Die kommunizierende Mehrzahl', 227.

[36] See for instance the contributions to Theo Sommer (ed.), *Denken an Deutschland: Zum Problem der Wiedervereinigung* (Hamburg: Nannen, 1966) and Helmuth Plessner, 'Wie muß der deutsche Nation-Begriff heute aussehen?', in *Merkur*, Vol. 21, (1967), 211–23. But, significantly, a confederation had also long been the SED's official solution to the German question.

[37] *Ibid.*, 232–3.

reached, Grass warned in 1967, then the national conservatives in the West and the 'Stalinist Right' in the GDR might well cooperate at the expense of Social Democracy and 'liberal federalism' and bring about a 'monstrous' national creation, whose existence would only arouse fear.[38]

In his advocacy of a confederation in 1990, Grass reiterated this vision almost point by point, employing the same basic concepts and drawing on the same – though radicalized – historical lessons. He substituted *Einigung* for *Einigkeit*, with *Einigung* as a process which still had to be carried out successfully by East and West Germans in order to reach an understanding which, in the 1960s still might have been a given. He now specifically referred back to Herder's conception of the *Kulturnation* and his celebration of diversity, wanting the Germans to be 'diverse and colourful'.[39] Moreover, a number of his arguments were akin to the axiomatic attitudes about German unification in the eighteenth century, when it was widely believed that German diversity and German individualism could not be forced into a nation-state. Wilhelm von Humboldt still saw diversity as a cultural advantage which the Germans held over the French, and even made the very same prediction which Grass was to make about the danger of a centrally administered Germany for its neighbours: 'Nobody could then prevent Germany from becoming a conquering country, which no true German could want'.[40] Also, many of Grass's arguments against what he termed the *Einheitsstaat* [unitary state] were similar to the ones the nationalist historian Heinrich von Treitschke, at that time still a national liberal, had tried to refute with his attack on 'particularism' in his famous essay *Bundesstaat und Einheitsstaat* [Federal State and Unitary State].[41] Treitschke had rejected the views that a *Kulturnation* did not need to be fulfilled through the creation of a state; that 'nature herself had condemned Germany to eternal division'; that Germany was 'the country of decentralisation'; that only in small states could spiritual *Bildung* reach its highest level; and that the division of Germany accounted for the 'beautiful diversity of our political life'.[42]

Grass's conception of a half-way house confederation accorded with his opposition to an 'all-or-nothing' attitude, which he thought was an expression of free-floating German idealism attaching itself to various causes, while a slow *Einigung* tied in with his view of progress as protracted and

---

[38] *Ibid.*, 233.

[39] Grass, *Gegen*, 16 and 37.

[40] Humboldt quoted by Hagen Schulze, *Staat und Nation in der europäischen Geschichte* (Munich: C. H. Beck, 1995), 182–3.

[41] Heinrich von Treitschke, 'Bundesstaat und Einheitsstaat', in Heinrich von Treitschke, *Historische und Politische Schriften* (Leipzig: Verlag von S. Hirzel, 1903), 77–242.

[42] *Ibid.*, 81–96.

piecemeal. The notion of compromise was also implicit in his advocacy of a 'third way' between capitalism and Communism, i.e. a democratic socialism, in which freedom, equality and prosperity would all be possible – even though the concept of democratic socialism, as with so many of its proponents on the Left, always remained undefined, since it supposedly was not an 'ideology' or a 'dogma'.[43]

Diametrically opposed to this conception of *Einigung* through a confederation (ensuring diversity, reconciliation and freedom) was what Grass consistently called the *Einheitsstaat* [unitary state, with the double meaning of a uniform state], a term implying not only political unity, but also a decidedly anti-Herderian uniformity. According to Grass, the actual process of unification was heading precisely towards such an *Einheitsstaat*, and he resisted this development for a number of reasons. First, the sheer pace of unification was inherently opposed to his notion of progress as piecemeal. Second, he criticized what he perceived as the lack of an underlying purpose for unification. In his view, the vacuum left by the lack of genuine ideas was filled with the 'fetishist cult' of the German Mark. Third, the *Einheitsstaat* would do violence to an already damaged GDR identity. Fourth, and, in his view, most significant, was the prospect of a return of aggressive German nationalism in a unified state. In that he also followed Jaspers who had argued in the early 1960s that unification contained an irreducible ambivalence: on the positive side, it meant freedom for East Germans, but simultaneously – and dangerously – it increased power for Germany as a whole.[44]

Grass, however, implied that the turn towards aggressiveness was inevitable: a unified Germany would automatically assume a position of immense power in the middle of Europe, which would arouse the fears of its neighbours and isolate Germany. This in turn would lead to German defensiveness which would ultimately result in aggression – a concern Grass shared with many left-wingers, and to which I shall return in the fourth chapter. Again, Grass had already made the same historical argument nearly twenty years earlier, when he claimed that 'German unity, as history teaches us . . . has always made internal crises grow into superregional conflicts'.[45] Now, however, Grass added a special moral twist to this essentially historical and empirical argument. He insisted that a people that had committed the crimes of Auschwitz had no right to live in a unified nation-state and that – because, in his interpretation, a unified Germany had been a precondition for the rise of National Socialism – unification would again lead to a catastrophe. In other words, Grass, mixing

[43] Grass, 'Sieben Thesen zum demokratischen Sozialismus (1974)', in *Essays*, 640–4.

[44] Jaspers, *Lebensfragen*, 201.

[45] Grass, 'Deutschland – zwei Staaten – eine Nation?', 447.

two distinct moral and historical claims, played 'Auschwitz' off against the right to self-determination, going so far as to posit that, while the right to self-determination was universal, there was one and only one exception: the Germans. In other words, he put himself in the paradoxical position of a selective universalist. The idea that a people could 'gamble away its right to the particular size of a national state' had also been stated by Jaspers, but Jaspers had not made the explicit moral link with Auschwitz and generally did not have a deterministic conception of history, which Grass increasingly espoused.[46]

Grass, then, essentially reiterated political positions which he had staked out in the mid-1960s. Arguably, it was the sheer similarity between the political constellation of the mid-1960s, with a long-lasting CDU government putting forward a policy of reunification shaped by the agenda of the West in both instances, which suggested such a reiteration of political views. More importantly, however, he also relied on deeper beliefs and concepts which had sustained his more general political stance, and which had in fact been subject to more change than the advocacy of a confederation which had remained remarkably similar in almost thirty years.

History, Hegelianism and German Drives

Among these positions was, first of all, Grass's peculiar attitude to history. Asked about Martin Walser's support for the process of unification, Grass charged that Walser was caught up by his feelings while he claimed to espouse a reasoned form of historical consciousness.[47] According to Grass, historical consciousness and memory were the key to a peaceful Germany and a rational national consciousness, in contrast to an irrational and potentially dangerous national sentiment. National consciousness had to grow slowly, and made its bearers immune to nationalist hysteria.[48] Styles of thought indebted to Hegel and historicism, on the other hand, would bolster nationalism and the German tendency towards extremes. In the 1960s Grass had explicitly rejected a Hegelian view of history, arguing that Bismarck, Marx and their more radical successors in the twentieth century had been Hegel's 'pupils' who used his thought for purposes of domination.[49] Instead, Grass, mixing existentialism and historicism in a somewhat contradictory manner, insisted that history was essentially absurd and had no overall course or meaning, but that it also taught hard

---

[46] Jaspers, *Lebensfragen*, 197.

[47] Grass, *Gegen*, 26.

[48] Grass, 'Des Kaisers neue Kleider', 115.

[49] Grass, 'Zwischenbilanz: Versuch, ein Nachwort zu schreiben (1967)', in *Essays*, 264–74; here 264.

lessons – with the writer having the intricate task of laughing at history's absurdity and at the same time elucidating its lessons.[50] Nevertheless, he equally affirmed human agency in history – even if it was futile – *and* answered Ernst Moritz Arndt's canonical German question 'What is the German's Fatherland?' by claiming 'whatever we make of it'.[51] In the same vein, from the early 1980s onwards, Grass had adopted a rather dialectical argument which contained both a claim about historical inevitability with regard to nuclear and ecological catastrophe, and a call to radical political action and the assumption of human agency – precisely so as to prevent what he had portrayed as inevitable.

Now Grass also saw history entirely in terms of an ineluctable logic, linearity and, to a certain extent, a national metaphysics. For him it was the unitary state which was the key to the crimes summed up in the name of Auschwitz, rather than the Nazis or ordinary Germans as such. In the same vein, the GDR population was the victim of a Stalinist system, rather than real human beings in the form of the leaders of the SED. History appeared as a matter of supra-human, ineluctable forces which meant that the *Einheitsstaat* had to founder inevitably. As Grass remarked, 'against all reassurances, even the well-intentioned ones, we Germans would be feared again', presuming that most reassurances would in fact be hypocritical, as a new 'DM-imperialism' would conquer Europe.[52] He claimed that 'we are going to be unified, strong and – even in the attempt to whisper – sound loud.'[53] This historical determinism curiously mirrored the strictures of the most fervent exponents of geopolitics and the fatal consequences of Germany's *Mittellage*, i.e. the country's position in the middle of Europe – and constituted one of the instances where the underlying assumptions of the Left and the Right came curiously close.

Such geopolitical determinism entailed that once the unitary state was achieved, there was not much citizens could do about it – it simply had to result in aggression, given geography, demography and the psychological make-up of the Germans and their neighbours. This also meant that the critical *Zeitgenosse* had no more influence on events, because by then, *ältere Triebkräfte* [older drives] inherent in the Germans would have taken over.[54] In other words, geopolitical determinism was reinforced by concerns about an almost mythical national German essence, with which certain 'drives' were associated. Ironically, it was precisely this deterministic, almost

---

[50] Grass, 'Was Erfurt außerdem bedeutet (1970)', in *Essays*, 418–28; here 428.

[51] Grass, 'Loblied auf Willy', 104.

[52] Grass, *Gegen*, 32.

[53] *Ibid.*, 37.

[54] *Ibid.*, 72.

fatalistic attitude with which Grass reproached the proponents of a fast unification. Their claim that 'the train has already left the station', i.e. that unification had become an inevitable political development, betrayed an attitude which Grass thought was both fatalistic and used to silence critics. Grass lamented and identified with those who were left behind at the station; however, in his own view, the train called *Einheitsstaat* had indeed left the station, and there was nobody and nothing which could stop it on its way to a new German nationalism.

The Dialectic of Auschwitz: Temporality and Taboo

Grass hinted at a continuing underlying doubt whether the Germans were really well intentioned at all, and consequently issued the imperative that they could not and should not trust themselves. In other words, Grass articulated the most extreme claim inherent in the culture of suspicion which the Left had fostered since the 1950s. This assumption, however, clashed with the belief that after Auschwitz, the Germans actually had the special privilege of an insight into themselves and that they *did* know what they were capable of doing – and consequently had to contain their ancient drives. In this scenario, they should be trusted not to trust themselves. It remained unclear, however, whether this meant that in a sense only the Germans could commit such crimes, i.e. that there was a particular primordial propensity (consistent with 'older drives'), or that the Germans had a special insight into the human condition as such. In other words: did Grass mean to 'nationalize' or 'universalize' the Holocaust? In one sense, Grass certainly – and paradoxically – 'nationalized' the Holocaust by adopting the most extreme anti-nationalist interpretation inherent in Jaspers's *Schuldfrage*: the Germans had incurred an indelible moral and metaphysical guilt, and accepting political responsibility for the past entailed a renunciation of the nation-state. But it might also condemn the Germans to a 'pariah'-existence in the indefinite future, an option which Jaspers had in the end rejected.[55] At the same time, instead of abandoning the concept of the nation altogether – as the 'post-nationalist' positions of many on the Left suggested – the Holocaust mandated the return to a German high culture inherent in the concept of the *Kulturnation*. But rather than being based on political impotence, as in the eighteenth and nineteenth century, the *Kulturnation* was now predicated on the Germans' distrust of themselves and consequently the renunciation of the nation-state framework.

Grass also consciously took up the more 'universal' arguments advanced by Jaspers, namely that the Germans could teach a lesson to humanity as

---

[55] Jaspers, *Die Schuldfrage*, 26.

a whole. Jaspers had argued that 'the history of the German nation-state has come to an end, not the history of the Germans. As a great nation we can do one thing for us and the world: make people realize that today the idea of the nation-state spells disaster for Europe and all other continents. The idea of the nation-state is presently an overwhelmingly destructive force in the world. We might begin to lay bare its roots and effect its negation'.[56] Grass followed Jaspers's advocacy of confederate structures as well as his call for a voluntary renunciation of nation-state sovereignty in the interest of the West as a whole. But Grass combined the moral arguments which had been made by Jaspers — and indeed, himself — in the 1950s and 1960s with a historical, determinist claim which had never been part of Jaspers's position: namely, that, through unification, the Germans would necessarily become aggressive yet again.

To some extent, Grass's thinking on the Holocaust was in danger of instrumentalizing the victims in a world-historical learning process. There seemed to be a perverse dialectic about Auschwitz, which came to ground what Habermas criticized as a 'negative nationalism of a community of fate', in which an anti-nationalist meaning was extracted from the Holocaust.[57] According to this view, Auschwitz was willingly recognized as a singular crime — but at the same time this crime was jealously guarded as a unique, almost metaphysical act which, yet again, had made the Germans a 'special people'. Also, there was a 'cunning' quasi-Hegelian drive inherent in the view that Auschwitz had enabled the Germans 'to know themselves', or rather, their mythical essence. In other words, the Holocaust — in any case, as a possession of the perpetrators, as primarily a German affair in which the victims disappeared from the picture — became part of a metaphysical view of history, which seemed directly opposed to the anti-idealism which Grass had always advocated. And as with Jaspers in his original view of German guilt, the preoccupation was with what 'being German' meant.

However, Grass's previous engagement with Auschwitz and the question of German guilt had been an even more complicated — and problematic — one, which went some way in explaining his strident stance in 1990.[58] It was inextricably bound up with his own experience under the Nazi regime, as well as his role as a writer. As he explained, significantly in a

---

[56] Jaspers, *Lebensfragen*, 219.

[57] Jürgen Habermas, 'Yet Again: German Identity — A Unified Nation of Angry DM-Burghers', in *New German Critique*, No. 52 (1991), 84–101; here 98. [initially as 'Der DM-Nationalismus. Weshalb es richtig ist, die deutsche Einheit nach Artikel 146 zu vollziehen, also einen Volksentscheid über eine neue Verfassung anzustreben', in *Die Zeit*, 6 April 1990].

[58] See also Thomas Kniesche, '"Das wird nicht aufhören, gegenwärtig zu bleiben." Günter Grass und das Problem der deutschen Schuld', in Hans Adler and Jost Hermand (eds), *Günter Grass: Ästhetik des Engagements* (Bern: Peter Lang, 1996), 169–97.

'Speech to a young voter who feels tempted to vote for the NPD [the extreme right-wing National Democratic Party]' in 1966, Grass had been a member of the *Jungvolk* at the age of ten, joined the *Hitlerjugend* at the age of fourteen, became a *Luftwaffenhelfer* at the age of fifteen and a member of the regular army at the age of seventeen, after which he was captured by the Americans. In other words, he had been 'too young to have been a Nazi, but old enough to have been formed' by the Nazi regime.[59] Only at age nineteen did he begin to realize 'what amount of guilt our people had knowingly and unknowingly accumulated, what burden and responsibility mine and the following generation would have to carry'.[60] But the year 1945 had in itself been no clear break; Grass's had been a 'delayed reaction' to the horror of the Nazi crimes, his own implication in them, and the fact that his entire moral world-view had been 'monstrous'. Ever since, Grass claimed, the dead were watching him when he was writing.

Partly because of his continuing 'delayed' horror over his own complicity, the meaning of Auschwitz actually assumed increased prominence in Grass's thinking over time. In other words, his reaction to Nazism remained an incomplete process – and the more this part of history receded in time, the more Grass sought to resist historicization. In October 1965, he argued much like Habermas in the late 1980s that through socio-political and personal continuities the crime of Auschwitz lived on in German society and had prevented the election of the emigrant Willy Brandt. Through the appointment in 1950 of the ex-Nazi Hans Globke as secretary in the Federal Chancellery 'the crime of Auschwitz prolonged itself into our own days, office and dignities were bestowed upon it'.[61] This continuing influence of the spirit which had produced Auschwitz was, in Grass's eyes, further legitimated by the 1966 election of Kurt Georg Kiesinger (who had been a member of the NSDAP from 1933 to 1945) as Federal Chancellor. Grass, in a number of open letters to Brandt, opposed a Grand Coalition, with Kiesinger as its head, for precisely this reason, and began comparing 1966 to 1933.[62] Finally, apart from the persistence of Auschwitz through Adenauer's 'restoration', the burden of guilt had another aspect altogether in that it imposed a special modesty on German intellectuals: rather than propose utopian plans for humanity, as student leaders like Dutschke had supposedly done, 'we Germans and also the post-

---

[59] Grass, 'Rede von der Gewöhnung', 205.

[60] Grass, 'Rede an einen jungen Wähler', 163.

[61] Grass, 'Rede über das Selbstverständliche', 141.

[62] Grass, 'Das Gewissen der SPD (1966)', in *Essays*, 173–5; here 174–5.

war generation still and for a long time to come are responsible for Auschwitz and Treblinka; that obliges us to speak quietly'.[63]

However, in addition to this national dimension of the Holocaust, it also continued to have a universal meaning. While Auschwitz was spatially and temporally delimited, in principle accessible to empirical investigation, committed by human beings and capable of being understood by human beings, it also remained a future potential. In 1970, Grass hinted for the first time that Auschwitz was 'temporally universal', when he claimed that 'it is necessary to comprehend Auschwitz in the historical past, in its present and not to exclude it blindly in the future. Auschwitz does not just lie behind us'.[64] He increasingly came to universalize Auschwitz, claiming that it was being repeated in the present, for instance in the civil war in Biafra in the late 1960s, and even capable of being surpassed in its inhumanity. It was no longer confined to the past, especially since 'progress' increasingly came to threaten human existence: the snail, Grass's previously chosen symbol of progress, was in fact too fast for mankind. Consequently he could claim, 'the future has already caught up with us . . . The difference in times seems to be abolished: past barbarism approaches us like a mirror image. We think we are looking back, but in fact remember a known future. Progress, it seems, lies already behind us'.[65] This multidimensional conception of time led Grass to adopt a new tense in his literary writing, which he called *Vergegenkunft*, which in German mixed the nouns for past, present and future. Grass had already defined the writer as someone who 'wrote against the passage of time'. But with his increasingly gloomy picture of the future of humanity, this definition took on a new meaning: if the future was already contained in the past, and the past returned in a barbaric future, then the writer could no longer simply function as a repository of authentic memory. He also had to write the future from the point of view of the past — and vice versa — and come to terms with the fact that time, which had been the resource of literature to survive all adversary political circumstances, was now — for the first time — running out in a world-historical process of self-destruction. Apocalyptical projections became the appropriate task of literature — not only to preserve literature's own basis, but also to take account of the supposedly changed structure of temporality as such.

At the same time, the presence of Auschwitz, if anything, became stronger rather than attenuated, as new generations were born in the

---

[63] Grass, 'Über das Ja und Nein (1968)', in *Essays*, 320–6; here 320.

[64] Grass, 'Schwierigkeiten eines Vaters, seinen Kindern Auschwitz zu erklären (1970)', in *Essays*, 458–61; here 461.

[65] Grass, 'Nach grober Schätzung (1975)', in *Essays*, 673–83.

Federal Republic. By 1979, Grass argued that guilt was being passed down the generations, comparing this process to the hereditary guilt depicted in the Old Testament. *Schuld* [guilt] now became like *Schulden* [debts] which could in fact never be paid off. Grass explicitly affirmed a German exceptionalism in this matter: other nations might have been more forgetful and therefore happier, but 'only the Germans are not allowed to escape' from their history.[66] This inescapability of history was linked to the uncertainty of the Germans about themselves, about what they might do or might have done, which was, after all, Grass's recurring question about his own youth: what if he had been slightly older? Would he have been a Nazi? – a question which haunted Grass to the extent that he wrote an alternative biography in which he was born in 1917 and became a National Socialist.[67] The retrospective anti-Nazism of his generation, he claimed, had been without much value. So the fact remained that he 'could not vouch for himself'.[68] And neither could the Germans generally 'vouch for themselves'.

As a *writer*, Grass had struggled with the issue of Auschwitz ever since the 1950s, when he had confronted Adorno's supposed 'prohibition' on writing poetry after Auschwitz.[69] While recognizing the crimes of Auschwitz as a unique *Zivilisationsbruch* and himself as part of the generation of its perpetrators, he had also rebelled against the ostensible 'taboo' posited by Adorno, since, in a sense, Auschwitz threatened Grass's whole artistic existence. He confronted this threat by adopting an attitude of what he called poetic 'asceticism' and scepticism.[70] In 1990, then, this way of dealing with the legacy of Auschwitz was meant to become the model for Germany as a whole: not a complete renunciation, but an ascetic compromise that would centre on the aesthetic and the affective, i.e. the *Kulturnation*, rather than the political, i.e. the nation-state. Grass seemed

---

[66] Grass, 'Wie sagen wir es den Kindern? (1979)', in *Essays*, 755–69; here 756. Grass's engagement for the peace movement at this time was also linked to the Holocaust. Like many on the Left, he claimed that nuclear War was essentially a 'Final Solution on a global scale', and since the Germans were responsible for Auschwitz, they also had a special responsibility to prevent such a War.

[67] Grass, 'Kein Schlußwort (1979)', in *Essays*, 770–4.

[68] Grass, 'Wie sagen wir es den Kindern?', 765.

[69] Adorno had argued that 'writing a poem after Auschwitz is barbaric'. See his 'Kulturkritik und Gesellschaft', reprinted in Petra Kiedaisch (ed.), *Lyrik nach Auschwitz?* (Stuttgart: Reclam, 1995), 27–49; here 49. Later Adorno, under the influence of the work of Paul Celan (who also influenced Grass during his time in Paris), 'repealed' his 'prohibition' in *Negative Dialektik* (1966; Frankfurt/Main: Suhrkamp, 1994). I cannot go into the complexities of Adorno's position and what it meant for German writers – but it would be a grotesque misunderstanding to claim that for twenty years, writers laboured under a 'taboo', as is sometimes suggested in the secondary literature. Grass's retrospective understanding – or misunderstanding – of Adorno was an exception, rather than the rule. See Braese *et al.* (eds), *Deutsche Nachkriegsliteratur und der Holocaust*.

[70] Grass, *Gegen*, 51–4.

to have transformed Adorno's moral and aesthetic prohibition into an explicitly political one and imposed it on the nation as a whole. This meant a blurring between a subtle philosophical position and a historical situation in which more or less plausible assumptions about Germany's power and its neighbours could be made. Grass, the critic of the radical students who were shouting Marx and thinking Fichte, himself freely mixed the political with the aesthetic – and the metaphysical.

Finally, Grass's 1990 warnings about a future Auschwitz also have to be understood against his beliefs about guilt and *Vergegenkunft* which he had formed since the 1960s, i.e. the belief that guilt could never be diminished, and the insight that, given the sheer magnitude of the crime of Auschwitz, past, present and future were intertwined in the temporal mode of *Vergegenkunft* not just for literature, but also for the nation as a whole. If Auschwitz was not remembered, the nation would also lose its future, and the barbaric past would return. Like many on the Left, Grass felt that unification and the 'return of the nation-state' would automatically entail a renunciation of the moral imperative to remember the past.

However, despite the fact that Grass could draw on a considerable moral and political authority, most commentators rejected this brand of historical determinism as well intentioned but essentially absurd. Foreign observers even reproached him with a 'typically German' perpetual attachment to guilt and suffering. In his insistence on Germany's inability to become like any other nation, they detected a reverse expression of the *Sonderweg*, an anti-nationalist nationalism, and the fascination with a tragic, special fate of the German nation.[71] Once again, the Germans were cast as the 'chosen people', as only they had committed the ultimate, unspeakable crime, and thereby gained invaluable insight into themselves, which should now lead them to a rejection of unification and a continuation of a life of tragic, eternal condemnation. Grass was, however, in a way only expressing what had long been an implicit left-wing consensus of post-war German intellectuals, namely that the division of Germany had to be accepted as a direct punishment for Hitler's and Germany's crimes. This quasi-moral view of the division seemed to be grounded more in the Hegelian assumption of world history as world judgement and a desire for punishment than a sober analysis of the power politics of the Cold War. Another common view held that the Wall functioned as a basic mechanism to protect the Germans from themselves, and that all the democratic and liberal achievements of forty years would be washed away by anything resembling political unification.[72] In both views, it was usually omitted that mainly East Germans and not the proponents of the theory

---

[71] Michael Ignatieff, 'Unheimliche linke Träume', in *Die Zeit*, 19 October 1990.

[72] Friedrich Dieckmann, 'Die Linke und die Nation', in *Merkur*, Vol. 48 (1994), 762–70; here 765.

of 'division as punishment' actually suffered from the division.[73] Most of all, the theory seemed a sign less of 'post-nationalism' than of the very 'negative nationalism' which conservative critics suspected was at the heart of post-nationalism. Grass, despite denying the Germans the right to unification, never went so far as to examine the question of nationhood as such. While clearly the concept of the *Einheitsstaat* was his *bête noire*, even this self-avowed 'constitutional patriot' still understood it wholly within the traditional German definition of the nation.[74]

While it was not unreasonable to see the post-war experience as a return to what Wolfgang Mommsen called 'a normal pattern of a plurality of German states with cultural–national identity', Grass's total attachment to the *Kulturnation* overlooked the fact that this concept almost by definition tends not only to be centred on cultural elites, but also to be imperial and exclusive.[75] That is to say, the discourse of diversity is a dangerous one, or at least a dialectical one. It can lead either to a rigid communitarianism in which disparate, diverse communities are kept separate and in which hybridization stands for cultural annihilation (Fichte's view, and, to a lesser extent, Herder's), or an attitude in which diversity serves to reaffirm the identity of a centre. Grass in his effort to keep the two Germanies politically apart in the name of traditional German diversity and federalism came closer to the latter view. He implicitly called for making foreigners living in Germany full citizens, but added that they 'could help to make us experience our still diffuse consciousness of nation in a new way. With their help we can be European and German at the same time'.[76] This well-intentioned, but deeply problematic idea of multiculturalism in which foreigners unwittingly add to and reaffirm the identity of the central culture seemed like a parallel to the instrumentalization of the victims of the Holocaust. Later, it was to become a major position among many left-wing intellectuals in the discussion about German citizenship and immigration.

Kulturnation: An Imagined Literary Nation

Still, there was an inner logic in the adherence to the illiberal idea of the *Kulturnation* as the '*übergreifende Gedanke*' [all-encompassing, unifying reason] for *Einigung*. For forty years, it had made sense to assume that

---

[73] Peter Schneider, 'Gefangen in der Geschichte', in *Der Spiegel*, 18 January 1993.

[74] On this definition as expressed in citizenship laws, see Rogers Brubaker, *Citizenship and Nationhood in France and Germany* (Cambridge, Mass.: Harvard University Press, 1992).

[75] Wolfgang J. Mommsen, *Nation und Geschichte* (Munich: Piper, 1990), 76. Even more problematically, the concept of the *Kulturnation* would have led to the question of German culture which existed outside a united Germany.

[76] Grass, *Gegen*, 85.

there were two German states in one *Kulturnation*, and to admonish the Germans for their lack of national consciousness, as Grass did when he claimed that 'every other nation would have tried to preserve and augment the existing commonalities across the existing political divisions'.[77] In 1965, he had first pointed to the fact that it had been writers and Enlightenment thinkers who had created a unified Germany in the eighteenth century, through the power of language, and against the separatist policies of the powerful.[78] Ever since, writers had assumed the role of reminding politicians of the cultural unity of the nation. When politicians embarked on 'short-sighted' and selfish separatist policies, as Chancellor Ludwig Erhard had supposedly done in the mid-1960s, the writers took a stand in defiance of political realities.[79]

As Grass had pointed out in *Headbirths*, in the early 1980s the only thing that the two Germanies had in common was a *gesamtdeutsche Literatur* [an all-German literature], but the materialism prevailing in both states made it impossible to recognize their membership in a common *Kulturnation*.[80] In this situation, intellectuals played a pre-eminent role in keeping this *Kulturnation* alive by referring back to a common cultural past and by mediating between the two German states. It was the literary tradition itself which called for this 'impotent defiance', this rejection of a literally concrete political reality.[81] And it was in literature that Germany as a whole (or rather as a diverse whole) was still alive. As he claimed, 'take them all when you search for Germany on a Sunday afternoon . . . Heine who's dead and Biermann who's alive, Christa Wolf over there and Heinrich Böll over here, Logau and Lessing, Kunert and Walser . . . Don't give a damn about borders. Only wish for the language to be extensive . . .'.[82] In that sense, Grass could claim that the German poets had always been the real patriots.[83] In his novella *The Meeting at Telgte*, dating from the late 1970s, Grass had described a meeting of seventeenth-century German poets who had resolved to keep Germany together through the German language after the ravages of the Thirty Years War.[84] While *The Meeting*

---

[77] Grass, 'Rede über das Selbstverständliche', 147.

[78] Grass, 'Des Kaisers neue Kleider', 114.

[79] *Ibid.*

[80] Grass, *Kopfgeburten*, 142.

[81] Grass, *Gegen*, 52.

[82] Grass, *Kopfgeburten*, 250.

[83] *Ibid.*, 150. Grass himself had participated extensively in meetings between East and West German writers throughout the 1970s and 1980s.

[84] Günter Grass, *Das Treffen in Telgte*, in *Werkausgabe in zehn Bänden*, Vol. 6, 5–137, trans. Ralph Manheim (London: Secker and Warburg), 1981.

at Telgte was a coded description of the meetings of the *Gruppe 47*, it was also an allegory for the role writers could perform in preserving national unity.

Creating and re-creating the nation together had indeed been the archetypal political role of German intellectuals, and especially writers. Particularly in the eighteenth and early nineteenth century, they had formed and preserved a German *Kulturnation* in the absence of political unification.[85] With this concept, a fruitful tension was set up between the intellectuals' construct of the *Kulturnation* and political reality, in particular the unity (encompassing diversity) of thought and feeling, as expressed in works of art, and the reality of political division. Cultural strength and unity became opposed to political impotence. In this scenario, intellectuals played a crucial role in preserving the hope for unification, but as soon as the cultural construct and the political came closer together, their role was diminished accordingly. The productive tension between the cultural and the political depended on the weakness of the political.

Grass's imagined confederation, in its versions of both the 1960s and 1990s, would have preserved this special role for intellectuals. It would have been their task to keep the common *Kulturnation* alive, and mediate between the two confederate states, slowly bringing about the mutual understanding between East and West, as well as the self-understanding of the federal state which was to be formed after the confederation stage. They were the ones to initiate and conduct a process of 'common reflection'.[86] For this task Grass had writers and intellectuals in mind whose experience spanned both Germanies, for instance Christoph Hein and Erich Loest. In an interview he claimed that he 'could think of a great number of writers who due to their biographies, their experiences, which they have made either in the one or the other or both states, are quite capable of giving content to this concept of *Kulturnation*'.[87]

As I argued in chapter one, the two main foci of identity in post-war West Germany were the Holocaust and the economic miracle.[88] Grass was trying to defend the strongest version of the 'Holocaust identity', namely the German as 'pariah', fearing that in the process of unification a strengthened 'economic identity', i.e. what Habermas was to call 'DM-Nationalism', would completely displace an identity which the intellectuals had made it their task to guard. In this defence, Grass, associating the

---

[85] The original distinction between *Kulturnation* and *Staatsnation* derived from Friedrich Meinecke, *Cosmopolitanism and the National State*, trans. Robert B. Kimber (Princeton: Princeton University Press, 1970). See also Giesen, *Intellectuals and the German Nation*, 90–9.

[86] Grass, *Gegen*, 97.

[87] *Ibid.*, 26.

[88] Giesen, *Intellectuals and the German Nation*, 145–63, 237–41.

'economic miracle identity' with domination, consistently tended to equate the forty years of SED dictatorship with the new dictatorship of capital. One kind of oppression would replace another, and the new division between rich West Germans and poor East Germans was just as dramatic as the one made out of steel and concrete. The now triumphant ideology of market capitalism was condemned to founder just as dogmatic Communism had foundered. Capitalism was as much a form of barbarism as the previous dictatorships, its structural violence even worse. But whatever one thinks about the question of whether political freedom depends on a certain level of social rights, this equation of a politically (and also economically) oppressive dictatorship and the mechanisms of a market economy was at least problematic. It blurred the distinction between a *Rechtsstaat* [constitutional state] and a dictatorship, between a state which upheld the rule of law – however imperfectly – and one which killed and tortured some of its citizens. Grass even went a step further in likening the Unification Treaty to Hitler's 'Enabling Legislation' of 1933, thereby equating the actions of the West German government with those of the Nazis. Again, this amounted to a simplification and blurring of distinctions which was precisely not conducive to the kind of reasonable debate which the 'critical contemporary' and citizen Grass had always advocated. Like many intellectuals who claimed 'reasonableness' in theory, Grass in many actual political interventions employed a language centred on parallels and metaphors from the past which never failed to shock, but also cast doubt on the self-ascribed reasonableness.

The equation of the dictatorship of capital with that of the SED also had numerous precedents in Grass's thought. He had frequently argued that both sides in the Cold War were steeped equally in ideologies, which, ultimately, both had their roots in Hegelianism. Grass's criticism of Communist states was regularly accompanied (and relativized) by the claims that he was *not* speaking from the platform of anti-communism, and that he was not afraid of 'applause from the wrong side'.[89] He tried to preserve a 'non-ideological' stance, sharing out criticism of East and West evenhandedly, but in the process often equating East and West altogether or claiming that East and West were converging in their undemocratic ways. The reverse side of this position had been that East and West might fruitfully learn from each other and converge in peaceful, evolutionary ways towards Grass's ideal of democratic socialism. In short, only first admitting one's own mistakes allowed the intellectual to then criticize others. But clearly, this balancing act could be taken too far – especially since the imperative for equidistance seemed to precede the examination of any particular situation.

[89] For instance in a call for freedom of thought directed at the president of Czechoslovakia in 1967, 'Geben Sie Gedankenfreiheit: Offener Brief (1967)', in *Essays*, 259–61; here 260.

Moreover, Grass's opposition to dictatorships of any sort was undercut by the curious opposition he had set up between the *Biedermeier*-type niche society of the GDR which it was imperative to preserve, and democracy and civic participation on the other. He seemed aware of the fact that the attractive features of the *Biedermeier* had depended on Metternich's repressive measures, leading one to believe that *Biedermeier* and democracy were mutually exclusive. Given this choice, however, how could the niche society be preserved without a proportionate sacrifice in democracy and civic life?

Finally, implicit in the whole argument about preserving identity was the assumption that an identity was formed by common historical experiences and bound up with certain structures experienced in common over time. These structures and shared identity could only be secure in a separate state. In one sense, this constituted an arch-nationalist claim. Actual developments after 1990 confirmed this view to a certain extent, as East Germans initially felt they had lost their distinctive identities and then experienced a widely shared nostalgia for the GDR. However, the crucial point is that they did so deliberately, first desperately trying to shed difference, then eager to recover it, and not because of some abstract a priori claim that East and West German identities had to be kept apart and preserved in separate states.

In one sense, Grass's stance showed a remarkable degree of consistency, and, one might add, sincerity. His position had essentially remained the same — but the world around him had changed dramatically, which is why he came to be precisely one of the apocalyptic prophets whom he had once contrasted with the responsible, reasonable citizen—writers. It was ironic that the reasonable *Zeitgenosse* and citizen with his advocacy of compromise ended up taking a stance which resembled the very 'all-or-nothing' attitude which he had so often criticized. Now it was either a confederation along Grass's lines of thinking or Kohl's *Einheitsstaat*, whose fate was already sealed. Now it was freedom or unification, but it could not be both.

While Grass's viewpoint came to be seen by the media as increasingly eccentric, in 1990 many of his assumptions were shared by intellectuals on the Left, not the least spokespeople of his own party, the SPD. He was in line with the basic policy outlook of the Social Democrats: his advocacy of slow, piecemeal reform was a variation of the SPD's previous prescription of cautious, step-by-step change.[90] And his prohibition of unification after Auschwitz was in one sense a metaphysical version of the policy of self-containment, to which successive SPD chancellors had subscribed. Both Grass's critical stance and the policies of the SPD in 1990 came to be seen as opposition to unification as such, as an imposition of asceticism on a society which resisted such prescriptions. The end result was that Grass as

---

[90] On this policy, see Timothy Garton Ash, *In Europe's Name: Germany and the Divided Continent* (London: Jonathan Cape, 1993).

a writer lost some of his moral and political authority, while the SPD lost significant electoral support in 1990.

Postscript: A Novel Campaign and a Nobel Prize

Unlike some other left-wing intellectuals, Grass did not retreat from the public sphere after political developments had turned out very differently from his prescriptions. He sought to continue his role as citizen, as long as he 'paid taxes in this country', and appealed to East and West German writers not to fall silent, but to remember their civic responsibilities. They had a 'common experience that the silence of the intellectuals at the end of the Weimar Republic had contributed to the fact that this fragile construction could be destroyed'.[91] He also continued to claim that in 1990 'politicians should have sought the advice of the writers'.[92] He saw the increasing social divisions between East and West Germans as evidence that the unification process in 1990 had been fundamentally flawed, that unity had in fact failed, and that his proposals had been morally, but also politically and socially preferable. The increasing social alienation of East Germans was a direct result of the fact that they had had no real say in the process of 1990. In 1992, he resigned his SPD membership over the party's approval of a more restrictive asylum law. He claimed that after the government had ignored Article 146 of the Basic Law in 1990, the Constitution had once again been breached by altering Article 16, i.e. the guarantee of political asylum, in 1993. Consequently, as a self-declared constitutional patriot, he felt that united Germany was built on illegitimate foundations. Like Habermas, he argued that an increasing disrespect for the Constitution also resulted in the erosion of the Constitution's powers of social integration.

Subsequently, Grass found himself at the centre of a major controversy surrounding his 'unification novel' *Ein weites Feld*, which was published in the summer of 1995.[93] The book had received much advance praise, but was then severely attacked by a number of critics. The magazine *Der Spiegel* featured a picture of Germany's most prominent literary critic, Marcel Reich-Ranicki, tearing the book apart on its front cover.[94] Grass felt that the critics were only rejecting the novel because of its anti-unification subtext: the negative reviews were part of a general 'witch-hunt of intellectuals'.[95]

---

[91] Günter Grass, 'Es gibt sie längst, die neue Mauer (1992)', in *Der Schriftsteller als Zeitgenosse* (Munich: Deutscher Taschenbuch Verlag, 1996), 250–62; here 251.

[92] *Ibid.*, 259 and 252.

[93] Günter Grass, *Ein weites Feld* (Göttingen: Steidl, 1995).

[94] Marcel Reich-Ranicki, '. . . und es muß gesagt werden', in *Der Spiegel*, 21 August 1995.

[95] 'Der Autor und sein verdeckter Ermittler', in Günter Grass, *Der Autor als fragwürdiger Zeuge* (Munich: Deutscher Taschenbuch Verlag, 1997), 247–87; here 256.

Observers sympathetic to Grass claimed that the purge of politics in literature, which had started with the *Literaturstreit* in 1990, was carried
further.[96] While the East German Christa Wolf had been publicly humili-
ated for essentially political reasons, it was now for Grass to be 'destroyed'.
Conservative critics, so the critics of the critics claimed, seemed to ignore
the literary merits of the book because they disagreed with its politics, and
also overlooked the basic distinction between author and narrator. Moreover, the politicians and right-wing intellectuals who in 1990 had seemed
like the 'victors of history', Grass felt, were now, after unity had failed,
blaming the man who warned of this failure all along – and whose gloomy
expectations had been easily outdone by reality.[97] Grass's critics in turn
reproached him for having used his protagonists as mouthpieces to lament
the fact that his warnings had not been heeded. He seemed to be 'sulking',
they claimed, and once again putting forward inappropriate historical parallels not only between unification in 1871 and 1990, but also between
Nazism and 1990s Germany. In other words, 'politicization' was a mutual
reproach. Nevertheless, for all the talk of a 'witch hunt', the final count of
positive and negative reviews turned out to be quite balanced, and the
book sold extremely well.[98] Grass frequently pointed out that many East
Germans had recognized their fate in the novel, whereas the West
Germans, in another act of arrogance, could only rage against it.

Grass displayed his civic anger yet again, when in a 1997 speech he
called the German practice of putting rejected asylum seekers into intern-
ment camps 'democratic' barbarism, comparing the law to racial laws
during the Nazi era. The heated response from the then secretary-general
of the CDU almost created nostalgia for the 1960s and 1970s, as a time
when intellectuals could still provoke genuine outrage among politicians.
But what some prematurely declared as a 'return of the intellectuals'
turned out to be short-lived.[99] Grass himself lamented the fact that younger
authors did not get involved in politics.[100] To younger writers and critics,
on the other hand, Grass seemed more and more like a thundering or at
least cantankerous patriarch, who kept repeating to his intellectual grandchildren the democratic lessons which they thought they had long learnt.
They in turn seemed to criticize him all the more stridently because they

---

[96] On the *Literaturstreit*, see Thomas Anz (ed.), *'Es geht nicht um Christa Wolf': Der Literaturstreit
im vereinten Deutschland* (Munich: edition Sprangenberg, 1991).

[97] Grass, 'Von der Überlebensfähigkeit der Künstler (1996)', in *Der Schriftsteller*, 297–307.

[98] Oskar Negt (ed.), *Der Fall Fonty: 'Ein weites Feld' von Günter Grass im Spiegel der Kritik*
(Göttingen: Steidl, 1996).

[99] Joachim Güntner, 'Grass-Wirbel. Zum Erwachen des engagierten Intellektuellen: Eine Nachlese',
in *Neue Zürcher Zeitung*, 29 October 1997.

[100] Günter Grass, 'Zwischen den Stühlen: Was heißt heute Engagement?', in *Die Zeit*, 29 April 1998.

were all too aware that they were living off his achievements as both writer and citizen.

Grass continued in a role that – however flawed any particular position he took might have been – was now even by his detractors accepted as that of the last truly representative figure in German literature, comparable only to Gerhard Hauptmann, Thomas Mann and Heinrich Böll.[101] This view was finally confirmed when Grass received the Nobel Prize in 1999 – which also gave intellectuals from other countries the opportunity to remind the critics just how much Grass had meant for their image of a democratic Germany, especially in Poland, where Grass had been elevated to the position of 'honorary dissident'.[102] But even the award failed to heal the rift between Germany's foremost *citoyen enragé* and his critics. They seemed more interested in measuring how long it would take before he would mention 'Auschwitz' after having touched Swedish ground – nine minutes – than in the question of what his work had meant for other countries' views of Germany.[103] Grass himself, not surprisingly, used his Nobel speech not just to criticize global capitalism, but also to justify his siding with the 'losers' of unification out of 'love for his own country'.[104] More importantly, he took the speech as an occasion for a great summing up – of his beginnings as a writer, his struggle with Adorno's dictum, his complex notion of time, and his not so complex suspiciousness, his apocalyptical anti-parliamentarism, and, above all, the need to keep 'the wound open' in the 'country of the book burning'. And underneath it all, and apparently immunizing Grass against any criticism, still ran one basic – and seemingly irrefutable – personal dictum, which he had best expressed three years earlier:

> Whoever was born in the Twenties of this century, whoever, like me, has survived the . . . War only by chance, whoever cannot be persuaded that – because of his youth – he was not also guilty of the tremendous crimes: someone like that is watched by too many dead when he is writing.[105]

---

[101] Stephan Speicher, 'Totentänze für die zivile Republik: Über Günter Grass, den Repräsentanten und Dichter des Nachkriegs-Deutschland, und die Beschwörung der Vergangenheit', in *Berliner Zeitung*, 16 October 1997.

[102] Adam Zagajewski, 'Lobrede auf einen strengen Deutschlehrer: Was wir Günter Grass verdanken, habt ihr nie begriffen', in *Frankfurter Allgemeine Zeitung*, 30 November 1999.

[103] Alexander Smoltczyk, 'Ein Butt und drei Bücklinge', in *Der Spiegel*, 13 December 1999.

[104] Günter Grass, 'Fortsetzung folgt', *http://nobel.se/laureates/literature-1999-lecture-g.html*

[105] Grass, 'Von der Überlebensfähigkeit der Ketzer', 304.

3 Jürgen Habermas and the Debate on the Constitution: 'DM Nationalism' versus *Verfassungspatriotismus*

Celui qui rédige les lois n'a donc ou ne doit avoir aucun droit législatif, et le peuple même ne peut, quand il le voudroit, se dépouiller de ce droit incommunicable, parce que, selon le pact fondamental, il n'y a que la volonté générale qui oblige les particuliers, et qu'on ne peut jamais s'assurer qu'une volonté particulière est conforme à la volonté générale qu'apres l'avoir soumise aux suffrages libres de peuple...

Thus the man who frames the laws has not nor ought to have any legislative right, and the people itself cannot, even should it wish, strip itself of this untransferable right; for, according to the fundamental compact, it is only the general will which binds individuals and there can be no assurance that an individual will is in conformity with the general will until it has submitted to the free suffrage of the people...

Jean-Jacques Rousseau, *The Social Contract*

Jürgen Habermas, Germany's pre-eminent and most polarizing post-war social philosopher, participated in every major academic debate since the early 1960s, especially those controversies which touched on the political self-understanding of the Federal Republic. Most notably, Habermas, having himself paved the way for radical rethinking of university life with his 1961 *Student und Politik* [Student and Politics] charged the students' movement with 'leftist fascism' in 1968, and triggered the *Historikerstreit* in 1986.[1] He rejected the apolitical tradition in German arts and academia as well as a 'strictly professional and institutional definition of politics', while at the same time remaining sceptical of a political activism which confused intellectual influence with political power. Thus Heinrich Heine with his detached, critical stance became a model for Habermas's inter-

---

[1] Jürgen Habermas *et al.*, *Student und Politik: Eine soziologische Untersuchung zum politischen Bewußtsein Frankfurter Studenten* (Neuwied: Luchterhand, 1961), where Habermas and his collaborators found that up to 30 per cent of students had antidemocratic attitudes at the beginning of the 1960s.

ventions in the public sphere: the intellectual was to supply public debate and the process of 'democratic will-formation' with arguments and criticisms, without pretending to possess the absolute truth and without a claim on the actual exercise of power.[2] In Habermas's view, rather than continuing the fateful split between intellectual life and politics, the intellectual would supplement the institutions of the state with a political culture of *Widerspruch* [contrarianism], while not denying the autonomy of the state on the one hand, and arts and academia on the other.

For Habermas, this 'supplementing' has often meant well-timed and polemically targeted strategic interventions to ignite debates in the public sphere. He has been known to carefully scan the pages of the *Frankfurter Allgemeine Zeitung* for the first signs of a strengthening of conservative forces eager to re-legitimate nationalism and historicism. Habermas, who rarely participated in more collective entreprises like signing petitions, often quickly – and sometimes ruthlessly – responded with letters to the editor and counter-articles in left-liberal publications like *Die Zeit*. This polemical practice frequently provoked the charge that the philosopher of unconstrained discourse was in fact himself policing the boundaries of the Federal Republic's public sphere. Habermas's fellow sociologist Heinz Bude even claimed somewhat mischievously that 'the theoretician of power-free discourse is in practical matters a follower of Carl Schmitt'.[3] In particular, Habermas seemed to fall short of his own normative standards for discourse in that he rarely seemed to assume the sincerity of his intellectual opponents, instead seeing their arguments as purely strategic and power-oriented.

Nevertheless, most critics recognized that beneath Habermas's polemical attacks, there was a genuine concern not just with day-to-day combat against conservatism, but also with protecting the *conditions of possibility* of a democratic culture and a public sphere in which one could argue reasonably about political ends.[4] It was not surprising, then, that in the

---

[2] Jürgen Habermas, 'Heinrich Heine and the Role of the Intellectual in Germany', in *The New Conservatism*, 71–99.

[3] Heinz Bude, 'Die Soziologen der Bundesrepublik', in *Merkur*, Vol. 46 (1992), 569–80; here 577. It would be worthwhile to study the numerous instances in which a close theoretical kinship between Habermas and Schmitt was insinuated. No doubt Habermas was influenced by Schmitt, and in turn chose Schmitt as one of his most formidable opponents. But the desire by commentators to group them together was more often motivated by a right-wing wish to detect in Habermas a secret enemy of the Constitution. Dieter Simon has rightly claimed that such unfounded accusations were the result of left–right Cold War dichotomies. See Dieter Simon, 'Die Einheit des Rechts in der Vielheit der Systeme', in *Frankfurter Allgemeine Zeitung*, 8 December 1992.

[4] Significantly, this was recognized even by Habermas's ideological arch-enemies at the *Frankfurter Allgemeine Zeitung*. See Gustav Seibt, 'Gespräch als Gesetz', in *Frankfurter Allgemeine Zeitung*, 16 June 1989. See also Robert C. Holub, *Jürgen Habermas: Critic in the Public Sphere* (London: Routledge, 1991).

summer of 1989, on the occasion of Habermas's sixtieth birthday (and the Federal Republic's fortieth), many commentators praised Habermas for his influence on the liberal-democratic development of West Germany, even as an 'intellectual constant, on which the Republic should be congratulated'.[5]

In the *Historikerstreit*, Habermas's most significant public intervention before the fall of the Wall, he had fiercely opposed those whom he perceived as the proponents of a 'sanitized' national identity and of cultural continuities with the pre-1933 past. While his most immediate target was Ernst Nolte, Habermas also included Michael Stürmer and Andreas Hillgruber among the 'revisionists' and thereby, *ex negativo* (and *ex nihilo*), established a historiographical-cum-political coalition which had not really existed before. Arguably, the most important, but not the most immediate, target was Stürmer who was widely perceived as having considerable political influence as the author of lead articles in the *Frankfurter Allgemeine Zeitung* and as an adviser to the Chancellor at that time. Stürmer in particular was presented as reducing the comprehensive 'mental opening' and the establishment of firm political ties to the West, which Habermas saw as *the* historical achievement of the Federal Republic, to strategic military and economic considerations. However, while forcing his diverse opponents into what appeared like a homogeneous group, Habermas ultimately succeeded in dividing conservatives more generally, as moderates like Federal President von Weizsäcker spoke out against attempts to draw a thick line under the past. Moreover, even the *Frankfurter Allgemeine*, which had initially provided the journalistic platform for Nolte and his defenders, eventually dropped the controversial Berlin professor from its pages.

Habermas was generally credited with having won the historians' dispute, not least because of his defence of a 'post-conventional', post-national identity based on constitutional patriotism. He had not formulated the concept of *Verfassungspatriotismus*, but, partly through the *Historikerstreit*, became its most prominent proponent. Since constitutional patriotism served as the basis for most of Habermas's arguments in the debates on unification, I shall first reconstruct a brief history of the concept. Subsequently, I shall turn to Habermas's interventions in 1990, and analyze them in terms of his long-held political and philosophical commitments. Finally, I shall offer a critique Habermas's arguments in 1990 about the meaning of constitutional patriotism, and the need for a referendum on unification according to Article 146 in light of his own previous positions. A consideration of Habermas's vision for the 'new Germany', sometimes called the 'Berlin Republic', will be deferred until the penultimate chapter.

---

[5] Peter Glotz, 'Rechtsfiguren für den Konflikt', in *die tageszeitung*, 21 June 1989.

A Short History of *Verfassungspatriotismus*: Towards a Post-national Republican Germany

The political scientist Dolf Sternberger, close associate of Karl Jaspers and doyen of democratic political theory in West Germany after the War, had introduced the concept of *Verfassungspatriotismus* on the occasion of the thirtieth birthday of the Federal Republic.[6] As early as 1959, however, he had thought about a 'patriotic sentiment in the constitutional state', and in the early 1960s had developed the notion of *Staatsfreundschaft* [friendship towards the state], understood as a 'passionate rationality' which would make citizens identify with the state and defend it against its enemies.[7] In such early versions of constitutional patriotism, the state was understood less in terms of the written Constitution, than as a Hegelian code of *Sittlichkeit* [public ethical life], its life and its spirit conceived in the sense of Montesquieu's 'spirit of the laws', rather than any institutions as such. To lend such arguments theoretical coherence, Sternberger drew on Aristotelianism, Hannah Arendt's republicanism and an emphatic notion of civic conduct, or *Bürgerlichkeit*.[8] To lend them historical legitimacy, Sternberger excavated a tradition of patriotism stretching back to Aristotle which was not linked to the nation. He argued that at least until the end of the eighteenth century, all forms of patriotism had been 'constitutional patriotism' understood as the love of the laws and common liberties.

As much as Sternberger was trying to transcend the *nation*-state, however, he was much less sceptical about the nation-*state*. In fact, while he was highly critical of Max Weber and his category of 'legal domination', his concept was still substantially indebted to traditions of German étatisme. Sternberger, who was born in 1907, had been marked by the experience of Weimar's failure. It was not surprising that he primarily focused on loyalty to the state and to the rule of law, rather than on civil liberties or the social rights which a constitution might guarantee. Sternberger had explicitly called upon friends of the Constitution (as opposed to the *Verfassungsfeinde* [enemies of the constitution] – a highly contested concept used in the 1970s for terrorists) to defend the state, thereby linking constitutional patriotism to the concept of militant democracy.

Nevertheless, a core meaning of constitutional patriotism had been

---

[6] Dolf Sternberger, 'Verfassungspatriotismus', in *Frankfurter Allgemeine Zeitung*, 23 May 1979.

[7] Dolf Sternberger, *Staatsfreundschaft* [*Schriften* IV] (Frankfurt/Main: Suhrkamp, 1980). See also Hans Lietzmann, '"Verfassunspatriotismus" und "Civil Society": Eine Grundlage für Politik in Deutschland?', in Rüdiger Voigt (ed.), *Abschied vom Staat – Rückkehr zum Staat?* (Baden-Baden: Nomos, 1993), 205–27; here 207–10.

[8] On Sternberger's theory of *bürgerlich*-humanist legitimacy – and its contradictions – see Jörg Pannier, *Das Vexierbild des Politischen: Dolf Sternberger als politischer Aristoteliker* (Berlin: Akademie, 1996).

established: while relating to abstract values, constitutional patriotism could be an ethos of loyalty capable of transcending the nineteenth-century nation-state, which, however, did not exclude national solidarity with the citizens of the GDR. In short, *Verfassungspatriotismus* meant an attachment to the democratic institutions of the Federal Republic, a republican consciousness which took pride in the achievements of rights and freedoms in the West German polity. But for Sternberger, this patriotism was to exist alongside German national feelings 'wounded' by the division; it was not to substitute for them.

During the *Historikerstreit*, Habermas appropriated the concept of *Verfassungspatriotismus*, both making it more popular and shifting its meaning. In accordance with Sternberger, he still insisted on *Verfassungspatriotismus* as a conscious affirmation of political principles, and, as in Sternberger's vision, the relationship constitutional patriots were meant to have to the Federal Republic was one of friendship, rather than love. But Habermas went further by insisting that constitutional patriots should develop 'post-conventional identities'. Put simply, this meant that citizens had to critically reflect upon and then transcend their particular traditions and group identities in favour of universal values, rather than subjecting themselves to conventional social expectations. Post-conventional, reflexive identities were most likely to emerge where national traditions were questioned, historical discontinuities and ambivalences acutely felt, and universal values increasingly endorsed. The paradigmatic case for all three conditions was of course the Federal Republic, which, at least according to Habermas, had developed a form of patriotism focused not so much on historical identities, as on rights and democratic procedures. In short, West Germans were able to develop a more abstract patriotism, which pointed beyond itself to even more abstract, inclusive, and increasingly universalist forms of political belonging.

But where Habermas added a much stronger universalist element to Sternberger's conception of constitutional patriotism, he also subtracted the étatisme still present in Sternberger's *Staatsfreundschaft*. The traditionally German idea of the state as a substantial, or even metaphysical entity above and beyond society, was to be dissolved into the *Rechtsstaat* [the rule of law], embodying universal norms and guaranteeing the rule of law, and into the *Sozialstaat* [welfare state], which was to render possible effective political participation. Where Sternberger's patriotism had centred on democratic institutions worth defending, Habermas focused on the public sphere as providing a space for 'domination-free discourse' and public reasoning among citizens. Territory, organisation and the monopoly of legitimate violence (including the violence against constitutional enemies), the traditional Weberian reference points for the state, were displaced by an open-ended process of communication, which was formally underpinned by the rights guaranteed through the *Rechtsstaat* and materially by the welfare provided through the *Sozialstaat*. Citizenship thus consisted of effective access to this communication process among free and equal citizens, rather than passive, inherited nationality. Where Sternberger's civic friendship had centred on the state, Habermas envisaged civic friendship as an outcome of unconstrained discourse leading to mutual civic recognition. In such a scenario, nationalism and other forms of particularism could only be perceived as a kind of political-cum-moral regression.

However, Habermas's conception of constitutional patriotism as striving towards ever more abstract and universalist forms of politics, did not exclude the possibility that West German *Verfassungspatriotismus also* remained rooted in a particular identity. In fact, like so many intellectuals, Habermas stressed that the particular – in fact unique – experience of National Socialism had to be the implicit reference point for such a German republican consciousness. Only after the ultimate barbarism of Nazism had Germany, at least its Western part, finally turned to the Enlightenment and firmly anchored itself in the West. He affirmed that 'our patriotism cannot hide the fact that in Germany democracy has taken root in the motives and the hearts of citizens, at least of the younger generation, after Auschwitz – and in a way only through the shock of this moral catastrophe'.[9] He added that 'the overcoming of fascism forms the particular historical perspective from which a post-national identity centred around the universalist principles of the rule of law and democracy understands itself'.[10] After all, conventional morality in the sense of obeying law and order, following 'common sense' or acting according to national traditions had all spectacularly failed in preventing the moral catastrophe of the Third Reich.

Therefore, as with Grass, there was a certain dialectic to the fascist experience: it had also been a 'chance', and, above all, it had been *aufgehoben*, i.e. both transcended and preserved, in a new post-fascist identity, which could only be based on traditions which had passed the critical 'filter' of Auschwitz. However, where Grass had first and foremost defended the 'Holocaust identity' of the post-war Germans as a cultural one, Habermas primarily affirmed the republican *political* identity of the citizens of the Federal Republic. Remembrance, linked to the importance of public communication, thus became the basis for a democratic consciousness, and democratic identity inextricably bound up with a German 'Holocaust identity', as well as the successful coming to terms with the past in the Federal Republic.[11] As in Walter Benjamin's theses on the philosophy of history,

---

[9] Jürgen Habermas, *Die nachholende Revolution* (Frankfurt/Main: Suhrkamp, 1990), 152.

[10] *Ibid.*

[11] Jürgen Habermas, 'Historical Consciousness and Post-Traditional Identity: The Federal Republic's Orientation to the West', in *The New Conservatism*, 249–67, where Habermas redefined Jaspers's collective responsibility as 'a kind of intersubjective liability' that 'arises from the historical complex of forms of life that have been passed on from generation to generation'. In 1990, Habermas also referred to Jaspers's dictum that Germans could teach the world that the nation-state was a 'calamity'. 'Yet Again', 85.

which were heavily influenced by Jewish mysticism, the dead had a claim on the living and the weak messianic power of the present, just as much as future generations. In Habermas's interpretation, Benjamin had above all radicalized the modern consciousness of time by orienting it towards the past as well as the future. For Benjamin as for Habermas, the dead – in this case the victims of National Socialism – had a stake in the present just as much as those yet to be born. The living, then, had to do justice to the dead by atonement through memory and a specific *Sühnebewußtsein* [consciousness of atonement].[12] Consequently, German constitutional patriotism was based on both politics *and* memory, or rather, what Habermas called Benjamin's 'anamnestic solidarity', and therefore also relied on values which, in Habermas's terms, could be called strictly 'pre-political'.[13]

For all these reasons, Germany could not develop a 'normal' national consciousness and instead had to deliberately fashion an identity based on universalism and informed by the fascist experience – they had, after all, 'learnt something special' from their 'national catastrophe', as Habermas's philosophical soul-mate Karl-Otto Apel once put it.[14] In Habermas's view, other countries were also forced in the direction of universalism by socio-economic forces, supra-national institutions, and changes in international communication.[15] However, it was Germany, having been politically purified in a somewhat dialectical manner through the Holocaust, which was likely to emerge as the first post-national, multicultural 'state-nation'.

Was constitutional patriotism simply a form of 'negative nationalism', an inversion of traditional nationalist doctrines, or, above all, just an artificial intellectual construct, as critics often claimed? It certainly was a patriotism based on reason and reflection, an identification with the 'civic state-nation' and pride in democratic institutions instead of supposedly 'pre-political' values such as territory, culture or *Volk*. But in that sense, it

---

[12] *Ibid.*, 155–6; Jürgen Habermas, *The Philosophical Discourse of Modernity: Twelve Lectures*, trans. Frederick Lawrence (1985; Cambridge, Mass.: MIT Press, 1987), 11–16. Habermas, however, also played down the theological and revolutionary elements in Benjamin's theses. See also his 'Walter Benjamin: Consciousness-Raising or Rescuing Critique', in Gary Smith (ed.), *On Walter Benjamin: Critical Essays and Recollections* (Cambridge, Mass.: MIT Press, 1988), 90–128, and the illuminating discussion by Max Pensky, 'On the use and abuse of memory: Habermas, anamnestic solidarity, and the *Historikerstreit*', in *Philosophy and Social Criticism*, Vol. 15 (1989), 351–80.

[13] Jürgen Habermas, 'Konservative Politik, Arbeit, Sozialismus und Utopie heute', in *Die Neue Unübersichtlichkeit* (Frankfurt/Main: Suhrkamp, 1985), 59–76; here 68.

[14] Karl-Otto Apel, 'Zurück zur Normalität? Oder können wir aus der nationalen Katastrophe etwas Besonderes gelernt haben? Das Problem des (welt-)geschichtlichen Übergangs zur postkonventionellen Moral aus spezifisch deutscher Sicht', in Forum der Philosophie Bad Homburg (ed.), *Zerstörung des moralischen Selbstbewußtseins: Chance oder Gefährdung?* (Frankfurt/Main: Suhrkamp, 1988), 91–142.

[15] Habermas, *Die nachholende Revolution*, 152.

was close to the Rousseauean idea that 'the love of one's country is the love of justice'.[16] It was an attempt at recreating a language of republican patriotism as it had existed prior to the nineteenth century, when the language of nationalism drove it out of European discourse.[17] The Federalists knew of it, and it is a recurrent theme in Mill, who conceived of a loyalty attaching itself to 'the principles of individual freedom and political and social equality'.[18] This institution-centred patriotism resurfaced from time to time in European history, but was usually swamped by a more nationalist, culture-centred rhetoric. Sternberger's and Habermas's concepts were both ingenious attempts to find a form of liberal loyalty and to deal with the problem of patriotism and identity in a divided nation haunted by a past of nationalist excesses. Only such a form of patriotism, Habermas thought, would not alienate Germany from the West, even if, paradoxically, the West itself remained wedded to largely 'pre-political' notions of nationality, or, in the French case, a republicanism not nearly or, at any rate, no longer, as ambitious in its universalist aspirations as Habermas's. In fact, the West could never be Western enough, or, as one acerbic observer put it, 'Habermas, it seemed, refused to let Germany join any club that would have it as a member'.[19]

Apart from this grounding in the history of European political thought, then, constitutional patriotism was not abstract in the sense that it was rooted in the special pride of having overcome fascism with democratic institutions, and, in particular, of having reflected, and where necessary, broken with particular German traditions. This break with intellectual traditions again made Habermas's vision different from Sternberger's in that he was especially concerned that political and intellectual-cum-cultural ruptures had to go hand in hand. It was also this distinctive emphasis on opposing discredited cultural traditions which made it radically different from much of the languages in the tradition of European patriotism.

Verfassungspatriotismus was not one man's maverick idea: it had become very much part of a West German liberal consensus that encompassed the editors of *Die Zeit*, writers, social scientists as well as politicians. The ingenuity of constitutional patriotism was not least that it suited the Left perfectly in allowing it a careful, conditional identification with the Federal Republic, which had in fact long become their home, while still permit-

---

[16] Habermas, 'Yet Again', 88.

[17] For a discussion of this discourse of patriotism, see Maurizio Viroli, *For Love of Country: An Essay on Patriotism* (Oxford: Oxford University Press, 1995).

[18] F. R. Leavis (ed.), *Mill on Bentham and Coleridge* (London: Chatto and Windus, 1962), 122.

[19] Mark Lilla, 'The Other Velvet Revolution: Continental Liberalism and its Discontents', in *Daedalus*, Vol. 123, No. 2 (1994), 129–57; here 146.

ting some distance and a primary identification with the 'other, better Germany', which this time was not Grass's *Kulturnation*, but one of democratic universalism.

Even earlier than Sternberger and Habermas, the political scientist Karl Dietrich Bracher had developed a notion of 'post-national democracy' which was based on the historical lessons drawn from Weimar and an identification with West German democracy not just as the opposite of dictatorship, but also as opposed to the old Wilhelmine *Obrigkeitsstaat* [authoritarian state]. Kurt Sontheimer, Martin Broszat and Wolfgang Mommsen all explicitly supported the concept or adjacent notions like *Staatsbürgernation*, even if none of them pushed the concept as far in a universalist direction as Habermas did. Moreover, these proponents of constitutional patriotism did not see the concept as a temporary or compensatory one tied to national division. Not surprisingly, *Verfassungspatriotismus* was then widely affirmed at the fortieth anniversary of the Federal Republic.[20] But there had also always been notable detractors. Those clinging to national sentiments, to 'history' — understood as an imperative to overcome the division, and as the belief that the concrete and the particular could not, and should not, be eradicated by supposedly rationalist designs — opposed constitutional patriotism. The historians Hagen Schulze and Hans-Peter Schwarz argued that the national and emotional 'abstinence' of the purely 'academic' *Verfassungspatriotismus* would leave the national question to more sinister political forces. Étatiste thinkers Helmut Schelsky, Josef Isensee and Hans-Joachim Arndt charged that the state had to be brought back in, since the universalist values of the Constitution were insufficient to sustain social cohesion.[21] Walser went so far as to attack the concept as 'embroidered blankets of solace over the gap of the division' and even as a 'fashionable notion of political masturbation'.[22] Clearly, constitutional patriotism was not as widely and deeply shared as some of the congratulatory remarks in the summer of 1989 might have suggested.

Rescuing a Republican Consciousness

Very early on after the fall of the Wall, Habermas became concerned about what unification might do to the republican consciousness which had formed in the Federal Republic. Two weeks after East Germans first rushed

[20] Karl Dietrich Bracher, 'Kein Anlaß zu Teuto-Pessimismus', in *Süddeutsche Zeitung*, 24 May 1989.

[21] For instance Helmut Schelsky, 'Über das Staatsbewußtsein', in *Die politische Meinung*, No. 185 (1979), 30–5.

[22] Martin Walser, 'Über Deutschland reden: Ein Bericht', in Martin Walser, *Deutsche Sorgen* (Frankfurt/Main: Suhrkamp, 1997), 406–27.

from East to West Berlin, Habermas voiced these concerns in a piece entitled 'The Hour of National Sentiment. Republican Ethos or National Consciousness?' However, he did not publish it then, but only sent it to some
of his friends. In this essay, Habermas expressed fears that West Germany
could abuse its economic power to blackmail the GDR into an *Anschluß*
[annexation], a term which evoked images of Hitler's annexation of
Austria. The *Anschluß* was opposed to the option of giving the citizens
of the GDR a true right of self-determination by supporting the process
of radical democratization irrespective of what the GDR citizens would
ultimately decide. The choices were therefore: either the Federal Republic gave every way a chance (including an ill-defined 'third way') or
dictated the terms of an *Anschluß*, for which, in his view, the Christian
Democrats and the *Frankfurter Allgemeine Zeitung* were pressing.[23] In the
event of such an *Anschluß*, Habermas feared that a traditional antinomy,
or split of identifications with either freedom *or* unity, might return to
Germany. In this scenario, the Federal Republic's republican consciousness,
which in the case of many West Germans was still more habitual than
rooted in reflection, might be revoked.

Habermas's main concern was that what he called 'habitual republicans'
might desert the republican consensus if the democratic Right no longer
kept a newly invigorated national-conservative Right in check. Ironically,
this danger arose precisely because of the Federal Republic's increasing
liberalization, which also meant that the CDU had moved more to the
centre.[24] In Habermas's view, the national-conservative *Republikaner auf
Abruf* [republicans ready to desert the republican consensus] might
increase their numbers and influence, and finally abjure their republicanism in a situation fraught with new, inevitably national questions. If
the government treated unification mainly as an economic problem to be
tackled by technocratic means and used economic power to curtail the
right to self-determination of GDR citizens, the opinions of habitual
republicans, who saw democracy merely as a political hull for an effective
economic system, might become the reigning discourse. Through such a
'cold Anschluß [annexation]', a republican consciousness which was just
gaining firm ground in West Germany would be damaged, maybe
irreparably.[25]

In Habermas's view, this was precisely the dangerous direction in which
West German policies were moving after November 1989. Consequently,
he made a number of public interventions early on in 1990 in order to

---

[23] Habermas, *Die nachholende Revolution*, 158.

[24] 'Political Culture in Germany since 1968: A Interview with Dr. Rainer Erd for the *Frankfurter
Rundschau*' in *The New Conservatism*, 183–95.

[25] Habermas, *Die nachholende Revolution*, 152.

criticize the unification process along the lines which he had first suggested in the paper to his friends. Like Grass, he was uneasy about the sheer speed of unification. But, as with many intellectuals, what was described as the seeming 'acceleration' of history, or a transformed sense of temporality, came to be a shorthand for more profound concerns: in Habermas' case, the real diagnosis was a number of 'normative deficiencies' which bedevilled the unification process. In a prominent article in *Die Zeit* he claimed that the whole process of unification was supported by 'chubby-faced' economic nationalism rather than a consciousness rooted in republican values. The currency union amounted to a new form of economic imperialism. Most damagingly, the Kohl government had managed to 'out-maneuver . . . the public sphere' and did not give the unification process a chance to develop 'any *democratic* dynamic of its own'.[26] Habermas accused the West German government of thinking in terms of nineteenth-century power politics and consciously destabilizing the GDR.[27] In short, the unification process seemed to be centred on the executive, driven by elites, and excluding the very entity which had been at the heart both of Habermas's theorizing and his democratic commitments: the public sphere, in which citizens could freely come to discursive, intersubjective political understandings.

To counteract these tendencies, Habermas suggested that 'an agenda for unification would have to give priority to the freely exercised right of the citizens to determine their own future by direct vote' as an act of democratic foundation, namely through invoking article 146 of the Basic Law and instigating a general discourse about the democratic future of Germany, instead of an annexation through article 23.[28] Only then could unification be 'understood as a normatively willed act of the citizens of both states, who in political self-awareness decided on a common civil union'. He contrasted a proceduralist account rooted in his philosophy of communicative action and underpinned by the classical voluntarist republican claim that citizens be the authors of the laws that bind them, with a paternalistic communitarian approach supposedly taken by the government, which aimed at extracting emotional support from pride in the Deutschmark.

However, beyond such immediate procedural necessities, Habermas was also concerned about the long-term effects on political mentalities. He wanted a popular referendum on the Constitution, because a renewed republican consciousness could then crystallize around it. An affirmation of republican values, however, was also necessary for a different reason altogether, related to the other 'mnemonic basis' of constitutional

---

[26] Jürgen Habermas, *The Past as Future*, trans. Max Pensky (Lincoln: University of Nebraska Press, 1994), 41.

[27] *Ibid.*, 42–3.

[28] Habermas, 'Yet Again', 95.

patriotism. In Habermas's words, 'the demise of the GDR stirs up other pasts . . . including pasts that ought not to serve as models for the future, pasts that shouldn't regain any power over the present'.[29] He explained this potential for historical regression by the fact that the GDR, by appropriating and misusing progressive ideas 'in the service of political self-legitimation, cynically denying these ideals through its inhuman praxis and thus bringing them into disrepute', had done enormous damage to emancipatory Enlightenment ideas and traditions in Germany. Habermas went so far as to claim that

> this dialectic of devaluation will end up being more ruinous for the spiritual hygiene of Germany than all the concentrated resentment of five or six generations of anti-Enlightenment, antisemitic, false romantic, jingoist obscurantists. The devaluation of our best and most fragile intellectual traditions is, for me, one of the most evil aspects of the legacy that the GDR brings into the expanded Federal Republic.[30]

The delegitimation of socialist and emancipatory ideals would create an opening for Western conservatives to sound the end of emancipatory progress and tap into reactionary and anti-republican traditions in German thought. Together with this delegitimation, Habermas feared, went an exclusion of the 'critical intellectual' from the public sphere. As he claimed in an interview,

> now there's no shortage of cultural luminaries ready to take the downfall of the GDR as a pretext for hustling to gloss over everything that doesn't fit into the elitist model of a specifically German cultural pessimism deeply rooted in historicist, late romantic thought. I'm afraid something of that old sour atmosphere is going to be seeping back in, and the 'cultured' will replace the 'intellectuals' once again.[31]

These 'luminaries' would be the same intellectuals who had already tried once before to 'normalize' Germany's past through 'historicism'. In other words, a unification process executed without or even against the public sphere, might potentially provoke the return of a whole cluster of German continuities, including the reappearance of the German mandarin, the very type against which Habermas and fellow left-wing intellectuals had defined themselves in the 1950s.

In his rhetoric, Habermas set a hypothetical unification process with a moral dimension against the actual one which he described as thoroughly

---

[29] Habermas, *The Past*, 37.

[30] *Ibid.*, 37.

[31] *Ibid.*, 39.

technocratic. Even historians now became 'managers of the past' and neo-nationalism was manipulated in accordance with opinion polls. National-ism, Habermas feared, was essentially to serve as a form of *compensation* for the normative and discursive deficits of the unification process. Opposed to this technocratic unification 'from above' was the spontaneous and self-transforming nature of a democratic political culture, i.e. that 'delicate fabric of mentalities and convictions that can neither be invented nor manipulated through administrative measures'.[32] In sum, an 'executed' and elite-driven process of unification meant a boost for a conservative vision, precisely at the moment when

> the old Federal Republic was well on the way toward a modern demo-cratic society with strengthened political participation, and toward a protest culture that reminded the 'two-thirds society' of the new tasks of the social and ecological domestication of capitalism . . . and new strategies beyond the privileged administrative forms of state-social pacification.[33]

According to Habermas, the population in the East supported the author-itarian approach of 'social pacification' and was only at the stage of the West German mentality in the Adenauer era.[34] Conservatives would invoke an idealized economic miracle in an effort to extend a 'normal' economic miracle identity to Germany as a whole, thereby returning German polit-ical culture to the authoritarian stage of the 1950s. In short, given what he had written to his friends in November 1989, all of Habermas's worst fears seemed to come true.

How is one to judge Habermas's intervention during this period? Which intellectual resources did he marshal to protect a republican consciousness? And were his arguments consistent with his previous theorizing? I shall first relate Habermas's position in 1990 to some of the deep concerns ani-mating his theoretical-cum-political project as a whole.

Nationalist Compensation versus Discursive Reconciliation

One of Habermas's extraordinary strengths as a thinker has been his ability to assimilate other theories and intellectual challenges to his thought, both to differentiate and synthesize, thereby continuously revising his own social-philosophical project. Nevertheless, it is striking that for all the

[32] *Ibid.*, 47.

[33] *Ibid.*, 57.

[34] *Ibid.*, 58.

changes, both politically and theoretically, which Habermas has undergone, there are also a number of distinctive and recurring patterns of thought. Before 1989, there had been three such patterns which appeared time and again both in Habermas's social theories and his political interventions: first, a need to differentiate and to avoid both theoretical and political one-sidedness and negativism; second, a desire to move from the particular to the universal, and to dissolve 'substantial' entities in procedures. This move was also linked to a fear of losing real gains made in advancing democracy and rationalization more generally, and instead be offered forms of emotional 'compensation'. Finally, as part of his work's deepest impulse, there was a desire for successful personal interaction, reconciliation and an almost Brechtian kind of 'friendliness'. I shall discuss these three aspects in turn and show how each contributed crucially to the subtext of Habermas's interventions in the unification debates.

Habermas always attempted to resist the political and philosophical negativism associated with left-wing Weimar intellectuals, including his intellectual father figures Horkheimer and Adorno.[35] Theoretically, he moved away from the dystopian vision offered in their *Dialectic of Enlightenment* by returning to the Weberian beginnings of Critical Theory, and recovering a different model of modernity.[36] Rather than one-sidedly reducing modernity to the all-pervasive triumph of instrumental reason, as Horkheimer and Adorno had supposedly done, Habermas attempted to offer a more nuanced picture, in which both instrumental and substantial rationality found their place. Here, the pathologies of modernity were no longer inevitable, as long as both forms of rationality did not come to usurp each other's proper place, and as long as, in Habermasian parlance, the 'lifeworld', i.e. the spheres of life in which non-strategic communication and solidarity were possible, and the 'system', i.e. the economy and the state, remained separate.[37] Despite all its pathologies, Habermas argued, modernity had meant real gains in rationalization and individual autonomy. And any totalizing critique which denied these gains might in fact become counterproductive and eradicate the very emancipatory achievements it failed to see. Similarly, Habermas reconstructed a form of Western Marxism which sought to overcome the productivist paradigm of externalization and self-realization through labour which had been derived from Hegel. Drawing on

---

[35] Habermas, *The Philosophical Discourse*, 106–30.

[36] This is necessarily a highly schematic account. One of the best discussions of Habermas's reconstruction of Critical Theory remains Seyla Benhabib, *Critique, Norm and Utopia: A Study of the Foundations of Critical Theory* (New York: Columbia University Press, 1986).

[37] Jürgen Habermas, *The Theory of Communicative Action, Vol. 1 Reason and the Rationalization of Society*, trans. Thomas McCanthy (1981; Boston: Beacon Press, 1984) and *The Theory of Communicative Action Vol. 2: Lifeworld and Sytem: A Critique of Functionalist Reason*, trans. Thomas McCanthy (1981; Boston: Beacon Press, 1987).

the pragmatism of C. S. Peirce and J. L. Austin's speech act theory, Habermas substituted a philosophy of intersubjectivity for the 'subject philosophy' still at the heart of the Marxist enterprise. And he finally took leave of any philosophy of history, even if his 'gains in rationalization' remained an almost liberal notion of 'progress' by another name.

In the same vein, Habermas, despite many disappointments and misgivings about the reality of democracy in West Germany, always sought to stress that the Federal Republic had been a real historical achievement for the Germans. He unashamedly called himself a 'product of "Re-education"', and argued that after 1945

> we have learned that the *bürgerliche* constitutional state in its French or American or English version is a historical achievement. This is an important biographical difference between those who had witnessed where a half-hearted *bürgerliche* Republic, like the Weimar Republic, can lead, and those who have formed their political consciousness only later.[38]

In other words, Habermas's political stance was shaped by the success of 'Re-education', but also by the memory of Weimar left-wing intellectuals having undermined democracy through a 'totalizing critique', which failed to differentiate and to defend what little had been achieved in the way of liberal democracy – with disastrous consequences.

This drive towards differentiation was also evident in Habermas's more directly political thought. While his early writings had been animated by a strong anti-parliamentarist impulse, which led some critics to compare him to Carl Schmitt, and by a desire to increasingly democratize the economy, the state administration and political parties, Habermas's political ambitions were increasingly scaled down. By the end of the 1980s, under the influence of Niklas Luhmann's systems theory, his position had become a much more nuanced one, but, his critics charged, also more mellow, even resigned: Habermas now claimed that in modern, highly complex societies, integration was accomplished through power, money and solidarity.[39] The first two, i.e. the bureaucratic apparatus and the economy, had developed their own systemic imperatives, and any attempt to displace these autonomous rationalities through democratization would lead to regression in overall rationalization. Only the 'life-world' was the proper realm for communicative power and solidarity. They were to be generated in a public sphere, in which citizens could put pressure on the

---

[38] Detlef Horster and Willem van Reijen, 'Interview with Jürgen Habermas', in Detlef Horster, *Habermas zur Einführung* (Hamburg: Junius, 1995), 97–126; here 101.

[39] For a summary of these changes by Habermas himself, see the preface to the 1990 edition of *Strukturwandel der Öffentlichkeit: Untersuchungen zu einer Kategorie der bürgerlichen Gesellschaft* (1962; Frankfurt/Main: Suhrkamp, 1990), 11–50.

political and economic systems, and defend the 'life-world' against the tendency by the system to 'colonize' it through 'bureaucratizing' and 'economizing' spheres of domination-free discourse and non-instrumental subjectivity.

In addition to the memory of Weimar mandarins, however, there was also that of German continuities under Adenauer's 'Chancellor Democracy'. Habermas was shocked by the continuity at the very political top, but also by the continuities in the universities. While he had been very familiar with − to some extent a democratic follower of − Heidegger and the cultural critique of Arnold Gehlen at the beginning of his studies in the early 1950s, a key moment came when he discovered that Heidegger had republished his lectures from the 1930s without a word of apology or explanation.[40] Habermas penned his first journalistic article (ironically, for the very *Frankfurter Allgemeine Zeitung* which was later to become his journalistic *bête noire*) to attack Heidegger.[41] Subsequently, his attachment to the philosophies of Gehlen and Heidegger was turned into opposition. Habermas rediscovered Western Marxism and then performed his own 'opening towards the (philosophical) West'. Politically, he also turned increasingly radical, in fact to such an extent, that Horkheimer became wary of an unreconstructed Marxist at the Institute of Social Research, and eventually forced Habermas's departure. While Habermas's theories evolved, however, his opposition to a certain type of theory never wavered after the 1950s: namely, theories which seemed to offer a truncated vision of modernity, and, instead of making good on the emancipatory and rational potential already contained in modern developments, offered forms of emotional compensation for modernity's undeniable pathologies and insecurities. Such compensation effectively amounted to a form of historical regression.

The pattern which Habermas opposed most vigorously was that established by theorists like Gehlen, Schelsky and Joachim Ritter: a modern technocratic order, in which, according to Gehlen, the emancipatory premises of the Enlightenment were dead, but its consequences in the form of instrumental reason still unfolding. In such a technocratic, 'post-historical' order all historical possibilities had been played out or 'crystallized', the intellectuals confined to their compartments of specialization and the promises of emancipation reneged on.[42] In particular, the emotional safety provided by traditions, religion and 'thick' collective identities were offered as compensation in times of modernization crises.

[40] Rolf Wiggershaus, *The Frankfurt School: Its History, Theories and Political Significance*, trans. Michael Robertson (1988; Cambridge: Polity, 1994), 537−65.

[41] Jürgen Habermas, 'Mit Heidegger gegen Heidegger denken: Zur Veröffentlichung von Vorlesungen aus dem Jahre 1935', in *Frankfurter Allgemeine Zeitung*, 25 July 1953.

[42] Arnold Gehlen, *Über kulturelle Kristallisation* (Bremen: Angelsachsen, 1961).

Habermas had first attacked such conceptions of modernity cut off from any further emancipatory promises in the 1950s. In the debate on whether West Germany was primarily a *Rechtsstaat* or a *Sozialstaat*, Habermas sided with his teacher Wolfgang Abendroth, who advocated the development of the *Sozialstaat* into a socialist democracy, opposed to Schmitt's pupil Ernst Forsthoff.[43] Forsthoff, according to Habermas, offered the substantive sovereign state as a means of social integration and compensation for the dislocations caused by social modernization. In the 1970s and 1980s, Habermas thought he recognized the same pattern, when, in his view, the intellectuals of the *Tendenzwende* recycled the arguments from the 1950s, detaching them from their compromised Nazi past.[44] In the 1980s, he claimed to have detected yet again a similar constellation of sentiments and charged a rather heterogeneous group of scholars with 'neoconservatism'. Habermas effectively grouped friends and enemies like Hermann Lübbe and Odo Marquard, who had been taught by Ritter, and who once again blamed the pathologies associated with a 'modernity pacified through compensation' on left-wing intellectuals. For them, too, religion, historical narratives and the comfort offered by pre-political collective identities were to serve as a kind of compensation for the inevitable dislocations and contingencies caused by rationalization.

Not least because of what can only be described as his own trauma of having been unaware of cultural and philosophical continuities while supporting the democratic political order, Habermas, then, made it his particular task to combat German cultural continuities. The Westernization of politics and culture had to be synchronized – in fact, they seemed almost dependent on each other for an authentic collective-learning process. Consequently, in every debate in which Habermas identified a danger for German democracy, his 'Four Horsemen' were not far off: Heidegger, Schmitt, Jünger and Gehlen would appear on the horizon of a seemingly Westernized cultural consciousness. It even seems that, rather than having engaged in a string of diverse debates, Habermas had engaged in *one* long debate with the 'cultural luminaries'.[45] Curiously, therefore, every political debate would also immediately be 'intellectualized' and cast in the language of 'ghostly returns' and what Habermas's American translator Max Pensky has aptly called a seemingly 'unrelievable anxiety over the possibility of a slip back into fascism'.[46]

---

[43] Jürgen Habermas 'Neoconservative Cultural Criticism in the United States and West Germany' in *The New Conservatism*, 22–47; here 33–4.

[44] Jürgen Habermas, 'Introduction', in Jürgen Habermas (ed.), *Observations on 'The Spiritual Situation of the Age': Contemporary German Perspectives*, trans. Andrew Buchwalter (1979, Cambridge, Mass.: MIT Press, 1984), 1–28.

[45] Max Pensky, 'Jürgen Habermas and the antinomies of the intellectual', in Peter Dews (ed.), *Habermas: A Critical Reader* (Oxford: Blackwell, 1999), 211–37; here 221–4.

[46] *Ibid.*, 225.

Having reconstructed some of Habermas's deepest and most sustained commitments, it is not difficult to see why he objected so fiercely to some of the developments in 1990. He construed the unification process as one in which political, bureaucratic and economic elites were executing policies without consideration either for an autonomous public sphere, in which citizens could publicly reason about what political outcome they desired, or for the 'life-world' which had evolved in the GDR. In fact, it seemed that the communicative power which had been constituted by the East German citizens' movements was purposefully extinguished by the West German parties and the bureaucracy. Given the lack of a public sphere to produce communicative power and solidarity, and given that economic and administrative power could not create solidarity by themselves, the default source of social integration had to become a pre-political, homogeneous national identity. Since, due to the division, there was no 'conventional identity' of shared experience during the last forty years to fall back on, national solidarity necessarily had to be construed in terms of continuities with the pre-1945 period. Moreover, as consent could not be formed in democratic deliberation, legitimacy was to be found in acclamation and 'manufactured' mass loyalty. Nationalism thus came to function as a form of compensation for the lack of a true discursive will-formation, and a slow rapprochement and reconciliation between East and West Germans. Such compensation in the form of 'chubby DM-nationalism', which was a more dangerous version of the 'cultural compensation' which neo-conservatives had ostensibly advocated in the 1980s, necessarily constituted a form of historical – and intellectual – regression.[47]

However, as critics pointed out even at the time, there simply was not nearly as much nationalist passion inflamed from above, let alone 'DM nationalism', in 1990 as Habermas seemed to suggest. It was equally implausible to sustain that Germans invested the DM with libidinal forces, as he had claimed at one point. While the currency was deeply associated with security and success after the trauma of two disastrous inflations within a generation, the Mark was hardly a means of aggression.[48] Apart from such factual points, there was the more important observation that a currency was actually more than an issue of economics, because it was tied to a whole basket of rights and liberties. In short, the currency was not as separate from the Constitution as the Habermasian vision suggested. Arguably, what blinded him to this point was precisely his desire for differentiation between politics, economics and the life-world, but also a somewhat Manichean division between the political and the economic,

---

[47] Habermas, 'Yet Again', 84.

[48] As recognized for instance by Habermas's left-wing ally Hans-Ulrich Wehler in 'Aufforderung zum Irrweg', in *Der Spiegel*, 24 September 1990.

in which the common pursuit of private self-interest could *only* be perceived as a morally inferior mode of social cohesion. This rigid (and in itself idealist and apolitical) separation between politics and economics, or 'the social', could be traced back to Hannah Arendt's thought, which of course required that political deliberation be cleansed of private self-interest.

More importantly, as much as Habermas strove to be politically subtle and discriminating, this kind of differentiation was always delivered *ex post facto*. The future-oriented warnings which he made in the present, however, were frequently polemical and often intentionally *not* discriminating in order to be effective. But to evoke the language of the *Stukas* in the context of 'DM Nationalism', as Habermas did in 1990, was crudely to instrumentalize – and devalue – the very mnemonic substance on which a proper version of constitutional patriotism depended. The rhetorical power of such insinuations depended on metaphors and historical analogies drawn from National Socialism, thereby equating what could clearly not be equated. This is the instance where Habermas came up against the 'paradox of the democratic, but uncivil intellectual' explained in the first chapter.

In sum, Habermas's interventions were animated by fears of nationalist compensation for the 'normative deficiencies' of the unification process, and of a 'de-differentiation', in which money and power became dominant and solidarity was extracted from a pre-political, homogeneous national identity. However, it is also important to stress what Habermas's interventions were *not* based on: they did not entail an idealization of the GDR niche society, despite Habermas's concern for undamaged forms of life, in which unconstrained communication was possible. Such romantic 'life-forms' could have easily been projected onto the GDR – but Habermas resisted the temptation. In the same vein, Habermas was not primarily concerned about the 'loss of a socialist utopia', as so many on the '68 Left were (see chapter four). He had for a long time sought to dissociate Critical Theory from philosophies of history, in fact, from totalizing philosophical systems altogether.[49] He had indeed been close to a kind of anti-anti-communism because he associated anti-communism with a repression of the Nazi past, a realignment of the Germans with the bourgeoisie in the European civil War, and even antisemitism. And Habermas made some clearly tactical attempts to salvage parts of the socialist impulse in his 1990 writings – but this salvation was essentially semantic, since he simply redefined the core of socialism as solidarity and communication. In other words, his own theory supposedly had long absorbed socialism's basic intuitions.

[49] Jürgen Habermas, 'Ein Interview mit der *New Left Review*', in *Die Neue Unübersichtlichkeit*, 213–57; here 224.

Aestheticizing *Verfassungspatriotismus?*

Habermas's notion of *Verfassungspatriotismus* was increasingly attacked during and after the debate on unification as a temporary notion specific to the Federal Republic, even as a 'patriotism for professors', and as an abstract rationalization which never commanded any real support.[50] The question, however, is not so much whether there can be such a thing as constitutional patriotism — I have suggested above that there is indeed a long, although sometimes buried, tradition of republican patriotism in European thought — but whether the concept was effectively adapted and applied by its adherents in 1990. In Habermas's case, he presented *Verfassungspatriotismus* in the same terms as he had before 1989, effectively arguing for nothing more than an extension of West German ideas to the East. In the best case, citizens in the GDR would come to accept this kind of patriotism; in the worst case, their hunger for Western lifestyles would be manipulated by conservatives, thereby damaging the Western republican ethos. Accordingly, in Habermas's thinking the GDR figured alternatively as the danger of political-cum-historical regression, as an anti-democratic contagion, or as a catalyst for a return to 'pre-political' values.

Generally, Habermas showed a marked lack of interest in the East German revolution. He somewhat dismissively called the East German and the East European revolutions *nachholend*, i.e. revolutions to catch up with the West and the ideas of 1789. Habermas emphasized that 'the catching-up revolution does not throw any new light on our *old* problems'.[51] However, could the core values of the East European revolutions not have been used to strengthen *Verfassungspatriotismus* in the sense of relating this abstract concept to shared democratic practices, and embed it in a new context of motivations and mentalities? After all, the East European revolutions had been about the reassertion of civil society and popular sovereignty in its most dramatic form, embodied in the revolutionary cry of 'We are the people'. The problem for Habermas lay in the fact that this reassertion was connected to 'conventional' nationalism, and that regaining freedom meant at the same time the return of national particularity and the sovereign nation-state.[52] Nationalism was first of all an instrument to resist Soviet imperialism, but dissidents and the leaders of the revolution, at least for some time, managed to draw the ideas of nationalism and democracy together.[53] Moreover, the East European revolutions were

---

[50] For example in M. and S. Greiffenhagen, *Ein schwieriges Vaterland*, 40.

[51] Habermas, *Die nachholende Revolution*, 7.

[52] Ralf Dahrendorf, 'Die Sache mit der Nation', in *Merkur*, Vol. 44 (1990), 823–34; here 824.

[53] See for instance Adam Michnik, 'Verführung zum Verrat. Der Fall der Intellektuellen im Zwanzigsten Jahrhundert', in *Neue Rundschau*, No. 2 (1992), 80–5; here 83.

characterized by the dissidents' ability to carve out ever more public space and ultimately to reconstitute a genuine public sphere and restore the institutions of civil society. One could argue that these developments presented a window of opportunity to fill what *was* after all an abstract concept of *Verfassungspatriotismus* tied to the one foundational event of the Holocaust with new emotional content. Such new affective associations could have complemented, rather than replaced, the emotional and mnemonic references to the Holocaust which it had to contain in Germany. After all, the very point of the Constitution, with its protection of basic rights and liberties, in constitutional patriotism was to enable a multiplicity of experiences in the 'life-world', as well as a pluralism of historical and cultural identity formations. In 1989 abstract universal principles might have been linked with the life-world, especially given that in the 1980s debate about the 'incomplete project of modernity' versus Lyotard's 'post-modern condition' Habermas had called precisely for such a connection between modern culture, and, implicitly, philosophy and politics, with the life-world and everyday *praxis*.[54] One could go even further and argue that the East German revolution might have become a 'foundation myth' of the new Germany, and that intellectuals, using *Verfassungspatriotismus* and life-world experience, could have achieved a democratic, liberal fusion for the new Germany, firmly anchoring the country in the tradition of civic patriotism. Habermas himself had once hinted that critique combined with an emphasis on social differentiation and actual democratic achievements was not sufficient: since progress had a tendency to annihilate its own past traces, an 'active remembering' and a symbolic representation of past struggles and victories was imperative which went beyond Benjamin's 'anamnestic solidarity'.[55] This means that there would have been intellectual resources available to counter the (in itself empty) charge of symbolic emptiness, rationalism and 'abstractness'. Not surprisingly, Habermas's critics in 1990 repeated these accusations, adding that he was out of touch with ordinary people, and, more importantly, with 'history'. Brigitte Seebacher-Brandt, for instance, played off 'the return of history' against the social philosopher for whom 'history' was 'essentially alien', thereby setting up precisely the antinomy which Habermas had always claimed to reject.[56] However, as I shall explain in the penultimate chapter, other left-wing and republican-minded intellectuals were eventually to fasten on the East German revolution as a 'founding myth' to remedy the 'republican deficit' which resulted from the unification process.

---

[54] See Jürgen Habermas, 'Modernity – An Incomplete Project', in: Hal Foster (ed.), *Postmodern Culture* (London: Pluto Press, 1991), 3–25; here 13.

[55] Habermas, 'Konservative Politik', 68.

[56] Brigitte Seebacher-Brandt, 'Ein Linker träumt vom Überleben der DDR', in *Rheinischer Merkur*, 14 September 1990.

Arguably, Habermas's lack of flexibility in 1990 also stemmed from a feeling of alienation towards the GDR.[57] Habermas later admitted that he simply felt no relationship whatsoever with the political developments in the East:

I mention this history of a lack of a relationship to remind you of the fact that people like us had more in common with the post-war history of Italy or France or the US than with that of the GDR. The history of the GDR was not our history. This is even more true for my children and the generation of my children. One has to have the right to say this without sentimentality.[58]

In a letter to Christa Wolf, Habermas re-emphasized that he had always seen 'the opening towards the traditions of the West as something liberating'.[59] Only through this opening towards the West could German intellectuals rediscover some of their own traditions in a way which would have been impossible had Schmitt and Heidegger been the only intellectual guides to the past.[60]

To say that 'the history of the GDR was not our history' was of course true in one sense. But it was remarkable for the leading West German social philosopher and political moralist to admit not having thought about the GDR as part of Germany at all, of never having included it on the road map to a post-national state.[61] Consequently, the GDR, as another country, clearly inferior to Habermas's idealized West, could merely be a detour on that route, or, worse, a setback.

Ralf Dahrendorf's wry assessment that Habermas was the true 'grandson of Adenauer' and the heir of the idea of Westernization proved to be surprisingly true. Unlike many other leftist intellectuals, however, Habermas did not just discover his attachment to the Federal Republic at the very moment when it was to become part of a united Germany (see chapter four). Despite his sometimes harsh criticisms of certain political aspects of the Federal Republic, Habermas had always sought to stress the real historical achievements in finally making West Germany a liberal

---

[57] For the resistance to aestheticization, see Richard Rorty, *Contingency, Irony, and Solidarity* (Cambridge: Cambridge University Press, 1989), 61–9.

[58] Habermas quoted by M. and S. Greiffenhagen, *Ein schwieriges Vaterland*, 273.

[59] Jürgen Habermas, 'Vom Gepäck deutscher Geschichte: Jürgen Habermas an Christa Wolf', in Christa Wolf, *Auf dem Weg nach Tabou* (Cologne: Kiepenheuer und Witsch, 1994), 140–9; here 145.

[60] *Ibid.*, 147. See also Jürgen Habermas, 'Zur Entwicklung der Sozial- und Geisteswissenschaftenin der Bundesrepublik', in *Texte und Kontexte* (Frankfurt/Main: Suhrkamp, 1991), 207–15.

[61] For similar criticisms from an East German intellectual, see Richard Schröder, 'Es ist doch nicht alles schlecht', in *Die Zeit*, 31 May 1991.

democratic, truly Western polity. There was no newly found apologia-cum-nostalgia for the Federal Republic in 1990, precisely because there had been a long-lasting attachment. But it was this attachment which made 17 million East Germans who seemed to have just emerged from the 1950s appear as a threat.

Republican *Renouveau à la* Rousseau or Kantian Continuity?

The practical (and procedural) demand on which Habermas's interventions in 1990 centred was the call to hold a referendum on an all-German Constitution, which would have established a new social contract between East and West Germany. On a very basic level, such a 'zero hour' as a mythical founding fitted well with the republican cast of some of Habermas's thinking. In republican models from Machiavelli to Rousseau, a correct 'foundation' plays a crucial role in moulding a proper civic consciousness. However, unlike in the case of an entirely new republic, or the case of the regeneration of a corrupt one, Habermas's referendum was aimed not so much at changing, but at *re-affirming* the existing Constitution, since Habermas and like-minded intellectuals could not have wished for a far-reaching change of existing principles. The referendum would have been more like a plebiscite with a preordained outcome, and a 'fast-track' introduction to constitutional patriotism for East German citizens. For Habermas, only a procedure of this kind would enable both West German and East German citizens to see themselves as the authors of the laws of the new, unified state. By extension, only a referendum would allow the East Germans to retain their dignity and to determine their own political fate.[62] Finally, a referendum could have allowed for both a revision of certain parts of the West German Constitution and the preservation of specific East German constitutional achievements, such as the right to work.

However, a number of objections could be (and in fact were) made to such a model. If the long-term aim of a referendum was the strengthening of constitutional patriotism, it was at least somewhat counterintuitive to open up the content of that very Constitution in a moment of extraordinary historical flux. Some commentators made the argument that precisely because West Germans were constitutional patriots, they should not risk their Constitution in a vote – and it was hard to imagine that Sternberger would have risked the Constitution in the way Habermas was prepared to do.[63] Moreover, as was frequently pointed out, at least the East

---

[62] Micha Brumlik, 'Basic Aspects of an Imaginary Debate', in *New German Critique*, No. 52 (1991), 102–8; here 102.

[63] Robert Leicht, 'Einheit durch Beitritt: Warum am Grundgesetz rühren?', in *Die Zeit*, 23 February 1990, and Peter Graf Kielmannsegg, 'Grundgesetz über alles', in *ibid.*

Germans had already clearly voted for accession in the March *Volkskammer* elections. One might have objected to this declaration of will, but then there was no good reason not also to object to any outcome of a referendum, and opt for a continuation of the division. One also might have made reasonable objections to the way the West German political parties essentially took over their East German 'sister parties' — but analytically (and historically) this invasion and distortion of an autonomous East German public sphere was a different issue: a campaign surrounding a general referendum would have suffered from the same deficiencies. Moreover, the old East German public sphere was in any case much more severely distorted than one colonized by Western parties could ever be; and the autonomous public sphere generated by the citizens' movements was only slow to develop.[64] It was then only a question of West Germans being asked to consent — but was it remotely conceivable that they might have withheld that consent? How could they have withheld consent for what was after all a part — or, to be more precise, the preamble — of the very Constitution they were supposed to affirm? And, if the argument was based on the claim that the Constitution generally was in need of revisions and progressive additions, why had the Left not raised this issue more forcefully before 1990? Finally, as a number of leftist intellectuals pointed out, there was in fact a high probability, given the prevailing conservative majority among the population in 1990, that a revised Constitution might have turned out to be *more* illiberal, or at least more conservative.[65]

On a theoretical level, the mythical founding exercised by a popular sovereign contradicted the purely proceduralist and rational light in which Habermas wanted his proposals to be seen.[66] In particular, a referendum to sign a 'new social contract' was severely at odds with Habermas's own recent account of a multi-layered, proceduralized type of popular sovereignty in 'Popular Sovereignty as Procedure'.[67] In this account, Habermas had posited that the moral substance of self-government, rather than being institutionalized in a single act of popular law-making (as in Rousseau's model), had to be realized in many steps of a collective, proceduralist process of will-formation. In such a process citizens could freely deliberate and 'lay a communicative siege' to the institutions of the state, which

---

[64] Charles S. Maier, *Dissolution: The Crisis of Communism and the End of East Germany* (Princeton: Princeton University Press, 1997), 168–214. It was ironically the insistence of the citizens' movements on 'dialogue' and their refusal to take power in 1989 that enabled the Western parties to overwhelm them.

[65] Peter Glotz, 'Der Ulrich der Deutschen', in *Die Zeit*, 18 May 1990, and Brumlik, 'Basic Aspects'.

[66] *Ibid.*

[67] Jürgen Habermas, 'Volkssouveränität als Verfahren: Ein normativer Begriff von Öffentlichkeit', in *Merkur*, Vol. 43 (1989), 465–77.

were always in danger of becoming autonomous administrative powers.[68] This 'siege' and pressure exercised through the communicative power of an undamaged public sphere was not a matter for intellectual elites, but should involve the widest possible participation of citizens. Social integration could no longer be accomplished through single acts of lawmaking by a sovereign people, as Habermas had still suggested in his earlier work. Unlike in such earlier, more 'radically democratic' models, the solidarity needed for social integration was to be generated through communicative action, rather than through a single, Rousseauean democratic will. Now, the procedures of deliberation themselves were to be the source of legitimacy, and would have made reasonable outcomes highly likely.[69] Sovereignty would have been dissolved into procedures, and the symbolic locus of power remained empty, rather than being filled with a mythical, united 'people'.[70]

Therefore, suggesting a plebiscite would have meant a return to the very concretist, voluntarist and substantial models of 'radical democracy' which Habermas had sought to overcome in his later accounts. This is not to deny that a 'coming to a self-understanding' about united Germany would have been normatively desirable and might have generated some of the solidarity which was sorely lacking in the 1990s. But such communicative action, gradually generated in a rapprochement between East and West, would have depended on undamaged public spheres, rather than a single act of popular will. It was in this sense that the insistence on Article 146, understood as a 'foundation through affirmation' contradicted Habermas's earlier views of 'popular sovereignty as procedure'.

Also, as Peter Graf Kielmannsegg has argued, only a negotiated contract between the two German states could have given the East Germans a voice in the unification process, while in a referendum a West German majority might have simply overwhelmed them.[71] Thus, the *Staatsvertrag* [the constitutional contract between the Federal Republic and the GDR about unification] was actually the liberal as opposed to the majoritarian option. Habermas objected that the East was so weak that the representative of the West Germans, Wolfgang Schäuble, essentially had concluded a treaty with himself. But the basic fact that there were more West Germans than East Germans and that only a minority of East Germans preferred an autonomous existence for the GDR, could not be dissolved by ever so many

---

[68] *Ibid.*, 475.

[69] *Ibid.*

[70] See also the account by Habermas's students Ulrich Rödel, Günter Frankenberg and Helmut Dubiel, *Die demokratische Frage* (Frankfurt/Main: Suhrkamp, 1989).

[71] Kielmannsegg, 'Vereinigung ohne Legitimität?', 68. See also Peter E. Quint, *The Imperfect Union: Constitutional Structures of German Unification* (Princeton: Princeton University Press, 1997), 47–54.

instances of discursive understandings in the public sphere. In this limited sense, the normative *did* have the power of the factual. And finally there is the almost trivial observation that in 1990, under world-political pressures, the conditions for calm deliberation were difficult to meet.[72]

Ralf Dahrendorf, Habermas's predecessor as the sociological 'star' at the Frankfurt Institute, once observed that in Habermas's political thought, Kantian and Rousseauean elements were both present and vying for predominance.[73] Arguably, his 1989 piece on popular sovereignty as procedure, which advocated going beyond Rousseau's republicanism, showed the accommodating, pragmatic Kantian, while in 1990 the Rousseauean Habermas flamboyantly burst onto the scene, with classical republican ideas about a founding and, one might argue, even a civic-republican legislator. Habermas, it seems, had always been a democrat first and foremost, and a liberal secondarily.

But Habermas also transferred what were legitimate concerns about the dignity and autonomy of the East Germans, and about the damage done to the public sphere in Germany, onto the political, and particularly the constitutional sphere. Ironically, this transfer was in many ways the opposite of what one might have expected given Habermas's recent theoretical writings. Rather than relying on civic action from below to 'lay siege' to the institutions of united Germany and gradually make use of procedures to protect the public sphere, Habermas advocated a referendum from above. Contrary to numerous critics who had charged him with neglecting institutions for the sake of an amorphous communicative process, the momentous founding was institutional – and, with its emphasis on cleansing the public sphere of sordid private, economic interests – utopian. But with that very argument, Habermas was in danger of falling victim to a concretist, even decisionist definition of sovereignty.[74] In the same vein, contrary to critics who have portrayed Habermas as an ultimately apolitical thinker, Habermas was prone to 'overpoliticization', putting an enormous burden on public deliberation and the law as the solution to

---

[72] On these issues, see Dieter Grosser, *Die Überwindung der Teilung: Der innerdeutsche Prozeß der Vereinigung* (Stuttgart: Deutsche Verlags-Anstalt, 1998), Dieter Grosser, *Das Wagnis der Währungs-, Wirtschafts- und Sozialunion: Politische Zwänge im Konflikt mit ökonomischen Regeln* (Stuttgart: Deutsche Verlags-Anstalt, 1998) and Philip Zelikow and Condoleeza Rice, *Germany Unified and Europe Transformed: A Study in Statecraft* (Cambridge, Mass.: Harvard University Press, 1997).

[73] Ralf Dahrendorf, 'Zeitgenosse Habermas', in *Merkur*, Vol. 43 (1989), 478–87; here 482.

[74] Briefly, decisionism refers to the idea that there comes a point when one has to go beyond rational deliberation and make an a-rational, or even irrational, decision as an imposition of sheer political will, which then becomes a value in itself, especially if this decision creates political order. Carl Schmitt and, in some interpretations, Hobbes, are the most prominent representatives of this view. In the stalemated debate between German constitutional lawyers on Article 23 versus Article 146, there indeed seemed to be a point where only political will, as opposed to a further careful weighing of arguments, could decide the issue.

challenges which were, at least on the surface, not necessarily political. Apart from this capacity of politics to generate social cohesion, there was also an underlying sense, betraying faint echoes of Hannah Arendt's thought, that engaging in politics was indispensable to a full moral life. At the same time, and once again contrary to the notion of Habermas as apolitical, he had a finely tuned sense for a tendency in German conservatism to conflate normal and constitutional politics, and a certain deformalization of law and political questions more generally – a tendency evident in the unification process, but also on numerous occasions afterwards.

The debate on the Constitution did not remain entirely without consequences, even if these consequences ultimately proved disappointing for most thinkers on the Left. In 1990 a 'Board of Trustees for a Democratically Constituted Federation of German States' was formed. The initiators aimed at a progressive revision of the Constitution, in particular a strengthening of civil society, but they also sought to contribute to a 'more perfect union' between East and West Germany by overcoming the 'stigma of the truncated foundation' (Thomas Schmid).[75] Article 146 of the old Constitution and Article 5 of the Unification Treaty then became the basis for a 'Joint Constitutional Commission of Parliament and Upper House', which started work in January 1992. However, the Commission soon fell victim to party politics and was widely seen as a failure. Left-wing critics had to concede that the political omissions and deficiencies could not be compensated with a belated constitutional politics.[76] If anything, a constitutional debate had been an ersatz locus for a true debate on the nature of united Germany. But such debates about symbolism and interpretations of the recent pasts, i.e. a catching-up on the process of 'coming to a self-understanding' which had been missed in 1990, were then displaced onto the debate about the capital, the commemoration of the Second World War in 1995, the Goldhagen debate in 1996, and, finally, the Walser debate, all of which amounted to 'delayed reactions' to unification (see chapter eight). For Habermas, too, the 'politically crippled discussions over a new Constitution' could not compensate for the 'absence of a union toward a common future made with will and consciousness'.[77] Permanent damage had already been done, and the 'birth defects' of unification seemed to turn into long-term handicaps.

---

[75] Bernd Guggenberger, 'Klammheimlicher Themenwechsel: Die Deutsche Verfassungsdiskussion zwischen Wiedervereinigung und Maastricht', in Bernd Guggenberger and Andreas Meier (eds), *Der Souverän auf der Nebenbühne: Essays und Zwischenrufe zur deutschen Verfassungsdiskussion* (Opladen: Westdeutscher Verlag, 1994), 14–20.

[76] *Ibid.*, 20.

[77] Habermas, *The Past*, 150 and 149.

Damage Done and Damage Limitation after 1990

After 1990, Habermas perceived a further erosion of republican consciousness. Intellectuals distanced themselves from the very West which Habermas cherished and, according to Habermas, argued that West Germany had been intellectually colonized by the West just as East Germany had been politically colonized by the Soviet Union. He identified Martin Walser and the Hegel scholar Dieter Henrich as advocates of such a 'convergence thesis', and expressed concern that a reactionary alliance between West German anti-Westerners and embittered East German intellectuals might take the next logical step and call for a return to irrational German intellectual traditions. In this scenario, Habermas's task as an intellectual became 'damage limitation', i.e. reducing the damage done to Germany's republican consciousness and its intellectual ties to the West. Habermas was battling at two frontlines on the intellectual field: first, he was defending his victory in the *Historikerstreit* against those who yet again wanted a return to nationalist 'normality'; second, he was opposing those GDR intellectuals who distrusted a Western emancipatory agenda out of cultural pessimism or because they simply equated liberalism with capitalism. In the years following unification, his concerns about the rise of a New Right were partly vindicated. The New Right did question the cultural and political ties to the 'victors of the West' (with Habermas as their prime polemical target), while East German intellectuals such as playwright Heiner Müller espoused what often seemed like a rather crude anti-Western cultural pessimism.

Subsequently, Habermas continued to point to the fateful legacies of the fast-track unification process, and to criticize what he perceived as further violations of the Constitution, which of course struck at the very heart of constitutional patriotism. On the other hand, new problems came to occupy the Left's foremost thinker, in particular the Maastricht Treaty and the possibility of a genuine European public sphere, with even more abstract forms of loyalty. Nevertheless, in 1996 when Habermas delivered the Tsaonam lecture in Seoul on the lessons of German unification, he was still adamant that unification pressed through by elites had left a fateful legacy of popular resentment, both between East and West Germans and against foreigners.[78] But, unlike Grass, he also claimed that the recovery of national unity had been 'unquestionably a legitimate objective', while 'at a distance of some six years, we can see that the government which initiated and steered the process assumed too much in the way of a pre-political background consensus'.[79] Consequently, he could claim that a more

---

[78] Jürgen Habermas, 'National Unification and Popular Sovereignty', in *New Left Review*, No. 219 (1996), 3–13.

[79] *Ibid.*, 10–11.

drawn-out process of communication would have allowed East and West Germans to learn what to expect of each other and to assume collective responsibility for unification. Given the history of the last ten years, it is hard to disagree with this assessment. But it was to Habermas's credit that, again unlike Grass, he conceded that 'it would be unfair to set the costs of this road to state unity against the hypothetical results of a normatively prescribed, but not actualized alternative'.[80]

It is worth pausing at this point to compare Habermas's and Grass's positions. There are a number of obvious differences, most notably Habermas's much more secure grasp of economics and of the importance of institutions, where Grass, not surprisingly, emphasized the cultural and the aesthetic in his advocacy of the *Kulturnation*. More significantly, where Habermas was unrelenting in his insistence on the synchronicity of the cultural and the political, always detecting, debating and destroying 'cultural continuities', Grass insisted on the non-synchronicity of culture and politics. For Habermas, it was the ghostly presence of the 'cultural luminaries' which threatened what seemed like the most stable of democratic polities, whereas for Grass, the political structures of the nation-state would necessarily endanger the *Kulturnation* which could only truly flourish in a confederation.

Similarities could be found in their rhetoric, as both talked about unification as an *Anschluß* and compared Germany's economic power to the military might of the Wehrmacht. And yet, in a testimony to the democratic nature of the post-war Left, both seized on the Constitution as a bulwark against the policies of the Kohl government. Most importantly, however, both seemed to interpret popular feelings as an expression of 'economic nationalism'. But not only was it questionable whether such feelings were really 'economic nationalism' — such 'economic nationalism' would precisely *not* have been traditional German nationalism, as both seemed to think. In any case, both saw prosperity and the pursuit of private interest as a necessarily inferior mode of social cohesion. Whereas Grass and Habermas marshalled a pure culture, Habermas advocated a pure politics against the sphere of self-interest.

In comparison to Habermas and many on the Left, however, Grass's position on the intellectual field was somewhat eccentric in that he was neither a post-nationalist nor an anti-nationalist. In fact, he explicitly sought to preserve the *Kulturnation* and a 'reasonable national consciousness', lest the Right substitute nationalism for a national vacuum. But this national consciousness was never permitted to find any political expression. Habermas claimed that Germans could be patriots because they had overcome National Socialism and fashioned their identity on the basis of a critical examination of their traditions. Grass wanted them to have a

[80] *Ibid.*, 12.

national consciousness on the basis of their common culture — and not least on the basis of permanently working through Auschwitz.

While Grass's central concept of the *Kulturnation* almost disappeared after 1990, Habermas's remained the theoretically strongest position of post-nationalism, capable of attracting and subsuming adjacent views such as republicanism and liberal, voluntarist conceptions of the nation. On the other hand, any intellectuals opposed to post-nationalism had to define themselves vis-à-vis Habermas, and it was not surprising that New Right thinkers chose Habermas as their prime ideological enemy. This choice was reinforced by the very fact that inside Habermas's concept of post-nationalism a conception of the Germans' enduring 'Holocaust identity' was hidden.

Seen from a generational perspective, both Habermas and Grass underwent their formative intellectual experiences in the 1950s and were influenced by Jaspers as well as Adorno and his dictum that ' "I think of Auschwitz" has to accompany all my thoughts' — which had influenced their peculiar conceptions of time. Both the concepts of anamnestic solidarity and *Vergegenkunft* meant that the past was present in more than a metaphorical sense. Moreover, the 1950s was also the past which was returning in the sense that both saw in unification a catalyst for a regression to the authoritarian mentality of that time. Nevertheless, a crucial difference remains: Grass was opposed to a German nation-state in principle, as, after Auschwitz, a German nation-state was categorically immoral and, politically, bound to be aggressive again, as a mythical German essence would re-assert itself. For Habermas, despite all his concerns about the 'futurity of the past', the future remained open in principle, and a larger German state, if it recovered and fostered constitutional patriotism, might progress on its path to a post-national, proceduralist republican future.

4 Melancholy, Utopia and Reconciliation: Left-Wing and Liberal Responses to Unification

Halb Klagelied, halb Pasquill, halb Rückhall der Vergangenheit, halb Dräuen der Zukunft, mitunter die Bourgeoisie ins Herz treffend, durch bittres, geistreich zerreißendes Urteil, stets komisch wirkend durch gänzliche Unfähigkeit, den Gang der modernen Geschichte zu begreifen.

Half lamentation, half lampoon; half echo of the past, half menace of the future; at times, by its bitter, witty and destructive judgements striking the bourgeoisie to its very heart's core, but always appearing ludicrous through its complete incapacity to understand the course of modern history.

Karl Marx and Friedrich Engels, *The Communist Manifesto*

Left-wing West German intellectuals rejected or were at least sceptical of unification for a wide range of reasons. Often the arguments were similar for East and West German intellectuals, and a number of unexpected coalitions emerged, some of which were transformed into more enduring political alliances in the new Germany. In this chapter, rather than focusing on the trajectories of towering intellectual figures such as Grass and Habermas, I seek to identify concepts and patterns of thought which were shared by a wide range of intellectuals. After analyzing a number of positions which opposed above all the chosen procedure of unification, I shall argue that most other arguments were inspired by a certain despair about the supposedly final loss of a socialist utopia and, more significantly, melancholy about the loss of a Federal Republic which had seemed to be safely on the path to a genuinely post-national and post-materialist democracy.

Arguments put forward by the Left in the debate on the supposed 'return of the nation-state' were often rooted in a particular left-wing consensus which had emerged in the late 1960s and 1970s, and which centred on anti-nationalism, anti-anti-communism and, finally, anti-fascism. This was primarily the consensus of the generation of 1968, which became intellectually most defensive after 1989. Liberal intellectuals, on the other hand, were more relaxed about a supposed return to 'nation-state normality' and attempted to reconcile the democratic traditions which had found a home in the Federal Republic with a more or less communitarian view of the nation. In contrast, liberal-conservative intellectuals, in particular historians, were eager to discard notions of post-nationalism and rather uncritically to draw on the historical or even 'naturalized' nation as a source of intra-German solidarity. While they claimed that with unification the German 'identity neurosis' had finally come to an end, they were in fact most eager to continue a 'psycho-social' discourse now focused on the need for Germany to 'grow up', gain 'self-confidence' and pursue its national interests.

Even as the unification process was still unfolding and severely criticized by most left-wingers, others on the Left came to question the Left's premises and to reproach their fellow intellectuals for past ideological mistakes. An acrimonious debate about what 'was left' ensued after the initial reactions to unification. The Right, not surprisingly, joined in this exercise of 'mutual self-criticism', putting the Left further on the defensive, questioning the central 1968 doctrine of anti-fascism, but, through this anti-anti-fascism, also distracting from its own ideological insecurities after the effective end of anti-communism. While they are beyond the scope of this chapter, the Gulf War of 1991 and the Yugoslav Wars further deepened the Left's crisis. Arguably, even a decade after unification, the Left has, by and large, yet to recover from its defensiveness in 1990 and the major reassessments which it undertook (or, for that matter, failed to undertake) subsequently.

Losing Time

Many intellectuals were sceptical about unification for reasons resembling the reservations of Grass and Habermas. In a stance consistent with their critical commitments, they resisted any attempts to see unification as 'natural', inevitable or beyond critical commentary.[1] In particular, they opposed what they saw as inappropriate haste in the unification process. Speed itself, however, became a symbol for other tendencies which the Left opposed: the fact that the political process was entirely centred on a supposedly unaccountable executive and above all, a supposed desire

---

[1] As Helmut Peitsch has pointed out, unification was often 'naturalized' and put beyond critical debate by the metaphors of Brandt's 'growing together' of the two Germanies, Augstein's 'train that has left the station' and the image of 'the inexorable river of time'. Helmut Peitsch, 'West German Reflections on the Role of the Writer in the Light of Reactions to 9 November 1989', in Williams et al. (eds), *German Literature at a Time of Change*, 155–86; here 164.

to escape from the past.[2] As Green politician Antje Vollmer put it, unification was 'the quickest way to transform past nightmares into colonizing activism while avoiding the labour of mourning'.[3] Some intellectuals drew a parallel between the executive-driven unification process in 1990, dictated by foreign policy considerations, and what they thought had been essentially the same pattern in 1870/71. As with the first unification, democracy and unity were supposedly once again competing, mutually exclusive principles, rather than being brought (and thought) together.[4] Like Habermas, left-wingers claimed that the sovereign had not been allowed to speak, partly for fear that 'it might have been indifferent to unification'.[5] Instead of a genuine plebiscite, there had been a profoundly undemocratic 'acclamation spectacle'.[6] Kohl, in his desire for rapid unification, had replaced the 'primacy of democracy' with a traditional 'primacy of the political' centred on secretive *Kabinettspolitik* [cabinet policy].[7] And like Habermas, these intellectuals were fundamentally concerned that 'unification from above' would cause political damage which even a later 'Re-education' [*sic*!] of East German citizens could not repair.[8] As in 1870/71, nationalism threatened to provide the very social cohesion which was lacking after a unification brought about from above.[9]

Beyond such 'Habermasian concerns' about the consequences which an 'executed' unification might have on German political culture, some West German intellectuals concurred with Grass that the GDR – or at least some elements of life in the GDR – were worth preserving for the sake of diversity. Antje Vollmer, who advocated an 'ecological confederation', thought of ecology not just in the sense of an environmental consciousness in both German states, but also in the deeper sense of 'preserving diversity and

---

[2] Arthur Heinrich, 'Alles eins?', in Arthur Heinrich and Klaus Naumann (eds), *Alles Banane: Ausblicke auf das endgültige Deutschland* (Cologne: PapyRossa, 1990), 7–18; here 9, and Lothar Baier, *Volk ohne Zeit: Essay über das eilige Vaterland* (Berlin: Wagenbach, 1990).

[3] Antje Vollmer, 'Tips für David: Plädoyer für eine ökologische Konföderation', in Frank Blohm and Wolfgang Herzberg (eds), *'Nichts wird mehr so sein, wie es War': Zur Zukunft der beiden deutschen Republiken* (Frankfurt/Main: Luchterhand, 1990), 117–25; here 119.

[4] Heinrich, 'Alles eins?', 12. Those on the Left who saw these as rival principles often reiterated Jaspers's argument that freedom had to have priority over unity, and that it could be realized in the GDR without unification. See Wolfgang Herles, *Nationalrausch* (Munich: Kindler, 1990), 9.

[5] Heinrich, 'Alles eins?', 11.

[6] *Ibid.*, 12.

[7] *Ibid.*

[8] *Ibid.*

[9] Lutz Niethammer, 'Geht der deutsche Sonderweg weiter?', in Antonia Grunenberg (ed.), *Welche Geschichte wählen wir?* (Hamburg: Junius, 1992), 23–54.

difference'.[10] She opposed 'richness through difference' to the monetary 'richness through expansion' which unification along government lines supposedly entailed.[11] Like Grass, she lauded the peculiarities of GDR culture, in particular its quality as a 'counter-culture' of 'modest growth'.[12] In the same vein, other intellectuals sided with the GDR as 'David' against the 'Goliath' West Germany, and, as far as possible, demanded a relationship of equality between the German states. The GDR, Vollmer suggested, had to discover the 'power of the weaker', while the Federal Republic should undertake reforms of its own. Only if both states were given room for reform and autonomous development, could the best of both ultimately be put together.[13]

Many left-wing intellectuals found themselves facing the same dilemma which Grass had confronted: true to their moral commitments, they sought to defend a weaker party against what appeared to be an overwhelmingly strong and overbearing power. In their bleak view of West Germany, the Federal Republic was 'economically more potent, politically secured through mass loyalty', and a state 'in which conservative-reactionary Fatherland ideologies, rigorous strategies to preserve power and expand the interests of capital coalesce'.[14] Against this 'unholy alliance of capital and cabinet', against 'colonization, *Anschluß* or *Ausverkauf* [sell-out]', they felt compelled to side with the weaker party. But the dilemma arose because this 'weaker party' was a state which had lost its legitimacy in the eyes of most of its population, though not in the eyes of its discredited elite. Consequently, West German intellectuals were eager to find positive elements which the GDR could offer in the unification process, and somehow establish some equality between East and West Germany. Logically, if the GDR had not much to offer in terms of 'socialist achievements', the Federal Republic had to be denigrated as being in urgent need of reform, in order for this logic of equivalence and equidistance to work.

One 'GDR achievement' was of course the East German revolution itself. West German intellectuals tried to reach out to the East German revolutionaries in order to sound a wake-up call for their own 'democratically disguised authoritarian state'.[15] Even if they were to lose a *socialist* utopia, Western intellectuals still thought they could regain the idea of revolution if they connected with the East Germans, and even treated the

---

[10] Vollmer, 'Tips', 120.

[11] *Ibid.*, 119.

[12] *Ibid.*, 118.

[13] *Ibid.*, 123–4.

[14] Oskar Negt, 'Der gebrochene Anfang', in Blohm and Herzberg (eds), *'Nichts'*, 19–44; here 28.

[15] Robert Jungk, 'Veränderung ist möglich', in *ibid.*, 126–32; here 126.

East German revolution as a new 'source of utopian hope'.[16] On a more concrete level, demands for equality of the GDR often translated into a demand for the Federal Republic to grant the East a *Lastenausgleich* [equalization of burdens] by reimbursing the GDR for the reparations which the GDR had been forced to pay to the Soviet Union.[17]

However, the most immediate injunction against a 'breathless Realpolitik', as Oskar Negt, a veteran of 1968, called the government's policies, was the demand to 'stop and hold one's breath'.[18] Referring to Walter Benjamin, Negt sought to oppose the notion of rapid, pragmatic progress in the 'empty, homogeneous time' of linear history, which Benjamin had described in his 'Theses on the Philosophy of History', with a notion of *betroffenes Innehalten* [a reflective pause].[19] Others demanded a *Zeitsouveränität* [sovereignty over time] for the GDR, even as its political and economic sovereignty was rapidly slipping away after the opening of the Wall.[20] Only additional time would enable the GDR to constitute itself as 'the revolutionary Germany' against a West Germany which supposedly still stood in an essentially antidemocratic tradition. The most radical opponents of unification even demanded that the Wall should have been kept intact and that Austria and Hungary should have been asked not to allow GDR citizens to flee to the West.[21] However, beyond such concerns about the political consequences of procedure, there were also deeper reasons why left-wing intellectuals sought to resist unification in principle.

Losing Utopia

During the second half of 1989 and 1990, many West German intellectuals expressed a desire to preserve the GDR as an independent state, or at least, following Grass, as part of a German confederation. Apart from ostensibly prudent reasons to do with peace and security in Europe, they

---

[16] *Ibid.*, 128.

[17] Vollmer, 'Tips', 12. See also 'Aufruf an die Regierung der Bundesrepublik Deutschland zur Zahlung ihrer Reparations-Ausgleichs-Schuld an die Deutsche Demokratische Republik', reprinted in Siegfried Prokop (ed.), *Die kurze Zeit der Utopie: Die 'zweite' DDR im vergessenen Jahr 1989/90* (Berlin: Elefanten Press, 1994), 220–2.

[18] Negt, 'Der gebrochene Anfang', 21.

[19] *Ibid.*, 22. See also Walter Benjamin, 'Theses on the Philosophy of History' in *Illuminations*, ed. Hannah Arendt, trans. Harry Zohn (London: Fontana, 1992), 245–55.

[20] Heinrich, 'Alles eins?', 12.

[21] Erich Kuby, *Der Preis der Einheit: Ein deutsches Europa formt sein Gesicht* (Hamburg: Konkret Literatur, 1990).

put forward arguments which, above all, were concerned with preserving the GDR as a political and socio-economic alternative to the Federal Republic.[22] Beyond this aspect of retaining a specifically socialist alternative, they also felt that the collapse of 'actually existing socialism' threatened utopian thinking in general, and even the condition of possibility for any immanent social critique.

Thus, a substantial number of intellectuals spoke out against unification essentially because they wanted to give the experiment of 'real', i.e. democratic, socialism as a 'third way' another chance. In this demand, West German intellectuals sided with many older East German intellectuals. Soon after the SED regime started to crumble these East German intellectuals published a manifesto *Für unser Land* [For Our Country] in which they demanded the realization of true socialism in a separate GDR.[23] West German intellectuals desired democratic socialism for its own sake, but, arguably, also to preserve a separate GDR as a 'utopian regulative' against which the Federal Republic could be measured. For them, salvaging an alternative in another country, in fact any alternative, even in the name of vague terms such as humanism and 'third way', became a priority. The writer Jurek Becker, who had emigrated from the GDR to West Germany, spoke for many left-wing intellectuals, both East and West, when he argued that 'somehow, across all experiences and beyond all insight, existed the hope that the socialist countries could find another path. That's over now'.[24] This loss of utopia was bound up with an almost apocalyptical despair that the only path now left would inevitably lead to disaster. As Becker specified his reasons for rejecting unification, he claimed that

the only answer I can give, is better suited to a poem than a political discussion: the most important thing about the socialist countries is nothing visible, but a possibility. There not everything has been decided like here. This uncertainty does not have to mean anything good, but it keeps the only hope alive that after us, human beings will continue to exist. Eastern Europe seems like a last attempt to me.[25]

---

[22] As the left-wing writer Uwe Timm pointed out, 'one has to remember that socialism in the GDR was an alternative to the FRG, admittedly an ugly, bureaucratically bloated alternative, but still an alternative, and that this "real" socialism, despite all ossification, would have been capable of self-transformation is not a mere assertion. That is demonstrated by the grassroots democratic movements . . .'. Quoted by Peitsch, 'West German reflections', 168.

[23] Konstanze Borchert *et al.* (eds), *Für unser Land: Eine Aufrufaktion im letzten Jahr der DDR* (Frankfurt/Main: IKO, 1994).

[24] Jurek Becker, 'Über die letzten Tage: Ein kleiner Einspruch gegen die große deutsche Euphorie', in *Neue Rundschau*, Vol. 101, No. 1 (1990), 90.

[25] *Ibid.*

For Becker and many other intellectuals the fundamental threat was precisely that the 'West had won', and would consequently be strengthened in what they saw as an ideology which already doomed mankind to end in an ecological disaster. The very fact that most East Germans only wanted to adopt Western political and economic principles would confirm the worst tendencies in the West, its complacency and lack of vision.[26] Not surprisingly, intellectuals sought to counter such 'triumphalism' and to side with the 'victim of history', i.e. the GDR.

In the same vein, many West German intellectuals thought it was imperative to reaffirm socialist principles at the very point when 'actually existing socialism' was swept away in Eastern Europe. In particular, they sought to salvage a notion of 'democratic socialism' which was defined as almost the opposite of 'actually existing socialism'. Walter Jens, a classicist and one of West Germany's foremost left-wing intellectuals, wanted to retain a vision of the 'third way', the position of an 'undogmatic Left', which was to continue its own path between 'brutal collectivism' and 'rude social Darwinism'.[27] To continue the project of such an uncontaminated Left, Jens argued, one had to distinguish carefully between socialism's 'appearance' and its 'essence', as well as its 'perversion' and its 'essence'. 'Is Christianity passé . . .', he asked rhetorically, 'because there have been inquisitions and witch burnings . . . genocide and torture in the name of the Trinity?'[28] Such arguments, however, despite ostensibly dissociating an undogmatic Left from the GDR, often came to resemble apologies for the GDR through moral relativization. Jens claimed that the Stasi were not much different from the West German police forces which brutally broke up anti-nuclear demonstrations.[29] This equation of East and West had a positive dimension as well: Jens called for a democratic movement of 'We are the People' in the West. In that sense, against all odds, intellectuals like Jens demanded that if democratic socialism could not be realized in the GDR, it might actually be realized in a unified Germany.

In the same vein, Negt argued that the end of 'actually existing socialism' might in fact herald the 'beginning of a new socialist age'.[30] While he conceded that 'everything has to be thought through again', he also defiantly argued that as long as Stalinism existed, capitalism had faced no serious competition, with the implication that a new socialism might in fact have depended on the end of perverted, 'actually existing

---

[26] *Ibid.*

[27] Walter Jens, 'Nachdenken über Deutschland: Warnung vor dem Winken aus dem Zuschauerraum', in *Neue Rundschau*, Vol. 101 (1990), No. 1, 91–3; here 92.

[28] *Ibid.*

[29] *Ibid.*, 93.

[30] Negt, 'Der gebrochene Anfang', 43–4.

socialism'. On a less sanguine note, Negt claimed that the present task of a united Left was the cultivation of a collective memory of socialism's utopian promises. Benjamin's famous *Angelus Novus*, propelled by the storm of progress blowing from paradise and looking back on the rubble of history, now also gazed upon the ruins of socialism. Certain socialist hopes, however, which 'had nothing to do with the accumulation of productive forces' and the 'myths mediated by the state about human crisis solutions', had to be preserved by the Left. This cultivation of memory referred in particular to '1968' as 'the utopia of another Germany'. In that sense, intellectuals like Negt and Jens wavered between a defiant stance, claiming that an age of true socialism was yet to come and in fact depended on overcoming 'actually existing socialism', and a melancholic call that the best the Left could do after the supposed world-historical triumph of capitalism was mnemonic cultivation – with memory and hope being two sides of the same coin. On a more long-term strategic level, as Norbert W. Kunz pointed out, the Left felt it needed to preserve utopia to become once again 'capable of exercising hegemony' in the future.[31] Consequently, he could claim that 'the battle against a lack of utopias will be a decisive one . . .'.[32]

The question remained, however, whether the Left should not have simply dissociated itself from the end of 'actually existing socialism' completely. Only by collapsing socialism into utopian thinking, and then admitting a connection between socialism and what had been constructed in the GDR, did the Left become vulnerable to the Right's charge that the collapse of actually existing socialism also meant the end of the actually existing Left in the West – and of any utopian thought. Such a dissociation, however, was made almost impossible by the fact that many left-wing intellectuals had in fact had a stake in the existence of the GDR – at least on a very abstract level. Apart from the socialist utopia, the GDR had for years been identified with being the peaceful German state. In that sense, just in the way that the GDR had for decades been fixated on the Federal Republic, intellectuals in the West were in two different ways also dependent on the East: in the case of the Right, to prove that socialism had failed and that the Federal Republic was clearly the champion of freedom, and, in the case of the Left, to argue that there was still hope for the socialist dream and, in some cases, that the GDR was the champion of peace. This tendency to reserve 'freedom' for West Germany and 'peace' for the East was typical of the compartmentalized thinking and the peculiar division of memory and political principles between the two German states. Rather than painting a more nuanced picture of East and West, many on the Left

---

[31] Norbert W. Kunz, 'Auf der Suche nach einer neuen Utopie des Sozialismus', in Martin Gorholt and Norbert W. Kunz (eds), *Deutsche Einheit – Deutsche Linke: Reflexionen der politischen und gesellschaftlichen Entwicklung* (Bonn: Bund, 1991), 147–67; here 148.

[32] *Ibid.*, 167.

fell victim to the false certainties of neatly allocating memories and political principles to the two states. In retrospect, it is easy to forget just how much the division of Europe affected modes of thought, shaping (and distorting) the patterns of interpretation that intellectuals applied. Dialectical *Blockdenken* [thinking in terms of blocs] and anti-attitudes were inseparable from the Cold War – but did not cease overnight with the fall of the Wall.[33]

In that sense, there had long been a neat ideological arrangement: West Germany allowed for social criticism, but was ideologically reprehensible. East Germany, on the other hand, could not be criticized by its own people and was not to be criticized by the Western Left. After all, it still held the promise of a utopian future (or at least the possibility that capitalism could be transcended, which gave theories of 'late capitalism' and other forms of 'analytical finalism' in the West some plausibility). Critique thus became a zero-sum game for a Left which had at least some abstract stake in the existence of the GDR.[34] Rather than thinking through these distortions and tacit assumptions after 1989, many on the Left engaged in an entirely abstract debate about the conditions of possibility for utopianism – a debate which displaced the not entirely unimportant question of which utopias the Western Left still had to offer. Utopianism – and more or less secular forms of messianism – had of course long been a strand in the German intellectual tradition, more so probably than in any other European intellectual culture.[35] In particular, the apocalyptical messianism of Walter Benjamin had seen a late flowering among the '68ers, whereas among the sceptical generation utopianism had been largely discredited. And it was no accident that Benjamin and his image of the *Angelus Novus* were so frequently invoked in and after 1990. While in the late 1960s, Benjamin's idea of a messianic disruption of 'empty, homogeneous time' had fired the students' Marxist-cum-messianic imagination, in the face of unification the Left counted itself among the victims of the very ideology of progress and the very historicism supporting the victors of history which Benjamin had lamented. However, there seemed to be something altogether too quick, perhaps even perverse, about this invocation of Benjamin and what had become an almost clichéd image of the *Angelus Novus*. After all, it had been the Left which until 1989 had relied on the tacit assumption that it was allied with the forces of history and that it represented post-national,

---

[33] Richard Wagner, 'Für eine Linke ohne Sozialismus', in *Kursbuch*, No. 104 (1991), 55–64; here 55, and Freimut Duve, 'Der kalte Krieg im Kopf', in *Vom Krieg in der Seele: Rücksichten eines Deutschen* (Frankfurt/Main: Eichborn, 1994), 83–109.

[34] Helmut Dubiel, 'Linke Trauerarbeit', in *Merkur*, Vol. 44 (1990), 482–91.

[35] On Weimar in particular, see Dagmar Barnouw, *Weimar Intellectuals and the Threat of Modernity* (Bloomington: Indiana University Press, 1988).

post-materialist progress. Now it seemed to shift effortlessly from an attitude of knowing superiority to counting itself among the victims – who of course, by definition, were innocent.

In short, utopianism had been part of a particular '68er mentality, for which actual continued theorizing on utopias was less important. But the abstract post-1989 debate on utopianism also displaced the question of whether a vague utopianism had not afforded the Left a radical conscience, while actually being rather comfortable in the conditions of the Federal Republic. Another way of putting this was that both East and West German intellectuals had a considerable interest in the status quo, and that in both cases criticism and complacency had gone hand in hand rather conveniently.

Arguably, on a deeper level, West German intellectuals were also at least somewhat attracted to the GDR (and, consequently, sought to preserve some of its legacy), because in its society writers and intellectuals were taken seriously – whether as state writers or dissidents – while in the West there remained a feeling of being left out, of a still 'homeless Left', however unjustified that perception in fact was. The GDR, or what West Germans projected onto it, held the promise of a state in which intellectuals were not alienated from the people and were involved in steering society towards a humane ideal. Thus, the end of the GDR constituted not just the loss of an intellectual ideal, but also a utopia of the intellectuals.

Losing the Federal Republic

For many intellectuals the disappearance of the GDR primarily meant that they had to come to terms with conditions in the Federal Republic. This proved particularly difficult for those post-1968 left-wing intellectuals who had somewhat grudgingly accepted the political order in West Germany, while they 'marched through the institutions', but who had largely retained their fundamentally critical stance or even a *Totalkritik* of the Federal Republic. The prospect of unification, however, meant they had to take a clear stance: a semi-detached attitude towards West Germany seemed to become untenable, as a vague sense of alternatives evaporated. Would they finally identify with this state as their own, or would they insist that it remained a second-best option and not nearly as promising as another, better, socialist Germany-yet-to-come? Or would they attempt to find positive elements in the GDR experience to yet again balance the relationship between what were ostensibly unequal political regimes and retain some moral equivalence?

Surprisingly – and, for some, even shockingly – most intellectuals took the first route, revealing all of a sudden that the strident critique of West Germany had gone hand in hand with a well-hidden attachment to the

'Bonn Republic', even a kind of complacency about West German achievements. Suddenly many who had for years adamantly reproached the Federal Republic for thinly disguised fascism passionately pleaded for actually existing constitutional patriotism.[36] Left-wing intellectuals spoke of a growing attachment to 'that bland, small, unloved, practical state, the Federal Republic of Germany', which they had experienced in the years prior to unification.[37] It seemed that only the opposition to unified Germany allowed the open and belated reconciliation with the 'old Federal Republic' — or, put differently and paradoxically, only the opposition to Kohl reconciled the Left with Adenauer.

Thomas Schmid, a member of the '68 generation, confessed that 'I have come to value the FRG despite its imperfections as a civil society'.[38] For these intellectuals, a fledgling West German civil society and growing post-nationalism, the increasing importance of citizens' initiatives, as well as feminist and environmental concerns were suddenly all under threat from unification and what they perceived as a diversion to traditional '1950s' issues associated with the economic miracle identity.[39] It seemed that 'soft' post-material issues and the hope of a 'more gentle republic' were suddenly replaced with traditional materialist concerns.[40] Especially the March 1990 elections, in which the CDU-led 'Alliance for Germany' won a decisive victory in the GDR, seemed to signify the return of Adenauer and Erhard with a vengeance, including their respective positions of a 'politics of strength' and 'prosperity for everyone'.[41] '89 was simply '68 turned upside down, and both seemed moments when history had 'accelerated' — only that left-wing intellectuals who had thought themselves far ahead of the times in and after 1968, suddenly seemed to be 'belated'.

In short, '1989' threatened '1968', and just as the Left thought it was 're-founding' the Federal Republic as a post-national, post-materialist polity, and was therefore slowly making peace with the 'unloved Republic', an abrupt 're-foundation towards the right' seemed to have overtaken them.[42] Suddenly 'normality had changed its owner', as Arthur Heinrich

---

[36] Rammstedt and Schmidt (eds), *BRD ade!*

[37] Patrick Süskind, 'Deutschland, eine Midlife Crisis', in *Der Spiegel*, 17 September 1990.

[38] Thomas Schmid, *Staatsbegräbnis: Von ziviler Gesellschaft* (Berlin: Rotbuch, 1990), 8.

[39] Wolfgang Benz, 'Sorgen im freudigen Augenblick', in Wilhelm von Sternburg (ed.), *Geteilte Ansichten über eine vereinigte Nation: Ein Buch über Deutschland* (Frankfurt/Main: Anton Hain, 1990), 53–9; here 56.

[40] Georg Fühlberth, *Eröffnungsbilanz des gesamtdeutschen Kapitalismus: Vom Spätsozialismus zur nationalen Restauration* (Hamburg: Konkret Literatur, 1993), 128.

[41] Fühlberth, *Eröffnungsbilanz*, 131.

[42] Heinrich, 'Alles eins?', 15.

put it, since a growing everyday reality of post-nationalism had been replaced by the supposed normality of the nation.[43] It also became clear then that the Left in fact hardly had a principled stance on 'post-nationalism' — it simply seemed to have become an everyday reality, at least for intellectuals for whom Paris and Tuscany were closer than East Berlin and Dresden.[44]

After establishing a coalition between the proponents of a 'gentler republic' and the East German revolutionaries in favour of continuing a left-wing re-foundation in the name of the 'other Germany' had failed, unification only held the prospect of regression. As Otto Kallscheuer pointed out, West German intellectuals were deeply disappointed that the *Volk* in the GDR, with its materialist desires, had not conformed to their preconceptions.[45] Since the Left had been unable to establish its own foundation myth of a new Germany, grounded in the experiences of the East German protest movement, some observers also changed their interpretation of the East German experience itself: it was no longer a genuine revolution, but merely a coup or collapse.[46] In the same vein, Kallscheuer saw Hannah Arendt's observations about the failure of revolutions confirmed: once again, a fledgling republicanism had been overtaken by the 'social question' and materialist needs.[47] Consequently, a 'republican deficit' was likely to haunt the new polity.

Not surprisingly, West German left-wing intellectuals began to view the accession of East Germany with increasing concern. Micha Brumlik, professor of educational studies in Heidelberg, argued from a rather clinical perspective that the psychological damage to GDR citizens needed to be assessed, and that 'the SED state' had been inscribed even in the souls of its opponents.[48] Other intellectuals mixed political with rather negative aesthetic judgements about greedy Western businessmen and

---

[43] *Ibid.*, 16.

[44] Süskind, 'Deutschland, eine Midlife Crisis'.

[45] Otto Kallscheuer, 'Die Linke, Deutschland und Europa: Versuch, einige Widersprüche zur Sprache zu bringen, in Blohm and Herzberg (eds), *'Nichts wird mehr'*, 133–49; here 135.

[46] Kuby, *Der Preis der Einheit.* This reinterpretation of the East German revolution, which was shared by the disappointed leaders of the East German citizens' movements, become more pronounced over time. In retrospect, Green politicians Thomas Ebermann and Rainer Trampert claimed, 'the "peaceful revolution" was a lie from the start. The East Germans wanted to share in the world power of their great brethren and were intoxicated with their own submission . . .' See their *Die Offenbarung der Propheten: Über die Sanierung des Kapitalismus, die Verwandlung linker Theorie in Esoterik, Bocksgesänge und Zivilgesellschaft* (Hamburg: Konkret Literatur, 1996), 280.

[47] Kallscheuer, 'Die Linke' 138.

[48] Micha Brumlik, 'Birth of a Nation? Gedankensplitter zur Einheit', in Heinrich and Naumann (eds), *Alles Banane*, 151–62; here 153.

the GDR masses eager for Western consumer goods.[49] Joseph von Westphalen, for instance, compared unification to a fit of collective German bulimia.[50] For him, 17 million 'unreconstructed' East Germans eager for capitalism and consumer goods meant a political as well as an aesthetic regression into the petty bourgeois 1950s.[51] The journalist Henryk Broder was to warn against a process of *Verostung* [Easternization], and thought that foreigners in Germany were the last chance against such a *Verostung*.[52]

Some voices, however, took a more proactive stance and demanded a vigorous 'Westernization' of the GDR, which, after all, contained the 'central lands' of the old German *Sonderweg*, and, by and large remained 'more German' and illiberal. If Germany had been the belated nation, then East Germany was doubly belated. As the historian Jürgen Kocka claimed, unification was nothing more than a 'means for the democratization of the GDR', and should not entail any loss of the Westernization of the Federal Republic. He refused to take anything on board from the GDR, instead emphasizing the achievements of West Germany, which was now in danger of being denigrated as a 'Rheinish-separatist half-state'.[53] But rather than being tempted by new special paths and lamenting the Federal Republic's deficiencies, West Germany's achievements should be borne in mind: 'in the light of our history and with a sober comparison one can know what one has had – and what one can lose'. By and large, however, as with a socialist utopia, left-wing intellectuals tended to retreat to a position where they defensively sought to cultivate the memory of past

---

[49] Ironically, these essentially aesthetic judgments were shared by young post-material West German writers and older, rather puritan East German intellectuals like Stefan Heym. See Stefan Heym, 'Ash Wednesday in the GDR', in *New German Critique*, No. 52 (1991), 31–5.

[50] Joseph von Westphalen, 'Das große Fressen: Letzte Polemik gegen die deutsche Einheit', in *Die Zeit*, 18 May 1990.

[51] In other cases, it was precisely the construction of an antithesis between a consumerist Western 'elbow society' and a more humane Eastern 'niche society' that was used to support arguments against unification and the consequent destruction of this niche society. Often more than a faint echo of old German ideological constructions could be found in such views, namely the antithesis of *Kultur* [culture, profound] and *Zivilisation* [civilization, shallow], *Gemeinschaft* [community] versus *Gesellschaft* [society] as well as *machtgeschützte Innerlichkeit* versus superficial outer freedom. As seen previously, Grass had praised the niche society as 'something *Biedermeierliches*', and Günter Gaus, originator of the concept, argued along similar lines. West German intellectuals' anti-capitalist views also coalesced with many East German perspectives, most importantly Heiner Müller, *Zur Lage der Nation* (Berlin: Rotbuch, 1990).

[52] Henryk M. Broder, 'Verostung', in Jörg-Dieter Vogel, Wolfgang Schütte and Harro Zimmermann (eds), *Neues Deutschland: Innenansichten einer wiedervereinigten Nation* (Frankfurt/Main: Fischer, 1993), 38–41.

[53] Jürgen Kocka, 'Nur keine neuen Sonderwege: Jedes Stück Entwestlichung wäre als Preis für die deutsche Einheit zu hoch', in *Die Zeit*, 19 October 1990.

victories. In short, the Left sought to reaffirm its own traditions, and reassure itself of its own identity.

However, apart from the fear of regression, there was another, arguably deeper strand of thought which made the Left reject unification. Similar to Grass, many intellectuals argued that the division had been a kind of world-historical punishment for the past crimes of the Germans. According to this logic, unification would spell the end of catharsis by division and necessarily entail what Wolfgang Benz called a 'cheerful wanting-to-forget the causes of the German division in the moment of its overcoming'.[54] Negt claimed that many of his generation had been convinced that 'the German division and the loss of the Eastern territories had been a mild punishment for historical crimes of the Germans which could never be expiated'.[55] Within this logic (or rather, metaphysics) of division as atonement, unification automatically had to mean a forgetting of the past, even an annihilation of the consequences of the past. Unification, in short, meant amnesty, and amnesty necessarily had to lead to amnesia.

In addition, as Antje Vollmer had candidly pointed out in 1985, the Left was essentially afraid of its own people and consequently distrusted democracy to some extent.[56] Thus, the reconstitution of a larger German state inevitably frightened the Left, with its fear of the *Biedermänner* [philistines] and ordinary people, and what Vollmer called its 'contempt and cynicism vis-à-vis the Germans'.[57] Where the sceptical generation had seen the gradual disappearance of the post-fascist democratic deficit, the '68ers had started out with a much larger degree of distrust, and, consequently, were even more concerned about a new democratic deficit in 1990 than older intellectuals. Since the '68ers had staked their position on anti-fascism and theories of the authoritarian personality, institutional safeguards had never meant as much to them as to older intellectuals in the first place. Thus, the '68ers, still the prime carriers of a radicalized culture of suspicion, put forward the most extreme version of the fear of a widening democratic deficit with the addition of East German *Biedermänner*.

Some radical left-wing thinkers went even further in an essentially negative or 'inverted' nationalism, denouncing the coming of a 'Fourth Reich'. Hermann Gremliza, editor of the left-wing magazine *Konkret*, engaged in what could only be called German anti-nationalist nationalism, or rather, self-hatred: 'As if German-hater was not the only morally acceptable attitude, which an observer of this reprehensible nation could assume. He does

---

[54] Benz, 'Sorgen', 59.

[55] Negt, 'Der gebrochene Anfang', 23.

[56] Antje Vollmer, 'Deutsche Linke und ihr Volk (1985)', in *Die schöne Macht der Vernunft: Auskünfte über eine Generation* (Berlin: Verlag der Nation, 1991), 62–9; here 65–6.

[57] *Ibid.*, 65 and 68.

not hate the citizens of the FRG and the GDR, but the stinking corpse "Germany" and those "Germans" who want to excavate and resuscitate it.'[58] Finally, the intellectuals who clung to the old Federal Republic as it was disappearing in the process of unification, were often the same intellectuals who had already shown their attachment to the status quo of the division of Europe during the 1980s, when they had been extremely reluctant to support East European protest movements such as Solidarity or Charter 77, because they saw them as a threat to peace and stability.[59]

In sum, left-wing West German intellectuals faced multiple potential losses, and were split on the question as to how they should respond to the prospect of unification. One part of the Left attempted to fasten onto the East German revolution, and establish a united German Left, also demanding a thoroughgoing reform of West Germany. Such intellectuals were quickly disillusioned and instead sought to salvage parts of the post-national and post-materialist programme the Left had advanced in the Federal Republic. They also increasingly came to see East Germany as a threat to this programme. Others were never interested in taking on board any political elements from East Germany, and instead demanded a vigorous 'Westernization' of the East. In most cases, however, the perceived loss of utopia and the threat to the Left's values led to a compounded sense of melancholy – which seemed the reverse side of earlier utopian hopes. Some intellectuals tried to continue a gesture of shock and provocation, comparing unification to a fit of bulimia, or reproaching the Federal Republic with being authoritarian, or predicting the inevitable foundering of the latest unification. The debate about utopia, interspersed with defiant statements that there could be no 'prohibition on utopias', continued for some time, meriting an extended series in *Die Zeit*, followed by sporadic calls to end 'left-wing mourning' and fashion a new creative role for the Left.[60] Arguably, mourning utopia replaced an engagement with new realities.

The 'loss of utopia', however, was the least important (and most academic) of the 'losses' which unification threatened. If anything, it only reinforced a long-term trend of the 1980s, when the postmodern suspicion of modernist 'metanarratives' and Habermas's declaration of an 'exhaustion of utopian energies' had already cast doubt on utopian thought.[61]

---

[58] Hermann L. Gremliza, *Krautland einig Vaterland* (Hamburg: Konkret Literatur, 1990), 23.

[59] Wolfgang Templin, 'Die Emanzipation der DDR und die hilflose westdeutsche Linke', in Helga Grebing *et al.* (eds), *Sozialismus in Europa: Festschrift für Willy Brandt* (Essen: Klartext, 1989), 162–7.

[60] Matthias Greffrath, 'Freunde, hört die Signale! Kleine Predigt zum Ende des linken Trauerjahres', in *Die Zeit*, 9 November 1990.

[61] The clearest indication of this exhaustion was probably Habermas (ed.), *Observations on the 'The Spiritual Situation of the Age'.*

Nevertheless, by falling into melancholy over the loss of utopia, the Left seemed retroactively to identify yet again with the GDR's supposed utopian potential. Making socialism, utopia and a 'better Germany' hidden in the GDR adjacent concepts enabled the Right to put the Left further on the defensive. On the other hand, the questions what to retain or discard from the traditions established in West Germany, how to interpret the 'Bonn Republic' in retrospect and whether the GDR should be integrated through 'Westernization' retained their salience long beyond the events of 1990. However, since it had staked so much on utopia and a retrospectively idealized image of the old Federal Republic, the Left found it difficult to contribute constructively to this discourse (with some significant exceptions, which I shall discuss in chapter eight).

Nevertheless, the central issue, other than the debate about the loss of utopia, and the underlying melancholy about the supposed end of the Federal Republic, was of course the question of nationhood and the value of the nation-state as such. Many of the Left's arguments about nationhood could be traced back to what I shall call a consensus of anti-fascism, anti-anti-communism, and, above all, anti-nationalism.

After '68: Anti-Nationalism, Negative Nationalism and Post-Nationalism

On a personal level, many intellectuals who belonged to the 1968 generation or were even younger than that, openly admitted that they felt no emotional connection to the GDR. As Kallscheuer pointed out, for the '68ers the Wall *was* a political crime, but not 'a problem in their own life history'.[62] They felt compelled to defend the GDR against 'Cold Warriors' and 'rollback politicians', but, apart from that, the GDR remained a 'black box': 'This other, supposedly better (officially) anti-fascist and (internally) antidemocratic *German* state did not interest "us" existentially very much'.[63] For them, unification was simply, as Antje Vollmer put it, a 'dream of old men', who after the fall of the Wall asserted the fact that they were still the generation in power against the generation of 1968.[64]

More importantly, on an intellectual level, members of the '68

---

[62] Kallscheuer, 'Die Linke', 134.

[63] *Ibid.*

[64] Antje Vollmer, 'Die Träume der alten Männer', in *Die schöne Macht*, 145–7, where she appealed to the generations of Kohl (and Brandt) 'Gehen Sie uns doch einmal aus der Sonne, meine Herren!'. *Ibid.*, 147. Also Herles, *Nationalrausch*, 10.

generation arguably lacked a conceptual framework to deal with the phenomenon of the nation-state. As an intellectual 'default option', they resorted to often unhistorical and indiscriminate rejections of nationhood. They polemicized against old demons in a way reminiscent of the immediate post-war period, using somewhat crude historical analogies and a certain linear logic. This thoroughly negative response was conditioned by a left-wing consensus, which had largely been formed in the late 1960s and 1970s, and which consisted of anti-nationalism, anti-anti-communism and anti-fascism. The specific issue in this section will be anti-nationalism, which was deeply ingrained in a West German left-wing mentality, and which, over time, had branched off into theories of post-nationalism and a more emotional attitude of negative nationalism.

Anti-nationalism was of course widespread after the Second World War, since nationalism was associated with militarism and National Socialism. However, this rejection of nationalism, which was in line with the policies of European integration which Adenauer actually pursued, did not mean that intellectuals rejected unification. If anything, for intellectuals ranging from Grass to Enzensberger, national identity and reunification were seen as oppositional topics, and intellectuals freely exhibited their own *Leiden an Deutschland* [suffering because of Germany], a term coined by Thomas Mann and taken up by the Left after 1945.

The situation was different with the generation of 1968. It was not that the student movement had been anti-nationalist as such (or even entirely pacifist, ecological and utopian), as many on the Left were to suggest in retrospect. They had been not so much 'fatherlandless', as 'fatherless', according to Alexander Mitscherlich's observations at the time.[65] Two of the most important student leaders, Rudi Dutschke and Bernd Rabehl, were so-called *Abhauer* – they had escaped from the GDR just before the building of the Wall.[66] In fact, Dutschke's career as a rebel had begun with his refusal to serve in the East German army, which made it impossible for him to undertake sports studies and become a sports reporter, which had been his initial career plan. After the building of the Wall, Dutschke demonstrated on its Western side, throwing UN leaflets and ropes across it.[67] In 1967, Dutschke, who might best be described as a Protestant national Marxist, also saw the student movement as having a consciousness-raising effect in both West and East Berlin, even as a

---

[65] 'Vaterlose Gesellen: Alexander Mitscherlich über den Frankfurter SDS-Kongreß und die Studentenrebellion', in *Der Spiegel*, 8 April 1968.

[66] Rudi Dutschke *et al.*, *Mein langer Marsch: Reden, Schriften und Tagebücher aus zwanzig Jahren* (Reinbek: Rowohlt, 1980).

[67] Gretchen Dutschke, *Wir hatten ein barbarisches, schönes Leben* (Cologne: Kiepenheuer & Witsch, 1996), 35.

potential mediator between East and West, with a revolutionary German unity as a distant goal.[68]

More generally, the students, longing for an imaginary community with Mao, Castro and Ho-Chi-Minh, also made a universal, anti-imperialist argument in favour of colonial self-determination, in the process offering apologetic enthusiasm for murderous regimes around the globe. This universalism, however, always stopped short of Germany itself, foreshadowing the selective universalism of Günter Grass. Moreover, as I shall explain in the chapter on the New Right, this argument left the way open to the reassertion of national identity and (anti-colonial and anti-American) German self-determination among the peace movement in the early 1980s. Overall, however, since fascism and the authoritarian character were not specifically German phenomena, the question of unification was hardly important. In that sense, the '68ers were not so much anti-nationalist, as a-national.

This changed with the Left's frustration and fragmentation after '68, and, particularly, during the 'long march' through the bourgeois institutions of the Federal Republic (with the intention of dissolving them).[69] During the 'happy ten years' of 1965 until 1975 the number of those employed in public service increased by a third, and the number of highly paid civil servants even doubled.[70] Unlike the so-called *Zaungäste* (sometimes even dubbed the 'lost generation') of those born around and after 1950, the '68ers found the path for marching through the institutions relatively unblocked. During that march, however, they abandoned more and more of their theoretical positions from the 1960s, while supposedly remaining faithful to the sentiments of '68. That meant a shift from the advocacy of Third World anti-colonial violence to strict pacifism, and from the mechanisms of supposedly fascist institutions to an ecological consciousness which could be nothing less than global. In short, the theories were gradually abandoned, the sentiments and the suspicion were not – maybe not a surprising outcome, since '68 itself had already been, above all, a 'psychodrama', as Raymond Aron pointed out at the time.[71] Thus, an instinctive aversion to nationalism, often couched in the language of 'anti-imperialism' and based on a new 'politics of emotion and morality', often

---

[68] *Ibid.*, 141–2 and '"Wir fordern die Enteignung Axel Springers": Spiegel-Gespräch mit dem Berliner FU-Studenten Rudi Dutschke (SDS)', in *Der Spiegel*, 10 July 1967.

[69] The best account of the many twists and turns of the post-68 Left is Andrei S. Markovits and Philip S. Gorski, *The German Left: Red, Green and Beyond* (Cambridge: Polity, 1993).

[70] Axel Schildt, *Ankunft im Westen: Ein Essay zur Erfolgsgeschichte der Bundesrepublik* (Frankfurt/Main: S. Fischer, 1999), 187.

[71] Aron quoted in H. Stuart Hughes, *Sophisticated Rebels: The Political Culture of European Dissent 1968–1987* (Cambridge, Mass.: Harvard University Press, 1990), 6.

came to substitute for any specific critique or theorizing.[72] What mattered was to remain faithful to an increasingly mythical moment within the steadily growing *Alternativkultur*, which was larger than anywhere else in Europe, and made for a strange mixture of political illiberalism and cultural libertarianism. While lamenting its own 'homelessness', just as the sceptical generation had done, the Left then in fact found a comfortable home in the Federal Republic. All this, however, meant that the language of nationhood was neglected and that the political field surrounding the concept was simply left to whomever might be able to capture it.

Secondly, the generation of 1968, in its reaction to the 'restorationist CDU state', subscribed to a strong form of anti-anti-communism. In a sense, the Right tried to pigeonhole the Left as 'crypto-Communists', and the Left, in a defiant way, identified with this label. But anti-anti-communism also constituted a backlash against the initial idealization of the United States during the 1950s, to the extent that the students would infamously shout 'USA-SA-SS'. Anti-fascism and anti-anti-communism went hand in hand: 'Auschwitz' was universalized through anti-fascism and immediately particularized again through anti-anti-communism, by locating the real present fascist threat in the United States.[73] In a sense, the tragedy of intellectual life in post-war West Germany was that anti-communism and anti-fascism became competing, even conflicting principles. This also explained why there was no strong anti-totalitarian and anti-communist Left theory, as there was in France, for instance – and as there had also been in Germany before the 1960s.[74]

Thirdly, anti-fascism became a basic attitude among post-war intellectuals, especially after the 1960s. They very much subscribed to Adorno's point that 'Hitler has imposed on human beings in their state of unfreedom a new categorical imperative: to think and act in such a way that Auschwitz is not repeated, that nothing similar happens'.[75] This anti-fascism was interpreted by the student movement as anti-capitalism in the sense that capitalism was just one step away from fascism and that the Federal Republic was not, as the sceptical generation believed, a post-fascist regime with a narrowing democratic deficit, but a potentially pre-fascist one with a widening deficit. This view provided another link to the GDR,

---

[72] Markovits and Gorski, *The German Left*, 11.

[73] Reinhard Lettau, 'Täglicher Faschismus: Evidenz aus fünf Monaten', in: *Kursbuch*, No. 22 (1970), 1–44.

[74] Sunil Khilnani, *Arguing Revolution: The Intellectual Left in Postwar France* (New Haven: Yale University Press, 1993), 128–36. For a forgotten strand of anti-totalitarianism, see William David Jones, *The Lost Debate: German Socialist Intellectuals and Totalitarianism* (Urbana: University of Illinois Press, 1999).

[75] Adorno, *Negative Dialektik*, 358.

since the students also tended to 'universalize' fascism. While taking little interest in life under conditions of 'actually existing socialism', some 1968 intellectuals tended to sympathize with the GDR's anti-fascist state-ideology. It would be unfair and has in fact been part of post-1989 right-wing mythmaking to suggest that all '68ers fell victim to the lure of the East Germany's official anti-fascist success story. Some parts, especially the 'anti-authoritarian' section of the German Socialist Student Federation led by Dutschke, proved resolutely immune to it. But just as for the French Left the headquarters of the Revolution had moved to Moscow, for a significant part of the German Left the headquarters of a proper *Vergangenheitsheitsbewältigung* could be located in East Berlin – which actually financed and influenced parts of the student movement and the sects into which it splintered after 1968.[76]

During the 1970s, then, as theories were abandoned and sentiments preserved, anti-nationalism had become thoroughly ingrained among the generation of '68. On the other hand, a small part of the Left underwent a national revival in the late 1970s and early 1980s, which I shall elaborate on in chapter seven. But it was only during the 1980s that post-nationalism received its first real theoretical elaboration. Significantly, however, it was older intellectuals like Habermas, Bracher and Sontheimer who were most concerned to flesh out notions of republican belonging beyond the nation-state and to provide some institutional foundations for such post-national values. Among younger intellectuals, on the other hand, post-nationalism was often taken for granted as a natural state towards which the Federal Republic was evolving.

The left-wing consensus which emerged from the constellation of these multiple 'anti-concepts' was nearly entirely defined *ex negativo*, as a negation of what the Right supposedly thought. These self-definitions consisting of the opposite of statements by the political opponent came to substitute for a genuine position based on an independent analysis. More than other intellectuals, the '68ers depended for their convictions on the particular 'positionality' of their claims on the intellectual field: since one could supposedly never go morally wrong by defining oneself against the nation due to the fact that nationhood and National Socialism had been inextricably linked, anti-nationalism seemed to guarantee anti-fascism, and thereby fulfilled the categorical imperative of 'never again'. At the same time, principled anti-nationalism became fatefully adjacent to anti-liberalism. But due to this 'contraphobic' positioning, as Dan Diner has

---

[76] Wolfgang Kraushaar, 'Von der Totalitarismus- zur Faschismustheorie: Zu einem Paradigmenwechsel in der Theoriepolitik der bundesdeutschen Studentenbewegung', in Claudia Keller (ed.), *Die Nacht hat zwölf Stunden, dann kommt schon der Tag: Antifaschismus – Geschichte und Neubewertung* (Berlin: Aufbau, 1996), 234–51, and Hubertus Knabe, *Die unterwanderte Republik: Stasi im Westen* (Berlin: Propyläen, 1999), 182–233.

called this particular left-wing move on the intellectual field, it also became impossible to develop a more differentiated view of the nation, or even to think nationhood and democracy together.[77] For the same reason, any rehabilitation of the nation would necessarily entail a proportional repression of the Nazi past. Like criticism during the Cold War, collective memory thus became a zero-sum game for the Left.

This is not to suggest that the intellectual and political initiative in post-war West Germany always lay on the Right and that left-wing intellectuals merely responded to it. But the behaviour of intellectuals in 1990 suggested that the consensus had become ossified, and that, to some extent as in Grass's case, intellectual positions had become mere ideological reflexes. Moreover, as intellectuals lacked the criteria to interpret developments in 1990, but still wanted to perform their traditional role of 'seeing through' and explaining complex realities, they often resorted to simply asserting the opposite of what the Right said. This could still appear as 'progressive', but had little to do with enlightenment in a Kantian sense. In fact, ritualistic assertion became a defence against reality.

Not surprisingly, then, in 1990 some younger intellectuals faced the problem of a lack of intellectual resources. Younger writers found the language of nationhood entirely inaccessible from within a post-modern, post-material and multicultural theoretical framework which had been formed in the 1980s. In such a framework, 'nation', 'identity' and other totalizing 'meta-narratives' were discredited. Wilhelm Schmid, for instance, a West German philosopher born in 1953, argued that the concept of 'identity' was simply an 'error', and that fascism, based on racism, was only 'the ultimate form of thinking in terms of identity'.[78] Following Foucault, these writers also distrusted the public role of the traditional intellectual *per se*.

Other intellectuals, most notably Peter Glotz, the leading policy intellectual and one-time general secretary of the SPD, combined a normative case against the traditional nation-state with an empirical prediction that the nation-state would be superseded.[79] He viewed the traditional nation-state as artificial, as suppressing diversity, as having an inherently aggressive potential, and as associated with a 'false normalization' for the Germans.[80] Glotz preferred to think in terms of a post-national age in which political and economic problems had become so complex that they could only be tackled effectively on a supra-national level. Intellectuals like Glotz granted citizens a certain amount of identification with their local surroundings or even their federal states and wanted them to be 'good

---

[77] Dan Diner, *Kreisläufe: Nationalsozialismus und Gedächtnis* (Berlin: Berlin Verlag, 1995), 102.

[78] Wilhelm Schmid, *Was geht uns Deutschland an?* (Frankfurt/Main: Suhrkamp, 1993), 115.

[79] Peter Glotz, *Der Irrweg des Nationalstaats* (Stuttgart: Deutsche Verlags-Anstalt, 1990).

[80] Peter Glotz, *Die falsche Normalisierung: Die unmerkliche Verwandlung der Deutschen 1989 bis 1994* (Frankfurt/Main: Suhrkamp, 1994).

Europeans' as well, while the level of identification with the country as a whole was seen as problematic, if not dangerous. However, this idea of escaping the nation-state by moving either up to supra-national institutions or down to regions and even 'tribes' betrayed a thoroughly anti-institutional attitude. As Dahrendorf pointed out, such attitudes tended to overlook the fact that the nation-state was constitutionally still the main guarantor of citizenship rights.[81] The Left, it seemed, was fascinated by either 'small nationalisms', which were seen as expressions of Herderian cultural diversity and autonomy, or larger multinational entities such as the Habsburg empire which were equated with multiculturalism. Both somewhat romantic attitudes, combining a flight into sentiment and abstraction, showed a lack of concern with constitutional matters, institutions and rights. This had already been the case in the 1980s, when, in one of the most profound paradoxes of the Federal Republic, a thoroughly post-national consciousness had developed in a country with a decidedly nationalist citizenship law.

In response to unification and the debate on the nation surrounding it, left-wing intellectuals generally relied on arguments rooted in post-nationalism or negative nationalism. At best, they attempted to formulate a form of German republicanism, or a civic conception of the nation. At worst, they rejected thinking about the nation altogether, in a reflexive reaction rooted in the old anti-nationalist consensus. Only time would tell whether this anti-nationalism would be an appropriate response. But even voices within the Left suspected that one had to somehow engage with nationalism in order to overcome it. As Wolfgang Thierse, East German intellectual, vice-chairman of the SPD and eventually President of the Bundestag, pointed out with regard to the return of a nationalism which oscillated between chauvinism and legitimate demands for self-determination:

The Left in the West opposes its traditional ideology of the end of the nation-state to this [rise in nationalism] and thereby often documents its rather unconscious fears about the 'uncertainties' of the changes in Eastern Europe. But that does not mean one becomes capable of politics . . . We have to accept this process in reality, because the liberation from socialism took place in the form of nationalism. It has to be the task of a reasonable policy that nationalism does not . . . become directed against the emancipatory process. But that presupposes that the Left does not just issue decrees that everything national is an outdated value of the nineteenth century.[82]

---

[81] Dahrendorf, 'Die Sache mit der Nation', 827.

[82] Wolfgang Thierse, Überlegungen zur Zukunft der Linken in Deutschland', in Michael Müller and Wolfgang Thierse (eds), *Deutsche Ansichten: Die Republik im Übergang* (Bonn: J. H. W. Dietz Nachf., 1992), 85–104; here 99–100. See also Dieckmann, 'Die Linke und die Nation'.

Coming to Terms with the Nation: Liberal and Liberal-Conservative Rejoinders

Liberal, and particularly older liberal, intellectuals were by and large more willing to accept a unified Germany. They did not seek to 'naturalize' the nation, but also refrained from demonizing the institutional framework of the nation-state *per se*. On the other hand, liberal-conservative thinkers, especially historians, adopted a self-consciously relaxed stance about the supposed 'return to normality', which they equated with the 'Bismarck Reich'. They attacked post-nationalism, and were more willing to draw on – in Habermasian parlance – 'conventional' feelings of national solidarity in the effort to integrate the GDR. Such views had a certain affinity with positions later adopted by the New Right, and, to some extent, there was a continuum of common concepts between certain liberal-conservative thinkers and the New Right. In that sense, the crucial fault line on the intellectual field was between liberals who advanced relatively nuanced conceptions of the role of the nation-state, and liberal-conservative and New Right intellectuals who 'naturalized' the nation. Liberal thinkers situated their conceptions of the nation between concepts of constitutionalism and heterogeneity, which, they felt, made it secure against potentially adjacent concepts such as ethnic homogenization, and the nation as a 'community of fate'. On the other hand, liberal-conservatives and the New Right, who often explicitly demanded homogenization in the vein of an étatisme indebted to Carl Schmitt, were clearly thinking in terms of an ethnically defined nation. They also resisted any further European integration not for fear of a 'democratic deficit', but because of a potential loss of German peculiarities.

Liberals like Dahrendorf rejected the reproach of 'DM-Nationalism', and tried to combine a relaxed stance about 'normal nationality' with the positive liberal traditions of the Federal Republic, in particular constitutional patriotism. He claimed that 'now that Germany is no longer a provisional, but a normal nation-state, it can also develop a normal constitutional patriotism'.[83] Subsequently, he advocated a conception of the 'heterogeneous nation-state' as a liberal solution which preserved the nation-state as a historical European achievement capable of guaranteeing civil rights, while guarding against a nationalist tendency of producing homogeneity through exclusion.[84] In this scenario, liberals would defend the nation-state against nations, and ensure that ' "citizenship" and "civil society" [English in the original] become a vocabulary which also in its German version has an unambiguous, radical and liberal

---

[83] Dahrendorf, 'Die Sache mit der Nation', 827.

[84] Ralf Dahrendorf, 'Die Zukunft des Nationalstaates', in *Merkur*, Vol. 48 (1994), 751–61.

meaning'.[85] While rejecting both an explicit 'Holocaust identity' and the notion of 'post-conventional identity', liberals nevertheless used a conceptual language with close affinities to Habermas's post-nationalist positions.

They frequently pointed out that for the first time, Germany could have both unity and freedom, that unity was not achieved against Germany's neighbours and that, again for the first time, a German nation-state would be part of the West.[86] Unlike left-wing intellectuals, they were accepting of the notion that 'the nation-state seems to continue to be the normal form of political organization of European societies', and that consequently, unification actually meant a welcome '*Anschluß* with 'European "normality"'.[87]

Others suggested a more explicit balance between liberal and communitarian elements. The Hegel scholar Dieter Henrich, for instance, sought to reconcile the political principles of republicanism which had found a home in the Federal Republic with a more relaxed attitude towards a concept of the nation placed between republicanism and a Hegelian communitarianism. With unification, he expected the recovery of particular German spiritual and intellectual possibilities, which had been lost during the division, but which could now make a fresh contribution to 'the *Selbstverständigung* of mankind in the new world situation'.[88] Unification was imperative mostly out of solidarity with the East Germans, but also to end the mental deformations which the West Germans had suffered due to the division.[89] The latter also meant that for the first time all Germans could account for their past, freed from the biased perspectives caused by the Wall.[90] Explicitly opposing Habermas, he argued that the East German desire for the Deutschmark and the desire for civil rights were connected, but agreed that an all-German plebiscite would lead to a 'deeper legitimacy' for the Federal Republic, too. An all-German affirmation would also show the West's solidarity with the East.[91]

In Henrich's vision, a republican constitution, strengthened by the East German revolution and its essentially *bürgerliche* character, should be combined with a 'life praxis' already inherent in the 'profile of the nation' –

[85] Dahrendorf, 'Die Sache mit der Nation', 827.

[86] For instance Hagen Schulze, 'In der Mitte Europas: Ein normaler Nationalstaat', in Josef Becker (ed.), *Wiedervereinigung in Mitteleuropa: Außen-und Innenansichten zur staatlichen Einheit Deutschlands* (Munich: Ernst Vögel, 1992), 159–73; Jürgen Kocka, 'Nur keine neuen Sonderwege', 188.

[87] Kocka, 'Nur keine neuen Sonderwege', 188.

[88] Dieter Henrich, *Eine Republik Deutschland: Reflexionen auf dem Weg aus der deutschen Teilung* (Frankfurt/Main: Suhrkamp, 1990), 12.

[89] *Ibid.*, 25.

[90] *Ibid.*, 31.

[91] *Ibid.*, 66.

which would allow the two Germanies to come together as 'one republic Germany'.[92] He insisted that in the system of values in united Germany, 'the republican component' was to have priority and be the *conditio sine qua non*.[93] But republicanism was to be realized in concrete practice or, rather, a Hegelian *Sittlichkeit* [public ethical life], in which there was a 'concordance' between the Constitution, the nation as an 'association of solidarity' and everyday 'life-forms'.[94] For Henrich – and this made his vision different from many left and right-wing arguments – unification held the promise of regaining a particular German culture, including such previously demonized values as *Innerlichkeit*. Nevertheless, unlike in ethnic conceptions of the nation, the new national 'self-description' of the Germans was to be reached discursively and result in the development of an 'association of common attitudes'.[95] Henrich and many other liberals tried to reconcile republicanism with a broadly communitarian vision of the nation, positioning themselves with a more relaxed and communitarian view of 'pre-political values' vis-à-vis Habermas and his post-nationalism, but clinging to voluntarist (and 'imagined') conceptions of the nation vis-à-vis the liberal-conservatives. Voluntarism, unlike with Habermas in his Rousseauean moment in 1990, usually took a more Kantian form.

The liberal-conservative historian Christian Meier, on the other hand, explicitly invoked nationality as a historical source of solidarity between East and West.[96] Nations, he posited, were 'communities of action' and 'communities of solidarity'.[97] Only thinking in the categories of the nation would allow the solution of the problems which unification posed. Those who were sceptical about the category of the 'nation' would have to be asked whether their scepticism 'was not just a rationalization of the wish of German petty bourgeois to be left alone'.[98] If the Germans failed to show national solidarity, they would attempt to 'escape from history'.[99] From this perspective, the idea of 'post-nationalism' would necessarily appear as a *Sonderweg*, even as the *Lebenslüge* [life-lie] of West

---

[92] *Ibid.*, 14–15.

[93] *Ibid.*, 30.

[94] *Ibid.*, 33–4.

[95] Dieter Henrich, *Nach dem Ende der Teilung: Über Identitäten und Intellektualität in Deutschland* (Frankfurt/Main: Suhrkamp, 1993), 17 and 21, 81–3.

[96] Christian Meier, *Deutsche Einheit als Herausforderung: Welche Fundamente für welche Republik?* (Munich: Hanser, 1990), 43.

[97] *Ibid.*, 102–3.

[98] *Ibid.*

[99] *Ibid.*, 51.

Germany.[100] While socialism had been the *Lebenslüge* of GDR identity, the corresponding 'life-lie' of West Germany had been post-nationalism and constitutional patriotism. Meier suggested that West Germany had never been post-national, but only of 'latent nationality'.[101] Overcoming the division was the first step towards a new confrontation with the past. Therefore, the idea of *Vergangenheitsbewältigung* itself mandated the reconstitution of a German national subject.

Conservative historian (and CDU policy adviser) Hans-Peter Schwarz also argued that a 'national normality' had been restored and offered a sanguine view of the future of a unified Germany. It offered the opportunity for the Germans finally to escape from their 'identity neurosis'.[102] The old Federal Republic, with its 'boring, complacent and unproductive' identity discussion, had clearly been in a state of 'geopolitical and geographical anomaly', in which German history had been forgotten as well. Moreover, West German 'space had no depth and no real border'. Only now did the country regain 'space' and 'width', state and people were once again one, and the 'professorial fiction' of constitutional patriotism could be discarded.[103] Not surprisingly, this also opened up the possibility that the Germans 'might discover anew what a state is', since now all classes could 'calmly and self-confidently' identify with state, history, *Volk* and the Constitution.[104] Thus, as he was ridiculing the very identity debates which conservatives had begun in the 1970s and 1980s, Schwarz in fact made one of the most typical conservative 'identitarian' claims inspired by German étatiste traditions. He subsequently argued that national normality had to mean the assertive pursuit of national interests, a demand often surrounded by metaphors about Germany's 'need to grow up' and to 'flex its muscles'.

Conservative responses to left-wing concerns about the nation revolved around the 'normality' and the 'naturalness' of the nation. Historians in particular were eager to discredit post-nationalism and cast a negative light on the Federal Republic as deficient in politics and in a geopolitical – and, it seemed at times, metaphysical – concept of 'space'. They also tried to bring a sense of closure and newly found calmness to the 'identity debates' in which they had previously been the most vocal participants, claiming that the 'normal' and 'self-evident' state of the nation had now been achieved. This calmness was polemically opposed to the Left's 'alarmism'

---

[100] *Ibid.*, 17.

[101] *Ibid.*, 49.

[102] Hans-Peter Schwarz, 'Das Ende der Identitätsneurose', in *Rheinischer Merkur*, 7 September 1990.

[103] *Ibid.*

[104] *Ibid.*

and subsequent melancholy about unification. Ironically, however, in their policy recommendations after 1990, often grounded in the claim that Germany was back in the position of the old Bismarck Reich, these intellectuals reverted to the very same psycho-social discourse of 'identity neuroses' which they had pinned on the Left during the unification debates.[105]

What was Left?

One of the most vocal groups in the unification debate, however, talked less about unification than about what it meant for the Left itself. While a self-critical revision was considered necessary by many observers, the Left's self-critique soon became a drawn-out process of recrimination and revenge. It seemed as if the culture of suspicion had turned inwards, and as if marking out demarcations vis-à-vis other intellectuals took precedence over theorizing. Arguably, this self-involved debate, in which anti-intellectual polemics abounded, created an intellectual vacuum to be filled by prescriptions from the Right.

The self-critique of the Left was pushed furthest by some members of the '68 generation, a few of whom had actually been leaders of the student movement. They had undergone a phase of left-wing melancholy before 1989, when they emerged as acerbic analysts of the failure of the Left to revise its ideals in the light of the collapse of Communism. They also adopted a self-consciously 'realistic' and sceptical stance, which, in an American context, might have been called 'neo-conservative', and, in the French context, been identified with the 'new philosophers'. Peter Schneider in particular, promoting Karl Popper's principle of falsification, criticized his fellow intellectuals for 'sleeping through an earthquake' and the inability to admit past mistakes publicly.[106] He also attacked them for what he termed *Lagerdenken*, a fixation on thinking in terms of left and right 'camps' and, consequently, a strict friend–enemy distinction. This *Lagerdenken*, according to Schneider, led to a rigid culture of consensus and to the fact that 'the question of what kind of camp a statement gets one in was and is much more important than the question of whether the statement was true'.[107] For Schneider, the legacy of *Lagerdenken* made the

---

[105] In particular Hans-Peter Schwarz, *Die Zentralmacht Europas: Deutschlands Rückkehr auf die Weltbühne* (Berlin: Siedler, 1994) and Arnulf Baring, *Deutschland, was nun? Ein Gespräch mit Dirk Rumberg und Wolf Jobst Siedler* (Berlin: Siedler, 1991).

[106] Peter Schneider, 'Man kann sogar ein Erdbeben verpassen', in *Die Zeit*, 27 April 1990.

[107] Peter Schneider, 'Die Angst der Deutschen vor den Idealen', in *Frankfurter Allgemeine Zeitung*, 13 May 1991.

debate in 1990 a ritualistic performance of positions and an exchange of ideological reflexes — a not implausible interpretation of the Left's reaction. Indeed, the insight that often the greatest fear for intellectuals — and the fear most important to overcome — was being unpopular within their own 'camp of opinion' proved true not just of the West German Left. On the other hand, Hans Magnus Enzensberger, once again a tiny step ahead of the Zeitgeist, made a number of plainly anti-intellectual interventions which played off 'the masses' against both political leaders and intellectuals.[108] True to his Maoist past and his tendency to go against whatever passed as received opinion among intellectuals, he praised the masses and ordinary people precisely for their greed and materialist pragmatism.

Schneider, and, to a lesser extent Enzensberger, came closest to achieving a critical revision of earlier views, and of the Left's blind spots in the past. However, their arguments often bordered on a self-contradictory, rigid anti-intellectualism in the case of Enzensberger, and a tendency to fight yesterday's battles, in Schneider's case. Like American neoconservatives and French 'new philosophers', they suddenly held their liberal convictions with the same dogmatism as they had once held their Maoist beliefs. The flight from any normative expectations at all into a hard-headed realism, the strenuousness of which betrayed the same determination to find certainties as previous ideological attachments, harked back to the 'cold conduct' of the 1920s. In particular, Enzensberger and others reverted to an anthropological pessimism familiar from thinkers like Gehlen, which both furnished a sense of certainty and immunized from future ideological disappointments.[109] It seemed that just because 'utopia' had failed, theory was thrown out altogether — but without theory, intellectuals could perform no work at all, and not even propose the most timid alternatives to actual policies. The new anti-idealism also stood in a continuity with the earlier Marxist materialism, which of course had itself been a form of anti-idealism. There was a danger that, for a lack of ideas, suddenly any critical stances came under suspicion, and that the only criticism left for the post-89 Left was left-wing self-criticism.

Treason or Failure? The Paradoxes of the Federal Republican Opposition

West German left-wing intellectuals rejected unification for a wide range of reasons. At the most basic level, developments in 1989 and 1990

---

[108] Hans Magnus Enzensberger, 'Gangarten — Ein Nachtrag zur Utopie: Wenn ein Alltag anbricht, der ohne Propheten auskommt', in *Frankfurter Allgemeine Zeitung*, 19 May 1990.

[109] Enzensberger, 'Ausblicke'.

challenged the modes of thoughts and the tacit consensus that had been built up since 1968. The collapse of 'actually existing socialism' prompted defiant reactions of post-nationalism, but also an emotional negative nationalism. Intellectuals first fell back on the main positions of the consensus, which was already disintegrating, and, after much confusion and sharp criticism, partially retreated into silence or the debate about 'what was left'. This created a vacuum at a time when the country more than ever depended on an interpretation of complex historical developments and an engagement with the politics of nationhood. While the Right referred to the past as a basis of identity, the Left also dealt with the question of nationhood in a retrospective way, i.e. by projecting the Bismarck Reich into the future, and reverting to the kind of demonization of Germany which had been prevalent immediately after 1945. Internally, the Left, put on the defensive, kept fighting the ideological battles of the past and contributed little in terms of linking the new nation-state to concepts of citizenship and civil society, which might have been conceptual ways out of the increasingly fruitless debate about 'what was left' – although it would also be an intellectualist illusion to assume that right-wing thugs would not have turned to violence in post-unification Germany, if only left-wing intellectuals had engaged more with the nation. In a sense, however, Left and Right curiously mirrored each other in their fixation on the past and collective German psychology at the expense of political and, in particular, institutional questions.

What precisely, in the end, however, was it that had supposedly done so much damage to the Left? It could hardly be the fact that it had been 'sidelined', as some critics claimed, since political defeat hardly had to translate into intellectual discrediting. After all, there had been many intellectual defeats before, and there were going to be defeats in the future – and in any case, even in its heyday, the Left had not enjoyed any unmediated political influence. In the same vein, it hardly made sense to reproach the Left for not having 'predicted' the fall of the Wall – after all, who had? Even for past decades of the Federal Republic, the claim that intellectuals had been particularly sensitive seismographs of political developments was hardly borne out by the facts – if anything, both the intellectuals of the sceptical generation and the '68ers had successfully *reacted* against established authority and ossified institutions, rather than foreseen major changes.

So what was different in 1990? First, there was the sense of the Left's defensiveness, an impression that the Left had become 'part of the problem, rather than part of the solution', as one of the former leaders of the student movement put it.[110] It was an inability to lend events any

[110] Christian Semler, 'Der Weg ins Freie: Verrat und Identität der Linken', in *Kursbuch*, No 116 (1994), 25–36; here 34.

plausible meaning and the sheer self-absorbed character of many leftist interventions which diminished the legitimacy of the Left. It was for this reason, also, that critics of the Left, both from the Right and within the Left itself, talked about 'failure', rather than 'treason'.

Moreover, there were the ambiguities involved in the Left's dissociation from ideal and actually existing socialism. If the idea of the nation had been fatally contaminated by National Socialism, as the Left always claimed, why was something similar not true for the idea of socialism – a question which did not have to imply an equivalence of socialism and National Socialism. The Left's desperate rescue of 'socialism' resembled attempts by conservative thinkers in the immediate post-war period to portray the nation as the first victim of National Socialism. In the same vein, many of the apologist arguments which the Left had always fiercely rejected with regard to the Third Reich – such as von Molo's claim about the 'inner emigration' which outsiders could not judge – were advanced in defence of East German intellectuals who had compromised with the regime. Once again, the logic of anti-anti-communism held sway. Rather than furthering their long-term credibility through an open reckoning with the past, strategic considerations to combat an 'offensive from the Right' took precedence. But it was precisely this priority of position-taking which, in retrospect, had proved so fateful for the Left in the Federal Republic.

Ultimately, what proved damaging to the Left was not the fact that it criticized unification and failed to rise to a 'national challenge' – as the Right charged, implying that criticism was illegitimate *per se* – but the fact that so much of its past and present criticism had been one-sided, driven by position-taking, and, above all, characterized by a lack of seriousness. The latter became clear with the suddenly revealed attachment of left-wingers to the Federal Republic: in retrospect, it turned out that for a Left which had periodically assessed the degree of its own homelessness, criticism had hidden affirmation, being against had really been the most subtle form of being in favour, and criticism and complacency had gone hand in hand – which is why criticism could be turned into apologia almost overnight.[111] Unlike the sceptical generation which had sought to defend the Federal Republic, the post-68 Left had never made this affirmation explicit. Nor had they theoretically engaged with the critical potential of liberalism and 'formal democracy', as, to varying degrees, the Left in France, Britain and the United States had in the 1970s and 1980s. It was, then, above all, this realization of a lack of political and moral seriousness in their previous criticisms, not the fact that the Left was critical of unification, which undermined the Left's credibility more generally.

---

[111] For instance Dieter Lattmann, 'Wie heimatlos ist die Linke heute?', in *Stuttgarter Zeitung*, 8 April 1972.

Finally, the wake of the unification debate also seemed to have an emotional dimension in the form of personal feelings of disappointment and rage – some intellectuals seemed to take it as a personal insult that things had not turned out as they had wished, and they resented that they had to re-examine long-held beliefs. All in all, Andreas Huyssen's in itself melancholic conclusion was correct that the 'rhetoric and behaviour of West German intellectuals . . . lacked sovereignty, perspective, and compassion; it betrayed self-indulgence and arrogance, a fatal aloofness from reality and a desperate clinging to projections, and, when under fire, melancholic self-pity and unrepentant self-righteousness'.[112]

---

[112] Huyssen, 'After the Wall', 110.

5 Martin Walser: German Sentiments and Opinions about Germany

Ich bin durch Widerspruch geworden, was ich bin. Dem wurde widersprochen. Dem widersprach ich. Aus mir spreche nicht ich, sondern der Widerspruch.

I have become who I am through contradiction. That was contradicted. I contradicted that. It is not me who speaks when I speak, it is contradiction.

Martin Walser, *Meßmers Gedanken*

When the Wall came down, it seemed that one writer could lay claim to having been a persistent advocate of unification. Martin Walser had for years publicly 'talked about Germany' and made many enemies on his supposed political home on the Left in the process, especially among the younger generation. When the prospect of unification began to loom large, this seemed to be the moment of Walser's triumph: the writer who had defended the 'common sense' of the *Volk* against intellectuals, and its desire to continue living as one nation, could finally feel vindicated, it seemed, when the *Volk* not only chanted *Wir sind das Volk* [we are the people], but also expressed its desire to be *ein Volk* [one people].

In an interview at the time, however, Walser insisted that he had not 'learnt how to triumph'.[1] This did not necessarily save him from being instrumentalized by conservatives, and from being presented as both the prophet and poet of unity. His book *Über Deutschland reden* [Talking about Germany] was quickly reissued in an expanded edition in November 1989 with a special banderole quoting an article by Joachim Fest in the *Frankfurter Allgemeine Zeitung*.[2] Fest had claimed that 'Walser is the only significant author of the Federal Republic who dared to voice the dramatic presence of the German question which was so often pushed into the

---

[1] ' "Triumphieren nicht gelernt": Der Schriftsteller Martin Walser über die Intellektuellen und die deutsche Einheit (1990)', in Martin Walser, *Auskunft: 22 Gespräche aus 28 Jahren*, ed. Klaus Siblewski (Frankfurt/Main: Suhrkamp, 1991), 257–66.

[2] Martin Walser, *Über Deutschland reden* (1988; Frankfurt Main: Suhrkamp, 1989).

uncertain future, before political developments confirmed it'.[3] The media and the public by whom Walser had often felt victimized in the past, now built him up as a counter-figure to the 'Cassandra' of unification, Günter Grass. Earlier in 1989, many of Walser's critics had already seen their worst fears confirmed when Walser attended a party meeting of the Christian Social Union [CSU, the CDU's Bavarian sister party] in Bad Kreuth. For them, Walser, variously portrayed as a literary historian of 'West German mentalities', and as a spokesperson of middle-class Germany, even of *l'Allemagne profonde*, had finally given himself hostage to the Right.

Whether or not Walser had done anything of the sort, the question remained how he could have been transformed into a conservative icon. After all, it had been the supposed 'Proust from Lake Constance' (in Enzensberger's words) who, in 1961, had almost single-handedly started the tradition of writers voicing their support for the SPD.[4] He had nearly always been among the signatories of protests by intellectuals, whether against re-armament or against the Vietnam War. He had written the introduction to the German translation of one of Elie Wiesel's books, and sided with various marginalized groups in West German society, editing the writing of workers as well as prisoners and even publishing the autobiography of a young murderess – with the 'Proust' of West German literature apparently doubling as a 'Foucault from Lake Constance'.[5] Walser had also once been close to the DKP, the West German Communist party, and had continuously affirmed his belief in 'democratic socialism', which he thought was the only way of actually realizing democracy.[6] Had Walser simply changed his views with age and moved to the Right, as most commentators assumed? Alternatively, was his trajectory indicative of larger intellectual shifts? Or had Walser's position always been more complex than the charge of 'left intellectual-turned-conservative' would suggest?

In this chapter, I seek to show that, rather than having started off as a left-wing radical and then consistently moved to the right, Walser had for a long time been the proud representative of the provincial German petty bourgeoisie, and defended a German form of interiority and, arguably,

---

[3] *Frankfurter Allgemeine Zeitung*, 6 November 1989.

[4] Walser (ed.), *Die Alternative*.

[5] Elie Wiesel, *Die Nacht zu begraben, Elischa* (Munich: Bechtle, 1963), Martin Walser (ed.), *Die Würde am Werktag* (Frankfurt/Main: Fischer, 1980) and Ursula Trauberg, *Vorleben* (Frankfurt/Main: Suhrkamp, 1968).

[6] Martin Walser, 'Wahlgedanken', in *Wie und wovon handelt Literatur: Aufsätze und Reden* (Frankfurt/Main: Suhrkamp, 1973), 100–18.

sentimentality. While his criticism of the reunification policies of the Adenauer era and the deformities of post-war West German capitalism had at one point converged with those of the *Gruppe 47* and other intellectuals, his critique had already been rooted in a different framework. Unlike Grass, but like Enzensberger and Peter Weiss, Walser moved sharply to the left in the late 1960s and early 1970s. However, he quickly became disillusioned with the DKP, and increasingly fastened on the issue of the nation, arguably as a form of compensation for unfulfilled promises of social reform.

However, Walser's trajectory also demonstrates that the constellation on the intellectual field had been reconfigured over time. Arguments in favour of the nation, but against 'reunification', which Walser, like so many left-wing intellectuals, had seen as part of a 'hypocritical Adenauer vocabulary' in the 1960s, were no longer acceptable by the time Walser had fully developed his 'talking about Germany' in the 1980s, when the '68ers had become dominant on the Left. Some of the criticisms directed against Walser at that time also highlight the rigidities which characterized the Left in the 1980s.

His critics, then, from both the Left and the Right, tended to attack him for the wrong reasons. The Right wanted to claim as one of its own a man who had consistently espoused 'democratic socialism'. The Left, on the other hand, rather than fastening on these underlying issues and engaging with the questions which Walser persistently posed, seemed to brand him a 'nationalist', even a 'revanchist', simply for articulating national questions and the plight of the East Germans.

I also seek to show that Walser's self-proclaimed 'longing for the nation' was intimately connected to his conception of writing in general and to his role as a spokesperson for the German lower middle class. Unlike in the case of Grass, one needs to investigate Walser's conception of writing as such. This conception initially overlapped with, and then came to dominate his public stance vis-à-vis the nation: the writer's defensive, 'disempowered self' and the divided nation not only sustained a dialogue over the decades, but came to share many characteristics.[7]

---

[7] Walser's literary critics persistently pointed out that his protagonists tended to be thinly veiled disguises for Walser himself. Walser often concurred with this criticism as far as his early works were concerned. Since, in addition, Walser often drew on his private experiences in his public pronouncements, one can, without collapsing the author into his characters, trace a much closer connection between Walser's personal views, his writing and his public stance than in the case of almost any other writer in the Federal Republic. Walser himself was candid about these connections in the innumerable interviews he gave during the course of his career. Ironically, the author most suspicious of the public sphere had made it one of his principles never to refuse an interview since his own experience as a young reporter in the 1950s.

Walser's Critique of West German Society: Competition between Dependent, Disempowered Selves

Walser was born in Wasserburg near Lake Constance in 1927, the same year as Grass. Like many right-wing intellectuals in the first half of the twentieth century, Walser came from an intensely Catholic petty bourgeois background. As he himself has written, this was an environment which instilled in him both a lasting feeling of anxiety, and an acute sense of the economic pressures under which the lower middle class suffered. His family ran an inn, and when his father, a hapless businessman, died at an early age, they were saddled with large debts. The fear of economic dependency and social disgrace in a small village community had been Walser's first 'experience of class', and would constitute major themes of his literary work.[8]

This 'experience of class' continued when he encountered teachers in school who adopted a self-consciously bourgeois attitude to compensate for their own petty bourgeois origins.[9] In the pattern typical of his generation, Walser had to break off his education and was drafted first into the *Heimatflak* [anti-aircraft defence] in 1943, then into the *Arbeitsdienst* [labour service] in 1944, and finally into the military itself, before he was captured by the Americans in 1945. After the War, he confronted city-life for the first time and began to study in Regensburg. Again, his life was severely disrupted when the currency reform made it impossible for his mother to finance his studies. Walser started to work as a reporter, and, covering provincial politics in the south-west of West Germany, gained an acute insight into the emerging social values of the new Federal Republic. Moreover, he felt he was left with a lasting awareness of the media's potential for the manipulation of consciousness.

Walser's early writings were influenced by Kafka and existentialism, but he soon emerged as a satirical diagnostician of West German society. This turn from the humanist concerns so typical of the early 1950s to a realist observation of society was not least inspired by Walser's participation in the 1958 Harvard International Seminar, to which Henry Kissinger had invited him. The *Gruppe 47* soon 'discovered' Walser; he won the group's prize as early as 1955 and proved eager to redirect the focus of his fellow writers away from the task of coming to terms with the War to an engagement with West German society. In particular, he chose to direct his literary attention to the ways in which the market economy psychologically deformed the heroes of his novels. These were the *Angestellten*, the white-collar workers, who had already been recognized in the Weimar

---

[8] Anthony Waine, *Martin Walser* (Munich: C. H. Beck, 1980), 8.

[9] 'Martin Walser und Tübingen', in *Auskunft*, 45–70; here 67.

Republic as a peculiar social group with its own values, caught between a proletariat which they feared and a bourgeoisie to which they aspired in a futile quest for social recognition.[10] Walser viewed these white-collar workers, in particular provincial salesmen and real estate agents, as paradigmatic for the emerging social order in West Germany and the human cost it exacted. He sought to draw attention to the almost automatic humiliation which resulted from their economic state of dependency. He claimed that 'the worst thing that could happen' to human beings was 'dependency' and concentrated on providing a chronicle of the everyday sense of powerlessness which individuals were experiencing as a result of economic competition.[11] While it would be simplistic to see Walser as an advocate of *Gemeinschaft* against *Gesellschaft*, he did uphold an ideal of non-alienated, to some extent communal subjectivity and individual dignity which fitted into community-oriented German traditions.

Throughout the 1960s, Walser's writings moved in a more radical direction, culminating in the early 1970s in the volume *Fiction*, which was his most experimental literary work, and the novel *Die Gallistl'sche Krankheit* [The Gallistl Disease], which was his most overtly political novel to date.[12] In *Die Gallistl'sche Krankheit*, the entry of the hero into a fraternal community of Communists emerged as the possible solution to the alienation and humiliation from which Walser's characters had suffered. For reasons I shall discuss further below, Walser moved close to, but himself never became a member of the DKP. The novel, however, also contained another theme which rivalled the main topic of ending alienation through a socialist community. Walser's protagonist Gallistl, in words almost identical with what Walser himself was to publicly affirm in the late 1970s, confessed that

> my sentiment reaches deep into Pomerania. I am familiar with Saxony although I have never been there. How often do I think of Magdeburg! I do not want to conquer the GDR. But I do not want someone prohibiting my sentiments from entering and exiting [the GDR] as they like. This ridiculous enmity. The German national character in competition with itself.

Toward the mid-1970s Walser turned away again from more overtly political subjects. It was only then that he came to experience commercial success and acclaim from literary critics who now celebrated his heroes as

[10] In particular Siegfried Kracauer's study, *Die Angestellten: Aus dem neuesten Deutschland* (Frankfurt/Main: Societats, 1930).

[11] 'Ein Gespräch mit Martin Walser in Neu-England', in *Auskunft*, 96–115; here 100.

[12] Martin Walser, *Fiction* (Frankfurt/Main: Suhrkamp, 1970) and *Die Gallistl'sche Krankheit* (Frankfurt/Main: Suhrkamp, 1972).

reflecting essential human dilemmas, rather than the particular conditions in the Federal Republic.[13] While abandoningCommunism in his literary work, Walser instead increasingly engaged with the issue of nationhood. In his 1978 *Seelenarbeit* [Work on the Soul], while still primarily dealing with a master-slave-relationship between a chauffeur and his boss, Walser also broached the question of Königsberg, the former German city in East Prussia, and described the work of an association of expellees. From then on, the issue of German division loomed ever larger in his literary work. This trend culminated in his 1987 novella *Dorle and Wolf*, a romance of unity, in which an East German spy marries a West German woman, defining himself as a citizen of another, unified Germany-yet-to-come for which he is really working.[14] Walser strongly suggested that Eros could make the Germans one again, as through the division East and West Germans had become 'half-people' without even being aware of lacking their other half.[15] He essentially collapsed the personal into the political, making individual and national love as well as sickness one. But by now, an all-German theme was almost expected from a writer who had come under severe attack from the Left for his supposed nationalism.

Walser as an Intellectual in Politics: The Accidental Representative

From the earliest stages of his career, Walser conceived of his writing as being inspired by a sense of absence, or *Mangel* [deficiency]. He claimed that it was only this sense of 'deficiency', meaning a deformed, abnormal reality, which moved him to write. It was past humiliations or failures, which, he felt, needed to be expressed in literature. The sense of powerlessness which characterized so many of Walser's lower-middle-class protagonists could be at least aesthetically reworked, although it might not necessarily be redeemed. Writing was a way of defending oneself against a hostile world, of forging weapons against the humiliations which were inevitably a part of life in a highly competitive society.[16] It was born of defensiveness and, at best, served as a form of compensation.

Walser chose salesmen and real estate agents as his preferred characters precisely because they felt more keenly than members of other professions that they, as individuals, were exchangeable, even superfluous in a capi-

---

[13] See Alexander Mathäs, *Der Kalte Krieg in der deutschen Literaturkritik: Der Fall Martin Walser* (Bern: Peter Lang, 1992).

[14] Martin Walser, *Dorle and Wolf* (Frankfurt/Main: Suhrkamp, 1987).

[15] See also Stephen Brockmann, *Literature and German Reunification* (Cambridge: Cambridge University Press, 1999), 37–9.

[16] Martin Walser, 'Auskunft zur Person', in *Auskunft*, 71–82; here 74.

talist system. In that, he claimed, they resembled the writer who also had become an essentially replaceable part of the modern economy. From early on in his public life, Walser sought to criticize a conception of the writer as a publicly present and transparent institution or even producer, whose 'success could be reported like the success of the Volkswagen factory'.[17] Walser repudiated the classical gesture of the representative bourgeois character or even national poet by authors like Goethe and Thomas Mann.[18] Instead of 'representing' a type or a sovereign individual, the writer should expose his fragmented, doubtful self and his sentiments, if he wanted to achieve any authenticity in the public sphere. He rejected a cult of the artist as either unique or representative individual. Instead, the author was always fully part of his own society, and through self-observation and the realistic description of his own feelings, could transform these sentiments into social critique. He could never simply provide unmediated 'meaning' in the public sphere – any pretension to do so was merely a subtle way of exercising power.[19] All he could aspire to was writing as a process of self-clarification, and the hope that the realistic description of everyday life in itself harboured meaning. Not least, this hidden meaning was historical, since the everyday and 'the social' were the present expressions of 'the historical'. Others in society might eventually share the meanings subtly articulated by the writer, and only in this limited sense could writing be said to be 'political'. The realistic description of the human deformities exacted by capitalist societies might then eventually help to abolish some of the 'worst conditions of the present'.[20] The influence of the writer in society was thus at best long-term. But precisely because of this invisible, weak influence the writer could come to the conclusion of his own interchangeability and superfluity.

The characteristics of the writer as 'negative' representative, as well as the normative claim to expose a supposedly authentic, 'disempowered' self in the public sphere were in fact specific to what Walser termed the 'inner constitution' of the Federal Republic and, in particular, Walser's position within it. Unapologetically, he claimed that he himself came from 'a petty bourgeois social stratum' and that most of his readers were lower-middle-class.[21] Since it could supposedly be 'theoretically and practically proven that writers could only ever write for their own class', it was only logical

---

[17] Martin Walser, 'Dem Sog ergeben', in *ibid.*, 7–21; here 19.

[18] For Mann's concerns about the dangers of the disempowered self, see Harvey Goldmann, *Politics, Death, and the Devil: Self and Power in Max Weber and Thomas Mann* (Berkeley: University of California Press, 1992).

[19] 'Interview mit Martin Walser (1965)', in *Auskunft*, 22–7; here 22.

[20] *Ibid.*

[21] Martin Walser, 'Realitätserfahrungen im Roman', in *Auskunft*, 31–6; here 33.

that Walser accepted this 'class barrier to the writer' and that all his writings had to come out of his own experiences within the petty bourgeoisie. Any attempts to transcend the class barrier in literary and personal self-redemption were doomed to lead to self-destruction. On the other hand, in this very futile attempt, the writer could demonstrate that in a particular, oppressive class constellation, a life with dignity was simply unliveable. Robert Walser and Kafka, in the heroic act of negating the connection to their class and therefore ultimately negating themselves, had shown through their very failure that a humane existence was impossible for the petty bourgeoisie in a society characterized by bourgeois domination.[22] His affirmation of – or resignation to – his own class opposition was paralleled by Walser's conscious affirmation of provincialism. Since the village had been his original way of being in the world, he felt that his experiences would be more authentic the smaller the circle in which he moved and which he described. Once again, the particular was to be the repository of meaning. The artistic and the private self were in that sense congruous in terms of being socially determined as well as, to some extent, disempowered. And only realism in writing and a certain limited level of authentic self-exposure in the public sphere could preserve this congruence.

This constellation of self, class and writing, however, did not mean that Walser could not also affirm his role as an intellectual. While critics often pointed to an inconsistency between his self-consciously petty bourgeois position, his literary writings, and his stance in the public sphere, Walser argued that one could be an intellectual in any class.[23] He adopted an almost Gramscian notion of the 'organic intellectual', when he claimed that 'I want to help in creating for my class that which it is lacking so much: a sense of its own historical importance'.[24] Walser's view of himself as a quasi-organic intellectual of the petty bourgeoisie, however, seemed to be contradicted by a form of engagement which had little to do with providing the petty bourgeoisie with a class consciousness from within. His support for major political initiatives and particular parties from the mid-1950s onwards seemed to conform more to the classical notion of the intellectual as transcending class boundaries and speaking to – and, more often, for – society as a whole. In the 1950s and 1960s, Walser very much conformed to the role of the intellectual as developing and consolidating a democratic consciousness for the Germans. Even when he subscribed to

---

[22] Martin Walser, 'Weit weg von der Berufskultur', in *Auskunft*, 37–44; here 44.

[23] 'Auskunft zur Person', 72.

[24] *Ibid.*, 73. He adopted an almost defiant stance against his intellectual detractors by claiming 'I do not want to leave my class', and once went so far as to say that 'yes, it provides me with a certain lust, to be a petit bourgeois then'. 'Ein Gespräch', 105.

what he vaguely defined as 'democratic socialism', his critique of West
Germany remained an immanent critique throughout, like Grass and
Habermas emphasizing the importance of the Constitution and admon-
ishing the state to live up to the commitments in the Basic Law. These
commitments, of course, included the goal of reunification, and Walser,
like Grass and most other intellectuals, attacked Adenauer and the official
policies of the government for having betrayed this goal. Therefore,
Walser's conception of himself as the spokesperson of the lower middle
class was rivalled by the conception of the intellectual as, to some
extent, a conscience of the divided nation, and as providing a model of
democratic citizenship in the public sphere. The latter stance did not
necessarily contradict the former, since the universal values instantiated in
the Constitution and Walser's call for social justice could of course embrace
the petty bourgeoisie, while not being limited to it.

Walser, then, was suspicious of the conception of a 'democratic elite'
which Hans Werner Richter had talked about, and, much to Richter's
dismay, called for the 'socialization' and 'democratization' of the *Gruppe 47*
itself in 1964.[25] The 'fool from lake Constance' as Richter has called
him, was even more suspicious of the culture of suspicion itself which
intellectuals of the sceptical generation sought to foster, since, in his
view, it implied unwarranted power for the intellectuals.[26] Putting his
own disempowered self on display was an ingenious way of disclosing
the power which the established intellectuals had illegitimately acquired,
or so Walser thought. But Walser, with his remarkable talent for self-
subversion and ostensible contempt for power, also discovered the power
of his own public powerlessness. Essentially, then, he sought to expose
the contradiction at the heart of democratic intellectuals' effort to democratize from above – but of course this very attempt also occurred 'from
above'.

Walser's suspicion came to be most clearly expressed in a powerful 1960s'
essay 'Draft for a Reproach', in which he criticized himself and his fellow
intellectuals as hypocritical.[27] They were 'idealists without ideals', signing
a political appeal from time to time, but generally complacent about their
powerlessness, even enjoying it. With this situation, Walser contrasted the
possibility that society and the state might actually invite intellectuals to
'cooperate'. In this hypothetical case, Walser predicted, their complacency
would be exposed. While the institutionalized anti-establishment of the
intellectuals in the early Federal Republic did very much 'cooperate' in the

---

[25] Martin Walser, 'Sozialisieren wir die Gruppe 47!', in *Die Zeit*, 3 July 1964.

[26] Hans-Werner Richter to Christian Mayer-Amery, 9 July 1964, in *Briefe*, 507–8; here 507.

[27] Martin Walser, 'Skizze zu einem Vorwurf (1960)', in *Erfahrungen und Leseerfahrungen* (Frank-
furt/Main: Suhrkamp, 1966), 29–32.

development of a democratic consciousness, Walser's self-criticism exuded not just an air of resignation, but also the suspicion that this 'cooperation', in the sense that intellectuals had been given well-defined roles in the public sphere as 'eminent nay-sayers', was precisely the problem. Walser, rather helplessly at this point, instead gestured towards a more authentic form of engagement.

In the late 1960s, Walser's disenchantment with the role of the intellectual as 'model citizen' grew even stronger. He criticized fellow writers who in his view had gone too far in the direction of a pragmatic accommodation of electoral politics. Walser attacked Grass's emphasis on the work of 'democratic nitty-gritty' for the SPD, claiming that the SPD had proven too adaptable to given realities.[28] In 1967, finally leaving behind the consensus about democratic institutions established among members of the sceptical generation, he argued that radical democratization could only be advanced through the threat of revolution: 'Whoever really wants evolution, has to work for the revolution'.[29]

As he moved away from the DKP in the mid-1970s, Walser's criticism of the role of the left-wing intellectual fulfilling a function in the public sphere became more pronounced. In 1980, he claimed that he had always defended himself against the designation as a leftist intellectual which had been externally imposed on him.[30] He argued that one could not consciously *assume* a function like that of the leftist intellectual. The only factor which had finally convinced him that he might indeed be one were the reactions to his views by conservatives.[31] But he himself, Walser claimed, had never done anything but 'come to terms with what happened to his mother, his father . . . and himself'.[32] In that sense, politics, and the experience of being slotted into left or right categories by the public, were an unintended consequence of his reworking of personal experience. But Walser still attempted to square his conception of the almost accidental petty bourgeois representative with the model of the writer as democratic citizen. He claimed that the 'petty bourgeois are also citizens, after all. We are citizens [English in the original], citoyens, and we are democrats if one is employed in a profession in which the historical plays some role'.[33]

[28] Martin Walser, 'Praktiker, Weltfremde und Vietnam (1966)', in Wagenbach (ed.), *Vaterland, Muttersprache*, 235–7.

[29] Martin Walser in response to the 1967 *TLS* article by Enzensberger in 'Ist die Revolution unvermeidlich'.

[30] 'Ein Gespräch in Neu-England', 104.

[31] *Ibid.*

[32] *Ibid.*

[33] *Ibid.*, 105.

Walser's German Concerns: The Politics of Sentimentality

In his early existentialist phase, and his subsequent critique of West German society, Walser had been almost entirely unconcerned about national issues. However, after the erection of the Wall, Walser increasingly came to grapple with Germany's division. And as in the case of Grass, a number of Walser's key commitments were formed in the early to mid-1960s. In particular, they were formed against the backdrop of what he saw as the 'hypocrisy' of official West German policies towards the GDR, and the on-going concerns about a past which most of his fellow citizens sought to repress.

In poems written immediately after the erection of the Wall, Walser, like Grass, suggested that Eastern and Western leaders were equally to blame for the division. The GDR leadership, Walser intimated, was both fearful and 'ideologized', while the West was hypocritical in denying the existence of the GDR as a state and building on an illusory 'policy of strength'. He lamented that the Germans were waiting for other countries to find ways for the Germans to communicate across the intra-German division, since they had lost or refused to develop a common language themselves.

In 1963, taking up the common theme of the 'belated nation', Walser argued that this lack of communication was due to the fact that the Germans had not had a proper chance to develop as a nation.[34] Before they had had an opportunity to become 'national Germans' and construct a proper state for themselves, the 'historical successors of nations', namely supranational ideologies, had become historically dominant. The fact that Germany had not been much of a nation appeared obvious when the country was divided and 'vaccinated' with two different ideologies. Since East and West rapidly grew apart, Walser could claim that 'today Germany no longer exists'.[35] The failure of Germany in the task of nation-building could largely be explained by the bourgeoisie's incapacity to act politically. Like many post-war observers, Walser claimed that because of their religious, inward-looking 'piety', Germans found it difficult to 'act politically, like Englishmen'.[36] Religious zeal had been secularized into anti-communism, which was also more akin to a religion.[37]

The logical corollary of Walser's claim was that even during the Third Reich, Germany had not been a nation, but merely tried to act as one, and had hence become a grotesque nationalist exaggeration. The lamentable,

---

[34] Martin Walser, 'Ein deutsches Mosaik', in *Deutsche Sorgen*, 90–112; here 90.

[35] *Ibid.*, 91.

[36] *Ibid.*, 112.

[37] *Ibid.*

but ultimately positive, result was that at least now, for a terrible price, Germany was protected against demagogues who tried to weld it into a nation, and had even been freed from the need to become a nation. All Germans could offer politically was to overcome their past. In the long run, however, their political weaknesses, or rather, their weakness at politics, could only be dissolved though 'Europeanization': 'The more Europe absorbs us, the more pleasant it will be to be a German'.[38]

In his early engagement with national questions, Walser clung to a number of widespread patterns of thought; he viewed the Germans as almost pathologically apolitical, and the possible escape from their Germanness through Europeanization, which, paradoxically, would also be an affirmation of 'politics' – because Walser implicitly defined politics as an art of the possible – as a reasonable accommodation to realities, which included other countries' fears and memories. This was precisely the reason why Adenauer's stance of non-recognition vis-à-vis the East had been, in Walser's view, 'apolitical'. Anti-communism had closed off room for reasonable maneuver, making enemies eventually act in accordance with the images that had been created of them.[39] Walser repudiated what he saw as the 're-training' of the Germans to treat Communists, rather than Jews and Slavs in the Third Reich, as enemies.

During the Auschwitz trials in the 1960s, Walser affirmed the need to confront the past and accept it as one's own. He was concerned that the Germans were trying to escape from history through judicial means, by isolating the 'subjective brutalities' of a small number of 'beasts', i.e. the camp guards and commanders. Instead of containing the past by blaming a few individuals, Walser advocated a specifically 'political reading' of the Auschwitz trials in the sense of refocusing on the state as the collective agent of the Germans, which had implicated all citizens. Consequently, 'everyone belonged in some partial way to the causes of Auschwitz'.[40] Walser effectively employed concepts associated with a conservative German state tradition, namely the identity of state and *Volk*, against the escape from responsibility and the past also advocated by conservatives. He also reaffirmed national solidarity, even with the perpetrators, so as to instill a sense of collective responsibility. Thus, he supported Jaspers's notion of collective political responsibility for the past.

Walser, then, turned more than ever before to 'national concerns' in the late 1970s. In fact, part of the reason why he had become disillusioned with the DKP was their lack of a truly home-grown, West German perspective. Walser could only accept an immanent West German critique, since out-

[38] *Ibid.*

[39] Martin Walser, 'Unser Auschwitz', in *Deutsche Sorgen*, 187–202; here 195–6.

[40] *Ibid.*, 200.

siders could never truly understand the situation in the country, while all the DKP was capable of was the mechanical repetition of official GDR positions. In other words, Walser sought to escape an intra-German version of *Lagerdenken*.

In this effort, he adopted his by now familiar stance of defiance: just as the writer was always defending himself, Walser now admonished the Germans, 'we do not have to accept what has happened'.[41] What looked like 'fate', i.e. the existence of two countries, was the result of a 'catastrophe', whose causes 'one could know'. But like the humiliations which had been the central concern of his literary work, Walser found it 'unbearable' that 'German history — as terrible as it was lately — should end in a product of catastrophe'.[42] He demanded that one counteract what only looked like fate. Defiance, however, could only be effected if the Germans allied themselves with the 'course of history' itself, and if they became capable of 'letting the historical process work for' themselves by 'injecting' their interest into this very process.[43] This ability was predicated on a historical consciousness and a 'historical desire' which the Germans had to preserve against the anti-nationalist and anti-historical language prevalent in the West German public sphere. In other words, it had to be cultivated in private, protected from the world of conformist opinions and the fast-moving, superficial realm of 'current affairs':

> If all of us only know what we know from the current flow of public opinion, then soon we will be only bright little lamps whose light and colour the powerful manipulate to illuminate their own interests. If someone has perceived the German problem from 1955 until 1975 only as the consumer of the so-called media, then today, if he has chosen conservative sources, he is waiting ... for the ... day of reunification, or he is, if he has been kept up to date by the liberal media, ready to dance forever as a drugged and dazed pragmatic around an open wound.[44]

Walser sought to reject both the official and hypocritical conservative language of 'reunification', and the left-wing tendency to accept the status quo. He criticized both as ultimately artificial, whereas the elemental 'need for Germany' had to be preserved in private hearts and minds uncontaminated by public discourse. This 'need' could be transferred from the consciousness of one generation to that of another, as a spiritual force which

[41] 'Eine aktuelle Aufgabe', in *Deutsche Sorgen*, 206–8; here 206.

[42] *Ibid.*

[43] *Ibid.*

[44] *Ibid.*, 207.

would be particularly replenished through the immersion in the cultural products of a previously undivided Germany. Walser's suspicions about the public sphere and its almost inherent lack of authenticity now combined with the idea of defiance vis-à-vis the 'unacceptable', as well as the need to articulate a 'deficiency', which had animated so much of his literary work. All were suffused with the language of private feeling, which remained the repository of authentic self-expression against both public argumentation in the name of reason and what seemed like 'political realism' supported by the 'facts' — the very facts, which, in the late 1960s, he had still brought to bear against 'feelings'.[45] His claims seemed naively defiant and politically innocuous at the same time, though in fact they were couched in absolute terms. Feelings, after all, brooked no compromise:

> But I feel an elemental need to be allowed to travel to Saxony and Thuringia under completely different circumstances than the ones which dominate in the present . . . Germany cannot be eliminated from my historical consciousness . . . I refuse to take part in the liquidation of history. Within me, a different Germany still has a chance.[46]

While Walser presented his thoughts in the language of the intensely personal and emotional, his pronouncements in the public sphere were after all a call for his fellow citizens to preserve the historical consciousness which kept the 'wound' of Germany open. It was, ultimately, a call to national participation. In a manner which seemed to be sheer idealism at the time, Walser, once called an *Empfindungspragmatiker* [a pragmatist of emotions], went so far as to say that 'the historical process directs itself according to one's need. Yes, it is even created out of this need. Consequently, it is really up to us'.[47] For now, preserving one's 'need' and resisting the 'powerful', which essentially had to mean the superpowers, remained a 'holding operation', which had to be encouraged by the poets — a hardly surprising choice, given that Walser's ultimate justification for his stance was cultural. As in Grass's conception of the *Kulturnation*, poets and artists had to create the 'spiritual space' in which the two Germanies could approach each other, making themselves the citizens of a utopian unified Germany-yet-to-come.

What role did Walser assign to the National Socialist past in his advocacy of a national, democratic, socialist future? He claimed that a rebirth of fascism in its National Socialist version was simply impossible. But he

---

[45] 'Auskunft über den Protest', in Martin Walser, *Zauber und Gegenzauber: Aufsätze und Gedichte* (Eggingen: Edition Isele, 1995), 35–7.

[46] 'Eine alltuelle Aufgabe', 207–8.

[47] *Ibid.*, 208.

conceded that a 'fascist tradition' had survived which could be activated in different antidemocratic disguises, whether as a fetishistic 'cult of the body', a return to the atavistic, or as plain narcissism.[48] Not surprisingly, it was in fact the intellectuals, Walser claimed, who were most likely to fall victim to this fascist style. But ultimately everyone, rather than a few prominent political figures exposed as former Nazis, harboured a fascist psychological potential. Like much of the '68 Left, and, to a lesser extent, Habermas and Grass, Walser claimed that 'we are still living under conditions which could produce fascism'. Consequently, the Germans in particular were called upon to show fascism as what it really was: 'a fall from history'. [49] Walser thus sought to firmly demarcate 'history', the driving force of his arguments in favour of the nation, against fascism, claiming that fascism was in fact the opposite of history.

Having come under increasing criticism for his supposedly 'national turn' in the 1970s, Walser took stock in 1979, wondering publicly whether he had in fact become part of the conservative *Tendenzwende*. Once again exposing his feelings in a seemingly self-critical manner, Walser claimed that he might well have been a hypocrite in the public sphere in the past, but that he actually thought this hypocrisy to have had more beneficial effects than his current 'moral fatigue'.[50] But, with his typical gesture of self-conscious public vulnerability, the 'prisoner of his feelings' admitted he could not avoid concluding that

> if for years one, as a co-worker in the construction of public opinion, aims at a public mode of expression (as opposed to a narcissistic one), there is the danger that this mode of expression becomes a thing for its own sake, and has less and less to do with the one who is practicing it.[51]

In short, Walser's public mode of expression had become inauthentic and deteriorated into a kind of 'knee-jerk' opinion-formation. He no longer recognized himself in his public, 'artificial' opinions which were part of a routine administered by powerful German 'mandarins'.[52] Against this dominant public opinion, intellectuals like Walser himself accumulated that which could not be publicly articulated, *das Verschwiegene*, which amounted to one's private 'samisdat'.[53] Ideally, the public sphere would

---

[48] 'Unsere historische Schuldigkeit', in *Deutsche Sorgen*, 210–2.

[49] *Ibid.*, 212.

[50] 'Händedruck mit Gespenstern', in *Deutsche Sorgen*, 213–27.

[51] *Ibid.*, 214.

[52] *Ibid.*, 216.

[53] *Ibid.*

allow for the confession of contradictions, rather than the administration of uniform opinions. In his vision, contradictions had to become part of the public sphere not least because German reality itself was so contradictory. Walser, once again in what seemed an intensely personal claim, argued that

> I do not believe that as a German of my generation one can have an undisturbed relationship with reality. Our national reality itself is disturbed. And if something as crucial as that is disturbed, it is possible that one does not gain real confidence in anything which is derived from this reality. What I lack above all, is confidence. But it appears to me that this is not because of me but because of present conditions. The conditions of the nation. They do not allow for confidence. This nation, as a divided one, is a permanent source of a destruction of confidence.[54]

Thus, the disempowered self which Walser had previously portrayed in his writings as a victim of capitalist competition now suffered from a 'national deficiency', and was directly projected onto the public sphere. To preserve any authenticity apart from the 'opinion business', Walser had to identify with the national 'contradiction between the two German parts' and confess his 'weakness and misery and helplessness'.[55]

Walser had previously employed the argument against the Weimar mandarins, the argument so crucial for post-war intellectuals to create an identity as democratic citizens, but now turned it against West German intellectuals themselves. Where Habermas and most other intellectuals had perceived a difficult, but ultimately successful rupture with the mandarin tradition, Walser saw continuity from 1918 to the present. He claimed that 'our national' helplessness was due to the intellectuals' alienation both from their history and from the people, i.e. *das Volk* whose very name seemed to have been discredited by the National Socialists. *Das Volk* were of course primarily workers, but of course even more so, the petty bourgeois despised by the intellectuals. Looking back on the Weimar Republic, Walser complained that 'where the intellectuals had Roaring Twenties, workers and petty bourgeois had a hopeless battle against the new incursions of a capitalism which had finally become international'.[56] The intellectuals, while of crucial importance in causing '1933', had escaped responsibility and blamed a supposedly 'fanaticized' petty bourgeoisie instead.

[54] *Ibid.*, 219–20.

[55] *Ibid.*, 220 and 221.

[56] *Ibid.*, 223.

Moreover, Walser now claimed that it was in fact an individualist, liberal society, hostile to religion and anything supra-individual, and its intellectuals which were responsible for 'repressing Auschwitz'.[57] To 'cope' with Auschwitz, one needed a sense of cooperation, solidarity and ultimately a feeling of common nationality. Only then could the Germans turn back again to their true 'national tasks'.[58] Walser suggested that ultimately nothing but the re-infusion of religion could help in coping with the past, but that the 'cultural apparatus', with Adorno as its high priest, had itself become something like a worldly church which blessed 'historical deficiency' among its adherents and condemned those who clung to the 'supra-individual' – whether in the form of God or the nation. But only the nation, God and history could remedy a situation in which the Germans saw themselves as the victims of 'processes', which Walser presumably identified yet again with 'international capitalism' and the 'victorious powers'. Liberal selves supposedly empowered by emancipation were in fact incapable of carrying the burden of the past on their own. Since Auschwitz had been collectively committed, as Walser had already claimed in 'Our Auschwitz', it could only be borne collectively. Shifting to an argument which came close to Jaspers's notion of metaphysical guilt, he argued that the supra-individual and transcendent would allow weak individuals to 'cope with the past'.[59]

Thus, by the late 1970s, Walser had finally fused his critique of the post-war public sphere with a full-blown advocacy of the feelings of the *Volk* as channeled through his own 'needs'. But the feelings he 'authentically' articulated in fact included a resentment of other nations grounded in the lack of German self-confidence as a nation – as Walser put it, 'I belong to a generation which was still born in Germany. As soon as I experience another nation, resentment awakens inside me'.[60] Walser in that sense had collapsed his conceptions of the writer as 'organic intellectual' of the petty bourgeoisie into that of the writer who felt a 'deficiency', and 'resisted'. This stance then in turn became identical with that of the intellectual who articulated his authentic feelings despite the pressures of a public sphere controlled by mandarins. All three conceptions now revolved around the nation – or rather, its absence. The 'lack of nation' constituted the primary deficiency and enabled Germans to 'resist' and redirect historical processes, but the memory of the nation also grounded the historical consciousness from which feelings and the 'need to overcome' the division arose. In the act of making these conceptions consistent, however, he had also

---

[57] *Ibid.*, 224.

[58] *Ibid.*

[59] See also the ambiguously titled 'Auschwitz und kein Ende', in *Deutsche Sorgen*, 228–34; here 231.

[60] 'Deutsche Gedanken über französisches Glück', in *Deutsche Sorgen*, 235–45; here 235.

resurrected patterns of thought which had conservative, and sometimes even antisemitic overtones. The opposition of the authentic private self and an untainted *Innerlichkeit* versus a superficial, even hypocritical public sphere was a staple of German thought from pietism to Heidegger and his contempt for the *Man* [the They] i.e. the inauthentic public with its shallowness and all-pervasive conventional wisdom. The notion of the authentic *Volk* versus the hedonistic, internationally oriented intellectuals, rather than being an accurate description of the 1920s, had itself been an ideological weapon of right-wing intellectuals in the Weimar Republic. And the articulation of private feelings that the disempowered self was incapable of rejecting, lest it succumb to the hypocrisy of the public sphere, was itself rooted in German pietist and quietist traditions. The emotional mode of what *was* after all a form of public intellectual engagement was also an effective self-immunization from argument. Not surprisingly, Walser was heavily attacked once he had presented his entire emotional-cum-intellectual edifice of a new German nationalism. And not surprisingly either, he retreated into a stance of, above all, the *victim* of the mandarins, who spoke for the victimized nation and who still dared to publicly expose his vulnerability.

Defending Self and Nation: History against Politics

Throughout the 1980s, the basic characteristics of the position Walser had outlined toward the end of the 1970s became more pronounced. Like many intellectuals on the Left in the early 1980s, Walser saw the Germans as being in need of liberation from both superpowers. In 1984, he wished the Germans a 'Polish persistence so that we survive the division nationally'.[61] At the same time, Walser's resentment of the victorious powers, East and West, increased, as he claimed that 'people who relish being Englishmen, Frenchmen and Italians, guard with relish that the German, cut in two, remains divided into halves. The right to self-determination, which of all human rights is now seen as the highest everywhere – the Germans should not have it'.[62]

Walser also came to advance a new interpretation of twentieth-century history. All great powers had been equally responsible for the First World War. Hitler, he claimed, was 'entirely a creation of Versailles', since the Germans had been 'condemned to feelings of inferiority' by the victorious powers of the First World War.[63] Just as fascism had been opposed to

---

[61] 'Deutsches Stilleben', in *Deutsche Sorgen*, 246–8; here 246.

[62] *Ibid.*

[63] 'Tartuffe weiß, wer er ist', in *Deutsche Sorgen*, 249–51; here 250.

history, it was now opposed to the nation: after the First World War, 'the nation had forgotten itself'.[64] After the Second World War, the victorious powers had once again 'not reacted more reasonably'.[65] The division had been a mere 'punishment', instead of the necessary 'rehabilitation', and remained an illegitimate 'intervention'.[66] Alternatively, Walser claimed that it was simply a result of the Cold War. In any case, it was not a historically or morally legitimate answer to the Third Reich. It was, in itself, deeply ahistorical: division, he argued, was the 'opposite of development, and, consequently, history'.[67] Unlike in the case of Austria, then, the division did not even allow the two Germanies to 'develop' a new and proper sense of self.

Walser now also sought to repudiate his earlier claim that Germany as such had never existed, or only existed as a patchwork of principalities. Privileging sentiment again, he argued that the 'longing for the nation' had been there much longer than an actual German state. In general, he had come to the view that for now the nation as such was 'the historically most powerful phenomenon', powerful in a 'geological, not political sense'.[68] Consequently, *Kulturnation* or even *Sportnation* [sports nation] were at best feeble forms of compensation, and, in the worst case, artificial constructions espoused by intellectuals and politicians as supposedly 'reasonable' solutions to the German predicament. Walser therefore opposed 'history' to present politics in a way consistent with his definition of 'politics' from the 1960s: politics was indeed the art of the possible and the seemingly reasonable, given present conditions. But 'history' now needed precisely to be defended against politics, because it contained a commonsense national continuity and the suggestion of what was 'historically' normal, i.e. an undivided Germany, which, from the point of view of politics, could only appear as 'unreasonable' in the present. Finally, Walser's 'psychosocial' argument about a 'lack of self-confidence' was sharpened into the claim that maybe Germany had lost a sense of self altogether. Revealingly, Walser compared the country to a patient who needed to be told by doctors who he really was. Thus, the 'injured' victim Germany, suffering from historical amnesia, could only perform empty rituals in the public sphere, rather than articulating how it felt about its history.[69]

---

[64] 'Deutschländer oder Brauchen wir eine Nation? Ein Gespräch über Staaten, Nation, Heimat und Literatur', in *Deutsche Sorgen*, 255–75; here 263.

[65] 'Tartuffe weiß wer er ist', 250.

[66] 'Über Deutschland reden', 412.

[67] *Ibid.*

[68] *Ibid.*, 426.

[69] 'Tartuffe weiß, wer er ist', 250–1.

Walser's tendency of basing arguments on emotions, as well as an articulation of what Walser thought were everyday experiences, also became more pronounced in conflicts with his intellectual opponents. He claimed that from a 'commonsense point of view' it was obvious that one was German, and that one only had to travel abroad to realize this. In 1986, when discussing the consequences of Yalta, he claimed that he had to say clearly 'what has happened there, is not acceptable, cannot be normalized', simply adding, with an air of resignation, 'me with my feelings'.[70] In the same vein, he defended memory against rationalist incursions, arguing that his 'memory could not be instructed with knowledge acquired in the meantime'.[71] The memory of a childhood during which Auschwitz had happened elsewhere, of necessity remained innocent. Walser, consistent with this position, identified himself as a 'historicist' precisely at a time when the legitimacy of historicization was at the heart of the *Historikerstreit*. In response to the debate, Walser claimed that he could contain the opinions of 'both Hillgruber and Habermas', since the German question could not be grasped from either Left or Right, but remained a common national task which transcended political divisions.

Finally, Walser renewed his critique of the public sphere during the 1980s: for Walser, opinions had become almost entirely independent of individuals, and were producing further opinions without any place for personal experience. Consequently, the disjunction between public articulation and authentic individual belief, which Walser had first suspected in the 1970s, had become even more serious. He compared a more authentic language still existent in East Germany, which contained genuine, involuntary memory, with a Western language addicted to judging and to making political statements. And 'the judgement' it was most 'addicted to' was of course the claim that the division was reasonable. This was again the realm of 'opinion', which once, in hisCommunist days, had simply been a function of capital, but which Walser now came to define more personally: '*opinion* may be called that content, which is represented in the sentence more through the will of the writer than through something concrete'.[72] The contrast was once again an authentic language which contained a peculiar German sensibility, and, in all of its texture, 'history'.[73] From this culturally pessimistic perspective, the West Germans were 'technicist-civilizationist-avantgardish', tropes which Walser seemed to have retrieved in an unreconstructed manner from earlier German conservative cultural critiques in the twentieth century.[74]

---

[70] 'Deutschländer oder Brauchen wir eine Nation?', 264–5.

[71] 'Über Deutschland reden', 406.

[72] *Ibid.*, 424 and 'Wahlgedanken'.

[73] *Ibid.*, 425.

[74] 'Das Sonntagsgespräch', in *Auskunft*, 182–91; here 185.

Nevertheless, the reactions to Walser's stance also highlighted some of the rules and rigidities which had come to characterize the intellectual field of the 1980s. The polarizing power of thinking in camps fully applied to Walser, who was now slotted into the right, rather than the left camp, and, after a while, defiantly adopted the label himself.[75] Even with regard to his 'democratic socialism' which he had espoused earlier in his career, Walser had been eager to exempt his thought from the logic which the Cold War imposed on many intellectuals. Just because the pressure to perform was even more pronounced in the East, this did not mean that there should be a taboo on criticizing this inhumane pressure in the West. However, a nuanced and balanced position which Walser had articulated with regard to democratic socialism and the national question could not be accommodated on the intellectual field. Rather than exposing some of the resentment and dubious historical assumptions underlying Walser's stance, his engagement with the nation was rejected by many on the Left – especially among the younger generation who had only known life in the Federal Republic – as nationalist *per se*.

Walser's Triumph (and on-going German Concerns): The *Volk* vindicated

As the East German Revolution gathered momentum, it seemed that Walser's positions were vindicated one by one. Already in October 1989, he perceived fellow intellectuals as sidelined, since for them 'an undivided Germany was either the least important or the least desired' goal. More importantly, the intellectual and emotional capacities of Walser's cherished *Volk* were confirmed: 'The *Volk* exists. That has now been proven'.[76] In December 1989, Walser could claim that 'we have experienced that the democratic means of expression of the *demonstration* is capable of unexpected precision. Hundreds of thousands, i.e the masses, have expressed themselves more truthfully and more precisely, and therefore more correctly, than all the intellectuals'.[77] And most importantly, 'history in the making' had triumphed over a 'politics' constrained by what had only just seemed reasonable.[78]

He also found that the intellectual debate surrounding unification confirmed the chararcteristics of German discourse which Walser had been criticizing. Referring indirectly to Grass, he charged that the debate only

---

[75] For instance 'Gedächtnis verloren – Verstand verloren: Jurek Becker antwortet auf Martin Walser', in *Die Zeit*, 18 November 1988.

[76] 'Deutsche Sorgen I', in *Deutsche Sorgen*, 430–8; here 435.

[77] *Ibid.*, 431.

[78] *Ibid.*, 433.

revealed that with the German question, 'we', i.e. the intellectuals, tended to quickly adopt positions chosen so as to enable a wholesale condemnation of those thinking differently, rather than with regard to substance.[79] Walser himself engaged in the substantive debate only to a limited extent. The correct course of action, i.e. self-determination and 'the formation of a national collective or *Verantwortungsgemeinschaft*' to take responsibility for the past, seemed self-evident to him. The question was rather how to make the 'self-evident self-evident': 'This seems to be the hardest'.[80] Apart from this articulation of the historically obvious, Walser could remain content with the fact that for once, 'German history was going well'.[81] Subsequently, he confirmed what his relatively reticent stance vis-à-vis actual policies had indicated: in 1993 he insisted that 'nobody in 1989 has made a better proposal than Helmut Kohl. Nobody!'.[82]

However, while German history might for once have had a happy ending, this did not mean that the public sphere had become any less distorting. If anything, Walser's criticisms shifted from denouncing a politics which had sacrificed history, to a more elaborated (and seemingly also more resigned) critique of his fellow intellectuals. He charged that with the modern media, consciousness had become entirely the site of clashing opinions, and therefore 'anaesthetized'.[83] Opinions almost automatically led to a form of self-righteousness, since they divided the world of other opinions into right and wrong. Opinions lived less off their actual content than their gestures, and the gesture of condemning someone else was the most appropriate gesture of all for opinions. Opinions, which did not insist on being right, were actually not opinions, but lived 'experience'. Not surprisingly, neither the writer nor the *Volk* needed 'theory and opinion'.[84] Thus, what had started out as doubts about his own authenticity within the public sphere in the late 1970s, had become a full-scale critique of the public sphere as such in 1990. Where Walser had once strongly believed in the importance of the public sphere as a *bürgerliche* achievement, he now admitted: 'For a while I believed that public opinion was something with which a democracy questioned its own legitimacy through a process of self-examination, thereby in fact achieving legitimacy. Now I sometimes already believe that it is an entertainment industry'.[85]

---

[79] *Ibid.*, 434–5.

[80] *Ibid.*, 437.

[81] *Ibid.*, 438.

[82] 'Deutsche Sorgen II', in *Deutsche Sorgen*, 453–67; here 462.

[83] 'Vormittag eines Schriftstellers', in *Deutsche Sorgen*, 439–52; here 439.

[84] *Ibid.*, 446.

[85] *Ibid.*, 448.

Walser increasingly articulated an almost Burkean conservatism, in which experience and the common sense of the people opposed the 'rationalism' of the intellectuals. At the same time, he adopted a gesture of resignation, since he saw himself as the victim of the very intellectuals purveying 'opinions'. In other words, where the disempowered self had once been the symbol of the fate of the petty bourgeoisie and then the nation at large, Walser now identified his own supposedly disempowered, doubtful self as persecuted by the left-liberal intellectual powers-that-be. He never denied that he himself remained an intellectual in the public sphere purveying his own opinion, but claimed that poetry and inwardness provided escape routes from the inauthentic world of opinions. He gestured towards Botho Strauß as a writer who articulated a semi-public sensibility beyond intellectual self-righteousness. Especially Strauß's 1985 poem *Diese Erinnerung an einen, der nur einen Tag zu Gast War* [This Memory of One, Who was Only a Guest for a Day] produced not just a 'feeling for history', but also a 'confidence in history'.[86] This confidence was shared by Walser, for whom the 'velvet' East German Revolution had been *das liebste Politische* [the dearest political], 'as long as I have lived'. But, alluding to Habermas, he claimed that for the 'democratic-enlightened-socialists', it had been 'DM nationalism'. In that sense, for all his self-proclaimed and self-conscious doubt, Walser not only claimed to be truly in touch with the *Volk*, but also to be the only genuine intellectual, if the intellectual was one to think for himself, rather than automatically to deliver opinions. Since the chief characteristic of the 1990s supposedly was the erection of taboos in the service of enlightenment, the genuine intellectual could only break these taboos to stay true to himself — after all, Germany was not a 'negro state of the nineteenth century'.[87] It was only logical, then, that Walser would also be intellectually persecuted. Implicitly comparing himself to East European dissidents, he had been and remained one of the 'samizdat Germans'.[88]

Postscript: Martin Walser, Skinheads and German Jews — Politicizing Victor Klemperer

In the early 1990s, reacting to the rise of skinhead violence in unified Germany, Walser argued that it had been the 'neglect of the national by all of us' which had left national questions to neo-Nazi ideologues, when,

---

[86] *Ibid.*, 451. See also Botho Strauß, *Diese Erinnerung an einen, der nur einen Tag zu Gast War* (Munich: Hanser, 1985).

[87] 'Über freie und unfreie Rede', in *Deutsche Sorgen*, 468–85; here 485, and 'Tabus sind gefährlicher als ich: Ein Gespräch mit Sven Michaelsen', in Rainer Weiss (ed.), *'Ich habe ein Wunschpotential'*, *Gespräche mit Martin Walser* (Frankfurt/Main: Suhrkamp, 1998), 47–54; here 50.

[88] 'Deutsche Sorgen II', 463.

of course, the Nazis had already betrayed the nation once. Rather than adopting a policy of 'confrontation' which the left-wing media favoured, Walser wanted *private* communication with the youngsters who had been excluded from public discourse. Rather than making the problem a prey for party politics and self-righteous intellectuals 'drunk on opinions', Walser argued that it was a national task for all Germans to reincorporate the right-wing radicals. And rather than punishing them with rationalist opinions, the intellectuals were to admit some of their own doubts and powerlessness along the lines that Walser's depiction of the disempowered self had suggested. Powerlessness was a precondition for real communication – a position which Walser indirectly admonished Habermas for failing to live up to. But since it was once again 'up to us' to solve the national crisis, powerlessness was, paradoxically, also a precondition for resuming the subject position which unification had reinstated for the Germans. However, even if the Germans had now returned to 'history' as a national subject and even if 'German history was going well', the question of how to treat the past remained. For Walser, reverting yet again to a view indebted to Jaspers, successive generations would inherit collective responsibility, but not collective guilt. Ideally, they would also cease to examine each other's conscience in the public sphere, and allow individuals to come to terms with their conscience in private. In that sense, he decisively discarded the second component of Jaspers's philosophy: the emphasis on public communication.

Arguably, however, the final reconciliation, so to speak, between Germans, their nation and their history, had to be accomplished through an engagement with the Jews and their fate at German hands: once again, the German question could only be answered, if the Jewish question which was nested within it, found an answer, too. Walser attempted his answer in his *laudatio* on Victor Klemperer in November 1995.[89] Walser clearly identified with Klemperer and his mode of expression, which supposedly was as full of self-doubt as was Walser's. Because of the scrupulousness which went with this self-doubt, Klemperer had achieved a level of precision in his expression, which, like the *Volk's* demonstrations in 1989, acquired a normative dimension. Because he had also always articulated his private doubts, his writings had ceased to be private and now achieved an authentic mode of expression in the public sphere. Klemperer, in short, could be trusted; he had created confidence through an authentic mode of

[89] The diaries which the Jewish professor of romance languages Victor Klemperer had secretly kept during the Third Reich caused a literary sensation in mid-1990s Germany, since they were seen as probably the best record of daily life (and discrimination) under the Nazis. Klemperer was posthumously awarded the *Geschwister Scholl Prize* in 1995. There was also criticism of Klemperer, however, for his anti-Zionism and his open cultural contempt for the *Ostjuden*. See *I Shall Bear Witness: The Diaries of Victor Klemperer 1933–41* and *The Diaries of Victor Klemperer 1942–45*, trans. Martin Chalmers (London: Weidenfeld and Nicolson, 1998, 1999).

expression.[90] But substantially, what could Klemperer be trusted to have articulated? A 'trust in German culture' and an affirmation of his 'Germanness', despite everything which the Nazis were inflicting on him and his wife, since, as Klemperer put it in his diaries, '"the Nazis are un-German"'.[91] Affirming Germanness had been a matter for Klemperer's individual conscience and a free choice. Walser — through Klemperer as a mouthpiece — insinuated that Zionists, at least on one level, were as much wedded to the determinism of blood as the Nazis. Klemperer was also said to have shared Walser's conception that without '1919' there would have been no '1933', and that any determinism about the inevitable 'road to Auschwitz' was a travesty of actual German–Jewish history. But Klemperer's diaries also taught the present that one should only be responsible for one's own conscience, and that all those now judging the East Germans' actions under the GDR and the Nazi regime were exhibiting a self-righteousness which lacked Klemperer's moral precision.

With Klemperer's example Walser sought to recover a basic trust in German culture itself but also the need for a privatization of conscience so that the newly united national community could be reconciled with itself. Not surprisingly, this longing for an untainted German culture 'obscenely harmonized' with Jewish culture came under sharp attack from Habermas.[92] What Walser's attempt at claiming Klemperer showed once again was that a recovery of Klemperer's *Deutschpatriotismus*, an affirmation of being German which — at least in Walser's conception — still contained space for doubt, seemed to depend on removing the 'filter of Auschwitz', through which according to intellectuals like Habermas, all cultural traditions had to pass.

Walser, Germany's consummate contrarian, ever irritating and ever irritable, had come a long way from being a democratic socialist and subscribing to the ideal of the intellectual as democratic citizen to the advocacy of the disempowered, doubtful self as the only authentic articulation of the writer in public. The man once opposed to *re*unification, had now become a 'samizdat German' who, because of his advocacy of national unity, felt persecuted by the media and rationalist intellectuals. But this strange trajectory was only partly due to Walser shifting the weight between the various roles and positions which had been implicit in his complex stance from the beginning. It was also due to the rigidities — and

---

[90] 'Das Prinzip Genauigkeit: Über Victor Klemperer', in *Deutsche Sorgen*, 565–601; here 585.

[91] Klemperer quoted by Walser in *ibid.*, 579.

[92] Jürgen Habermas, 'Aufgeklärte Ratlosigkeit: Warum die Politik ohne Perspektiven ist', in *Frankfurter Rundschau*, 30 November 1995.

sometimes hypocrisies — which over time came to characterize left-wing public discourse, and which Walser often highlighted through his seemingly innocuous recourse to sentimentality. However, Walser's trajectory also left a decidedly ambiguous legacy, which younger right-wing intellectuals could easily appropriate. He had taken on the role of the victim of a left-wing intellectual media conspiracy which was to be further developed by New Right intellectuals. He had drawn emphatic normative distinctions between a 'historical sentiment', national language and everyday experience on the one hand, and politics, 'unhistorical fascism' and the alienated intellectuals on the other. And the very 'return to history' which Walser had celebrated in somewhat sentimental terms, was to become a clarion call for those wanting to change the course of German foreign policy. Potentially, the sentiments which Walser had articulated couched in the language of the doubtful, disempowered self, could serve to re-empower the nation-state Walser had longed for against all odds. However, as I shall discuss in chapter eight, he was ultimately to be taken to task for this position by the official representative of Jews in Germany. What was seen as Walser's 'intellectual nationalism' and his one-sided appropriation of German Jews like Victor Klemperer for the sake of patriotism was not to go undisputed.

6 Karl Heinz Bohrer: Recovering Romanticism and Aestheticizing the State

*Die Cultur und der Staat — man betrüge sich hierüber nicht — sind
Antagonisten ... Das Eine lebt vom Andern, das Eine gedeiht auf
Unkosten des Anderen. Alle grossen Zeiten der Cultur sind politische
Niedergangszeiten: was gross ist im Sinn der Cultur, War unpolitisch, selbst
antipolitisch ...*

Culture and the State — one should not deceive oneself about this — are
antagonists ... One lives off the other, one flourishes at the expense of
the other. All great periods of culture are times of political decline: what
was great culturally speaking, was apolitical, even antipolitical ...

Friedrich Nietzsche, *Götzen-Dämmerung: Was den Deutschen abgeht*

Karl Heinz Bohrer, professor of German literature at Bielefeld University,
journalist and editor of the 'German Journal for European Thought',
Merkur, has become one of the most influential intellectuals in post-unification Germany — as well as 'the most important thinker of the aesthetic'
in the German-speaking world, as one critic put it.[1] In particular, he has
often been portrayed as the 'mastermind' behind the 1990 German
Literaturstreit. The dispute had been set off by the younger critics Ulrich
Greiner of *Die Zeit* and Frank Schirrmacher of the *Frankfurter Allgemeine Zeitung* who attacked the East German writer Christa Wolf for
having indirectly supported the regime.[2] More generally, the critics dismissed most of German post-war literature, East *and* West, as sentimental
and ideological, and called into question the role of the West German intellectual as providing a model of critical citizenship. In the *Literaturstreit*,
older writers like Grass, Walter Jens and Stefan Heym, who contended that
a witch hunt had been unleashed in the Republic's *Feuilletons*, often

---

[1] Franz Schuh, 'Der letzte Ästhet: Zu den Schriften Karl Heinz Bohrers', in *Die Zeit*, 2 April 1998.

[2] On the *Literaturstreit* and other literary consequences of unification, see Stephen Brockmann's
excellent *Literature and German Reunification*. The reason for not dealing here with the *Literaturstreit* as such is that, unlike in Bohrer's case, the positions of Schirrmacher and Greiner had no
immediate implications for conceptions of German national identity or politics in general — which
is not to deny that their interventions were themselves eminently political.

pointed to Bohrer as the sinister spirit behind the 'campaign', and many academic observers have followed them in this assessment.

The subject of this chapter, however, will not be to what extent the critics' arguments showed affinities with Bohrer's aesthetics. Rather, I seek to demonstrate how Bohrer seized on German unification as an opportunity to repeat his cultural critique of the Federal Republic and advocate unification as a remedy for its cultural shortcomings. Bohrer's cultural critique of the West Germany of the 1980s, however, was itself rooted in a peculiar and provocative philosophical stance on the proper relation between aesthetics and politics which he had been developing since the late 1960s. From his first major political interventions with regard to the student rebellion onwards, Bohrer insisted on a strict demarcation between aesthetics and politics, and at the same time subverted this very distinction by welcoming aesthetic renewal as a precondition for exposing and emphasizing the particular quality of the political. The evolution of Bohrer's thought has partly paralleled and partly overlapped with French poststructuralist and Anglo-American pragmatist and postmodern perspectives, in particular the position of Richard Rorty. The complex conceptual structure advanced by Bohrer, however, cannot simply be collapsed into either of these strands of contemporary theorizing. His specific aim has been the recovery of peculiar German traditions, in particular traditions conventionally labeled as 'dark' and 'irrational', for a German brand of what in Bohrer's terminology amounts to 'modernism', rather than 'postmodernism'. Partly for the tactical goal of provoking the liberal *juste milieu*, Bohrer has drawn on the early German Romantics, Nietzsche and the French Surrealists in order to develop his brand of literary criticism. He has consistently rejected conventional historical analogies and labels; instead, he has sought to 'shock' what appears to be his theoretical enemy, the liberal post-war intelligentsia, by playing with a self-consciously 'conservative revolutionary' vocabulary. Not surprisingly, this aesthetic theory has been charged with 'neoconservatism', just as many postmodern philosophers have often been reproached with neoconservatism, most prominently by Habermas. However, unlike in the case of other scholars whose political positions might be quite arbitrarily related to their literary criticism, Bohrer's aesthetic theories paved the way for a certain stance towards politics: recovering Romanticism as a model of modernity became a precondition for his political call to aestheticize the state, and, at the same time, defend the autonomy of the political from moral considerations.[5]

---

[5] However, I shall not here provide a critique of Bohrer's aesthetics as such. To put it schematically, the most common objection to his aesthetics has been that the self-referential purity he advocates is simply unattainable, and that his notion of 'suddenness' cannot be collapsed into the aesthetic moment as such. See for instance Martin Seel, *Die Kunst der Entzweiung: Zum Begriff der ästhetischen Rationalität* (Frankfurt/Main: Suhrkamp, 1985), 55–61.

In this chapter, I first outline Bohrer's position on aesthetics, then analyze his cultural-cum-political critique of West Germany and finally examine his stance vis-à-vis German unification. After analyzing his pro-unification position, I demonstrate how Bohrer's diagnosis of West German 'provincialism' and his call for the autonomy of the political became sources of concepts and arguments for the Right in post-unification Germany.

Arguing for the Autonomy of the Aesthetic

From his time in the late 1960s as editor of the literary section of the *Frankfurter Allgemeine Zeitung*, Bohrer has been preoccupied with the separation of life and literature, art and non-art, as well as issues of fantasy versus everyday life, and individuality versus solidarity.[4] Also from the 1960s onwards, Bohrer became increasingly critical of sociological and Marxist approaches to literature, and the peculiar German tradition of *Ideologiekritik* [critique of ideology] associated with the Frankfurt School.[5] He also rejected any materialist aesthetics and psychological perspectives on art. This critique of the traditional left-liberal approach to literature in post-war Germany was coupled with a general suspicion of any *littérature engagée* and normative claims about the socially responsible intellectual.[6] Bohrer viewed this model both as elitist and as essentially belonging to the nineteenth century.[7] He criticized the role of post-war West German literature as the (bad) conscience of the nation, and reproached German intellectuals with a 'provincial belatedness'.[8] Bohrer charged that 'as a result of the past and present German flight into the reactionary and apolitical — a pre-eminent part of that flight is the reverential or academic reception of late romantic aestheticism — the French debate about engaged

---

[4] Karl Heinz Bohrer, *Die gefährdete Phantasie, oder Surrealismus und Terror* (Munich: Hanser, 1970), 7–8.

[5] For *Ideologiekritik*, see Raymond Geuss, *The Idea of a Critical Theory: Habermas and the Frankfurt School* (Cambridge: Cambridge University Press, 1981), 26–44.

[6] Bohrer, *Die gefährdete Phantasie*, 20. While rejecting any overtly moral engagement, Bohrer did defend the radical aesthetic visions of intellectuals like Benjamin, Adorno and Herbert Marcuse, which, he conceded, were eminently political, against calls for 'constructive critique' so typical of the anti-intellectual pamphlets of the 1970s. See for instance 'Staatsräson und Moral: Am Beispiel Bölls', in *Frankfurter Allgemeine Zeitung*, 2 February 1972 and 'Was heißt hier "Verantwortlichkeit der Intellektuellen"?', in *Frankfurter Allgemeine Zeitung*, 26 September 1972.

[7] However, he also articulated some fundamental doubts about the political potential of writing. In 1968 he claimed that 'it is illusionary to regard writing as something other than an attempt at an extreme individualization. This is valid irrespective of the content, i.e. it is also valid for a political topic, where the author — seemingly going beyond himself — is "engaged"'. *Ibid.,* 89.

[8] *Ibid.,* 26.

art was taken up quite late in Germany and sentimentalized'.[9] Discussing the famous controversy between Sartre and Camus, Bohrer unambiguously sided with Camus, while rejecting the latter's 'heroic nihilism, his pathos of the absurd' and 'naive stoicism'.[10] He emphatically applied the phrase with which Camus had denounced Sartre, 'Sartre or nostalgia for the universal idyll', to the 'contemporary West German literature of bliss or shabbiness'.[11] This literature, Bohrer argued, was distorted by the 'bad conscience' of the German intelligentsia after the Second World War and focused on political content, rather than on 'the formal arrangement of the aesthetic material' or, as Bohrer specifically wanted art to be understood, 'art as appearance [*Schein*]'.[12] Instead of accepting art as being about beauty — and as ultimately 'autonomous' from 'reality', the West German literati clung to 'false utopias' and 'chiliasm' by focusing on 'real' content:

> What do the false utopians and chiliasts mean by utopia? They jump to the wrong conclusions by taking the promises immanent to art, the anticipation of the future that is peculiar to art, too literally and by insisting stubbornly that either the world must change here and now to fulfill these promises, or else all of art is worthless. They do not realize that the madness of a Rimbaud or an Artaud or a Nietzsche are to be taken seriously only as a style, as an ecstasy, as a semantic or theatrical event, or not at all. Instead, the false utopians understood the utopian concept and all its representative elaborations merely in their content, alternating between a vague claim to private happiness and claims of social perfectibility.[13]

Bohrer sough to defend the 'aesthetic boundary' between art and life, and prevent any crossovers, whether in the form of overtly politicized literature, or in the supposedly 'authentic' confessional and biographical literature so typical of West Germany in the 1970s.[14] At the same time, Bohrer rejected any subordination of art to philosophy, as in Hegel's notion of 'art as the appearance of the Idea', through which art became a 'thing of the past', because it was less capable of grasping the truth than abstract thought. Bohrer extended this separation from philosophy to any concepts contained

---

[9] Karl Heinz Bohrer, 'Don Quixote's Mistake: The Problem of the Aesthetic Boundary', in *Suddenness: On the Moment of Aesthetic Appearance*, trans. Ruth Crowley (New York: Columbia University Press, 1994), 87–110; here 93.

[10] *Ibid.*, 94.

[11] *Ibid.*

[12] *Ibid.*, 93–5.

[13] *Ibid.*, 95.

[14] *Ibid.*, 95–6.

in a traditional philosophy of art.[15] He insisted that 'it is only through closing the boundary between art and reality that the aesthetic appearance becomes visible; this appearance is the scandal of the beautiful'.[16]

Bohrer's approach to aesthetics involved three central claims: the necessity to close art off from moral, political or any other 'real' criteria; his insistence on the irreducible individuality and subjective joy of aesthetic perception; and, finally, his conception of the aesthetic experience in terms of the 'suddenness' with which art affects us, i.e. a characterization of the aesthetic experience as akin to an 'epiphany'.[17] According to Bohrer, it was precisely 'the sudden', the 'dangerous moment' or even 'terror' as an aesthetic experience of time free from theory, 'the absolutizing of the now to an appearing moment, to the poetological structure of the epiphany' which characterized all of modern literature.[18] And this discovery of the sudden, the exception and the dangerous moment, while itself being in danger of fascist abuse (as in Schmitt and Heidegger), also enabled a modern 'literary, aesthetic hypostatization of the moment in the artistic act' which 'can be free of a primary ideological load'.[19] Bohrer claimed that the early German Romantics, and in particular Friedrich Schlegel, had first set the decisionist categories of the 'here and now' against any philosophies of history – and, by implication, utopias and any remnants of theology and eschatology. This figure of thought – which variously appeared as the 'here and now', the surrealist 'shock', an autonomous 'aesthetic subjectivity', or 'evil' as an aesthetic phenomenon which could not be morally judged – became increasingly radicalized, but always remained at the heart of Bohrer's theoretical project: namely, a conception of aesthetics as pure presence, instead of representation, i.e. the idea of the immanent, self-reflexive aesthetic sign that pointed to nothing beyond itself, and was radically divorced from 'reality', and therefore, *inter alia*, politics.[20] Unlike some conservatives, Bohrer always refused to see art as a form of 'compensation' for the disorientation characteristic of modernity, and, unlike the Left, rejected it as a vehicle of emancipation: it was to be equally separate from grand philosophical-cum-historical projects

---

[15] *Ibid.*

[16] *Ibid.*, 97.

[17] 'Suddenness' he defined both as 'a category for the phenomenality of the work of art in consideration of its aesthetic effect' but also as marking 'the barrier against a concept of time distorted by the history of philosophy or a theoretical system'. See *ibid.*, x.

[18] Karl Heinz Bohrer, 'The Prehistory of the Sudden: The Generation of the "Dangerous Moment" ', in *Suddenness*, 39–69; here 59.

[19] *Ibid.*, 61.

[20] Radicalization here refers to the fact that for instance in his 1978 investigation of Ernst Jünger's early work Bohrer was still prepared to take into account historical developments to explain literary artefacts, whereas subsequently literature became utterly divorced from politics in his work.

and everyday hedonism and comfort. Against this ambitious theoretical background, Bohrer undertook a number of controversial, and, in his own view, taboo-shattering, literary investigations. In this, he seemed to act strategically from the start, but also with an utmost seriousness which impressed his numerous critics and few followers alike.[21]

First, he tried to liberate Ernst Jünger from the label of 'pre-fascist'. Rather than judge Jünger's *oeuvre* by its political effects, or slot him into a specifically German, right-wing tradition of irrationality, Bohrer sought to show him as symptomatic of a European intellectual crisis in the first half of the twentieth century, and as one of the discoverers of 'the sudden'. Once again, he insisted on the autonomy of the aesthetic, and claimed that in Jünger's case, artistic talent could overcome a writer's own ideology.[22] Bohrer tried to rehabilitate what critics from Lukács's *Destruction of Reason* onwards had described as Jünger's decisionism by arguing that decisionism was a genuine problem for modern consciousness, i.e. a consciousness which had been formed by Romanticism and become thoroughly aesthetic.[23] According to Bohrer, Jünger had tried to respond to this problem by setting a pure *Anschauung* of beauty against the notion of reason. This aesthetic response, however, should not be put under the suspicion of ideology, as most post-war literary critics had claimed, and be characterized as anti-modern or as part of the Counter-Enlightenment, but seen as itself part and parcel of an evolving modernity.[24]

Subsequently, Bohrer sought to rehabilitate the mythical structure of art, thereby shattering what he perceived as the supposed taboo on myths as anti-modern and irrational. He employed the same pattern of argument, claiming that the early Romantic notion of a 'New Mythology', taken up by Nietzsche and the Surrealists, opened radically new perspectives for the reflection on aesthetic phenomena, and that myth and modernity, far from being opposed, were in fact bound up with each other.[25] However, where Horkheimer and Adorno had made a somewhat similar claim — and lamented the foundering of the Enlightenment in a state of all-pervasive instrumental rationality — Bohrer celebrated myth and fantasy as part of a modern, liberated consciousness.[26] He then went on to systematically

---

[21] Schuh, 'Der letzte Ästhet'.

[22] Karl Heinz Bohrer, *Die Ästhetik des Schreckens: Die pessimistische Romantik und Ernst Jüngers Frühwerk* (Munich: Hanser, 1978), 18.

[23] *Ibid.*, 19.

[24] *Ibid.*

[25] Karl Heinz Bohrer, 'Vorwort', in Karl Heinz Bohrer (ed.), *Mythos und Moderne: Begriff und Bild einer Rekonstruktion* (Frankfurt/Main: Suhrkamp, 1983), 7–11.

[26] Max Horkheimer and Theodor W. Adorno, *Dialektik der Aufklärung: Philosophische Fragmente* (1944; Frankfurt/Main: Fischer, 1988), English translation *Dialectic of Enlightenment*, trans. John Cumming (New York: Continuum, 1976).

recover Romanticism as part and parcel of modernity: he first argued that modern consciousness had been thoroughly formed by the great innovations of Romanticism, fantasy and irony. But this very consciousness increasingly came into conflict with the technological-cum-rationalistic discourse of modernity, thereby setting a poetic modernity against a scientific-rationalistic one. Rather than dismissing Romanticism as reactionary and irrational, Bohrer set out a theory of complex, competing visions of modernity.[27] Subsequently, he sought to weaken the 'suspicion' manifest in philosophy since Hegel that Romanticism was merely obscure and irrational. He claimed that the critique of Romanticism, in the name of either a teleological idealism or a scientific positivism, was in fact itself a part of German anti-modernism or 'belatedness'.[28] The critique of Romanticism elaborated by Hegel and Heine prevented German philosophy's acceptance of a consciousness of contingency, of the fantastic and aesthetic reflexivity, as well as the categories of subjectivity and evil – in other words, all the categories which for Bohrer constituted an autonomous aesthetic consciousness. Bohrer thus turned the traditional theory of a German romantic *Sonderweg* on its head: rather than viewing Romanticism as an irrational part of German consciousness from the nineteenth century onwards, or even as a pre-condition of fascism – as Lukács had claimed – Romanticism was now interpreted as quintessentially modern. It was then precisely the peculiar deficit in aesthetic-literary consciousness and the attempt to domesticate the aesthetic through philosophical categories in the nineteenth century which constituted the special path of German development.[29] And in what became a typical argument used by the Right in post-unification political discourse in Germany, Bohrer claimed that it was in fact the Left that had been the heir to the negative traditions and continuities of German history.[30]

Bohrer on '68: Surrealist Politics

It would be wrong to suggest that Bohrer first developed a full-blown stance on aesthetics before launching into political commentary. On the contrary, from the late 1960s onwards, when Bohrer started to stake out his views on a consistently demarcated aesthetics, his defence of pure art had been complemented by a particular perspective on politics in the Federal

---

[27] Karl Heinz Bohrer, *Der romantische Brief: Die Entstehung ästhetischer Subjektivität* (Munich: Hanser, 1987).

[28] Karl Heinz Bohrer, *Die Kritik der Romantik: Der Verdacht der Philosophie gegen die literarische Moderne* (Frankfurt/Main: Suhrkamp, 1989), 11.

[29] *Ibid.*, 18.

[30] *Ibid.*

Republic. In 1968, when he published his first major political intervention in the journal he was one day to edit, he attacked liberal critics for having misunderstood the nature of the student rebellion. He argued that their initial solidarity with the radical students had been driven by emotion, rather than political analysis.[31] Whereas the 'reactionaries' had at least clearly perceived the potential of a civil War between a revolutionary minority and a bourgeois majority, liberal and conservative critics confronted the student movement with the 'most dangerous objection' of all, namely that they stood in the tradition of the Conservative Revolution. For Bohrer, this was to tarnish the radical students with the very label which their opponents, namely the conservative *Burschenschaften* [fraternities], deserved. This historical genealogy amounted to a major ideological confusion, and, Bohrer argued, perpetuated an old liberal error. But it had also enabled what he called an 'interesting' and 'secret' West German psychology, which sought to collapse National Socialism into Communism, to be at least somewhat relieved of the burden of the Nazi past.[32] Bohrer emphatically rejected the labels of 'terror' and 'fascism' for the students, but conceded that they engaged in traditional popular front tactics, as well as a kind of 'political surrealism'. More importantly, Bohrer charged liberal critics with an inability to part with their historical analogies, which only 'obscured the phenomenon'. He clearly sympathised with the student movement, not least because of its antibourgeois shock tactics and its attempt to 're-politicize' the stale, supposedly de-ideologized and 'depoliticized atmosphere' of the 1960s.[33]

The same blindness to political reality which led the liberals to a misinterpretation of the student movement characterized the entire political establishment of the late 1960s. Bohrer claimed to detect a certain spiritual and intellectual 'damage', which also translated into political damage, and which at bottom was due to a deformed language. According to Bohrer, social and political phenomena were described with clichés and imprecise metaphors from the apolitical ' "sphere of the private", the "soul", the "spirit", of "fate" . . .'.[34] This language, thoroughly apolitical, ideologically saturated and potentially threatening to civil liberties, Bohrer claimed, actually had its origins in National Socialism. However, one strand of the student movement, which declared its approach as 'rational' and 'scientific', tended to share some of the characteristics of the politicians' language: the language of the formalist dogmatics of the rebellion, Bohrer

---

[31] Karl Heinz Bohrer, 'Die mißverstandene Rebellion', in *Merkur*, Vol. 22 (1968), 33–44; here 33.

[32] *Ibid.*, 36.

[33] Karl Heinz Bohrer, 'Die linke Minderheit: Theorie und Praxis der Rebellen von Berlin', in *Frankfurter Allgemeine Zeitung*, 23 June 1967.

[34] Bohrer, 'Die mißverstandene Rebellion', 39–40.

argued, was equally 'ideologically frustrated, unoriginal, tending towards submissiveness and closed off from reality'.[35] Against these two languages which Bohrer condemned as both apolitical and aesthetically impoverished, he celebrated the 'political surrealism' of the radical, 'exotic' and experimental wing of the movement. This part of the movement took its inspiration from the beatniks (and, ultimately, Dada and the Surrealists) and suffered from what only on the surface appeared as an apolitical 'discontent with culture'.[36] Their methods of argumentation, not directed towards dialogue with 'the establishment', but towards tactical maneuvers to deconstruct an ossified political language, thus in fact exposed the truly political. They refused to accept seemingly reasonable deliberations, which liberal critics demanded, as long as the language of deliberation had not been radically renewed. Thus, aesthetic provocation was an indirect route towards the political, cutting through the fog of clichés designed to escape from actual social and political phenomena. Only if liberal intellectuals freed themselves from historical analogies, an ossified language and political defense mechanisms, could a true political dialogue be established. In Bohrer's view, even before this potential dialogue, the exotic, radical, and supposedly irrational strategies of some of the students had already led to major shake-ups and reforms in the universities. Thus, the aesthetic shock, rather than what Jean Améry had called the arid 'jargon of dialectics' in Critical Theory propounded by some of the official student leaders, had led to actual political change.[37] Ultimately, it was then an aesthetic provocation, a playful use of expressionist, surrealist and conservative revolutionary language which opened up a new phenomenology of the political.

Clearly, at this stage aesthetics and the political were not yet divorced in Bohrer's thought, and the former could in fact lead to a renewal of the latter. He openly celebrated the surrealist elements of the student rebellion, even their decisionism, but parted company with them on utopias and the philosophies of history which underpinned their political project. Nevertheless, as the student rebellion progressed, he increasingly came to reject this link between aesthetics and politics, arguing that the self-interpretation of the students' surrealist acts as 'political' was 'belated'. In other words, 'political surrealism' was merely surrealism and no longer 'political'. Instead, he criticized the Left's yearning for the 'simple life', their anti-civilizational stance and, once again, their utopianism.[38]

---

[35] *Ibid.*, 43.

[36] *Ibid.*, 40.

[37] Jean Améry, 'Jargon der Dialektik', in *Merkur*, Vol. 21 (1967), 1041–59.

[38] Marianne Kesting, 'Revolutionäre Geste als Kunst: Karl Heinz Bohrers Auseinandersetzung mit der "Kursbuch-Linken"', in *Die Zeit*, 3 July 1970.

Bohrer's clarion call 'let us not use philosophy to legitimate the beautiful' and his rejection of any *Ideologiekritik* set him against the mainstream
of German literary criticism in the 1970s and 1980s, and allowed him to
adopt the role of the taboo-breaker and *enfant terrible*. Having attacked
the mainstream of literary criticism, Bohrer then undertook a cultural critique of West German politics. Just as much as his unashamed aesthetics
of the beautiful had gone against the grain of West German literary
theory, this critique was designed to go against the grain of the post-war
liberal-democratic consensus of the Federal Republic.

The Cultural Critique of West Germany: Apolitical Provincialism

As has often been pointed out, Bohrer's view of the West German polity
during the 1980s was strongly coloured by his experiences as a foreign correspondent for the *Frankfurter Allgemeine Zeitung* in London. He used the
urbane, cosmopolitan Western culture of France and Britain as a foil to
satirize West Germany. Bohrer's charge against the Federal Republic was
threefold: first, it was thoroughly provincial and petty bourgeois as far as
the stature of its political elites was concerned. Second, it lacked the kind
of modern (and modernist) culture usually associated with a metropolitan
environment such as Paris and London, and consequently its literature was
as petty bourgeois and provincial as its politics. This was particularly
obvious in the mixture of politics and art in *Gesinnungsästhetik*
[aesthetics of conscience] (a pun referring to Max Weber's *Gesinnungsethik*
[ethics of conscience] from *Politics as a Vocation*). This 'ideological aesthetics' demanded that a work of art not be judged on purely aesthetic
criteria and the strength of a subjective vision of the world, but on the
grounds of whether the author exhibited the correct political convictions.
Thus, culturally speaking, Germany had been cut off from modernity and
remained a 'belated nation'. However, while literature had been politicized,
an aesthetic dimension, in a misguided reaction to National Socialism, had
been annihilated from the representation of the state. German political
life was characterized by the sheer ugliness of its representatives, and the
petty bourgeois, provincial nature of its cultural expressions.[39] Third, West
Germany, with its excessive moralism and sentimentality, which were also
characteristic of the petty bourgeoisie, had lost a sense of the political as
such. This was particularly obvious in its failure to understand that sovereignty, as Carl Schmitt had claimed, ultimately meant that a state could
take the decision to go to War. Bohrer, causing an outcry back in West
Germany, defended Margaret Thatcher's Falklands War against what he
called the West German '*Mainzelmännchen* [innocuous comic characters]'

---

[39] Karl Heinz Bohrer, 'Die Ästhetik des Staates', in *Merkur*, Vol. 38 (1984), 1–15; here 4.

who had lost all sense of power, national sovereignty and 'history'. He claimed that the German body politic had no organs, a pun which played on the double meaning of organs as institutions, but also as 'guts'. The state exhibited a glaring vacuum where its power to act should have been located. Instead, the West Germans, in their apolitical chiliasm, longed for an idyllic world in which conflicts of interest had been overcome in favour of universal harmony, deliberation and problem-solving through social therapy. This longing and its corresponding rigid Protestant morality made them unable to deal with the world of politics, especially foreign policy, in all its chaos and contingencies. Chaos, 'suddenness', fleeting moments and contingent encounters which required quick, sovereign decisions – these were of course also the characteristics of the modern metropolis. In other words, Bohrer, crossing his own 'aesthetic boundary', claimed that German cultural provincialism and political backwardness were intimately related: Bohrer's political polemics were based on cultural criticism.

Provincialism and mediocrity, however, did not simply contrast with a vigorous metropolitan culture. From his deeply ironic perspective, Bohrer praised what he perceived as the decadence and refinement of London's culture in the late 1970s, which the sterile success story of West Germany simply could not compete with.[40] Bohrer, investigating what he called 'the psychological and spiritual structures of Western Europe', praised the rotten remnants of the British Empire. He admired both the supposed English resistance to 'theory' and the supposedly 'sovereign' behaviour of individuals still trained as 'gentlemen'. The most recurrent theme of his observations on the English relishing their own decadence, however, was the English interest in history, based on the fact that there the past was so much part of the present. Whereas the Germans of the Federal Republic, including their intellectuals, were incapable of thinking back before the year 1945 – apart from satirically, or in an accusatory, but in any case 'unhistorical manner', the English engaged with the past in a narcissistic, but ultimately socially effective way. England, in short, was truly self-conscious of its own historicity. Bohrer posited that it was 'normal' for peoples to be interested in history, something the Germans with their spurious love of Europe could not appreciate. He also relished whatever seemed still to hold the promise of an adventurous subjectivity for the sovereign individual, even the prospect of a civil War in Britain.[41] Ironically, foreign observers ridiculed Bohrer's projections onto England, pointing out that 'the "*Herr*

---

[40] See in particular the collection of Bohrer's articles for the *Frankfurter Allgemeine*, *Ein bißchen Lust am Untergang: Englische Ansichten* (Munich: Hanser, 1979), which he wrote in London after he had been fired by Joachim Fest from the literature section of the paper for being too esoteric.

[41] *Ibid.*, 13, 83, 133, 166, 173–5.

Kulturkorrespondent" was obviously none too familiar with the *"Kultur"* he was supposed to correspond about'.[42]

Bohrer, the expert on early Romanticism, thus cast a romantic eye on a Britain soaked in history and national symbols as opposed to a Germany that, ironically, exhibited all the traits which the Germans at the beginning of the century had associated with the commercialism of the English. In this way, Werner Sombart's famous opposition between the English as merchants and the Germans as heroes had been reversed: Germans for the most part were now Hegelian bourgeois, or even Nietzschean last men, eager to avoid the harsh realities of politics and slowly regressing to the level of innocent childhood.[43] Where the British were discovering new possibilities of refinement, even erotic lust, in their own decadence, and emotionally confronted the layers of their own past, the 'faceless' Germans now symbolized sterile efficiency, health and a complete forgetting of the past. West Germany remained not much more than a *'Europäisches Arbeitslager und strategisches Aufmarschgebiet* [a European labour camp and strategic theatre of operation]'.[44] As critics pointed out at the time, Bohrer's portrayal of England had been an aesthetic projection through and through, and, ultimately, a futile call for the renewal of a 'national mythology' and German *Geist* out of the spirit of decadence from across the Channel.[45]

For Bohrer, Germany's repudiation of heroism in favour of provincialism was not a historical accident. It was the direct consequence of the fact that National Socialism had destroyed a liberal *Großbürgertum* [as opposed to a petite bourgeoisie] and cut the country off from modernity. West Germany was unconsciously continuing the *Sonderweg* of being apolitical, of replacing politics with morals and *raison d'état* with legalism, making it, in Bohrer's judgment, immature and impotent at the same time. Its elites came from the provincial *Länder* and had proven their competence in the judiciary or the bureaucracy, rather than the liberal *Großbürger*, who, as in the Weberian model, had to 'represent' their political mettle in parliament. West German politicians, for whom Helmut Kohl was truly representative, had displaced political questions into private ones, lost all sense for symbolic forms, and were caught in an impractical 'politics of abstraction', rather than the *bürgerliche* 'concretism' and practical morality which Bohrer preferred.[46]

Bohrer's eclectic position made him a political *enfant terrible* throughout

---

[42] See Martin Esslin, 'A German Correspondent Reports from London', in *Encounter*, No. 5 (1980), 72–7.

[43] Bohrer, 'Die Ästhetik des Staates', 12.

[44] Bohrer, *Ein kleines bißchen Lust*, 128.

[45] Reinhard Baumgart, 'Das Einhorn brüllt, der Löwe tanzt', in *Der Spiegel*, 20 August 1979.

[46] Karl Heinz Bohrer, 'Provinzialismus (III): Das Vakuum', in *Merkur*, Vol. 45 (1991), 348–56; here 349.

the 1980s, as he attacked some of the cherished notions of both Left and Right. What intellectuals from both Left and Right praised as one of Germany's greatest strengths, namely its regional diversity and lack of great power pretensions, was dismissed by Bohrer as provincialism. What many Germans saw as an old-fashioned display of imperialism in the Falklands War, Bohrer celebrated as a truly political decision. And what advocates of constitutional patriotism praised as an enlightened post-national consciousness, Bohrer derided as a 'colonized consciousness', based on deep insecurities, and as yet another progressive utopia. Against this flight from one's own nationality, and against the antiseptic and philistine West German taming of 'culture' as something that could be administered, Bohrer set his project of recovering Germany as a 'spiritual-intellectual possibility'.[47] This recovery could consist neither in the reconstruction of once-and-for-all lost traditions like German idealism, nor could 'culture' be institutionalized as a party programme. But the Germans should reconnect with the exploration of the 'I', which Kant and Fichte had started, to the aesthetic subjectivity which had been at the heart of Germany as a 'spiritual possibility': 'Only when one dares to say I, instead of pointing to statistics, might the gray veil of German boredom disappear'.[48]

However, Bohrer's underlying assumptions were not just antithetical to West German culture, but also to some principles of West German democracy, as he self-consciously tapped into pre-war and nineteenth-century traditions of thought. He partially adopted the theoretical framework associated with Carl Schmitt, who in turn was indebted to thinkers of the Counter-Enlightenment such as de Maistre and Donoso Cortés. In particular, the idea of the autonomy of the political as an existentialist category not to be infected with moralism or legalism was, to some extent, a cornerstone of Schmitt's political thought.[49] Schmitt also held War to be

---

[47] Karl Heinz Bohrer, 'Deutschland – noch eine geistige Möglichkeit: Bemerkungen zu einem nationalen Tabu', in *Frankfurter Allgemeine Zeitung*, 28 April 1979.

[48] *Ibid.*

[49] Carl Schmitt, *The Concept of the Political*, trans. George Schwab (1934; New Brunswick, NJ: Rutgers University Press, 1976). The autonomy of the political constituted Schmitt's initial conception of politics in his battle against liberalism, until Leo Strauss pointed out in a review of Schmitt's book that in fact a quasi-Weberian theory of autonomous spheres remained mired in the ideology of liberalism. Schmitt subsequently changed his concept to one of 'intensity', in which any sphere could become effectively politicized, as long as an antagonism was sufficiently strong to group people into friends and enemies. See Heinrich Meier's brilliant *Carl Schmitt & Leo Strauss: The Hidden Dialogue*, trans. J. Harvey Lomax (Chicago: The University of Chicago Press, 1995). Bohrer, of course, also explicitly dealt with Schmitt in his work, namely when describing Schmitt's *Political Romanticism* as the latest part of the long line of German condemnations of Romanticism in his *Kritik der Romantik*. Schmitt himself had apparently contacted him after his *Surrealismus und Terror*, as he presumed the young aesthete was further developing his own positions, but then distanced himself from Bohrer after he published *Ästhetik des Schreckens*. See ' "Das ist das letzte Gefecht": Zeit-Gespräch mit dem 'Merkur'-Herausgeber Karl Heinz Bohrer über des Verschwinden des Bürgertums und die Rolle des Intellektuellen in der Krise', in *Die Zeit*, 7 March 1997.

the paradigm for the political, which he conceptualized as the establishment of a friend–enemy relationship. Bohrer followed this view of the political as containing an irreducibly agonal core. Given the necessity of an adversary, he was compelled to complain that because of their neurotic view of National Socialism, Germans had banned the category of 'enemy' from public discourse, even from their thinking. A culture of endless debate in search of a universal Habermasian consensus had replaced a 'sense of contradiction, of enmity, of politics'.[50] Not surprisingly, Schmitt had also warned against 'the idyllic goal of complete and final depoliticization'.[51] The complaint against contaminating an autonomous sphere of the political with 'legalism' and 'moralism' was equally a core argument in inter- and post-war conservative critiques of liberalism. Moreover, the idea of aestheticizing the state could be traced back at least as far as Treitschke and a particular German 'state metaphysics', which was inextricably linked with a 'state aesthetics of the sublime' of the state 'overwhelming' its citizens as much through aesthetic display as actual power.[52] Finally, the relentless critique of 'abstract moralism' in the name of the 'concrete', of 'life itself' was one of the claims of irrational *Lebensphilosophie* to which Bohrer's brilliant essays sometimes came down. Still, 'conservative' or 'young conservative', as Habermas designated intellectuals who accepted the cultural, but not the political consequences of modernity, would hardly do justice to the complexity of his thought. Rather, his desire to separate the political from 'moralism' and to emancipate aesthetics from philosophy and politics, could also be seen as 'classically modern'.[53] After all, the idea of autonomous spheres of the moral, the aesthetic and the scientific (and, one might add, the political) constitutes a thoroughly Kantian (and, later, Weberian) view of modernity.[54] In that sense, Bohrer's cultural and political position would best be described as

---

[50] Bohrer, 'Die Ästhetik des Staates', 14.

[51] Schmitt, *The Concept of the Political*, 54.

[52] Walter Bußmann, *Treitschke: Sein Welt- und Geschichtsbild* (Göttingen: Muster-Schmidt-Verlag, 1981), 160–70.

[53] Karl Heinz Bohrer, 'Die Ästhetik am Ausgang ihrer Unmündigkeit', in *Merkur*, Vol. 43 (1990), 851–65. On the notion of 'classical modernity', see Detlev J. K. Peukert, *The Weimar Republic: The Crisis of Classical Modernity*, trans. Richard Deveson (1987; London: Penguin, 1991).

[54] Bohrer himself, however, rejected any association of his theories with the notion of autonomous spheres, either in the form of Habermas's principled or Peter Bürger's pragmatic continuation of Weberian notions of the differentiation of cultural spheres of values. See Bohrer (ed.), *Mythos und Moderne*, 8. Here I disagree with Charles Larmore who sees Bohrer as interested in an anti-Weberian and anti-Habermasian 'disunity of modern reason', where art challenges science and morality. As I have pointed out above, Bohrer himself would not see art as pointing beyond itself to challenge other forms of 'reason', even if de facto his conceptualization of art could fulfil that function. See Charles Larmore, 'Modernity and the Disunity of Reason', in *The Morals of Modernity* (Cambridge: Cambridge University Press, 1996), 189–204.

nostalgia for a 'classical modernity', associated with the culture of High Modernism, sovereign political decision-making learnt through imperial rule, and the *großbürgerliche* metropolitan culture of Paris and London – Bohrer in fact once described himself as a 'modernist in a nostalgic sense'.[55] And it was a nostalgic, but at the same time anti-utopian modernism, self-consciously realist and 'cold' in politics – somewhat reminiscent of the gestures of sober resoluteness which had characterized intellectuals in the Weimar Republic such as Helmuth Plessner, who had defended the claims of an impersonal *Gesellschaft* against the advocates of a warm *Gemeinschaft* from both Left and Right.[56] Thus, his position was the paradoxical one of a pro-modernist conservative, who was trying to conserve a frozen state of early twentieth-century modernity as opposed to further emancipation through the politicization and democratization of other spheres of life, as advocated by the Left. But as in the case of Schmitt and the 'cold' intellectuals of the interwar period, Bohrer's advocacy of a separation of spheres sometimes suddenly collapsed into an existentialist celebration of conflict and an aestheticization of politics – which were akin to Weber's illiberal side, rather than a Kantian view of modernity.

Bohrer's Response to Unification: Recovering National Memory

When the Wall came down, Bohrer called for unification on the grounds that any other solution would be a continuation of the apolitical German *Sonderweg*, and that unification would enable Germany to become a nation again. In an article in the *Frankfurter Allgemeine Zeitung*, he argued that the Left's fear of unification was grounded yet again in an aversion to the 'chaos of a nonregimented, non-patronized' modern world and metropolitan culture in particular.[57] Bohrer rejected the notion of the *Kulturnation* advanced by Grass and many other left-wing intellectuals, because its advocates longed yet again for a harmonious utopia and ignored the fact that the small federal German states of the nineteenth century had been police states associated with narrow-mindedness and 'authoritarian characters'.[58] According to Bohrer, the Left wanted 'to preserve the GDR as a kind of

---

[55] ' "Das letzte Gefecht" '.

[56] Bohrer in fact comes as close as any major intellectual to reviving the Weimar model of the 'cold intellectual' as described in Lethen's *Verhaltenslehren der Kälte*. See Helmuth Plessner, 'Grenzen der Gemeinschaft: Eine Kritik des sozialen Radikalismus', in *Gesammelte Werke*, eds Günter Dux *et al.*, Vol. 5 (Frankfurt/Main: Suhrkamp, 1985), 7–133.

[57] Karl Heinz Bohrer, 'Why We Are Not a Nation – And Why We Should Become One', in Harold James and Marla Stone (eds), *When the Wall came down: Reactions to German Unification* (New York: Routledge, 1992), 60–70; here 63 [first in *Frankfurter Allgemeine Zeitung*, 13 January 1990].

[58] *Ibid.*, 65.

nature sanctuary for socially and economically dreamed-of yesteryears, a sanctuary in which the Federal Republic can daily renew its necessarily guilty conscience'.[59] He charged the Left yet again with 'chiliasm', 'sentimentality' and with longing for 'power-protected inwardness'. He countered the claim that division constituted a punishment for crimes in the past with the strangely literal argument that the loss of East Prussia and Silesia had been sufficient as a form of restitution, as if moral and geopolitical claims could be weighed on the same scales. Contrary to Grass's charges about the inherent aggressiveness of the future *Einheitsstaat* and Habermas's advocacy of West German continuity, Bohrer held that a state comprising the Federal Republic and the GDR would constitute an entirely new country. But, significantly, this denial would not entail a denial of the past. On the contrary, the new state could finally end the highly 'neurotic self-destruction' of the Germans as a nation, which was intimately related to their attempted escape from politics so as to 'erase the unbearable – the crimes of the father'.[60] For Bohrer, Germany as a nation, and therefore German memory, had been annihilated through the division, and the Germans were desperately trying to be apolitical and innocuous in an attempt to escape from the past. Only by again becoming a nation could the Germans overcome the 'plague of a notorious loss of memory' and their all-pervasive provincialism. And only then could they salvage specifically German traditions such as irrational Romanticism, which less hidebound foreign intellectuals, primarily the French, were appropriating for their postmodern theoretical innovations. Finally, unification would put an end to 'pacification through innocuousness', which amounted to a veiled call for national self-assertion.[61]

But what was Bohrer's underlying definition of the nation? He argued that the category of nation was constituted by 'the symbolic and reflective constants of a collective ability to remember'.[62] The nation was primarily a cultural phenomenon, which, however, could not exist outside a state. A cultural memory, according to Bohrer, could only be cultivated in a unified Germany, in which the sublime might also finally return to the representation of the state. In this way, Bohrer drew direct links between nationhood, statehood, political style and collective memory. He argued that acquiring a German national identity was a matter of being able to 'remember together'.[63] The necessarily distorted memories of the two

---

[59] *Ibid.*, 63.

[60] *Ibid.*, 66.

[61] *Ibid.*, 68–9.

[62] *Ibid.*, 68.

[63] Karl-Heinz Bohrer, 'Und die Erinnerung der beiden Halbnationen?', in *Merkur*, Vol. 44 (1990), 183–8.

partial nations had to come together again, and, by establishing a common memory, *Gemeinsamkeit* [common attributes and togetherness] could be attained. In fact, the ability to remember and *Gemeinsamkeit* depended on each other. Only such a 'labour of memory' could form the basis of a new sense of self-worth and end the state of a Federal Republic which 'politically and individually still suffered from the consequences of the Third Reich, insecure of its identity', and a GDR which was even more damaged.[64] Thus unification took on the character of national therapy, a reconciliation with each other, which at the same time had to be a reconciliation with the past. Like a split personality, to use Bohrer's categories of national psychology, the divided Germany had two distorted views of the past, and therefore of its present, which could be healed only in an act of mnemonic commonality. Thus the national soul would find ease in a reunified state.

In this way, Bohrer entirely reversed the Left's argument that Germany should atone for Auschwitz by renouncing unification. Taking up an article by the sociologist − and former assistant of Habermas − Ulrich Oevermann, who had argued that the opponents of unification aimed at continuing the *Sonderweg*, Bohrer claimed that only a united Germany could take on the task of mourning for the victims of the Holocaust.[65] According to Oevermann, Germany had to assume the 'structural, political and practical responsibility of the unified nation', as opposed to the 'permanent production of moralizing feelings of guilt'; refusing unification would constitute nothing less than moral escapism. Not surprisingly, both Bohrer and Oevermann rejected and ridiculed the concept of constitutional patriotism, with Bohrer arguing that Germany needed to develop a new, universalist conception of nationhood along the lines of the French and British. Germany had never succeeded in 'universalizing its ethnic-spatial identity through political and constitutional concepts'. Thus, strictly speaking, there had never been a modern German nation at all. Previous attempts to universalize such a conception had been Fichte's idealism and National Socialism.[66] Both had been characterized by 'chiliasm', utter 'seriousness' and had ended in disaster.[67] After National Socialism, the Germans had regressed to the self-understanding of a 'regionalist, naïve' people, as in the first quarter of the nineteenth century, and abjured all sense of danger

---

[64] *Ibid.*, 184.

[65] Ulrich Oevermann, 'Zwei Staaten oder Einheit? Der "dritte Weg" als Fortsetzung des deutschen Sonderweges', in *Merkur*, Vol. 44 (1990), 91–100.

[66] For this theory to work, Bohrer had to reconceptualize National Socialism as having been based on a universalist political ideology, rather than racism.

[67] Karl Heinz Bohrer, 'Gibt es eine deutsche Nation?', in Siegfried Unseld (ed.), *Politik ohne Projekt? Nachdenken über Deutschland* (Frankfurt/Main: Suhrkamp, 1993), 225–35.

and hierarchy in favour of innocuousness. However, now was the time to break out of the provincial self-understanding of the Federal Republic and attempt another universalization of a German conception of nation, which could then, like Britain and France, be culturally attractive to other nations. In other words, where Habermas sought to embed universalist values in the nation-state framework, i.e. nationalize universalism, Bohrer sought to universalize nationalism. Only then could practical issues in domestic and foreign policy be tackled successfully. Thus, for all his emphasis on the autonomy of the political, the precondition for a return of the political was a cultural one. The Germans had to redefine themselves, embrace political risks and face up to the past under the category of nationhood. In a way, Bohrer wanted his country to go back to the beginning: what France and Britain had done centuries ago, Germany had yet to accomplish: a successful process of nation-building.

Bohrer's analysis was driven by the desire for what he hoped would be a truly modern — and modernist — German culture. But importantly, the return to a — in Habermas's terms — 'conventional national identity' was not linked to a repression of the past. If anything, Bohrer's call for national identity was made in the name of memory and of assuming a particular national responsibility. He always sought to distance himself from those conservatives who in the *Historikerstreit* — and once again in 1990 — attempted to link national identity with forgetting. He explicitly repudiated intellectuals like Hermann Lübbe who deduced a triumph of 'conventional morality' from the demise of the GDR, arguing that the end of Communism did not imply a 'revision of our radical-liberal criteria'.[68] But neither, he argued, was there a necessary link between the question of German identity and a relativization of Nazi crimes, as a 'hysterical (and demagogic) Left' had claimed in the *Historikerstreit*. In that sense, at least, he still remained within the moral framework of collective responsibility which Jaspers had formulated in *The Question of German Guilt* — even if it was the opposite end of that framework in relation to Grass, and even if he drew the opposite conclusion from Habermas: the past mandated national identity, rather than post-nationalism, and, *pace* Jaspers, also a return to the nation-state. And it mandated both a cultural reconstitution for Germany and a political nation-state framework for that reconstitution.

However, Bohrer's ultimately cultural objectives contradicted his insistence on the autonomy of the political. For all his criticism of apolitical attitudes, Bohrer actually criticized politics from a thoroughly cultural

---

[68] Karl Heinz Bohrer, 'Widerspruch zu Hermann Lübbe', in *Merkur*, Vol. 44 (1990), 530–3; here 530. During the *Historikerstreit*, Bohrer had provided Hans Mommsen and Hans-Ulrich Wehler with space in *Merkur*.

point of view. He seemed to think that culture could improve politics — and vice versa: with unification political culture and cultural politics simply collapsed into each other, and the 'aesthetic boundary' dissolved. Moreover, given his former praise of English decadence, it seemed that only a weakening of the state, rather than a reconstitution of the German nation-state could possibly bring about the renaissance of culture, including the decadent modernist refinement for which Bohrer longed. He himself countered the objection that he was conflating the aesthetic and the political with yet another cultural argument, namely the apodictic statement that criticism from a cultural point of view was simply 'common sense' in Anglo-Saxon countries.[69] But he never exactly explained why salvaging the irrational tradition of German Romanticism or a spiritual renewal depended on the framework of a unified state. And he never explained how the *Bürgertum*, as the likely carrier of a new national culture, was to be reconstituted. Thus, sociological questions — the 'social' — also remained outside the autonomous categories of the political and the aesthetic. As in his aesthetic theories, there came a point where, despite all his undoubted analytical ambition, Bohrer would probe no further, instead advancing decisionist definitions and retreating into assertions about *das Unhintergehbare*, i.e. what could not be further analyzed. He would relentlessly deconstruct the theoretical positions of his opponents, but insulate his own categories — and the borders between them — through mere, or even essentially irrational, assertions. As his critics never failed to point out, this was the true 'Counter-Enlightenment'-dimension, or even mystification, in Bohrer's work: the categorical refusal to question one's own categories any further, instead reasserting them and ridiculing the concept of 'critique' altogether as an ideological West German obsession. This refusal to question further could of course be seen as an instance of 'anti-foundationalism' in the vein of Richard Rorty and other pragmatist-cum-postmodernist thinkers.[70] But Bohrer could neither agree with Rorty's call for a privatization of the aesthetic as self-creation nor could he relax and rely on a liberal national tradition in the way that American pragmatists might.[71] Alternatively, Carl Schmitt's charge of 'occasionalism' against the Romantics could have been applied to Bohrer: after all, the prospect of unification provided merely an 'occasion' for the aesthetic imagination to work on, and the transgressive call for real 'power politics' was in itself

---

[69] Karl Heinz Bohrer, 'Provinzialismus (IV). Ohne Geheimnis', in *Merkur*, Vol. 45 (1991), 537–46; here 537.

[70] Richard Rorty, 'The priority of democracy to philosophy', in *Objectivism, Relativism, and Truth* (Cambridge: Cambridge University Press, 1991), 175–96.

[71] Rorty, *Contingency, Irony, Solidarity*.

suffused with aestheticism.[72] But if unification truly was a historical window of opportunity, a means to deal with the weaknesses of the West German polity, the question became: why would an extension of the provincial Federal Republic remedy these weaknesses, especially if the GDR preserved some of the worst German anti-Western traits? In the end, like his aesthetics, Bohrer's proposed reconstitution of the German *Geist* out of the spirit of unification remained both elitist and enigmatic.

Consequences: Leaking the Aesthetic

Bohrer's enigmatic political fragments and aesthetic images were particularly powerful in defining the situation post-1990 and contributed influential concepts and arguments to the vocabulary of the Right. In particular, he first made the claim that it was in fact the neglect of national identity which was likely to breed nationalist violence and a breakdown of civilization.[73] In this Bohrer established a connection between national consciousness and sublimation, or self-control within civilization, which was also employed by Walser when he claimed that the neglect of national symbols was behind the culture of young right-wing thugs. Foreign policy intellectuals such as Christian Hacke repeated the point when they argued that because of West German political parties' neglect of national values, right-wing extremism could rise again.[74] Second, the idea of provincialism came to denote the activities of German politicians, depending on the point of view of the speaker. Hacke used it, '68 left revisionists used it, and it ended up as a cliché freely banded about in intellectual debates. Third, Bohrer talked about *gute Menschen* [good persons] to deride the practitioners of 'Protestant inwardness' and representatives of 'a moralism of absolute values'.[75] This terminology was taken up, shortened to *Gutmenschen*, and used by journalists who wanted to attack political statements in literature, *Gesinnungsethik*, i.e. a supposed ethics of conviction, and, in some cases, any kind of left-wing political engagement involving emotions. Fourth, Bohrer had established a conceptual link between what the sociologist Helmut Dubiel was later to call 'state sovereignty' and 'moral sovereignty', arguing that only though political unification could Germany gain the moral capacity necessary to deal with the past.[76] Politics,

---

[72] Carl Schmitt, *Political Romanticism*, trans. Guy Oakes (1925; Cambridge, Mass.: MIT Press, 1985).

[73] Bohrer, 'Und die Erinnerung der beiden Halbnationen?', 185.

[74] Christian Hacke, *Weltmacht wider Willen* (Berlin: Ullstein, 1993), 544.

[75] Bohrer, 'Und die Erinnerung der beiden Halbnationen?', 183.

[76] Helmut Dubiel, 'Über moralische Souveränität, Erinnerung und Nation', in *Merkur*, Vol. 48 (1994), 884–97; here 889.

morality and memory came to be linked in a novel way, which also opened a discourse about a 'moral lag', in which Germany's domestic moral constitution had not yet caught up with its new external sovereignty.

Karl Heinz Bohrer became one of the central figures in the debate on unification and the cultural definition of the new Germany for a number of reasons: he offered an ingenious and highly ironic cultural critique of the old Federal Republic. This critique could be taken up by intellectuals eager to change the political climate in post-unification Germany by distancing themselves from the supposedly apolitical and provincial Western precursor of the 'new Germany'. He also rehabilitated the 'irrational' traditions of German thought from early Romanticism to Ernst Jünger, thereby allowing intellectuals to tap into new genealogies. Bohrer's conceptual frameworks, couched in the language of 'taboo-breaking', bypassed any traditional discussions structured around the opposition of modern versus antimodern, and undermined the 'Western genealogy' of most left-liberal intellectuals in Germany by pinning the clichés associated with a *Sonderweg* on them. Finally, he offered a version of the autonomy of the political, which chimed with right-wing desires to free politics from moral and legal constraints, and at the same time advanced a kind of compensation in the form of an aestheticization of the state. Again, this argument was self-consciously constructed to bypass any objections which could have made use of Walter Benjamin's famous charge of an 'aestheticization of the political', since, according to Bohrer, Benjamin had merely rejected the 'false aestheticization' of politics. Most importantly, Bohrer claimed throughout that it was in fact his own theories, his eclectic recovery of Romanticism and other traditions and theories which were thoroughly modern. He thus pinned the label of *Sonderweg* and other symbols of antimodernism squarely on the Left. It was this virtuoso play with the concepts and categories – as well as the clichés – which structured intellectual discourse which accounted for Bohrer's success in influencing central debates.

And yet, for all his advocacy of the irrational, and of a recovery of specifically German traditions, as well as a more 'realist' power politics, there was one essential difference between Bohrer and some conservatives in the old Federal Republic as well as the New Right after 1989. His stance was never characterized by any resentment vis-à-vis the West, or vis-à-vis those West German intellectuals who had imported 'Western traditions' – even if some, such as Habermas, had supposedly gone too far in suppressing a genuinely German heritage. In fact, the West, and especially Bohrer's idealized Western Europe, always promised a world beyond the narrowness of German idealism, and the German longing for utopias, a world of classical nineteenth-century liberalism and modernism, and finally – of secularization. As he explained in a rare personal statement,

> I think that when we youngsters after 1945 saw the American gods emerge from the sea, who chewed gum and were friendly and played this wonderful music . . . then for the first time we took a step towards secularization. That meant: not only away from the gods of fascism, but towards a humanity without God . . . And you know, the Americans won the War by emerging from the sea playing jazz, in front of these brave, but dumb and completely anachronistic German soldiers. That was the triumph of secularization. To be human without gods.[77]

---

[77] ' "Das letzte Gefecht" '.

7   From National Identity
to National Interest:
An Anatomy of Germany's
New Right

*Und doch, gelingt einst das Werk der nationalen Reform, so wird zwar die
Schande ein Ende haben, daß ein großes Volk durch sein Grundgesetz zu
der defensiven Politik eines Kleinstaats verurteilt wird, aber unsere Macht
wird nach wie vor fürs Erste eine ziemlich bescheidene sein. Denn so
schnell nicht verharschen die Wunden, welche die Sünden und das Unglück
von Jahrhunderten geschlagen haben.*

And yet, if one day the task of national reform succeeds, the disgrace
will indeed come to an end, that a great people is condemned to the
policies of a small state through its basic law, but our power will remain
modest in the beginning. For the wounds which the sins and misery of
centuries have inflicted, will not crust over so quickly.

Heinrich von Treitschke

Much has been written about the so-called New Right in Germany in
recent years. Its rise has caused alarm both within the country and abroad,
particularly in the United States, where, arguably, alarmism has catered
well to a local audience.[1] While the New Right played less of a role during
the unification debate as such, its rise in the early nineties has been directly
linked to unification.[2] Some observers have gone so far as to see it as a
'structural feature' of the transition to a unified Germany, while others
have drawn a suggestive parallel with the period after unification in 1871.[3]

---

[1] For German and American alarmism, see Wolfgang Gessenharter, *Kippt die Republik? Die Neue
Rechte und ihre Unterstützung durch Politik und Medien* (Munich: Knaur, 1995) and Jacob Heilbrunn,
'Germany's New Right', in *Foreign Affairs*, Vol. 76, No. 6 (1996), 80–98.

[2] However, the attack on older intellectuals who had defended the division was the intellectual
starting point for many New Right arguments. See for instance, Rainer Zitelmann, 'Uncomfortable
Questions', in James and Stone (eds), *When the Wall came down*, 106–7, initially as 'Unbequeme
Fragen' in *Die Welt*, 13 October 1990.

[3] John D. Ely, 'The "Black-Brown Hazelnut" in a Bigger Germany: The Rise of a Radical Right as
a Structural Feature', in Michael G. Huelshoff *et al.* (eds), *From Bundesrepublik to Deutschland:
German Politics after Unification* (Ann Arbor: University of Michigan Press, 1993), 235–68.

As with post-Bismarckian despair, intellectuals, and paradoxically conservative intellectuals in particular, rather than celebrating a political success, attacked unified Germany for being a 'soulless, self-satisfied, and philistine state'.[4] And now as then — or so the parallel would suggest — it is the historians who seek to legitimate not just a German nation-state in its consolidation phase, but also its aggressive turn to 'geopolitics' and an assertion of a historically defined national interest — partly to compensate for its supposed lack of national identity.

This chapter analyzes the rise (and, I argue, fall) of the New Right. It also specifically questions some of the historical and social scientific categories relied on by observers to explain it. Given the New Right's own invocation of the likes of Carl Schmitt and Ernst Jünger, the movement has most often been compared to the 'Conservative Revolution' of the 1920s, but also linked to the 'extremism of the centre' sometimes employed to explain the rise of fascism.[5] I argue that few of these analogies prove convincing. Just as the New Right has remained fixated on its supposedly hegemonic predecessors on the left, namely the generation of '68, critics of the New Right have tended to exaggerate the parallels with earlier extreme right-wing movements. Rather than using blanket terms such as the 'Conservative Revolution', based on a number of vaguely defined common features, I argue that a comparison between the post-unification New Right and earlier right-wing intellectual movements *in the Federal Republic* is most instructive in determining the prospects — and limits — for the New Right project. Therefore, I shall analyze a number of traditions of conservative and right-wing thought in West Germany, to which the ideology of the New Right will then be related. These traditions are purely heuristic devices, since individuals in one tradition could often also be found in another, for instance étatiste intellectuals indebted to Schmitt's public law theories might also be 'neo-Fichtean' nationalists. But these traditions do provide an intellectual map to situate the New Right beyond alarmism or apology.

I shall first present an overview of New Right thinking, drawing on its two main manifestos, the volume *Westbindung* [Ties to the West] for foreign policy and *Die Selbstbewußte Nation* [The Self-Confident Nation] for domestic policy and cultural criticism. A genealogy of the New Right will then be followed by a conceptual anatomy of New Right ideology, before I evaluate some of the categories which have been put forward to classify the New Right. Finally, I suggest a range of reasons for why the

---

[4] Elliot Neaman, 'A New Conservative Revolution? Neo-Nationalism, Collective Memory, and the New Right in Germany since Unification', in Hermann Kurthen *et al.* (eds), *Antisemitism and Xenophobia in Germany after Unification* (New York: Oxford University Press, 1997), 190–208.

[5] Hans-Martin Lohmann (ed.), *Extremismus der Mitte: Vom rechten Verständnis deutscher Nation* (Frankfurt/Main: Fischer, 1994).

movement failed in its self-conscious quest for 'cultural hegemony' and is likely to remain marginal in the foreseeable future.

Die Selbstbewußte Nation: Inventing a New German Right

The argument so far has been that the Left had been caught off ideological balance by the prospect of unification, and subsequently had turned in on itself. It did not concentrate on providing any visions for a unified Germany, and, consequently, space opened up on the intellectual field for the Right. In this volatile situation, a clarion call was sounded, which was to have far-reaching effects upon the intellectual climate of Germany. In early 1993, the playwright Botho Strauß published his highly controversial essay 'Anschwellender Bocksgesang' [Rising Song of the Goat, with the double meaning of Impending Tragedy] in, of all magazines, *Der Spiegel*.[6] For some interpreters, the piece effectively combined all the elements which had constituted the ideology of the interwar intellectuals of the 'Conservative Revolution': a tragic view of history, xenophobia, an idealization of asceticism and duty, a distinction between the 'leaders' and 'the masses', and, above all, nationalism, with Strauß also figuring as the latest protagonist in a long line of antimodern 'aesthetic fundamentalists', which included figures such as Stefan George, Ludwig Klages and Hugo von Hofmannsthal.[7] More perceptively, Strauß's essay was seen as a mixture of René Girard's anthropology of sacrifice and the 'sacred', and ingenious *topoi* which had in fact long been part of Strauß's literary work.[8] Others again saw in the piece a hypersensitive poet's conscious provocation of the intellectual *juste milieu* of the old Federal Republic, which found its predictable response in an outcry from the left-liberal media.[9] In any case, 'Anschwellender Bocksgesang' remained a reference point for voices that warned of an impending Conservative Revolution as much as the representatives of the self-styled 'New Democratic Right'. Quoting extensively

---

[6] Strauß, 'Anschwellender Bocksgesang'.

[7] M. and S. Greiffenhagen, *Ein schwieriges Vaterland*, 281–2; Stefan Breuer, *Anatomie der Konservativen Revolution* (Darmstadt: Wissenschaftliche Buchgesellschaft, 1993) and *Ästhetischer Fundmentalismus: Stefan George und der deutsche Antimodernismus* (Darmstadt: Wissenschaftliche Buchgesellschaft, 1995).

[8] Richard Herzinger and Hannes Stein, *Endzeit-Propheten oder die Offensive der Antiwestler: Fundamentalismus, Antiamerikanismus und Neue Rechte* (Reinbek: Rowohlt, 1995), 190–200. See also René Girard, *Violence and the Sacred*, trans. Patrick Gregory (Baltimore: Johns Hopkins University Press, 1977). For Strauß's poetic views on the German question before 1989, see *Diese Erinnnerung an einen, der nur einen Tag zu Gast War*, 46–51.

[9] For a critique of the Left's reaction to Strauß's essay as another instance of 'helpless anti-fascism', see Claus Leggewie, *Druck von rechts: Wohin treibt die Bundesrepublik?* (Munich: C. H. Beck, 1993), 118.

from Strauß's essay – as well as including it as the opening chapter – New Right intellectuals launched their own collection of essays entitled *Die Selbstbewußte Nation* [The Self-Confident Nation] in 1994. The book and its foreign policy counterpart *Westbindung*, published one year earlier, contained a great number of essays of varying quality, although none of them could be called scholarly in a strict sense. Some observers rightly pointed to the diversity of approaches and differences in the degree of conservatism, arguing that the New Right had failed 'to find authors who could agree on what the New Right was Right about'.[10] However, the suspicion remained that this very heterogeneity constituted a conscious ideological strategy to liberate the Right from the 'intellectual ghetto' to which it saw itself so often confined after 1945. Even so, there were a number of common strands and reference points which make it possible to speak of a unified ideological programme, or even a 'conservative manifesto'.

The New Right's interpretation of the state of Germany had three basic elements: a fundamental critique of contemporary culture and in particular the media, criticism of the political establishment, and criticism of foreign-policy-making, with the latter two derived from the first. Overall, however, it was in the mixture – and mutual support of – cultural and political arguments which gave the New Right's analysis its inner logic and its distinctive flavour. Since Germany was supposedly in the grip of a feminine, excessively caring *Binnenmoral* [internal family morality] and a hedonistic liberalism, relentlessly enforced by a totalitarian leftist media monopoly, Germany failed to project power and become a proper 'militant democracy' both inside and outside. Consequently, it was in danger of losing inner security due to its lax stance on crime, and outer security due to its pervasive pacifist ideology.

The editors of *Westbindung* argued that the identification with Western liberal values had taken on 'an almost totalitarian character', with the cultural connection to the West as a new secular utopia.[11] Germany's public sphere was dominated by a left-liberal media, which, in its zeal for 'political correctness', had set up a 'discourse-apartheid', through which members of the Right were systematically silenced and excluded.[12] Representatives of the New Right not too subtly equated the supposed leftist dictators of public discourse with the National Socialists' 'directing of

[10] David Schoenbaum and Elizabeth Pond, *The German question and other German questions* (London: Macmillan, 1996), 45.

[11] Introduction 'Wir Deutschen und der Westen', in Rainer Zitelmann, Karlheinz Weißmann and Michael Großheim (eds), *Westbindung* (Berlin: Propyläen, 1992), 9–17; here 10.

[12] Ulrich Schacht, 'Stigma und Sorge. Über deutsche Identität nach Auschwitz', in Heimo Schwilk and Ulrich Schacht (eds), *Die Selbstbewußte Nation* (Berlin: Ullstein, 1994), 57–68.

consciousness'.[13] In essence, they set up a homogenous, quasi-totalitarian enemy, charging that this was precisely what the Left was inflicting on them. Consequently, the New Right could present itself as automatically anti-totalitarian.

Since the Left's dogmatic dealing with the Nazi past had supposedly started to resemble National Socialism in its method, i.e. its fanatical will to destroy the ideological enemy, it was actually the New Right which not only did justice to the victims of National Socialism, but, in a sense, was also among the victims. Members of the New Right therefore presented themselves as defending the authenticity of Auschwitz against the 'media terrorists' and 'consciousness manipulators' who instrumentalized the Holocaust to enforce their discursive power, thereby also contributing to a more open, even liberal intellectual climate in Germany.[14] Breaking 'taboos' and contesting historiographical theories such as the *Sonderweg* could then be presented as brave and even as progressive *qua* transgressive.[15] Thus, the New Right first sought to redefine the intellectual field in its favour by presenting itself as a victim in a discursive battle with the left media, thereby taking on the appearance of a truly liberal force, only to aim at gaining the very kind of 'cultural hegemony' from which they claimed to suffer. From the very start, then, the New Right project was a highly self-conscious — and contradictory — one.

Now that the scene of ideological battle had been set, a specific interpretation of culture and politics was presented. For the New Right, West Germany was above all dominated by a hedonistic liberalism and had lost its cultural identity. The American-inspired liberalism 'of maritime origins' appeared as a foreign imposition which in its universalist thrust destroyed all difference: specific merits of German culture such as inwardness and irrationalism were eradicated, and the sublime banished from the arts. The New Right appropriated the concept of difference from the anti-imperialist and anti-racist theories of the Left, setting itself up as the defender of 'difference and particularity'. In short, the Right appropriated a concept of the ideological opposition in order to turn the concept against the very intellectual group which had invented it.[16] Unlike the Left, however, they interpreted difference as referring first and foremost to national difference.[17] This postmodern-cum-conservative defence of the

---

[15] Ronald Bubik 'Herrschaft und Medien. Über den Kampf gegen die linke Meinungsdominanz', in *Die Selbstbewußte Nation*, 182–94; here 183–4.

[14] Rainer Zitelmann, *Wohin treibt unsere Republik?* (Berlin: Ullstein, 1994), 185.

[15] Bubik, 'Herrschaft', 183.

[16] For the invention of this intellectual move by the French New Right, see Pierre-André Taguieff, *La République menacée* (Paris: textuel, 1996).

[17] Ernst Nolte, 'Links und Rechts. Über Geschichte und Aktualität einer politischen Alternative', in *Die Selbstbewußte Nation*, 145–62; here 160.

national as a form of particularity worth preserving was designed to avoid charges of racism by substituting 'culture' for 'race' as the substance of an ideology focused on 'differences'. But it was then also mixed with older anti-universalist arguments advanced by Counter-Enlightenment thinkers like Joseph de Maistre.

In the Right's interpretation, the hedonistic culture of the Federal Republic entailed a loss of a sense of tragedy and of the value of suffering, claims which echoed not only Strauß's, but also Bohrer's 'provincialist' diagnosis. This loss of a sense of tragedy was brought about by an 'insurance' and 'security mentality', which had led to the 'infantilization' of the Germans. Institutionally, this mentality was supported by the welfare state, and ideologically fostered by an American-inspired addiction to the 'pursuit of happiness' in a society pervaded by a feminine ethics of caring. Germans, deluded by liberalism, conceived the state as an enlarged family, a charge which Arnold Gehlen had first levelled against the old Federal Republic. At the same time, this *Binnenmoral* did not afford any real security, as social cohesion and a sense of authority were weakened. Germany had degenerated into decadence, since a utopian form of liberalism and media 'humanitarianism' were undermining the state.[18] At the heart of this diagnosis was a particular philosophical anthropology found throughout *Die Selbstbewußte Nation* which was heavily indebted to Arnold Gehlen's thought. Gehlen, sometimes portrayed as a 'German Hobbes', saw a 'deficiency' in instincts and therefore behavioural indeterminacy as constitutive of human beings who consequently were in desperate need of authority and strong institutions to provide orientation.[19]

A foil for the Germany in which authority had broken down was Austria, which was still a homogeneous nation-state guaranteeing inner and outer security, and a country of authentic experience not distorted by an 'opinion-industry'.[20] The New Right drew a connection between Austria's particular culture protected from 'universal humanistic liberalism' and its neutrality, thereby reinforcing the perception that cultural and political ties to the West were bound up with each other. The Austrian body politic had remained 'healthy', because the Austrians had not been subject to 'Re-education' and had not since engaged in 'collective self-flagellation'.[21]

---

[18] Karlheinz Weißmann, *Rückruf in die Geschichte: Die deutsche Herausforderung: Alte Gefahren — Neue Chancen* (Berlin: Ullstein, 1993), 176–85.

[19] Arnold Gehlen, *Man: His Nature and Place in the World*, trans. Clare McMillan and Karl Pillemer (New York: Columbia University Press, 1988).

[20] The New Right's 'opinion industry' was of course modelled on Adorno's critique of the 'culture industry'.

[21] Peter Meier-Bergfeld, 'Über das Hissen der schwarz-rot-goldenen Flagge in Wien', in *Die Selbstbewußte Nation*, 195–226; here 212.

The strong Austrian state acted politically by distinguishing between inside and outside, as well as friend and enemy, while in Germany identity and consequently the ability to make such discriminations had disappeared.

The rather crude image which emerged was one of a Germany that, excessively security-oriented, had lost all sense of the political, of power and of the necessity of projecting it. Its internal *Hypermoral* [hyper-moralism], its legalism and addiction to security were shared by an elite which lacked self-confidence.[22] On a metaphorical level, democracy had led to the infantilization of Germans, because they tried to avoid the recognition of — and the confrontation with — evil.[23] In this 'psycho-social logic', Germany, like an adolescent, needed to grow out of its neurotic fixation on the past and become 'self-confident'. A 'self-confident' elite was needed to lead a country in which 'identity, social cohesion and transcendence', in one word, *Gemeinschaft*, were reinforced. The supposedly utopian ideal of a civil society had to be abandoned in favour of the homogeneous nation, which was always and everywhere a 'community of fate and mutual protection'.[24] Only such a self-confident nation could then project power, engage in geo-politics and meet new international challenges by making sovereign decisions. This also meant putting an end to 'the mystical idealization' and 'fetishization' of ties to the West. After what they hoped was the 'fall of the Federal Republic', the New Right explicitly called for a 'new foundation' which entailed establishing continuities with the pre-war past.

Consequently, the contributors of *Westbindung* also had to dismantle the idea of a *Sonderweg*, which was attacked as epistemologically flawed and historically untenable, and yet polemically applied to the Federal Republic itself, arguing that post-national West Germany had been yet another historical aberration. These scholars took seriously the Left's dictum that 'whoever denies the thesis of the *Sonderweg*, breaks the back of the political consciousness of the Federal Republic'.[25] While Germany was not necessarily to sever all ties to the West, it should seize on unification as a new beginning, and shed its child-like dependence on an idealized 'West'. In foreign policy, this meant above all overcoming the Germans' supposed 'fear of power', instead 'normally' pursuing a

[22] This charge was also first made by Gehlen in *Moral und Hypermoral* (Frankfurt/Main: Athenäum, 1969), where Gehlen differentiated between *Binnenmoral* and other forms of ethics, criticizing their supposed conflation by the Left.

[23] Rüdiger Safranski, 'Destruktion und Lust. Über die Wiederkehr des Bösen', in *Die Selbstbewußte Nation*, 237–48; here 238–9.

[24] Michael J. Inacker, 'Macht und Moralität. Über eine neue deutsche Sicherheitspolitik', in *Die Selbstbewußte Nation*, 346–89; here 368.

[25] Sontheimer, *Von Deutschlands Republik*, 62.

realistically defined 'national interest' and establishing a clear national scope of action.[26] Intellectually, it also amounted to a call to rediscover supposedly 'realist' thinkers in the German tradition, such as Ludwig Dehio and Gerhard Ritter.[27]

Parallel to these directly cultural-cum-political claims, a 'meta-discussion' on intellectual strategy ran through both *Westbindung* and *Die Selbstbewußte Nation*. Representatives of the New Right openly claimed that they had to learn from the Left, and in particular the generation of 1968, one central lesson, namely the need to capture public discourse in a systematic way, rely on a 'capillary diffusion' of their ideology, and 'march through the institutions'.[28] They also sought to replicate the attempt by the French *Nouvelle Droite*, inspired by Antonio Gramsci, first to gain cultural hegemony, and then, in Gramscian terms, turn from a War of position to a War of movement. Defining themselves self-consciously as 'young' and as 'the generation of 1989', they developed scholarly and journalistic strategies to move public discourse to the right.[29] This is not to suggest that their stance merely amounted to a generational rebellion, but it is quite clear that many of their essays which detailed ways of gaining discursive power also served as career manuals.

However, where for the *Nouvelle Droite* biology, and, to some extent, ancient history, had been the academic disciplines – and therefore the cultural or 'meta'-level – on which they advanced their political claims, the prime task of the New Right was charting a new historiographical path for the Third Reich. In particular, they attacked the historical claims which constituted the backbone of constitutional patriotism.[30] From the start,

---

[26] Gregor Schöllgen, *Angst vor der Macht: Die Deutschen und ihre Außenpolitik* (Berlin: Ullstein, 1993). For links to the discourse of *Mitteleuropa* and geopolitics see Heinz Brill, *Geopolitik heute: Deutschlands Chance?* (Berlin: Ullstein, 1994).

[27] *Ibid.*, 102.

[28] As Dieter Stein, editor of the primary New Right publication *Junge Freiheit* claimed: 'It is often conveniently forgotten that conservatism was grouped not around parties, but around journals, circles and courageous personalities . . . the centre cannot be a party, but has to be a diverse political, cultural and media "capillary system"'. Dieter Stein, 'Niederwerfung der Konservativen', in *Junge Freiheit* No. 4 (1992), 2.

[29] Roland Bubik, *Wir 89er: Wer wir sind – was wir wollen* (Berlin: Ullstein, 1995).

[30] Not surprisingly, the French *Nouvelle Droite* chose biology and ancient history, and *not* contemporary history, at a time when the 'Vichy syndrome' was finally coming into the open in the early 1970s, while the German Right launched their revisionism when a negative reading of German history was coming under attack in the early to mid-1980s. See Henry Rousso, *The Vichy Syndrome: History and Memory in France since 1944*, trans. Arthur Goldhammer (Cambridge, Mass.: Harvard University Press, 1991). For the French New Right's 'host of problems' of 'fragmentation of collective memory', 'lack of a popular base', 'ideological incoherence' and 'the taboo on any movement or culture that smacked of fascism', see Robert Gildea, *The Past in French History* (New Haven: Yale University Press, 1994), 329–39.

then, the New Right sought political legitimacy through the struggle over 'culture', which primarily came to mean 'history', rather than staking out present constitutional positions or policy prescriptions.

A Detour via History

Most members of the New Right were in fact young historians who grew up during the years of the *Tendenzwende* in the 1970s and experienced the *Historikerstreit* during their early academic careers. Mostly, they perceived the dispute as a witch hunt of academics who dared to utter unorthodox historical opinions. They also came strongly to believe that any change in the present and future self-understanding of Germany was to be affected through changing perceptions of the past. In other words, they fully subscribed to Michael Stürmer's claim that 'in a country without history, he who fills the memory, defines the concepts and interprets the past wins the future'. Karlheinz Weißmann, for instance, argued that 'the necessary integration of the Germans will be accomplished through a common national history or it will not be accomplished at all'.[31] Therefore, while publishing polemical political essays, members of the New Right also continued the parallel project of 'historicizing', or rather 'normalizing', National Socialism in their scholarly work.[32] Not surprisingly, Ernst Nolte came to be a crucial reference point for this movement, praised for his courage and objectivity given the attacks by the defenders of a supposed left-wing orthodoxy. Nolte himself had also drawn specific historiographical-cum-political lessons from the revolutions of 1989, namely that the notion of the *Bürgertum* and a 'defensive nationalism' needed to be rehabilitated, theses that the New Right was to develop further.[33] But in a rather insidious move, New Right historians also claimed the legacy of Martin Broszat and other historians such as Tim Mason and Detlev Peukert, who had died relatively young and left unfinished *oeuvres*. Like these historians, they were interested in the modernizing effects of National Socialism as well as its 'historicization'.[34] Broszat had initially given credibility to the idea of 'historicization', while Peukert, from a quasi-Foucauldian perspective, had

---

[31] Weißmann, *Rückruf*, 49–50.

[32] Most notable in this context was Zitelmann's redefinition of Hitler as a modern social revolutionary, *Hitler: Selbstverständnis eines Revolutionärs* (Darmstadt: Wissenschaftliche Buchgesellschaft, 1990).

[33] Ernst Nolte, 'Die unvollständige Revolution', in *Frankfurter Allgemeine Zeitung*, 24 January 1991. Nolte also reiterated his central claim that '1933' had to be seen as a hostile imitation of 'the more important Russian year 1917'.

[34] Michael Prinz and Rainer Zitelmann (eds), *Nationalsozialismus und Modernisierung* (Darmstadt: Wissenschaftliche Buchgesellschaft, 1994).

cast National Socialism as a pathological part of modernity, and the human and social sciences in particular.[35] By claiming that National Socialism had simply been an extreme expression of the 'totalitarian aspect' of modernity, New Right historians could link the project of 'historicization' with the totalitarianism paradigm and the postmodernism debate, so that their theses would also resonate with leftists turned right-wing under the influence of post-structuralism.[36] Moreover, historical reinterpretation had to extend to the early years of the Federal Republic, and particularly the common view of West Germany as a foreign policy 'success story' due to Adenauer's opting for the West. Rainer Zitelmann sought to rehabilitate the role of 'Adenauer's opponents' who had fought for German unity, and, so the historiographical subtext went, had been vindicated by unification vis-à-vis Adenauer's blind followers who had bound themselves with 'fetishistic' ties to the West.[37] Aside from the stress on German sovereignty, such studies also implied that after Communism's defeat, conservatism should end its temporary anti-Communist alliance with liberalism and the West, and return to its central pre-1945 beliefs.[38] Moreover, against Ralph Giordano's thesis of the 'second guilt' which the Germans had incurred through repressing the past in the post-war period, a different reading had to be established, according to which the 1950s were actually characterized by an adequate *Vergangenheitsbewältigung*.[39] Finally, moving into the more immediate past, the 1968 student movement had to be historically discredited in a single historiographical stroke with the discrediting of the idea of anti-fascism.[40] Where the '68 Left had interpreted anti-fascism as

---

[35] Martin Broszat/Saul Friedländer, 'A Controversy about the Historicization of National Socialism', in *New German Critique*, No. 44 (1988), 85–126, and Detlev J. K. Peukert, 'The Genesis of the "Final Solution" from the Spirit of Science', in Thomas Childers and Jane Caplan (eds), *Reevaluating the Third Reich* (New York: Holmes & Meier, 1993), 234–52.

[36] Uwe Backes, Eckhard Jesse and Rainer Zitelmann (eds), *Die Schatten der Vergangenheit: Impulse zur Historisierung des Nationalsozialismus* (Berlin: Propyläen, 1990).

[37] Rainer Zitelmann, *Adenauers Gegner: Streiter für die Einheit* (Erlangen: Straube, 1991).

[38] As Ulrich Raulff noted, this claim went beyond what Nolte would have endorsed. See 'Auch eine geistige Welt', in *Frankfurter Allgemeine Zeitung*, 13 April 1994. Nolte also did not see unified Germany as 'another country' and a new state in the way the New Right wanted to. See Ernst Nolte, 'Untergang der Bundesrepublik? Zur Frage der Kontinuität in der Nachkriegsgeschichte', in *Frankfurter Allgemeine Zeitung*, 5 September 1990.

[39] Manfred Kittel, *Die Legende von der 'Zweiten Schuld': Vergangenheitsbewältigung in der Ära Adenauer* (Berlin: Ullstein, 1993), criticized Ralph Giordano, *Die zweite Schuld oder von der Last ein Deutscher zu sein* (Hamburg: Rasch und Röhring, 1987).

[40] Criticism of 1968 was clearly bound up with a larger critique of anti-fascism in the case of Klaus Rainer Röhl, *Linke Lebenslügen: Eine überfällige Abrechnung* (Berlin: Ullstein, 1994). Röhl had previously been the editor of the left-wing magazine *konkret* (and the husband of Ulrike Meinhof). In 1993 he completed a dissertation on the cooperation between Nazis and the KPD in 1932, with Nolte as his supervisor. For a critique of anti-fascism, see Hans-Helmuth Knütter, *Die Faschismus-Keule: Das letzte Aufgebot der deutschen Linken* (Berlin: Ullstein, 1993).

necessarily anti-nationalist, the New Right now equated 'anti-fascist' with 'anti-German'. Taken together, New Right historians, widely represented in the Ullstein publishing house, could then offer a complete alternative reading of the history of the Federal Republic, from the heroic role of Adenauer's opponents to the disastrous effects of 1968.[41]

This alternative reading of history was presented with a particular *Gelassenheit*, i.e. calmness and even 'coolness', against the supposed *volkspädagogische* [popular pedagogical] intentions of left-wing historians. Previous historians were criticized for having imposed themselves as judges, while New Right historians could assume a tone of sobriety and 'realism', which was in turn linked with a self-consciously 'realist' position in foreign policy. Foreign policy intellectuals like Gregor Schöllgen played on the double-meaning of sovereignty, both as national sovereignty, and as a superior attitude of calmness, which allowed the sober calculation of interests.[42] 'History', both as a Rankean exploration of the authentic history of National Socialism and as a guide to the national future, was then seen as superior to the quintessentially West German – and 'pedagogical' – disciplines such as sociology or political science, a repository of unchanging and politically untainted truths. It was also played off against utopian thought, and fitted with Strauß's desire to reconnect with the '*lange Zeit*' [a mythical *longue durée*].[43] Consequently, the post-unification period was above all 'the chance of the German historians'.[44]

However, while some of the early works of Zitelmann and his followers were well received across the historical profession, it became clear relatively soon that emphasizing the modernizing aspects of National Socialism was to some extent a renewed effort to relativize National Socialism after the *Historikerstreit* had been won by the Left.[45] Especially when Ullstein, where Zitelmann had gained an important position, began publishing a whole battery of books with the double aim of attacking the Left and advancing 'historicization', the impression was reinforced that contemporary history was being instrumentalized by an academic-cum-political network of New Right intellectuals. While some left-wing

---

[41] Maria Zens, 'Vergangenheit verlegen: Zur Wiederherstellung nationaler Größe im Hause Ullstein', in *Blätter für deutsche und internationale Politik*, Vol. 38 (1993), 1364–75.

[42] Schöllgen, *Angst*, 33–4.

[43] Claudia Mayer-Iswandy, 'Ästhetik und Macht: Zur diskursiven Unordnung im vereinten Deutschland', in *German Studies Review*, Vol. 19 (1996), 501–23; here 510.

[44] Schöllgen, *Angst*, 118.

[45] Zitelmann's Hitler book was well received, while the book he co-edited on the 'brown elite' was even widely acclaimed. See Roland Smelser and Rainer Zitelmann (eds), *Die braune Elite: 22 biographische Skizzen* (Darmstadt: Wissenschaftliche Buchgesellschaft, 1990).

commentators clearly went too far in demonizing this supposed 'con-spiracy', there could be little doubt that what Dirk van Laak aptly named a 'circle' (of reviewing, citing and promoting each other's work) had formed with the open ambition of conquering 'cultural hegemony'.[46]

However, while this detour via history was clearly seen as a precondi-tion for future policy change, 'history' on its own could not answer the demand for policy substance. What patterns of conservative thought, and particularly post-war West German right-wing thought, did the New Right attempt to draw on and renew for the 1990s? Or did they in fact reach back even further and seek connections to the anti-liberal and anti-parliamentarian thought of the Conservative Revolution, precisely because earlier attempts to establish a 'democratic Right' in West Germany had foundered? To fully understand the New Right, one needs to understand the history of post-war conservatism – and its dilemmas, of which repre-sentatives of the New Right were highly aware. Therefore, I will describe three traditions of right-wing conservative thought in the old Federal Republic.[47]

The Statist Tradition: The Spectre of Carl Schmitt

In post-war conservatism, the étatiste tradition was by far the most impor-tant ideological cluster both in terms of academic reputation and in terms of actual influence on policy. It was pervasive in a significant number of law departments, and some of the lawyers subscribing to its central tenets – most prominently the Social Democrat Ernst-Wolfgang Böckenförde – sat on the Constitutional Court.

Representatives of this tradition mostly took as their starting point the teachings of Carl Schmitt. Schmitt had declared the death of the Leviathan, i.e. the end of modern European statehood at the hands of orga-nized interest groups, and resigned himself to the failure of its replace-ment through a *Reich* as the new form of political unity. Schmitt's followers instead tried to come to terms with what they saw as a structural change of modern statehood – into modern 'industrial society' and the *Verwaltungsstaat* [administrative state].[48] Like Schmitt, however, they pre-served a suspicion of the 'self-organizing society' based on a negative philosophical anthropology and a Hobbesian view of the axiomatic

---

[46] Dirk van Laak, 'Nicht West nicht Ost oder Zaungäste auf Bindungssuche', in Lohmann (ed.), *Extremismus der Mitte*, 88–104; here 92–3.

[47] This exercise will necessarily remain schematic and incomplete. In particular, I have to leave out Christian conservatism and what is often called the 'racist fringe'.

[48] Reinhard Mehring, *Carl Schmitt zur Einführung* (Hamburg: Junius, 1992), 13–30.

relationship of state protection and unquestioned citizen obedience. Thus Schmitt, despite many anachronisms and much mythical baggage, could remain the inspiration of étatiste thought in post-war Germany, because during every 'state' and 'legitimation crisis' – real, imagined, or even wished-for – his basic arguments against 'excessive pluralism' and political disintegration could be resurrected. They were reiterated against the emancipatory claims of social movements and individuals as undermining the unity and security which only the state guaranteed. But in moments of crisis, conservative statists were also tempted to put reason of state above the rule of law.

Already in the 1950s, during the debate about whether the Constitution primarily mandated a *Rechtsstaat* or a *Sozialstaat*, Schmitt's pupils, above all Ernst Forsthoff and Werner Weber, drew on Schmittian thought to fight the establishment of an extensive welfare state, since it was an 'iron law' that more *Sozialstaatlichkeit* meant less *Staatlichkeit* [stateness].[49] Moreover, initially part of a rather secretive network of 'circles' and private 'academies' which defined themselves against the intellectual climate in the 1950s Federal Republic, the Schmittians increasingly came out into the open in the 1960s.[50] The journal *Der Staat* was established as the main forum for the statist school, which despite the common use of a legal and political vocabulary indebted to Schmitt, accommodated a range of ideological persuasions. On the one hand, Böckenförde and the 'neoconservative' Hermann Lübbe tried to 'liberalize' Schmitt's teachings and appropriate his decisionism and his teachings on the 'state of the exception' to strengthen the underpinnings of a 'militant' liberal democracy.[51] They combined this 'liberalization' with the claim that what their critics derided as 'neoconservatism' was in fact the intellectual preservation of an authentic liberalism, whereas the 'progressivism' of the '68 generation would have 'totalitarian' consequences.[52] On the other hand, neo-Fichtean

---

[49] Ernst Forsthoff, 'Verfassung und Verfassungswirklichkeit der Bundesrepublik', in *Merkur*, Vol. 22 (1968), 401–14, and *Rechtsstaatlichkeit und Sozialstaatlichkeit* (Darmstadt: Wissenschaftliche Buchgesellschaft, 1968). Forsthoff's defence of the *Rechtsstaat* might have appeared like a classically liberal or at least libertarian position. However, his substantial view of the state was mirrored by an image of society as a natural hierarchical organism. See Peter Caldwell, 'Ernst Fortshoff and the Legacy of Radical State Theory in the Federal Republic of Germany', in *History of Political Thought*, Vol. 5 (1994), 615–41.

[50] Dirk van Laak, *Gespräche in der Sicherheit des Schweigens: Carl Schmitt in der Geistesgeschichte der frühen Bundesrepublik* (Berlin: Akademie, 1993).

[51] For instance Ernst-Wolfgang Böckenförde, 'Der verdrängte Ausnahmezustand: Zum Handeln der Staatsgewalt in außergewöhnlichen Lagen: Carl Schmitt zum 90. Geburtstag gewidmet', in *Neue Juristische Wochenschrift*, Vol. 31 (1978), 1881–90.

[52] For instance Hermann Lübbe, 'Carl Schmitt liberal rezipiert', in Helmut Quaritsch (ed.), *Complexio Oppositorum: Über Carl Schmitt: Vorträge und Diskussionsbeiträge des 28. Sonderseminars 1986 der Hochschule für Verwaltungswissenschaften Speyer* (Berlin: Duncker & Humblot, 1988), 427–40.

nationalist Bernard Willms drew on the nationalist strands in Schmitt's thought, and polemically played off his agonal concept of the political against the supposedly apolitical tenets of Critical Theory.[53] Conservatives outside public law circles also took up prominent Schmittian themes such as the critique of liberal institutions to deal with 'the exception'.[54] Most of these thinkers were united by an aversion to the democratic political science of the post-war period, which they perceived as apolitical and as simply reflecting the Allies' Re-education efforts.[55] They claimed that for a proper political science, the question of 'identity', established through friend–enemy decisions, had to be primary. As Hans-Joachim Arndt, referring to a 'lack of identity', paradigmatically explained: '. . . the primary question about the unity of Germany is: whether at all and who?, and only secondly it then becomes how that somebody is to exist constitutionally'.[56] However, while the right-wing intellectuals focused on recasting 'identity' through attacks on Re-education and the national victimization of the Germans remained marginal both in the academy and in the public sphere at large, intellectuals employing Schmitt's conceptual tools in thinking about institutions had considerably more influence. Rüdiger Altmann's concept of the *Formierte Gesellschaft* effectively became government policy for a short period in the mid-1960s, while Lübbe's liberal decisionism and his ideas on education were widely discussed in the 1970s, as the state had to defend itself against terrorism and as education reforms were foundering. Finally, the *Tendenzwende* of the early 1970s was led by conservative figures who sought to modernize conservatism after the party-political failure of the NPD in 1969, but still took Schmitt as a guiding political spirit. Already then the logic of breaking 'taboos' was at the centre of conservative strategies. And Schmitt, both as the enigmatic *éminence grise* residing in his 'internal exile' in his Westphalian home town of Plettenberg and as the author of notorious critiques of the then 'hegemonic' liberalism, was one of the greatest taboos of all.

---

[53] For one of the earliest criticisms of Critical Theory for its 'political deficit' by one of the later neo-nationalists, see Bernard Willms, *Kritik und Politik: Jürgen Habermas oder das politische Defizit der 'Kritischen Theorie'* (Frankfurt/Main: Suhrkamp, 1973). Willms criticized the reduction of politics to praxis and the further reduction of praxis to communication.

[54] Armin Mohler, for instance, claimed that '. . . "power" is precisely the rest of reality, which "cannot be solved" [rationally]', and linked this misrecognition of power to a lack of engagement with the 'exception'. See *Was die Deutschen fürchten: Angst vor der Politik – Angst vor der Geschichte – Angst vor der Macht* (Stuttgart: Seewald, 1966), 195 and 199.

[55] The foundational text of right-wing political science was Hans-Joachim Arndt, *Die Besiegten von 1945: Versuch einer Politologie für Deutsche samt Würdigung der Politischen Wissenschaft in der Bundesrepublik Deutschland* (Berlin: Duncker & Humblot, 1978).

[56] *Ibid.*, 80 and 92.

Technocratic Conservatism: The End of *Posthistoire*

Closely connected to the statist tradition was the technocratic conservatism of the 1950s and 1960s. It was formulated by theorists who had mostly been active National Socialists, but who, after National Socialism's excessive 'primacy of the political', renounced any room for politics in the face of supposed *Sachzwänge* [objective, and particularly technological, constraints] and the ideal of social planning. With the triumph of 'secondary systems' (Hans Freyer), i.e. a technical 'second nature', and the 'crystallization' of all cultural options (Arnold Gehlen), these right-wing Hegelian thinkers theorized the arrival of a state of *posthistoire*, which precluded any further ideological development and especially further 'emancipation'.[57] In other words, technical necessities had finally crowded out any room for politics, and, according to Gehlen's philosophical anthropology, only left individuals the option of having themselves 'consumed' by institutions.

When the political calm of the 1950s and early 1960s was challenged, technocratic conservatives resorted to the argument that the intellectuals constituted a new parasitic 'quasi-aristocracy' or 'priesthood' oblivious of − and in fact harmful to − the smooth functioning of industrial society.[58] They also charged the Left with having systematically captured and distorted public discourse, which inspired a number of academics associated with the *Tendenzwende* to 'reclaim' central concepts from the Left.[59]

Subsequently, technocratic conservatism was weakened by the rise of environmentalism and the realization that the diagnosis of *posthistoire* had only seemed plausible during the period of extraordinary stability associated with the long post-war boom. But, at least as far as its arguments about economic necessities were concerned, technocratic conservatism was revived in the early 1980s, coupled with a form of communitarianism as the emphasis on national cohesion and a new scepticism about the philosophical claims of the Enlightenment − advocated by philosophers like Odo Marquard.[60] Moreover, it was fused with the 'culture as compensation' argument originally put forward by Joachim Ritter and his school in the 1950s. These ingredients constituted the conservatism of the 1980s, which

---

[57] Hans Freyer, *Theorie des gegenwärtigen Zeitalters* (Stuttgart: Deutsche Verlags-Anstalt, 1955) and Muller, *The Other God That Failed*.

[58] Arnold Gehlen, 'Das Engagement der Intellektuellen gegenüber dem Staat', in *Merkur*, Vol. 18 (1964), 401–13, and Helmut Schelsky, *Die Arbeit tun die anderen: Klassenkampf und Priesterherrschaft der Intellektuellen* (Opladen: Westdeutscher Verlag, 1975).

[59] Gerd-Klaus Kaltenbrunner (ed.), *Sprache und Herrschaft: Die umfunktionierten Wörter* (Munich: Herder, 1975).

[60] For instance Odo Marquard, *Abschied vom Prinzipiellen* (Stuttgart: Reclam, 1981).

largely failed to deliver its promises for those who had hoped for a true 'spiritual-moral turn' after the CDU had re-conquered power in 1982. There was what was often called a 'traditionalism of modernity', but neither an advocacy of traditional morality, nor an economic libertarianism or 'neoliberalism'. Unlike in Britain and the United States, German conservatism was not successfully 'recast' in the 1970s and 1980s.[61]

The Nationalist Tradition: Beyond Left *and* Right

The statist position often shaded into a nationalist tradition which drew its intellectual resources from German idealism and increasingly came to unite sections of the Right and the Left. While nationalism was largely discredited after the Second World War, from at least the mid-1960s, a standard claim of the Right became that the Germans had lost a sense of their own history, and that a 'recovery of history' was a precondition of national self-confidence. Armin Mohler, the 'secretary' of post-war West German conservatism and the crucial figure in harmonizing various strands of right-wing thought, already argued in 1966 that 'a nation is sure of itself if it lives in accordance with its history'.[62] This loss of history was due to the sceptical generation's 'negative nationalism', or even 'black', i.e. antinationalist, 'messianism'.[63] And already then, the present 'psycho-social' condition of the Germans was described as one of being 'afraid of power' and being 'afraid of history', while conservatives claimed to have properly recognized 'reality', including the necessary breaking of taboos.[64]

With this conceptual structure in place, conservatives first went on the offensive again in the late 1960s, taking Caspar von Schrenck-Notzing's *Charakterwäsche* and Arnold Gehlen's *Moral und Hypermoral* as two foundational texts to overcome the 'overcoming of the past'.[65] They criticized

---

[61] Robert Devigne, *Recasting Conservatism: Oakshott, Strauss, and the Response to Postmodernism* (New Haven: Yale University Press, 1994).

[62] Mohler, *Was die Deutschen fürchten*, 130. The book was dedicated to Schmitt, 'from someone who admits that he has learnt from him'. On Mohler's shaping of post-war conservatism see van Laak, *Gespräche*, 256–62. Not surprisingly, it was Mohler who had predicted (or wished for) the rise of a New Right. Already in 1990, he had talked about the fact that 'a new generation of young right-wingers' was growing up again in Germany, which risked 'uncomfortable thinking'. Armin Mohler, *Liberalenbeschimpfung: Drei politische Traktate* (Essen: Heitz & Höffkes, 1990), 5–6.

[63] Mohler, *Was die Deutschen fürchten*, 134–5.

[64] *Ibid.*, 171. Exactly twenty years later, this dialectic of taboo and 'reality' still constituted one of the major claims in Mohler's rhetoric. See Armin Mohler (ed.), *Wirklichkeit als Tabu: Anmerkungen zur Lage* (Munich: R. Oldenbourg, 1986). Contributors criticized the asylum law, the 'repression of the state' by the Germans and, inevitably, the loss of nationalism.

[65] Armin Mohler, 'Deutscher Konservatismus seit 1945', in *Tendenzwende für Fortgeschrittene* (Munich: Criticón, 1978), 67–80; here 76 and 79 and Caspar von Schrenck-Notzing, *Charakterwäsche: Die amerikanische Besatzung in Deutschland und ihre Folgen* (Stuttgart: Seewald, 1965).

earlier West German conservatism for having been fenced in by anti-communism and for its lack of a positive relation to the nation as well as its fixation on Christianity.[66] Conservatism had simply meant a timid preservation of the status quo, rather than actively shaping politics like the Conservative Revolutionaries had done in the 1920s. Instead, conservatives needed to become self-consciously theoretical – and 'ideological' – again to win the future. At the same time, they had to learn lessons from the establishment of the *Nouvelle Droite* and its Gramscian strategy of concentrating on conquering cultural hegemony, rather than direct party-political success. Mohler in particular sought to shift German conservatism away from the *Gärtnerkonservatismus* [gardener's conservatism], the preserving conservatism he associated with *Abendland* and Adenauer. He had gathered theoretical ammunition first as private secretary to Ernst Jünger, and subsequently as a correspondent for various German newspapers in Paris where he witnessed the rise of de Gaulle and the beginnings of the Fifth Republic.[67] He argued that the Germans should develop their own brand of Gaullism, nationalist, neutralist and authoritarian, and proposed Franz Josef Strauß – for whom he wrote speeches – as a potential German version of the General. However, while Mohler and Gerd-Klaus Kaltenbrunner, as apprentices of the *Nouvelle Droite* and the spiritual masters of a 'reconstruction of conservatism', decisively influenced the *Tendenzwende* of the 1970s, they never managed the transition from cultural influence to actual political power.

Nationalism, however, also experienced a revival on the Left, and in the late 1970s, a neo-nationalism which sought to distance itself from the NPD and attract young Germans, in particular students, fed into the Green movement.[68] Other sectarian groups, which specifically aimed to bridge left and right, sought to establish a 'national revolutionary tradition', in which the situation of the Germans was presented as parallel to that of Third World liberation movements. In this scenario, Germany was militarily – and psychologically – a colonized country, culturally oppressed by both the United States and the Soviet Union, and in danger of losing its identity. A sympathy for the victims of world history, a desire to preserve the particular, and an often crude anti-capitalism coalesced into a vague ideological sentiment which proved appealing to both Right and Left. While the self-proclaimed 'national revolutionary' splinter groups disappeared by the beginning of the 1980s, their ideological protagonists had set the stage for the unprecedented flowering of the peace movement and the high tide of nationalist-cum-neutralist sentiments in the life of the old Federal

---

[66] *Ibid.*, 67.

[67] Armin Mohler, *Die Fünfte Republik: Was steht hinter de Gaulle?* (Munich: Piper, 1963).

[68] Hans-Georg Betz, 'Deutschlandpolitik on the Margins: On the Evolution of Contemporary New Right Nationalism in the Federal Republic', in *New German Critique*, No. 44 (1988), 127–57; here 129–33.

Republic. In an exceptionally successful ideological move, one of the national revolutionary intellectuals, Henning Eichberg, had first introduced the concept of 'national identity', which was to be at the centre of numerous debates of the 1980s.[69] Eichberg's original defence of German national identity had been the preservation of particularity through decentralization and regionalism. He had borrowed the notion of 'ethnopluralism' from the *Nouvelle Droite*, to describe – and prescribe – a rigidly separated plurality of primordial collective identities, linking the 'liberation struggles' of 'small peoples', ecology and anti-capitalism, while repudiating any kind of universalism. In the wake of the disappointment of many left-wing hopes during the 1970s, conservatives increasingly seized on the theme of 'identity', linked it to the rising interest in German history at the end of the decade, and for once achieved the prime goal of post-war West German conservative strategists: 'identity' entered mainstream discourse, as the theme was picked up by respectable academics and journalists.[70]

However, German nationalism received its real boost in the wake of the NATO twin-track decision. In the shadow of what seemed like an impending 'nuclear Holocaust' (with the parallel to the Judeocide intended), arguments about all Germans as victims of superpower imperialism could now be successfully linked with the concept that German unification or at least German neutrality was a precondition for world peace.[71] In this spirit, the Left rediscovered its nationalist roots, while the Right stressed its stance in favour of defending particularity, rather than the axiomatic agonal belief in man as a 'dynamic and dangerous being' (Schmitt). In this atmosphere, Left and Right could both subscribe to the appeal 'Save Peace – Unite Germany!' which appeared in the *Frankfurter Rundschau* in 1984, and in which national revolutionary, neo-conservative and leftist intellectuals called for a German peace treaty and a German confederation.[72] Most of these intellectuals also advocated that Germany tread another 'third way' and act as a mediator between East and West.

[69] Henning Eichberg, *Nationale Identität: Entfremdung und nationale Frage in der Industriegesellschaft* (Munich: Langen Müller, 1978). 'Identity', as a fashionable concept, only dated from the work of Erik Erikson and symbolic interactionism in the 1950s.

[70] Initially, 'identity' often brought together conservative and more extreme right-wing intellectuals. See for instance Peter Berglar, *et al.*, *Deutsche Identität heute* (Stuttgart: von Hase und Koehler, 1983), which united Stürmer, Nolte and von Krockow with Willms and Rohrmoser.

[71] See for instance Wolfgang Venohr, *Die deutsche Einheit kommt bestimmt* (Bergisch-Gladbach: Gustav Lübbe, 1982).

[72] In 1985, the volume *Ohne Deutschland geht es nicht* united followers of a 'national democratic socialism' with conservatives. Wolfgang Venohr advanced the formulae 'German division = latent danger of War' versus 'German unity = secure peace', not least because Germans would not shoot each other. See 'Ohne Deutschland geht es nicht', in Wolfgang Venohr (ed.), *Ohne Deutschland geht es nicht* (Krefeld: Sinus, 1985), 17–43.

Subsequently, this neo-nationalist discourse spread through journals and conferences, although its initiators remained largely outside the mainstream of academia and publishing.[73] However, their diagnosis of a West Germany 'psychologically unbalanced' and 'in need of identity' became increasingly current among CDU thinkers and conservative intellectuals. Identity, by way of a more 'normal' relationship to history was to lead to increased 'self-confidence'.[74] These issues then furnished the substance of the *Historikerstreit*.

Finally, a related strand of nationalist thought was a particular form of postmodern cultural pessimism, which was almost unconcerned with national sovereignty, but espoused the need to preserve cultural particularity. This aesthetic nationalism was composed of a strong Romanticism, anti-Americanism, and even antisemitism. It was also capable of combining the romantic heroization of figures such as the urban terrorist and Jünger's 'Anarch', with the adulation of the German *Volk*.[75] Younger cultural pessimists were often influenced by French post-structuralism, while both older and younger representatives of this strand, such as Gerd Bergfleth and Hans Jürgen Syberberg, were able to link their cultural pessimism with environmental concerns.[76] Cultural pessimism, like nationalism at large, allowed the lines between Left and Right to become fluid, and enabled a number of disillusioned members of the generation of '68 to join the ranks of the Right.

In sum, German conservatism in the post-war period remained defensive, fixated on overcoming the 'overcoming of the past' and eager to re-establish a strong, sovereign state capable of casting out the enemy and maintaining a clear demarcation between itself and the 'self-organizing society' within. It regularly failed in its resentment-driven attempts to inscribe a narrative of German victimization in public discourse, but met with considerable success when it drew on powerful German étatiste traditions to describe — and prescribe — institutions. In general, conservatism, even when trying to present itself as truly avant-garde and nonconformist,

---

[73] Philosophically, 1980s neo-nationalism found its foremost protagonist in the political scientist Bernard Willms, who drew on Fichtean idealism-cum-nationalism as well as Schmitt's concept of the political. See Bernard Willms (ed.), *Handbuch der Deutschen Nation*, 4 Vols. (Tübingen: Hohenrain, 1986). Institutionally, neo-nationalism was advocated in a range of journals such as *Nation Europa*, *Mut*, *wir selbst*, and *Criticón*.

[74] Karl Lamers, (ed.), *Suche nach Deutschland: Deutsche Identität und die Deutschlandpolitik* (Bonn: Europa Union Verlag, 1983).

[75] Diederich Diederichsen, 'Der Anarch, der Solitär und die Revolte: Rechte Poststrukturalismus-Rezeption in der BRD', in Richard Faber *et al.* (eds), *Rechtsextremismus: Ideologie und Gewalt* (Berlin: Edition Hentrich, 1995), 241–58.

[76] Gerd Bergfleth, *Zur Kritik der palavernden Aufklärung* (Munich: Mattes & Seitz, 1984) and Hans Jürgen Syberberg, *Vom Unglück und Glück der Kunst in Deutschland nach dem letzten Kriege* (Munich: Matthes & Seitz, 1990).

only had a *delaying* effect, rather than a 'conservative revolutionary' or truly reactionary one. Unlike what Mohler and others wished for, conservatism was never on the attack or engaged in 'radical activism' on the model of the Conservative Revolution. And even for Mohler, who was eager to emulate the supposed theoretical coherence of the *Nouvelle Droite*, conservatism often amounted to little more than 'realism' combined with a vague yearning for a more authoritarian political system. To put it another way, institutionally, conservatism often at least partially succeeded in its attempt at 'containing' the 'liberalization' sought by the Left, but in its 'psycho-social' approach, designed specifically as a revisionist 'roll-back' of Re-education, it was generally much less influential. Nationalist resentment remained ineffective, but resistance couched in terms of the strong state finding new ways of containing social interests such as in the 'aligned society', sometimes proved very successful.

The main reason for the overall failure of post-war conservatism was not specific to Germany, but rather the general conservative 'dilemma' which Martin Greiffenhagen has identified: conservatism remained fundamentally and negatively fixated on the present, unable to escape it.[77] Just as the 'Counter-Enlightenment' had to fight on the Enlightenment's terrain, reasoning against reason, so the German Right found it difficult to re-educate the re-educated. There was, however, a further, particularly German post-war dilemma for conservatism. How could conservatism escape the fact that it had been tainted by its ideological (and personal) association with National Socialism? The loss of traditions which had been abused by the Nazis, in particular historicist and Protestant perspectives on the nation-state, further exacerbated the fundamental dilemma. Only in the 1970s, with the *Tendenzwende*, could one speak of a conservatism that was relatively untarnished historically, since the 'neoconservatives' were for the most part 'liberal institutionalists' of the sceptical generation disappointed by reforms.

There was, however, even another dilemma in the question how conservatism was to define – and distance – itself vis-à-vis the antinationalist, anti-statist conservative Rheinland Catholicism of Adenauer, who had successfully recast the religious conservatism of the Weimar *Zentrum* [the Catholic Centre Party], made the CDU into a people's party and advocated the Westernization of Germany. A typically conservative insistence on gradual change and anti-rationalism would not suffice, given that – supposedly – so much of Re-education had penetrated German society and was pushed further by the Left. One strategy was the insistence on national identity and unification, represented in the nationalist–neutralist strand of conservatism. Another was the reassertion of a strong state against the 'CDU state' which had accommodated far too many special

---

[77] Martin Greiffenhagen, *Das Dilemma des Konservatismus in Deutschland* (Munich: Piper, 1971).

interests. The former resource of the Right, i.e. the insistence on national identity and unification, had disappeared after 1990 – thereby cutting away a major concrete policy plank and presenting both the Old and the New Right with a kind of 'melancholy of fulfilment'. Consequently, the ideological challenge for the New Right became how it would face this 'triple dilemma' – and, further, if and how it would define itself vis-à-vis the post-war conservatism just described. Or would it primarily attempt to connect with current thinkers such as Bohrer and Strauß, thereby avoiding a doubly tainted genealogy?

Reclaiming Conservatism: An Anatomy of the New Right

The common conceptual core of the New Right was the nation – linked to the notion of 'normality' through the claim that the nation-state remained the essential and 'normal' subject in history. The nation-state was not defended as a framework for civil rights, as liberals like Dahrendorf had done, but as a homogeneous 'community of protection and fate'. Most New Right intellectuals did not advance a peculiar definition of nationalism, whether voluntarist, ethnic or even racist, but this very emptiness of the conceptual core could itself be seen as an attempt to keep the movement open to a number of ideological persuasions, and avoid charges of racism. The ideological peculiarity of the New Right consisted of its defence of pure, almost contentless particularity, coupled with a narrative of on-going German victimization.[78] The New Right could link up with the neo-nationalism of the 1970s and 1980s, without a commitment to completely compromised fringe figures. It could also build bridges to – and form a front cutting across party lines with – new or old 'left-wing patriots' like Brigitte Seebacher-Brandt and Tilman Fichter.[79]

The centrality of the nation as undefined, but homogeneous particularity was underpinned by a perspective on the political as being of an irreducibly agonal, even tragic nature, and a philosophical anthropology which posited man as both weak and aggressive. While in this respect their political programme was relatively coherent, members of the New Right found it difficult to give a theoretically sophisticated account of it – or to offer any theoretical innovation at all, for that matter. Partly this was due to their self-appointed role as defenders of 'common sense', with the goal of capturing public discourse, rather than convincing an academic audience. But there was also a larger ideological problem in that nationalism – in

[78] Eva Geulen, 'Nationalism: Old, New and German', in *Telos*, No. 105 (1995), 2–20.

[79] Brigitte Seebacher-Brandt, *Politik im Rücken, Zeitgeist im Sinn* (Berlin: Ullstein, 1995), and Tilman Fichter, *Die SPD und die Nation: Vier sozialdemokratische Generationen zwischen nationaler Selbstbestimmung und Zweistaatlichkeit* (Berlin: Ullstein, 1993).

the absence of any further claims about institutions or even identity — would not yield concepts and ideas which could be operationalized, i.e. incorporated into party political programmes.

Members of the New Right linked their advocacy of the nation with the reinterpretation of the Nazi past analyzed above, on the one hand, and, on the other, with claims retrieved from the major thinkers of post-war conservatism. With regard to the latter, however, they mainly used fragments which were essentially part of a resentment-driven cultural critique, rather than the statist theories which thinkers like Forsthoff, Altmann and Lübbe had advanced. For instance, representatives of the New Right only tried to re-use standard cultural arguments from Gehlen's and Schelsky's complaints against an excessive pluralism, the supposed hegemony of left-wing intellectual 'priests' and citizens' 'insurance mentality'. Put in this way they failed to achieve their explicit aim of taking on the legacy of 'cold conservatism', which provided a realist political analysis, rather than sentimental 'Toryism'.[80] Given its relative weakness in addressing social questions, the New Right could not find much in the diagnoses of industrial society advanced by sociologists such as Freyer. Also, the celebration of technocratic capitalism by Freyer, Gehlen, and Forsthoff became an obstacle to appropriating their concepts and patterns of thought, as long as the Right sought to link up with ecological and anti-Western segments of the Left, which espoused a critique of technology. Instead, the New Right associated technology with liberalism, individualism and hedonism, all of which — in a bow to ecological conservatives — were held responsible for leading to an ecological apocalypse.

Moreover, where Gehlen had perceived a 'crystallized modernity', in which all fundamental historical options had been played out and society had entered a state of *posthistoire*, members of the New Right asserted that Germany, at least in the field of foreign policy, was 'called back into history'. True, *posthistoire* and *Rückruf in die Geschichte* [Return to History] were on entirely different levels of analysis, but, if anything, this attested to the poverty of more abstract thought in New Right ideology and its difficulties in finding 'elective affinities' with more substantial forms of conservative thought. Instead, they recycled many of the vague, general concepts which had been central to Mohler's and others' post-war conservatism (and, in fact, most kinds of conservatism): the defence of the 'concrete' and the 'particular' against the abstract, the emphasis on the irreducible nature of power and the irrational as well as the unpredictable nature of reality. Even the New Right's self-presentation as an avant-garde and as authentically 'liberal' was familiar from previous conservative thought in the Federal Republic. And finally, just as the old Right had

---

[80] Karlheinz Weißmann, 'Arnold Gehlen: Von der Aktualität eines zu Unrecht Vergessenen', in *Criticón*, No. 153 (1997), 31–6.

attacked their predecessors as *Gärtnerkonservative*, the New Right now dismissed the old Right as *Nischenkonservative* [niche conservatives].

It was also highly questionable, then, whether the parallel between the New Right and the Conservative Revolution, which so many commentators seemed to consider *de rigueur*, was even remotely illuminating. In most cases, the parallel was simply asserted, rather than proved with reference to particular parallel thought patterns. Protagonists of the New Right themselves had been eager to claim the legacy of the Conservative Revolution, as first delineated by Mohler.[81] They argued that referring to the Conservative Revolution fulfilled the double function of breaking a taboo and signalling that conservatism was no longer confined to preserving the status quo. As Weißmann pointed out, 'whoever talks about the relevance of the Conservative Revolution . . . wants to give an *Aufbruchssignal* [a signal to set off], to prepare an act of intellectual liberation and self-liberation'.[82]

However, while the New Right might indeed have seen reference to the Conservative Revolution as a 'mobilizing myth', observers of the New Right should not take this self-characterization at face-value. For one thing, there are the rather obvious historical differences between the period after the First Word War and after the Cold War. What has been conspicuously absent for the New Right is a *Fronterlebnis* [experience of the front in the First World War], apart from the experience of fighting in the trenches of history faculties supposedly dominated by 'political correctness'. Where in the 1920s the extremes touched each other, with *linke Leute von rechts* and *rechte Leute von links*, both animated by a free-floating anti-bourgeois and anti-Western radicalism, there were far fewer crossovers from Left to Right in the nineties. And finally, while ideas of *Mitteleuropa* made a comeback in some parts of foreign policy discourse, the ideological background of the *Reich* – with all its historical (and emotional) connotations – had disappeared.[83] Unlike after Versailles, there were simply no further reasonable claims to make about foreign policy revisionism after 1990, and in that sense, unification left the New Right with few actual political proposals to make, which then in turn led to an overemphasis of 'psycho-social' arguments. Moreover, the idea that in the past the Federal Republic had not vigorously pursued its national interests was itself a curiously romantic and unrealistic one. The style and rhetoric of foreign policy making had of course fundamentally changed in the post-war period – but, as foreign

[81] Armin Mohler, *Die Konservative Revolution in Deutschland 1918–1932: Grundriss ihrer Weltanschauungen* (Stuttgart: F. Vorwerk, 1950).

[82] Karlheinz Weißmann, 'Gab es eine Konservative Revolution? Zur Auseinandersetzung um das neue Buch von Stefan Breuer', in *Criticón*, No. 138 (1993), 173–6; here 176.

[83] Matthias Zimmer, 'Return of the *Mittellage*? The Discourse of the Centre in German Foreign Policy', in *German Politics*, Vol. 6, No. 1 (1997), 23–38.

observers noted, the low-key and ostensibly harmony-oriented style of German foreign policy actually served the interests of West Germany much better than an open and aggressive pursuit of these interests could ever have done.[84] Finally, on a cultural level, the Conservative Revolution, in its rhetoric and ideology, could build on expressionism and the Youth Movement. But the New Right had no previous generational revolt it could refer to and no original literary style – except possibly Strauß.

In short, then, the New Right drew on the cultural criticism of thinkers like Gehlen and Schelsky, largely subscribed to a 'psychosocial approach' inspired by Mohler and other opponents of Re-education, concentrated much of their energies on rewriting German history (though they did so in a generally much more sophisticated manner than previous revisionists) and largely left institutional questions to one side. They generally took an ecumenical approach by uniting 'cultural pessimists', 'normalization nationalists' in foreign policy, and Schmittian statists.[85] They were above all concerned to alter the 'mood' of foreign policy-making in favour of 'normalization', i.e. nationalization, and a new 'self-confidence'. But essentially, the New Right's difficulty lay not so much in defining what it was Right about, as some observers have claimed – but in being New.

Why the Right Failed (Again)

Arguably, the high watermark of the ideological tide of the New Right was 1994. The movement had gained momentum with Strauß's essay, still controlled strategic positions at Ullstein and *Die Welt*, and was benefiting from the fact that the government had adopted a number of policies previously seen as outside the political mainstream (most notably, the change of the asylum law). However, by 1995, the tide was turning. Indicative of the fact that the re-interpretation of the past had failed to take hold was the initial success, but ultimate failure of the prominent newspaper advertisement 'Against Forgetting' on the occasion of the fiftieth anniversary of the end of the War, which recast '1945' as the beginning of suffering for East Germans and expellees, rather than 'liberation'. This campaign had sought to bring the narrative of German victimization into the mainstream by uniting New Right with more established, including Social Democratic, public figures.[86] New Right members also lost some of

---

[84] For instance Garton Ash, *In Europe's Name*.

[85] For a classification of schools of foreign policy thinking in Germany after 1989, see Gunther Hellmann, 'Goodbye Bismarck? The Foreign Policy of Contemporary Germany', in *Mershon International Review*, No. 40 (1996), 1–39.

[86] See '8. Mai 1945 – Gegen das Vergessen', in *Frankfurter Allgemeine Zeitung*, April 7 1995. Prominent conservative politicians who signed the appeal were Alfred Dregger and Carl-Dieter Spranger. The former SPD defence minister Hans Apel later withdrew his signature.

their positions at Ullstein, and, in early 1996, the national-liberal wing of the FDP failed to carry out the much publicized plan to take over the party in Berlin. Why, then, did the New Right fail, at least for the foreseeable future?

One of the primary causes was arguably a fixation on their chosen ideological opponent, the generation of 1968, which translated into an excessive attention to positionality on the intellectual field. By painting a picture of a vast left-wing conspiracy, they ultimately fell victim to their own creation. As much as the New Right claimed to represent the *pays réel*, public against published opinion, there were actually very few people in Germany who felt oppressed by members of the generation of '68. But the New Right spent most of its energy on lashing out against Habermas and his followers, rather than providing any concrete policy prescriptions. Consequently, members of the New Right often came off as petty and resentful, as members of a generation-in-between (or *Zaungäste*) who were too young for '68, still steeped in the sometimes nasty radical student politics of the 1970s, and too old for the relatively apolitical mid-to-late 1980s. In short, they came off as academic 'angry white males', clearly uncomfortable with the gains feminism – and simply women in general – had made during the 1970s and 1980s in the Federal Republic. While the self-portrayal as victims was meant also to resonate with Germans who supposedly had been the victims of Allied Re-education efforts and, by extension, even the Second World War, this metanarrative of victimization ended up sounding more like self-pity (and led to the fact that the Right's own failures in the 1990s were immediately incorporated into this on-going double narrative of victimization). And just as the victimization narrative failed to capture the public imagination, the choice of 1989 as a reference point for a generational-cum-political movement proved to be a mixed blessing. While it was both obvious and tempting to refer to 1989 as shorthand for a substantial break in German history, the simple truth remained that most members of the New Right had not spent the late 1980s confronting the police on the streets of Leipzig or Berlin, but battling left-wing professors in West German seminar rooms.

In the same vein that a fixation on the '68ers replaced future-oriented prescriptions, taboo-breaking seemed to take the place of theorizing. If the lesson of the *Nouvelle Droite* really had been the importance of conquering cultural hegemony, then it was only half applied: as Mohler kept pointing out, theoretical innovation, which then trickled down into 'culture', had accounted for the success of Alain de Benoist and his allies, whereas the old German Right had remained fixated on the 'consciousness of national wounds', instead of establishing a 'school of thought'.[87] But theoretical innovation was clearly missing from the thinking of the New Right. Nationalism in itself was simply not enough, and the

---

[87] Armin Mohler, 'Gleichheit und Differenz', in *Criticón*, No. 129 (1992), 22–3; here 23.

'metapolitical' strategy failed precisely because it was not sufficiently political.[88] While the young historians polemically played off 'history' against the social sciences dominant in the 1960s and 1970s, they in fact found it exceedingly difficult to find a usable past, or even enlightening historical analogies. They clearly were tempted by ideas of *Mitteleuropa*, by geopolitical and realist thought in international relations – but for all their self-consciously sober talk about the world being risky and dangerous, they in fact never defined the national interest, or formulated strategies which would have been significantly different from the policies pursued by the Kohl government – with the important exception of European integration.[89] Moving away from the West and possibly playing the role of a 'bridge' or 'balance' between East and West were often hinted at, but never spelled out in any coherent fashion. 'National interest' and 'normalization' never failed to provoke, but ultimately remained vacuous terms, or rather provocative signals pointing in no direction in particular. Part of the problem was that the New Right remained caught in the psycho-social language of 'self-confidence' and 'growing up'. Consequently, what would have seemed like a logical move from 'national identity' to 'national interest', linking the old neo-nationalist discourse of the 1980s with more 'realist' and assertive foreign policy-making in the 1990s, remained at the level of 'identity' due to the lack of sufficiently appealing alternative 'interests'.

In the end, then, a self-consciously Gramscian strategy of gaining cultural hegemony largely failed due to a lack of ideological innovation. For all their negative fixation on the supposed 'left-wing media' and their desire to emulate the success of a left-wing conquest of hegemony, they seemed to ignore a basic, but important observation which Habermas had made in the late 1970s with regard to the ideological leaders of the *Tendenzwende*:

They declare an interest in the occupation of semantic fields, in strategies of denomination, in reconquering the power to define – in short, in the planning of ideology by means of the politics of language. It is true that in the course of the protest movement a shift occurred in the political register of concepts. But I have never understood how one can seriously believe that basic political–theoretical concepts can in the long

[88] This was belatedly recognized by the New Right, for instance Dieter Stein, 'Der metapolitische Holzweg der Rechten', in *Junge Freiheit*, 14 February 1997. On nationalism's need for a further 'host ideology', see Michael Freeden, 'Is Nationalism a Distinct Ideology?', in *Political Studies*, Vol. 46 (1998), 748–65.

[89] For an effort to distance an explicitly nationalist, but at the same time pro-European CDU position from the New Right and its 'anti-Western' *Sonderweg*, see Wolfgang Schäuble, 'Der Platz in der Mitte: Sonderwege und Staatsräson', in *Frankfurter Allgemeine Zeitung*, 6 July 1994.

run be altered unless they absorb complex argumentations and are shaped to reflect innovations and learning processes. The objective spirit can hardly be trimmed to the left or the right by linguistic–political advertising agencies.[90]

The second major reason, apart from a lack of ideological innovation, for the failure of the New Right was its lack of institutional support. While it is true that the New Right for a time gained considerable influence at Ullstein and *Die Welt*, efforts to capture a party-political vehicle failed. The main effort here had been an attempted takeover of the Berlin FDP with a national-liberal programme harking back to the much more conservative FDP of the 1950s, and ever since this has failed, there have been sporadic attempts to subvert parts of the FDP in other states. So just as on the ideological level there was no Leo Strauss and no Hayek, on the party-political side no German Jörg Haider emerged either.

It was arguably, however, yet again the structural dilemma of German (and, to some extent, any) conservatism which was at the heart of the New Right's failure. It remained negatively fixated on the present (and on the Nazi past, which it tried to 'normalize' qua modernization), and, in the absence of ideological innovation and institutional support was unable to create or recreate the institutions which it then would have been worth preserving.

All of this is not to say that one should be complacent about the threat of right-wing violence in Germany, or that extreme right-wing parties do not have the chance of capturing a protest vote or the vote of Germans with genuinely authoritarian beliefs. But it is to say that for now any right-wing ideological shifts engineered from above, with the spirit of Schmitt and Gramsci hovering above, so to speak, have little chance of success. Those genuinely worried about the resurgence of right-wing sentiments in Germany should probably look towards East German youth culture, rather than at Ullstein history books and the cultural pages of West German newspapers.

[90] Habermas, 'Introduction', in *Observations on 'The Spiritual Situation of the Age'*, 14.

8 Preparing for the Political or Privatizing Memory: German Intellectuals Confront the Berlin Republic

The acrimonious debate on unification was followed by ever more 'debates' at an ever more rapid succession on issues connected to the meaning of unification and the national identity of the larger Germany. There was a bitter dispute over the Gulf War, which further deepened the divisions among the Left, as many on the Left fell back on their traditional pacifism and even anti-Americanism, while those who had already turned more sceptical in 1989 supported the War. Shortly afterwards, there was a national debate on whether the capital should move to Berlin, centred on a free vote in the *Bundestag*. Legally, there should have been no vote at all, as the Constitution mandated Berlin as the capital of the united country. Nevertheless, the parliamentary debate, in which the proponents of the move to Berlin won by a narrow margin, became an important instance of public argument about the symbolic parameters of the new Germany. Subsequently, a fierce debate on the asylum law ultimately reaffirmed the ethnic exclusiveness of the German demos. This was followed by yet another debate on the meaning of the end of the Second World War on its fiftieth anniversary and a dispute on the role of the Wehrmacht in the War, prompted by a highly controversial exhibition on the atrocities committed by the Wehrmacht – which finally broke down the moral separation between the regular army and the SS.[1] Not least, there was the enormously emotional debate on Daniel Goldhagen's *Hitler's Willing Executioners*, which made the Germans doubt that their ordinary forebears could be separated from criminal Nazis in the past, but also reassured them that ordinary Germans were good democrats in the present.[2]

---

[1] Klaus Naumann, *Der Krieg als Text: Das Jahr 1945 im kulturellen Gedächtnis der Presse* (Hamburg: Hamburger Edition, 1998), Hannes Heer and Klaus Naumann (eds) *War of Extermination: The German Military in World War II 1941–1944* (1995; Oxford: Berghahn, 1999).

[2] Daniel Jonah Goldhagen, *Hitler's Willing Executioners: Ordinary Germans and the Holocaust* (New York: Knopf, 1996) and Ulrich Herbert, 'Academic and Public Discourses on the Holocaust: The Goldhagen Debate in Germany', in *German Politics and Society*, Vol. 17, No. 3 (1999), 35–53.

Most of these debates were quickly labelled as another *Historikerstreit*, and often intellectuals and left-liberal opinion at large did indeed seem to feel compelled to fall in line with the old alignments of the historians' dispute – sometimes with paradoxical outcomes, as when they sided with Goldhagen against the original left-liberal protagonists of the *Historikerstreit* who, by and large, dismissed the findings of the Harvard political scientist. None of these debates, however, seemed to have the larger meaning of the original historians' dispute, and all tended to fade from public consciousness rather quickly. In fact, some observers considered these debates thoroughly artificial and engineered by the very media which came under attack in them, notably in Peter Handke's indictment of the media over their supposedly unjust portrayal of Serbia, or, earlier in the decade, in Strauß's 'Anschwellender Bocksgesang'. Ironically, at the same time the notion that somehow the intellectuals chose to be 'silent' remained a common perception throughout the 1990s, prompting even Germany's foremost tabloid to run the headline: 'Why are our poets silent?' – an astonishing query, given that 'silence' had so far always been something of which intellectuals accused other intellectuals.[5]

But intellectuals did not remain silent, on the contrary. In this chapter, I shall discuss two debates which might have a more lasting impact – and which are directly related to unification *and* to the future of Germany. In a sense, they should be seen as delayed and displaced reactions to unification. The first is about the concept of the political and the nature of politics as such, which intellectuals linked to conceptions of the new Germany now embodied in the notion of the 'Berlin Republic' – a notion fiercely contested by those who wanted to stress continuities with the old Federal Republic. This re-examination of the political was a direct result of the supposed rupture of 1989.[4] The earthquake, which, according to Peter Schneider, intellectuals had missed in 1989, ultimately shook the foundations of politics as such, since many intellectuals came to question the category of 'the political' itself and asked whether the nation-state remained the appropriate framework for politics at all – which, finally, seemed to be a question of institutions, rather than identity. Secondly, I examine the heated dispute between Martin Walser and Ignatz Bubis, spokesman of the Central Council of Jews in Germany, which took place in the autumn of 1998. This controversy revolved around the very question of German nation-state 'normality', but also – perhaps for the first time – went to the heart of the German question by dealing more openly than ever before with the 'Jewish question', which had always been nested within it. However, both debates, while suggesting new political pathways for Germany, also demonstrate

---

[5] 'Warum schweigen die Dichter?', in *Bild-Zeitung*, 20 November 1998.

[4] Ulrich Beck, 'Die unvollendete Demokratie', in *Der Spiegel*, 18 December 1989.

the way intellectual discourse is still structured by central arguments and concepts inherited from before unification, and from the *Historikerstreit* in particular.

The *Begründung* of the Berlin Republic

The German word *Begründung* has a double meaning. It signifies not only foundation, but also giving reasons, providing a rationale. Toward the end of the 1990s Germans approached the *Begründung* of what was variously called the 'new Federal Republic', the Third Republic, or, most commonly, the Berlin Republic. Of course, one could argue that the real historical break had already occurred eight years ago, with the unification of the two Germanies in October 1990 as its official completion. But while the 3rd October 1990 might have been a formal foundation, there had of course, according to many intellectuals, been insufficient time for the other, normative dimension of *Begründung* in the 'rush to unity'.[5] More importantly, there was a real sense in which the move of the Federal Government to Berlin in 1999, was a highly symbolic, almost constitutional *Begründung* of the Berlin Republic in a way that the anticlimactic unification celebrations in October 1990 never were. Moreover, 1999 was the official starting date for European Economic and Monetary Union, thereby pointing beyond the German question, which might or might not have found a final answer, to a much larger European question, which certainly had not found an answer yet. Consequently, intellectuals confronted 'a double foundation' that loomed ever larger and posed the challenge of laying down normative foundations, into which lessons drawn from 1989 could be incorporated.

The early and mid-1990s, then, saw a growing literature which dealt explicitly with the Berlin Republic. What was most striking about this 'foundational' literature, however, was how often reflections on the future of Germany were linked to a discourse about what was to constitute the foundation of politics, or rather, 'the political', as such. This curious linguistic construction of 'the political', i.e. the transformation of the adjective 'political' into the noun 'the political', was made famous – or rather, notorious – by Carl Schmitt's 1927 book *The Concept of the Political*.[6] Before Schmitt, the concept of 'the political' was in use – but in the German tradition of positivist legal theory from the nineteenth century onwards, it was simply equivalent to state action.[7] Georg Jellinek, one of the most important positivist legal theorists at the turn of the century, could still write that 'in

---

[5] Konrad Jarausch, *The Rush to German Unity* (New York: Oxford University Press, 1994).

[6] Carl Schmitt, *The Concept of the Political.*

[7] Kari Palonen, *Politik als Handlungsbegriff: Horizontwandel des Politikbegriff in Deutschland 1890–1933* (Helsinki: The Finnish Society of Sciences and Letters, 1985).

the concept of the political one has already thought the concept of the state', a view also shared by Max Weber.[8] Schmitt was the first to point out the circular reasoning from the state to the political and back. He detached the political from the state, and opened his most famous work with the dictum that 'the concept of the state presupposes the concept of the political'.[9] Schmitt went on to argue that 'the political is the most intense and extreme antagonism, and every concrete antagonism becomes that much more political the closer it approaches the most extreme point, that of the friend–enemy grouping'.[10] Just as much as Schmitt exercised a subterranean influence on constitutional thought in West Germany, this 'concept of the political', defined as a friend–enemy relationship, came to haunt West German political science. Dolf Sternberger in particular tried to wrest the concept from the Right and redefine the political as the 'area of all endeavour to seek and secure peace'.[11]

After 1989, there was an almost inflationary use of the expression 'the political', and the number of books dealing with its nature grew exponentially.[12] But what lay behind the supposed crisis of the concept of the political? On the one hand, German intellectuals responded to what in the early and mid-1990s was perceived as widespread dissatisfaction with politics, the phenomenon which came to be known in an untranslatable phrase as *Politikverdrossenheit*, literally 'being fed up with politics', which meant, above all, a sharp decline of the electorate's trust in parties and politicians. Intellectuals, and in particular left-wing intellectuals, however, also engaged with the 'political' because they felt the need to rebut the conservative charge of 'failure' and of having been 'apolitical' before and during unification. Most importantly, globalization and the increased exposure of Germany to world politics and the world economy became reasons for engaging with 'the political'. As in many other countries, it was feared that globalization would narrow the scope for national politics, or even mean 'the end of politics', as governments were required to adjust to the *Sachzwänge* [objective necessities] of a global economy. The great irony, it

---

[8] Andreas Anter, *Max Webers Theorie des modernen Staates: Herkunft, Struktur und Bedeutung* (Berlin: Duncker & Humblot, 1995), 51.

[9] Schmitt, *The Concept of the Political*, 19.

[10] *Ibid.*, 29.

[11] Dolf Sternberger, *Die Politik und der Friede* (Frankfurt/Main: Suhrkamp, 1986), 76.

[12] For instance Ulrich Beck, *Die Erfindung des Politischen: Zu einer Theorie reflexiver Modernisierung* (Frankfurt/Main: Suhrkamp, 1993); Oskar Negt and Alexander Kluge, *Maßverhältnisse des Politischen: 15 Vorschläge zum Unterscheidungsvermögen* (Frankfurt/Main: S. Fischer, 1992); Andreas Göbel, Dirk van Laak, Ingeborg Villinger (eds), *Metamorphosen des Politischen: Grundfragen politischer Einheitsbildung seit den 20er Jahren* (Berlin: Akademie, 1995); Thomas Meyer, *Die Transformation des Politischen* (Frankfurt/Main: Suhrkamp, 1994); Peter Kemper (ed.), *Die Zukunft des Politischen: Theoretische Ausblicke auf Hannah Arendt* (Frankfurt/Main: Fischer, 1993).

seemed, was that just as the 'belated nation' took its 'second chance' (Fritz Stern) and finally achieved a secure nation-state, in which liberal democracy and national identity could be reconciled, the very nation-state model came to disintegrate more generally under international pressures. In the extreme version of this argument, Germans finally had their polity – but there was no politics left. Alternatively, the Left was prone to suggest that globalization, far from being merely a matter of 'objective necessities', was a profoundly political project, driven by particular interests, which had to be questioned and contested.

In the first part of this chapter, I shall categorize these various double or even triple foundational exercises, and analyze the ideological strategies which have been prominent in the emerging discourse on the Berlin Republic *and* the attempt to fix the meaning of the political. I shall start with what one might call the Old Right, i.e. the liberal-conservative opinion-makers of the old Federal Republic, before moving on to the three main responses by the Left. I argue that explicitly, or implicitly, all these approaches situated themselves with reference to what are usually seen as the two German classics of 'thinking the political', Schmitt and Hannah Arendt. This is not to say that either a Schmittian or an Arendtian conception of the political exhausts this concept. While Schmitt is often called 'the first philosopher of the political', the case of Arendt is much less clear-cut.[13] Arendt in fact did not seek to provide one definition of 'the political'. She made a great number of claims about 'politics', and was adamant that politics was primarily action in a public realm, very much on the model of the Greek *polis*, and the meaning of politics freedom and disclosure.[14] Both Schmitt and Arendt, for all their normative differences, however, shared the view that politics could not be reduced to matters of state, or to being one autonomous 'system' or realm of activity among others in a highly differentiated society, with their own distinct values (such as the economic, the legal, but also the erotic), as the neofunctionalist sociologist Niklas Luhmann, and arguably Max Weber, thought.[15] And in particular, the political had an existential quality which was lacking in liberal accounts of politics.

In any case, I shall pay careful attention to the particular concept of the political proposed by German intellectuals after 1989. Even if it is

---

[13] Heiner Bielefeldt, *Kampf und Entscheidung: Politscher Existentialismus bei Carl Schmitt, Helmuth Plessner und Karl Jaspers* (Würzburg: Königshausen und Neumann, 1994), 19.

[14] This picture of Arendt as nostalgic for all things Greek is of course a caricature and contains as much truth as any good caricature – but I cannot go into Arendt exegesis here. For excellent accounts affirming Arendt's modernism or even postmodernism, see Seyla Benhabib, *The Reluctant Modernism of Hannah Arendt* (Thousand Oaks, CA.: Sage, 1996) and Dana R. Villa, *Arendt and Heidegger: The Fate of the Political* (Princeton: Princeton University Press, 1996).

[15] Niklas Luhmann, *Social Systems*, trans. John Bednarz, Jr., with Dirk Baecker (1984; Stanford: Stanford University Press, 1995).

seen as a 'system', or a separate sphere, the question remains whether politics is crucial in steering society, a notion liberals, republicans and even statists might agree with, but one which a sociologist like Luhmann denied. Or is the political conceived essentially as an attribute, which makes another thing political, or as a peculiar relation, or as a substance, or even as a sort of energy and raw material, as Oskar Negt and Alexander Kluge argued?[16] Were such ideas attractive, precisely because 'the political' could then be played off against *die Politik* as official politics, i.e. the political sub-system? As I shall demonstrate below, many on the Left made this seemingly paradoxical move by claiming that the political had disappeared, or was at least being 'drained', from politics.[17] But then where had it escaped to?

Old Right, Newly Political

Henning Ritter, in an article in the *Frankfurter Allgemeine Zeitung*, asserted that 'the expectation directed towards the future Germany can be formulated as follows: that the Berlin Republic will be more "political" than the Bonn Republic'.[18] According to Ritter, this was not only due to the fact that Germany had regained its sovereignty. The Berlin Republic would also be particularly political in contrast with its predecessor, the first post-war Republic with its 'apolitical' basic features. The Bonn Republic was one of the few instances in which Walther Rathenau's dictum that the economy is fate (*die Wirtschaft ist das Schicksal*) actually had turned out to be true. Ritter argued that Bonn had developed a certain utopian tendency in its post-national idealization of its own occupation status, which was projected as the future of nation-states in general. In retrospect, Ritter argued, the Bonn Republic would be praised as a 'paradise', although no one had noticed its utopian qualities at the time of its existence.

Many conservative intellectuals adopted this contrast and the notion of a future that was somehow more 'political'. What did the political refer to in this context? It signified above all regained national sovereignty, but, even more importantly, an increased potential for conflict, with regard to both a new role for Germany on the world stage and conflict within Germany. 'Normality is regained', but 'normality, i.e. Berlin Republic instead of Bonn Republic, means most of all the normality of instability'.[19] This prediction

---

[16] Negt and Kluge, *Maßverhältnisse*.

[17] In particular Meyer, *Die Transformation*.

[18] Henning Ritter, 'Translatio rei publicae: Der Umzug von Regierung und Parlament als Gründungsakt der Berliner Republik', in *Frankfurter Allgemeine Zeitung*, 18 December 1996.

[19] Johannes Gross, *Begründung der Berliner Republik: Deutschland am Ende des 20. Jahrhunderts* (Stuttgart: Deutsche Verlegs-Anstalt, 1995), 42. For Gross's earlier assessments, see for instance *Die Deutschen* (Stuttgart: Scheffler, 1968).

of 'normality as instability' was made by Johannes Gross in his *Begründung der Berliner Republik* [foundation of the Berlin Republic], which constituted the most comprehensive conservative statement on the Berlin Republic. Gross — journalist, political pundit and friend of the elderly Carl Schmitt — had followed the development of the old Federal Republic with many books commenting the state of the Germans, and could be taken as a generally reliable, but also original and entertaining, guide to centre-right sentiments. Internally, the normality of instability predicted by Gross resulted from the disappearance of the corporatist consensus underlying the old Federal Republic, as the parties, the unions and the Churches — in short, the whole system of patronage and corporatism — were weakened. With this weakening, the legitimacy of the political system was increasingly not a matter of legality, but of security: only the state that functioned in the sense of providing its citizens with security would be accepted.[20] Gross repudiated Rathenau's dictum and reaffirmed Napoleon's that in fact politics is fate (*Die Politik ist das Schicksal*). For Gross, following Ernst Forsthoff and Forsthoff's teacher Schmitt, the old Federal Republic was apolitical, because the state became merely an instrument for the satisfaction of social needs. The state, increasingly indistinguishable from society, was pervasive in its interventions, and yet weak in its unwillingness to exercise authority.[21] According to Gross, redistribution, which knew neither friends nor enemies, but only ever more recipients, was apolitical, while decision-making, and the realization of different political options was indeed political. As much as West German politicians might have rejected the friend–enemy thinking of Carl Schmitt, in their support of an indiscriminate welfare state they had actually preserved a National Socialist legacy: the idea of the *Volksgemeinschaft* [national community].[22] Chancellor Kohl in turn represented a truly political figure, because he pursued interests and engaged in ruthless friend–enemy thinking, while of course publicly denouncing it.[23]

Gross sounded a wake-up call for Germany to face the reality of power politics and finally define its national interests, which was another way of saying that the country should have thought more clearly about who its friends and enemies were. On the other hand, due to the EU, Germany was said to experience a loss of political substance in the form of decision-making capacity, which could be partially compensated for by increased national representation. In other words, while the substance of the political as decision-making capacity in the face of conflict was taken away by Brussels, the aestheticization of state power in the new capital could at least

[20] *Ibid.*, 53.

[21] *Ibid.*, 61.

[22] *Ibid.*, 62.

[23] *Ibid.*, 71–2.

preserve the façade of politics. Not by chance, the cover of Gross's volume depicted the fake Berlin *Stadtschloß*, i.e. the false palace facade which Berliners could contemplate for a while to see whether they might enjoy a real copy of the royal palace which the GDR authorities had blown up in the 1950s. However, while Europe limited the scope of the political in foreign policy, Berlin would retain at least a 'reservation of the political' in domestic policy. Also, in Gross's wish and prediction, Berlin would be both the German Washington and New York, a metropolis which finally united the elites of business, the media and politics, and which could satisfy his nostalgia for a more *großbürgerliche* age. Salon hostesses would keep open houses, the political class was supposed to open itself up to the public sphere, and the often merely moralizing media representatives might finally gain more respect for political realities.

Gross's analysis had a mildly Schmittian subtext, but, more importantly, followed the very pattern of thought established by the *enfant terrible* of the German intellectual establishment Karl Heinz Bohrer. As I discussed in chapter six, already in the early 1980s, Bohrer had combined a cultural critique of the old Federal Republic as provincial and apolitical, with an affirmation of the autonomy of the political from moral considerations. He had also called for a new political class capable of sovereign decision-making, which would be similar to the metropolitan elites of London and Paris. On this reading, the state needed a new form of representation and aestheticization, but also a new self-confidence. Thus, for conservatives, the political remained, above all, a synonym for conflict. They insisted that the political remained the monopoly of the state, as authoritative decision-making remained the answer to the challenge of increased external and internal conflict. The state's capacity to provide security in an increasingly uncertain world remained its prime source of legitimacy. All of this was well within the mainstream of conservative thought drawn from the West German statist tradition and enriched by elements of Bohrer's seminal cultural-cum-political critique. Conservative responses to the Berlin Republic, then, turned out to be surprisingly conventional.

Habermas: The Berlin Republic between Normality and Post-nationality

Jürgen Habermas still best represented those West German intellectuals who argued for preserving the political principles underlying the old Federal Republic, combined with a further transfer of sovereignty to European institutions. For Habermas, the legacy of hasty unification and the absence of a republican re-foundation meant that a comprehensive political *Selbstverständigung* [discursive agreement] still had to take place about what the 'normality' — a term he now used half-ironically — of the approaching Berlin Republic should be.[24] Thus, 1990 remained a lost opportunity to reaffirm the Western values of the old Federal Republic and to begin the life of the larger Germany with a democratic *Selbstvergewisserung* [self-assurance].

As always, the quest for a new discursive self-understanding was bound up with German historiography – and Habermas's insistence on the need to break with German cultural traditions in the face of conservatives supposedly yet again drawing on the wrong pasts. Habermas now saw two 'revisionary readings' emerging which undermined the old Federal Republic as a Western success story: one was the return to a national history, in which continuities with the Wilhelmine era were affirmed and the Federal Republic necessarily appeared as the real *Sonderweg*; the other was the narrative of a global civil War, inspired by Schmitt and, more recently, Nolte, which yet again placed the Nazis on the side of the Western bourgeoisie in its fight against Bolshevism. Instead, Habermas sought to affirm the radical break of 1945 and relativize the regaining of national sovereignty in 1990: '1989 will remain a fortunate date only as long as we respect 1945 as the genuinely instructive one'.[25] Moreover, the nation-state had simply outlived its usefulness in dealing with problems which transcended national boundaries. In the face of globalization, new forms of social cohesion were necessary to preserve both democracy and the rule of law: not surprisingly, this new social cohesion was to be a post-national, republican one. To cope with global challenges, new supranational, more 'abstract' public spheres and new forms of social solidarity would have to be created at the European level.[26] Thus, the 'normality' of the Berlin Republic could not be thought without Strasbourg and Brussels.

Where did this leave the political? Habermas hardly needed a theoretical discourse of the political after 1989, because his conception of communicative action already contained an implicit engagement with Arendt and Schmitt. Whether or not the view of Arendt's major German disciple, Ernst Vollrath, was correct that Habermas had fundamentally misread Arendt, the fact remained that Habermas was one of the few thinkers on the Left who had creatively engaged with Arendt's notion of *praxis*.[27] In his turn to legal and political theory in the early 1990s, Habermas reaffirmed his commitment to a procedural and deliberative democracy, at the

---

[24] Habermas, *A Berlin Republic*, 164–5.

[25] *Ibid.*, 181.

[26] For a further elaboration, see Jürgen Habermas, *Die postnationale Konstellation* (Frankfurt/Main: Suhrkamp, 1998).

[27] Ernst Vollrath, 'Hannah Arendt bei den Linken', in Antonia Grunenberg and Lothar Probst (eds), *Einschnitte: Hannah Arendts politisches Denken heute* (Bremen: Edition Temmen, 1995), 9–22.

same time rejecting a republicanism which he saw as 'ethically overburdened'.[28] He equated Arendtian republicanism with the category of a 'political self-organization of society', as a 'polemical understanding of politics as directed against the state apparatus'.[29] Habermas criticized what he saw as Arendt's tendency to fuse state and society, and her neglect of the importance of institutionalizing procedures for public reasoning, as she relied solely on communicatively generated power.[30] Against such an account of both popular sovereignty and *Sittlichkeit* [public ethical life], Habermas, in a renewed commitment to differentiation and proceduralism, wanted practical reason to retreat from the *Sittlichkeit* or concrete political ethos of a community, and have it institutionalized in the procedures which ensured the communicative presuppositions of democracy, i.e. the procedures that ensured a proper deliberative democracy.[31] Law, and the Constitution in particular, could be a transmission belt between the communicative power generated in civil society and the state with its administrative power. Habermas's vision, with its enormous emphasis on law and its retreat from notions of a collective democratic subject, in many ways indicated what one might call both the 'legalisation' and 'liberalization' of the Left – confirming that Habermas's Rousseauean moment in 1990 had indeed been a radically democratic exception to his own theory. His thought was no longer very far removed from the liberalism of a Rawls or Dworkin, and, arguably, the status quo of the old Federal Republic. It certainly remained closer to that status quo than to any grand republican renewal à la Arendt, for which some of Habermas's allies on the Left were hoping.

Beck's Invention of the Political

There was also what one might call an implicitly Arendtian approach to the post-1989 constellation. This approach aimed at a renewal of democratic theory and at transcending an étatiste nation-state framework, but without resorting to the idea of 'post-conventional identity' associated with post-nationalism. This was particularly evident in the case of the self-styled iconoclast sociologist Ulrich Beck, who had become something like

---

[28] Jürgen Habermas, *The Inclusion of the Other: Studies in Political Theory*, eds Ciaran Cronin and Pablo De Greiff (Cambridge, Mass.: MIT Press, 1998), 239, with the translation modified.

[29] *Ibid.*, 247.

[30] Jürgen Habermas, *Between Facts and Norms: Contributions to a Discourse Theory of Law and Democracy*, trans. William Rehg (1992, Cambridge, Mass.: MIT Press, 1996), 146–51.

[31] Habermas, *The Inclusion of the Other*, 246.

a sociological prophet in the public sphere since his successful 'risk society-thesis'. Beck's major sociological treatise *Risk Society: Towards a New Modernity* was fortuitously timed: it was published shortly after Chernobyl and crystallized the environmental anxieties of the 1980s, but at the same time painted an optimistic picture of what Beck called a 'different modernity'.[52] This 'different modernity' was to be a 'radicalized modernity' which transcended industrial society, and was brought about by the silent revolution of a 'reflexive modernization', i.e. by 'simple modernization's' unintended consequences, which would add up to a structural rupture, and, somewhat as in Habermas's thought, redeem some of the as yet unfulfilled promises of the Enlightenment. This idea of a 'persisting but transformed modernity' arguably satisfied a longing among the post-socialist Left for engaging with the 'heritage of the philosophical discourse of modernity', and for holding on to the project of modernization, while at the same time radically criticizing it.[53] On another level, *Risk Society* repudiated the paralysis of systems theory, which confined 'politics' to the function of one system among others, and Marxism, which could not conceive of a 'modernization of modernity' without a socio-political revolution.[54] Vague as the theory might often have seemed, Beck's emphasis on new spaces opening up for political action, on subterranean changes which would suddenly erupt, and on the delegitimation of experts chimed well with '1989'.

In the 1990s, Beck called for nothing less than the 'invention of the political', arguing that 'our fate is that we have to invent the political anew'.[55] He defined the political in a manner both limited and optimistic as the capacity to shape social reality, conspicuously leaving out questions about the legitimation of power and interests.[56] He subsequently made the very theoretical move that had been at the heart of Schmitt's project: he detached 'the political' from the notion of the state, and then played the political off against the state. Schmitt made this move in response to a crisis in the peculiar formalistic positivism of the German tradition of con-

---

[52] Ulrich Beck, *Risk Society: Towards a New Modernity*, trans. Mark Ritter (1986; London: Sage, 1992).

[53] Peter Osborne, 'Times (Modern), Modernity (Conservative)? Notes on the Persistence of a Temporal Motif', in *New Formations*, No. 28 (1996), 132–41; here 132.

[54] Luhmann, *Social Systems* and, more recently (and more political) Helmut Willke, *Ironie des Staates: Grundlinien einer Staatstheorie polyzentrischer Gesellschaft* (Frankfurt/Main: Suhrkamp, 1992).

[55] Ulrich Beck, 'World Risk Society as Cosmopolitan Society? Ecological Questions in a Framework of Manufactured Uncertainties', in *Theory, Culture & Society*, No. 4 (1996), 1–32; here 11, and Beck, *Die Erfindung*.

[56] Beck, *Risk Society*, 190.

stitutional law, without truly transcending its categories and its perception of the political.[37] He had deinstitutionalized the political only to think state and the political together again, by defining (and reasoning in a circular manner) the state as the political unity capable of authoritative friend–enemy distinctions. At the same time, however, he had made the concept of the political freely available to movements like the National Socialists.

Beck sought to avoid Schmitt's étatiste approach, and any constraining of the political in an either–or logic. In fact, he identified such a move with the functional differentiation typical of systems theory, thereby implicitly associating Luhmann with Schmitt.[38] Beck instead relocated 'the political' in what he called 'sub-politics', and what Schmitt would have called the 'self-organizing society': sub-politics referred to the arena where the political, defined by Beck as large-scale social change, actually took place: economic-technological development, the natural sciences, but also private life. Thus, the side effects of economic-technological development, rather than rational will-formation in parliaments, were the source of the transformative power of a radical modernity.[39] While this critique of parliament was also a classic trope of Schmittian thought, Beck suggested that with increased civic participation rights, citizens could become capable of exerting power over these 'subpolitical' processes.[40] This claim about the political paralleled Beck's overall claim about the nature of 'reflexive modernization': it constituted a profound transformation of society, without any outward revolutionary change: he left the political system intact, but behind its facade, the 'hollowing out' of the political silently proceeded. Also, the differentiation process of modernization gave way to one of de-differentiation, in which, ideally, politics became decentralized and open for widespread decision-making: these decisions were to be open to democratic negotiations, so that 'sub-politics' became an arena in which a new political subjectivity could constitute itself.[41] The political, in short, could

[37] Ernst Vollrath, 'Wie ist Carl Schmitt an seinen Begriff des Politischen gekommen?', in *Zeitschrift für Politik*, Vol. 36, No. 2 (1989), 151–68. Also Peter C. Caldwell, *Popular Sovereignty and the Crisis of Constitutional Law: The Theory & Practice of Weimar Constitutionalism* (Durham: Duke University Press, 1997).

[38] It is noticeable, however, that Beck incorporated Schmittian thought patterns without acknowledging them, for instance Schmitt's conception of modernity as a quest for 'neutralizations'. Beck, *Erfindung*, 263–8, and Carl Schmitt, 'Das Zeitalter der Neutralisierungen und Entpolitisierungen', in *Positionen und Begriffe im Kampf mit Weimar–Genf–Versailles 1923–1939* (1940; Berlin: Duncker and Humblot, 1988), 120–32.

[39] Beck, *Risk Society*, 185–90.

[40] Carl Schmitt, *The Crisis of Parliamentary Democracy*, trans. Ellen Kennedy (1926; Cambridge, Mass.: MIT Press, 1985).

[41] Beck, *Erfindung*, 157.

be reinvented without a revolution. Thus, rather like Gross's, Beck's Berlin Republic would represent the state as make-believe: behind the façade, the political had escaped into society.

What was needed, however, was what Beck verbosely called a 'politics of politics', i.e. a politics that changed the very rules of politics and at the same time controlled the 'shape of the political'. This reflexive politics was at least partially equivalent to Arendt's conception of politics. While Beck did not make any civic republican or even civic humanist claims, he did describe politics as a realm of action and freedom, and predicted 'the return of individuals into society'.[42] Like Arendt, he rejected a Marxist or functionalist framework and emphasized the scope of action for individuals. Beck's emphasis on action and the individual also fitted into a larger paradigm shift, in which the social sciences — and history — placed greater value on individual action, rather than structure, and on culture, rather than economics. Arguably, this reorientation was a result of both the social sciences' failure to predict 1989 and the desire of disenchanted younger scholars — other than New Right taboo-breakers — to assert themselves against social history.[43]

At first sight, Beck seemed to offer a response to 1989 which was future-oiented, allowed the Left to escape the psycho-social discourse of identity, and transcended *both* the traditional state and the nation by offering an implicit theory of sociologically grounded post-nationalism. However, the suspicion remained that the theory of 'reflexive modernization' was merely an extrapolation of the experiences of the Federal Republic of the 1980s: Beck's risk society was also a rich society, which could afford the kinds of anxieties that he used to explain the loss of faith in industrial society and a traditional political class. Also, his sociology of a 'modernized modernity' was in one sense dialectical in a rather old-fashioned manner: the systems of modern industrial society produced their own 'risks', i.e. their own negation. In the 'sublation' of this contradiction, humanism and individual agency were miraculously resurrected. While this theory seemed to offer the Left insights into the future of institutions and the changing nature of the state, the question remained whether Beck underestimated the resourcefulness of 'simple modernity', and was still searching for the elusive 'third way' that once animated the theorists of a legitimation crisis in late capitalism; he seemed to have simply substituted the ecological crisis for the contradictions of capitalism, and reassured disillusioned Marxists that, even with the façade of official

---

[42] *Ibid.*, 149.

[43] For a response from the proponents of social history, see Hans-Ulrich Wehler, 'Von der Herrschaft zum Habitus', in *Die Zeit*, 25 October 1996.

politics and industrial society intact, revolutionary change was indeed under way.[44]

Finally, Beck's redefinition of the political – with its strong aesthetic overtones – appeared altogether too optimistic, emphasizing the creative elements of politics at the expense of the coercive ones. To overlook the presence of violence in politics seemed to qualify him for Max Weber's charge that whoever denied this presence was politically infantile.[45] Moreover, as much as Beck sought to provide a sociological argument for a more participatory politics, he had little to say about the constitution of various public spheres in the realm of sub-politics. In this instance a heavy dose of empirical sociology might have rescued the theory from an empty voluntarism and from illusions about the capacity of individuals to overcome obstacles and to decide democratically on the assessment of new risks. Consequently, Beck, who seemed to open up genuinely new vistas for the Left beyond contrition over the loss of utopia and conversion to nationalism and who eventually came to have a significant influence in Anglo-American debates through the work of Anthony Giddens, could hardly claim to have produced a political theory at all.

A More Republican Germany? The Left's Constitution of Liberty

Some intellectuals, referring most directly back to 1989, argued for a 'Berlin spirit' which was to draw on the constitutional achievements of the Federal Republic as well as the collective memory of the revolutionary action of East Germans in 1989. Here, the GDR revolutionaries were portrayed as acting spontaneously and as experiencing their capacity to act politically, thereby opening up new republican perspectives.[46] For these intellectuals, the 'belated nation' could finally arrive on the basis of the common experience of republican freedom and an act of mutual recognition: West Germans had to acknowledge the 'great achievement' of the East German revolution, while East Germans had to recognize the free

---

[44] Beck admitted as much in a footnote. See Ulrich Beck, 'Vom Veralten sozialwissenschaftlicher Begriffe: Grundzüge einer Theorie reflexiver Modernisierung', in Christoph Görg (ed.), *Gesellschaft im Übergang: Perspektiven kritischer Soziologie* (Darmstadt: Wissenschaftliche Buchgesellschaft, 1994), 21–43; here 41.

[45] Max Weber, 'The Profession and Vocation of Politics', in Peter Lassman and Ronald Speirs (eds), *Weber: Political Writings* (Cambridge: Cambridge University Press, 1994) 309–69.

[46] Bernward Baule, 'Freiheit und Revolution: Die Bedeutung von 1989 für die Berliner Republik' in Bernward Baule (ed.), *Hannah Arendt und die Berliner Republik: Fragen an das vereinigte Deutschland* (Berlin: Aufbau, 1996), 82–106; here 86.

institutions of the old Federal Republic.[47] In other words, where conservatives demanded *Selbstbewußtsein* [self-confidence] for the state, the republicans asked for a *Selbstanerkennung* [self-recognition] of the Republic.
For advocates of a new Berlin republicanism, intellectuals like Habermas
and Gross remained thoroughly caught up in the experience of the old
Federal Republic.[48] Rather than projecting the features of the Bonn
Republic onto Berlin, a recognition of the genuinely new and a broad
public discourse were required. In this project, Hannah Arendt was singled
out as a guiding spirit and as providing a possible answer for the meaning
of politics.

Arendt's thought was taken up for two reasons in particular: first, 1989
was interpreted according to her theories as a historical moment in which
non-violent revolutionaries spontaneously brought about something
entirely new, experiencing what Arendt called 'natality'.[49] In line with
Arendt's unorthodox definition of power as 'acting in concert', the GDR
revolutionaries experienced the 'power' they could constitute by acting collectively, their capacity for responsible political judgement, and the feeling
of public happiness which went along with it.[50] Finally, they realized what
it meant to constitute a public space and to move in it. In an Arendtian
view of unification, this experience of politics was crowded out by 'the
social', i.e. economic necessities, just as the French Revolution was distorted
and ultimately destroyed by people's 'real wants'.[51] While in Germany,
there was no effort to 'solve the social questions by political means', and
therefore no terror, it still remained true that no constitutional discussion,
either at the national level or in German town hall meetings, had taken
place.[52] Given these deficits, some Arendtians could only hope that narrat-
ing 1989 over time would keep this experience of politics alive, and that
spaces for political action as freedom could be strengthened within the
institutional framework of the Berlin Republic. But they also hoped that
the legacy of the East German revolution and the 'communitarian' elements of life in the GDR could help socially to integrate Germany as a
whole. In short, where the intellectuals of the sceptical generation
had officially advocated 'democratic socialism', but de facto advanced
liberalism to narrow the post-fascist democratic deficit, Arendtian

---

[47] Bernward Baule, 'Einleitung', in *Hannah Arendt und die Berliner Republik*, 7–13; here 8.

[48] *Ibid.*, 10.

[49] Hannah Arendt, *The Human Condition* (1958; Chicago: Chicago University Press, 1989), 176–8.

[50] For Arendt's concept of power, and her distinction between power and violence, see Hannah
Arendt, *On Violence* (New York: Harcourt Brace, 1970).

[51] Hannah Arendt, *On Revolution* (1963; New York: Penguin, 1990) 109.

[52] *Ibid.*, 112.

intellectuals after 1989 advocated a mixture of liberalism and communitarianism to remedy the 'republican deficit' and the intra-German divisions left by unification.

On another level, Arendt's claim that totalitarianism meant a radical break in historical continuity and the Western philosophical tradition was applied to 1989 in reverse. In other words, Arendt, as the theorist of natality, was viewed as offering a way out of the sterile historical categories of progress and process inherited from the nineteenth century. Her concepts – and peculiar phenomenology of the political – were mobilized against those intellectuals who responded to the radically novel, the great caesura of 1989, with the familiar categories of nationalism and geopolitics on the Right, and anti-fascism and post-nationalism on the Left.[53]

But could the post-1989 constellation be a genuinely new departure for the Left? After the Left had shunned her for being a Cold Warrior, an elitist and an Aristotelian philosophical anthropologist, did a rediscovery of Arendt now provide republican resources for a renewal of an emancipatory project beyond the sterile discourse of national identity and 'third ways'?[54] The answer could hardly be affirmative. As in the work of Habermas and Beck, Arendt's republicanism was shorn of its more radical elements, and not much more remained than a classical Habermasian call for more political participation. Her emphasis on a human plurality of opinions, on the formation of political judgement and on the power of narrative were alluded to, but hardly explored in their meaning for a more republican Germany. On the other hand, the danger a republicanism of virtue might pose was not discussed at all. Thus, arguably, the relationship between Arendt and the Left remains a history of *rendezvous manqués*.

Moreover, the Right's reaction to Beck and the Arendtians was predictable. Conservatives appealed to Forsthoff's critique of the old Federal Republic to reassert the authority of the state, and defended the state as protecting traditions and individuality against the Beckian individuation which left only interchangeable, atomized individuals.[55] As the Berlin Republic approached, tame initiatives from the Left were countered by conservative claims familiar, all-too-familiar from the old Federal Republic.

[53] Antonia Grunenberg, '"Macht kommt von möglich ..."', in Grunenberg and Probst (eds), *Einschnitte*, 83–95; here 83.

[54] See Ernst Vollrath, 'Hannah Arendt bei den Linken', 9–10, and Michael Th. Greven, 'Hannah Arendt – Pluralität und Gründung der Freiheit', in Kemper (ed.), *Die Zukunft des Politischen*, 69–96; here 88–9.

[55] Jan Ross, 'Staatsfeindschaft: Anmerkungen zum neuen Vulgärliberalismus', in *Merkur*, Vol. 51 (1997), 93–194.

Between Schmitt and Arendt: Taming the Political

In the 1990s, German intellectuals not only engaged in a discourse about foundations for the Berlin Republic, but also contested the meaning of what was to count as the foundation of 'the political' *per se*. Most intellectuals situated themselves vis-à-vis the classic thinkers of 'the political'. In the case of left-wing intellectuals, Carl Schmitt was usually cast in the role of *bête noire*. This was particularly so with Habermas who remained, one might say, negatively fixated on Schmitt. In his turn to legal and political theory, Schmitt was once again deemed the opponent most worthy of a lengthy refutation. In general, however, Habermas continued on the theoretical path towards post-nationalism which had been interrupted, but not fundamentally diverted by unification. In conservative contributions, Schmitt continued to be present in major arguments concerning the critique of the self-organizing society usurping the state and a foreign policy which failed to take account of ineradicable conflict. Conservatives – other than the New Right – generally resigned themselves to further European integration, but reverted to some of Bohrer's aesthetic arguments in order to compensate for the supposed loss of the political to Brussels.

On the other hand, a number of left-wing intellectuals attempted to recover Hannah Arendt's republicanism for the new polity, building partly on the literature on civil society, partly on what they perceived as the already Arendtian foundations of Habermas's theory of communicative action. Arendt's republicanism became an antidote to a new wave of nationalism in Europe and to the general 'erosion of the political', but also promised new perspectives in the wake of the 'exhaustion of utopian energies'.[56]

This polarization between Schmitt and Arendt clearly had something to do with the fact that 1989 could be given a Schmittian or an Arendtian reading. In Schmittian constitutional thought, 1989 meant that sovereignty in Eastern European states was reconstituted by homogeneous nations reasserting themselves as *pouvoirs constituants*.[57] But it could also be read as the beginning of ethno-nationalist enmity, of a friend–enemy logic and an ultimate shrinking of political space in the Arendtian sense: Schmitt, in other words, was the prophet of ethnic cleansing, and post-Communism was the period in which man, that 'dynamic and dangerous being', was no longer held in check by an authoritarian state.[58] On an Arendtian reading, in the peaceful revolutions of 1989 ordinary people had

---

[56] Peter Kemper, 'Vorwort', in *Die Zukunft des Politischen*, 7–12.

[57] Carl Schmitt, *Verfassungslehre* (1928; Berlin: Duncker & Humblot, 1970), 51.

[58] Beck, *Die Erfindung*, 227.

acted in concert, generated power and engaged in acts of collective founding and constitution-making. *Pace* the Schmittian interpretation of a
homogeneous will of the people asserting itself, 'the people' were a plurality of citizens' groups gathered at the Round Table.[59] This substitution
of plural and self-reflexive 'concerted action' for unitary popular sovereignty enabled the revolutionaries to avoid the logic of friend–enemy
thinking and the unleashing of violence in revolutionary civil War.[60] Moreover, 1989 was a spontaneous moment when individuals reasserted the
power to set a new beginning.

The question, however, remained whether any of the intellectuals
engaging with Schmittian and Arendtian thought actually followed the
two theorists in their more radical claims. Schmitt's followers emphasized
the étatiste, agonal and broadly Hobbesian elements in his thought – but
not in a way which deviated significantly from post-war West German
statism. In so far as Schmitt's theories of *Großräume* [great geopolitical
spaces] were revived, they were reduced to a 'realist' reading which could
as easily be found in Kissinger or Samuel Huntington.[61] Apart from marginal right-wing figures, nobody was willing to resuscitate the radical
vitalist and authoritarian elements of Schmitt's constitutional thought, or
his emphasis on the substantial homogeneity of the demos, let alone his
idiosyncratic Roman Catholicism.

In a way, the same held true for Arendt. Her followers desired a Berlin
Republic which was actually more republican, but hardly made any claims
for civic humanism, a radical decentralization in councils, or an institu-
tionalization of continuous political action. Thus, arguably followers of
both Schmitt and of Arendt, while remaining in a broadly liberal-
democratic framework, did not identify any potential for making the
Berlin Republic above all a more liberal polity. In particular, they never
quite confronted what to many observers seemed the real cause of a shrinking of political space, namely market-driven globalization as such. As with
Habermas in the unification debate, an emphatic concept of the political
was marshalled against the economic sphere of mere private self-interest,
but the latter was not discussed as such, and the spheres of politics and
economics remained rigidly divorced. But this divorce also ultimately rendered the overburdened conceptualization of the political politically impotent. And yet, paradoxically, tameness in the engagement with two great
thinkers, who in their very different ways were both illiberal, might
have been cause for liberal praise, since inadvertently, both latter-day

---

[59] Ulrich K. Preuß, *Revolution, Fortschritt und Verfassung: Zu einem neuen Vefassungsverständnis*
(Frankfurt/Main: Fischer, 1994), 84–8.

[60] Arendt, *On Revolution*, 158–9 and 202–14.

[61] Erich Vad, *Strategie und Sicherheitspolitik: Perspektiven im Werk von Carl Schmitt* (Opladen:
Westdeutscher Verlag, 1996).

Schmittians and Arendtians demonstrated how much German political thought had become liberalized.

Nevertheless, just as a form of communitarianism eventually entered the political rhetoric of Bill Clinton and Tony Blair, the 'return of the political' actually became part of the election campaign of 1998. Senior SPD intellectual Erhard Eppler outlined a 'return of politics', while the SPD and Green opposition politicians Siegmar Mosdorf and Hubert Kleinert predicted its 'renaissance'.[62] Both their books adopted what one might call a 'vulgar Beckian' view of politics as the 'capacity to influence' and sought to repudiate systems theory. However, while the Old Right, Beck and the republican Left all sought to transcend debates on normality and the nation through an explicitly political approach to the Berlin Republic, the contestation of national identity continued. With the 'Walser debate' in the autumn of 1998 it arguably reached its most decisive phase since 1989, because it involved not only the tangled issue of 'normality', but also the Jewish question which had been at the heart of the German question about normality for so long.

The Walser Debate: Normalizing Memory?

In the summer of 1998 Martin Walser was given the Peace Prize of the German Book Trade, one of Germany's most prestigious literary awards. Critics now recognized Walser not only for having been the foremost chronicler of the old Federal Republic, but also for his 'talking about Germany' and his insistence on unification during the 1970s and 1980s.[63] Walser's ouevre had supposedly been the true 'literary subtext' of West Germany: just as Walser's anti-heroes had been disempowered selves and victims incapable of decisive action, the Federal Republic had been without decision-making capacity and 'without history'.[64] In the same vein, Walser's constitutive self-doubt and even the self-hatred of his literary protagonists were read as symptoms of larger social-psychological phenomena in the Federal Republic. Most importantly, precisely because Walser, the 'enlightened conservative' (Grass), embodied both former West German culture and had insisted on unification, he seemed in a unique position to build a bridge between the Federal Republic and the Berlin Republic.

---

[62] Erhard Eppler, *Die Wiederkehr der Politik* (Frankfurt/Main: Insel, 1998); Hubert Kleinert and Siegmar Mosdorf, *Die Renaissance der Politik: Wege ins 21. Jahrhundert* (Berlin: Siedler, 1998).

[63] Jochen Hieber, 'Gegen den Abstieg gespielt und gewonnen', in *Frankfurter Allgemeine Zeitung*, 24 March 1997.

[64] Frank Schirrmacher, 'Walser: Friedenspreisträger 1998', in *Frankfurter Allgemeine Zeitung*, 5 June 1999.

Walser's speech, however, also had a more concrete political background. In September 1998, Helmut Kohl, the almost literal embodiment of post-unification continuity, had finally been voted out of office, and a new generation of politicians – the first without any personal memories of the Second World War – was taking over the reins of government. Through numerous public pronouncements on cultural politics, Social Democratic politicians had strengthened the perception that an SPD–Green government might seek the ever elusive 'nation-state normality' and a new 'uninhibitedness'. In particular, they seemed to take an excessively critical view of the Holocaust memorial to be built near the Brandenburg Gate, which, by 1998, had been subject to intense dispute for more than a decade.[65] In August, *Der Spiegel's* cover posed the question whether there was now 'too much memory'.[66] The new Chancellor further nourished speculation about a new German 'assertiveness' by declining an invitation to attend French commemorations of the eightieth anniversary of the First World War, and by claiming in his first 'state of the nation address' that Germany should be a 'self-confident nation', no better, but also no worse than others. In short, if the 'new Germany' was to redefine itself, this seemed to be an auspicious constellation.

In Walser's speech, which was designed both to provoke and to resist easy paraphrasing, the disempowered self was once again on full display.[67] Walser portrayed himself as the victim of public expectations and predetermined roles of what intellectuals in Germany should be and say. In an act of the 'soul thirsty for freedom', Walser emphatically rejected the role of 'conscience of the nation', arguing that intellectuals adopting such a stance were always in danger of viewing their conscience as purer than that of the people. Were they not, Walser asked – or rather, insinuated – in fact trying to escape the collective of the perpetrators and suffering from the illusion – even if only for split seconds – that they could be among the victims, too? In as direct an attack as possible without actually naming names, Walser criticized Grass and Habermas for 'instrumentalizing' Auschwitz in order to advance subjective, rather arbitrary political positions – for instance, a fundamental dislike of unification. He even hinted that intellectuals parading as the 'conscience of the nation' might be wilfully exaggerating the circumstances surrounding the violence against the homes of asylum seekers, and that they were attacking the German nation

---

[65] On the debate, see Michael Jeismann, *Mahnmal Mitte: Eine Kontroverse* (Cologne: DuMont, 1999). On the ambiguities associated with Holocaust memorials, James E. Young, *The Texture of Memory: Holocaust Memorials and Meaning* (New Haven: Yale University Press, 1993).

[66] *Der Spiegel*, 24 August 1998.

[67] Martin Walser, 'Die Banalität des Guten: Erfahrungen beim Verfassen einer Sonntagsrede aus Anlaß der Verleihung des Friedenspreis des Deutschen Buchhandels', in *Frankfurter Allgemeine Zeitung*, 12 October 1998.

as a whole in a way in which no other nation could possibly be attacked. These attacks were especially scandalous because the Germans had now undoubtedly become 'normal'. But in addition to the intellectuals performing their cruel work in the *Erinnerungsdienst* [memory service, a concept evoking the Nazi *Arbeitsdienst*], the media had made the remembrance of the Holocaust deteriorate into empty public rituals.

In the somewhat passive-aggressive, even defiant language of private emotions, which had always been his most potent public weapon, Walser confessed that he sometimes had to turn away from the 'permanent representation of our disgrace'.[68] In this highly emotional – and supposedly risky – self-revelation, he argued that intellectuals who were permanently representing shame in fact wanted to 'hurt us' – and possibly themselves. Against this background of empty public rituals and 'national masochism', he then proceeded to develop his own framework for remembrance. Drawing on Heidegger and Hegel – a dubious genealogy considered further provocation – Walser argued that one's conscience could simply not be delegated and that engaging with one's conscience always mandated a retreat into the self. 'Public acts of conscience' necessarily had to become 'symbolic' and thereby corrupt the true labour of conscience, which was incapable of public representation.

Walser then argued – once again – that writers revealed their true morality only in their literary works. Repeatedly alluding to the language of National Socialism, he held up this truth against the 'soldiers of opinion' and the 'wardens of opinion and conscience'. Real moral claims could only be negotiated between reader and author. And only the non-instrumental language of literature could truly communicate the author's morality – not the 'interview' and the corrupt language of the public sphere in general. Walser, who had never refused an interview and used almost every occasion to make his feelings public, claimed that his task was to surrender to language, rather than abuse language to have his opinions confirmed. But, as in Walser's previous pronouncements, language *was* history, and history was national.

By means of claims entirely consistent with his positions since the 1970s, Walser essentially questioned the public role of intellectuals *per se*. But the fact that he linked this attack with the issue of remembrance only proved to what an extent intellectuals in the old Federal Republic had become identified with the role of *publicly* linking democracy and a German 'Holocaust identity'. While they had never explicitly claimed the role of the 'conscience of the nation', as Walser alleged, they certainly had sub-

---

[68] This was in itself not a new claim by Walser: for instance, he had already turned off the TV series *War and Remembrance* for the same reason while travelling in the United States. See Martin Walser, 'Reise ins Leben', in *Zauber und Gegenzauber*, 142–63. Walser's deeply ambivalent relationship to America would be worth investigating in this context.

scribed to Jaspers's original ethos, namely that *public* communication about the past, complemented by private moral self-examination, was the constitutive act of assuming collective responsibility. Walser, somewhat negatively fixated on this tradition from Jaspers to Habermas, now effectively called for a privatization of conscience − and memory.

At the same time, he was defending the authenticity − and authority − of his own memories against moral accusations and 'instrumentalizations'. In his latest book *Ein springender Brunnen*, Walser had offered a highly poetic, but thinly veiled description of his own childhood under the Nazi regime, i.e. the supposed 'normality' of growing up in an inhuman regime, which had been part of the formative experience of the sceptical generation.[69] Walser had also previously drawn a distinction between *Gedächtnis* and *Erinnerung*.[70] The first was simply the 'storage house' of information about the past, while the second was an involuntary, supposedly authentic articulation of memory. The latter was not open to retrospective manipulation by additional historical information, i.e. the realization with hindsight of having lived in a world in which Auschwitz had become possible: in short, 'memory could not be commanded'.[71] In his speech he sought to defend the authenticity of *Erinnerung* to which one simply had to surrender in the same way that one had to surrender to language. As many observers pointed out, however, the very fact that he was talking *publicly* about remembrance and was calling *publicly* for a privatization of memory came close to a performative contradiction.

However, such subtle philosophical observations were soon overshadowed by the fact that Ignatz Bubis, head of the Central Council of Jews in Germany, criticized the speech, calling Walser an 'intellectual arsonist'.[72] In fact, while everybody present at Walser's speech had offered a rapturous standing ovation, Bubis and his wife alone had remained seated and silent. He later claimed that Walser, by advocating 'a culture of looking away' had lent intellectual respectability to views commonly only aired by extreme right-wing politicians.[73] He subsequently added that Walser's charge of the 'instrumentalization of Auschwitz' had clearly referred to the claims by non-Jews who had been slave labourers during the Third

---

[69] Martin Walser, *Ein springender Brunnen* (Frankfurt/Main: Suhrkamp, 1998). See especially the reflections on time and memory at the beginning and end of the book.

[70] 'Erinnerung kann man nicht befehlen: Martin Walser und Rudolf Augstein über ihre deutsche Vergangenheit', in *Der Spiegel*, 2 November 1998.

[71] *Ibid.*

[72] 'Geistige Brandstiftung: Bubis wendet sich gegen Walser', in *Frankfurter Allgemeine Zeitung*, 13 October 1998.

[73] Igantz Bubis, 'Wer von der Schande spricht', in *Frankfurter Allgemeine Zeitung*, 10 November 1998.

Reich. Finally, he publicly accused Walser of a latent antisemitism supposedly inherent in his 'intellectual nationalism'.[74]

The confrontation between Walser and Bubis, both born in 1927, provoked a rapid succession of further prominent interventions. The SPD patrician Klaus von Dohnanyi sought to defend Walser and pointed out the unbridgeable differences in moral perceptions of Jews and non-Jews after 1945. But rather than moderating the dispute, he provoked further outrage on Bubis's part, when he wrote that the Jews would have to ask themselves what they would have done, 'if after 1933 "only" the handicapped, the homosexuals and the gypsies had been carried off to the extermination camps'.[75] Dohnanyi both expressed approval of Walser's 'instrumentalization' charge and reaffirmed a German 'Holocaust identity' defined by the fact that the Germans stemmed from the perpetrators of 'this shameful time'.

Conservative observers quickly concluded that the dispute demonstrated the final failure of the project of *Vergangenheitsbewältigung*, or that it had in fact been doomed from the start.[76] Others saw the dispute as evidence that the memory of Jews and Germans would remain divided for the foreseeable future because 'suffering created a common memory, but shame destroyed it'.[77] On the other hand, former President Richard von Weizsäcker, who in 1985 had given the seminal speech acknowledging 1945 as 'liberation', failed to mediate despite an intervention couched in extraordinarily reconciliatory and non-committal language.[78] His references to the 'damage' done to German youth and to Germany's image abroad by the dispute remained ineffectual, when they might have been sufficient to settle the dispute a decade earlier.

In the end, Walser and Bubis met both privately and publicly.[79] As was to be expected, they failed to resolve the dispute, but Bubis retracted his accusation of 'intellectual arson', while insisting that many Germans might have misunderstood Walser as calling for the drawing of a thick line under the past. Walser, on the other hand, defiantly reiterated that many people had found his speech 'liberating'. He frequently appealed to the 'thousand letters' which he had received in response to the speech, thereby yet again immunizing himself from criticism by the political 'opinion

---

[74] 'Moral verjährt nicht', in *Der Spiegel*, 30 November 1998.

[75] Klaus von Dohnanyi, 'Eine Friedensrede', in *Frankfurter Allgemeine Zeitung*, 14 November 1998.

[76] Eckhard Fuhr, 'Deprimierend', in *Frankfurter Allgemeine Zeitung*, 10 November 1998.

[77] Ulrich Raulff, 'Das geteilte Gedächtnis', in *ibid.*

[78] Richard von Weizsäcker, 'Der Streit wird gefährlich', in *Frankfurter Allgemeine Zeitung*, 20 November 1998.

[79] 'Wir brauchen eine neue Sprache der Erinnerung: Das Treffen von Ignatz Bubis und Martin Walser', in *Frankfurter Allgemeine Zeitung*, 14 December 1998.

soldiers' with references to a semi-private public sphere, playing off a supposed 'silent majority' against the mandarins in the public sphere. Walser
and Bubis eventually agreed — albeit reluctantly — that a new language of
commemoration would have to be found. It was clear, however, that
Bubis referred to a new public language, whereas Walser insisted on a
new private language of conscience (the Wittgensteinian contradiction
notwithstanding).

Did this debate then signify some epochal shift of the tectonic plates of
the intellectual field? Was it yet another *Historikerstreit*, or in fact the first
fundamental debate of the Berlin Republic, as many editorials kept pointing out? If so, did it prove that — yet again — national questions about normality, rather than the questions which the proponents of 'the political'
had raised, were to be at the heart of public discourse in the Berlin
Republic? Clearly, it might be too early to tell. But there was certainly
something familiar about the debate's rhetoric. Walser's claims and those
of some of his supporters repeated a pattern of talking about the past
which was first established in the historians' dispute, and by Nolte in particular: the use of pseudo-hesitant rhetorical questions, advancing two steps
(in order to break a 'taboo') and retreating one step at a time; and, when
challenged, claiming that one had been completely (and willfully) misunderstood, that quotes had been taken out of a complicated context, and that,
in any case, disputing the meaning of the Holocaust was not the same as
denying its existence.[80] The next phase in this familiar pattern was a kind
of 'meta-discourse' about the appropriate rules of intellectual engagement,
about the character of the conflict, rather than about its substance, and the
mutual attribution of sinister motives, as well as the ultimate moral
reproach that one's opponent was not only instrumentalizing the Nazi past,
but in fact also showing some unspecified 'family resemblance' with the
Nazis themselves. In short, the rules of the culture of suspicion applied in
full force to the debate — and especially to those who sought to question
the culture of suspicion itself.

There was also a familiar parcelling out of concepts during the debate:
Walser and his supporters denounced the concept of 'collective guilt'
arguing that there was no such thing, despite the fact that neither Bubis
nor the Left had actually made this charge. The Left, on the other hand,
claimed the concept of 'collective responsibility', but found it increasingly
difficult to give it concrete meaning. In particular, it was unclear whether
collective responsibility at this point implied any directly political imperatives, or whether it meant finding the right symbolic responses to
the Shoah, and then how different private memories, such as Walser's,
should relate to public representations. In the same vein, Walser and his

---

[80] Christian Meier identified this pattern brilliantly in his 'Die Republik denken', in *Frankfurter
Allgemeine Zeitung*, 29 April 1994.

supporters seemed to assume that just because memory was personal and because, as Walser put it, 'as long as something is, it is not what it will have been', memory should be preserved in some pre-representational purity – and thereby be insulated from questions of political responsibility. The Left, on the other hand, criticized Walser's account of memory as 'lacking Auschwitz' – as if there was no room for legitimate competing memories, or even mis-memories, for that matter.

Nevertheless, there were also significant differences from the *Historikerstreit*. Most importantly, the Walser debate was not about historical argument at all, but about appropriate forms of commemoration. While Habermas and the historians had of course also argued about the present through the past, in the Walser debate there was a sense that the meaning of historical events as such was not at issue. The debate was entirely *reflexive*, as the participants seemed highly conscious not only of previous intellectual debates, but also of the dilemmas associated with previous forms of commemoration. In short, at issue were above all the representations of previous representations of the Holocaust, the very history and future of its public memory, rather than the event itself.

Unlike in the *Historikerstreit*, there was also the further problem of arguing about feelings. Walser, with his familiar distrust of the public sphere, had started the argument on the level of the unarguable, when he staked his public position on non-negotiable private emotions. It was then not surprising that a German debate became – once more – very personal and vituperative. Then again, perhaps Walser had never been interested in a debate in the first place, but in establishing a moral boundary – between the silent majority who shared his feelings, and those who put 'our shame' on display. In the same spirit of drawing a line, he essentially expatriated Bubis in their discussion by eliding the fact that both were, after all, German citizens – a point Bubis was at pains to emphasize. He also chided Bubis for 'still having dealt with completely different issues', when Walser was already coming to terms with the German past – to which the Holcaust survivor Bubis replied that at that time he had not yet been able to face the past. It was this aggressive, even self-satisfied appropriation of *Vergangenheitsbewältigung* that constituted a novel aspect of the debate – a sense that German intellectuals, having served in the *Erinnerungsdienst* for so long, could now legitimately call for closure. After all, Walser had already once called for German–Jewish reconciliation through the symbol of Klemperer – and just as the Germans now should be ready to forgive each other, as suggested by Walser's call for clemency in the case of an East German spy, with which he had begun and ended his speech, so the Jews should finally forgive the Germans. This, then, was where Walser's talent for self-subversion, his desperate struggle to cleanse himself of the 'dirt' of the German past had finally led: his speech came as close as anything to a rebirth of the authentic voice of the German mandarin intent on a harmonious national community, with his supposedly apolitical contempt for 'politics' and his adulation of 'history', and the resentment of those still bent on disturbing a personal and national 'peace of mind'.[81]

An especially bitter twist was added to the debate by the fact that the sceptical generation was probably now fighting its last battle – about which memories and intellectual legacies were to be passed on. Almost nobody in the Walser debate was under sixty. In one sense, the participants were speaking less as intellectuals, basing their claims on competence and an appeal to some form of 'general interest', as they had done in the *Historikerstreit*, than as individuals basing their interventions on private experience. The 'vulnerability' which the participants claimed for themselves, and the need for a gentler way of treating each other, was due to the fact that the debate was essentially about their very own individual life trajectories – and memories. To use the distinction coined by Jan Assmann, their 'communicative', i.e. living personal memory, would soon pass into 'cultural memory', i.e. public representations of the past.[82] But it seemed that precisely at the moment when communicative memory began to pass into cultural memory, there was an unprecedented crescendo of communication, a final battle about the content of cultural memory. Even at the time, the debate itself was already seen as a legacy – even if it was a legacy of unresolved antinomies and misunderstandings. This impression of finality was confirmed when Ignatz Bubis died six months later and was laid to rest in Tel Aviv. He refused to be buried in Germany for fear of desecration of his grave.

Above all, confusion and structural incompatibilities seemed to characterize these debates on collective memory. There was a tendency to conflate collective or national memory, and individual, living mass memory on both sides of the political spectrum. The Left seemed to assume that collective memory could become personal memory, a pure, inner experience, as if one had actually lived through the events in question, whereas Walser seemed to think that private memory could substitute for collective memory. With his demand to restrict public rituals in favour of private memory, he implied that private memory would need no public incentives whatsoever. Through the stark dichotomy between the purity of private conscience on the one hand and empty public ritual on the other, Walser nourished the suspicion that he was uncomfortable with the imperative to remember *per se*, and that by demanding an impossible purity, he was actually aiming at ending memory altogether. His claims were based on

---

[81] Walser's claim that he 'belonged to this dirt' and was 'besieged by the past' can be found in 'Ich bin umstellt von Vergangenheit: Ein Gespräch mit Jörg Magenau und Detlev Lücke', in *'Ich habe ein Wunschpotential'*, 33–46; here 40.

[82] Jan Assman, *Das kulturelle Gedächtnis: Schrift, Erinnerung und politische Identität in frühen Hochkulturen* (Munich: C. H. Beck, 1997).

yet another version of his earlier (and familiar German) view of the public sphere as inherently shallow and contaminated by instrumentality. But he also relied on a caricature of the previous public role of German intellectuals. Jaspers, and those influenced by him, such as Sternberger and Habermas, had always seen the dichotomy between public memory on the one hand, and private memory and moral self-examination, on the other, as a false one. Moreover, they had rarely insisted that public communication about the past had to be monolithic – rather, arguing about the past, rather than any particular argument, would be the appropriate way of assuming collective responsibility. Finally, as Jaspers had pointed out, while the public sphere of course allowed for shallow and morally unacceptable claims, everything that was 'base in the public sphere could only be corrected through the public sphere'.[83] In this sense, a fundamental chasm opened between intellectuals in Jaspers's tradition and Arendtian republicans concerned about 'public space' on the one hand, and, on the other, Walser and all those distrustful of the public sphere in ways which were reminiscent of Weimar intellectuals' suspicion of the *Man*.

This last point was not least stressed by Karl Heinz Bohrer, who intervened in the debate at a relatively late stage. He argued that Walser's intellectual mistake had consisted in making the necessary public and symbolic discourse about the Holocaust subject to the criterion of personal sincerity.[84] As always, he added a special twist by turning the arguments of the Left against itself. Instead of persisting with a left-wing public culture of guilt, which he saw as having failed, the Germans should return to a culture of shame, very much like the 'cold conduct' which had been so prevalent after the First World War. The culture of guilt had principally foundered for two reasons. On the one hand, it had not allowed for multiple memories, but had been centred on one event. Consequently, it resembled an obsession more than reflective memory. What Bohrer saw as a fixation on the Holocaust made a memory of Germany's larger national history impossible, which in turn rendered a proper memory of the Holocaust impossible. Additionally, only a 'self-conscious' – rather than a self-confident – nation could remember at all. The Left's aversion to the nation, then, had also destroyed a proper, public memory of the Holocaust – a fact which Bohrer found confirmed in the insouciance of the new government consisting of '68ers. Paradoxically, he claimed, an attitude which took Auschwitz as the foundational myth of post-war Germany made memory itself impossible.

So, in the end, what did the Walser debate signify with regard to the

---

[83] Dolf Sternberger, 'Jaspers und der Staat', in Klaus Piper (ed.), *Karl Jaspers: Werk und Wirkung* (Munich: Piper, 1963), 133–141; here 137.

[84] Karl Heinz Bohrer, 'Schuldkultur oder Schamkultur und der Verlust an historischem Gedächtnis', in *Neue Zürcher Zeitung*, 12 December 1998.

symbolic stakes involved in defining the Berlin Republic? On one level, German intellectuals still remained very much caught in the discourse of a vague national psychologizing, talking about 'confidence' and 'normality', which, because of their very emptiness, contributed to the acrimonious nature of German debates. They were also still searching for an ever-elusive 'normality'. In fact, it turned out that the Walser debate and the debate on the political, while seemingly most personal and private in one case and most public and political in the other, were actually profoundly similar in one respect. Both were about defining what should count as 'normal', or, in other words, what was *not* in need of justification and *not* open to political action.

The debate also showed that the memory of Germans and 'Jews in Germany' remained fundamentally divided – which was neither surprising nor a state of affairs which either side could or should want to change unilaterally. 'German memories' themselves were of course also still conflicting. But rather than some forced national reconciliation, or, as Walser suggested, privatization of memory for the sake of authenticity, competing public articulations of memory might in fact remain the hallmark of a liberal polity. And just as memories would always be conflicted and contested once they were publicly articulated, so a shared language about the past, which Bubis and Walser supposedly sought, would have to be a language of disagreement. Defining themselves by their disagreements and remaining faithful to them, seemed like the only, but not necessarily deficient way, for Germans who of course also disagreed amongst themselves, and 'Jews in Germany' (or 'German citizens of Jewish faith', as Bubis put it) who also disagreed amongst themselves, to see themselves as a collective.

Intellectual Refoundations? In Search of Another Republic

'For me, the Berlin Republic means: We have to combine the democratic traditions of the old Republic and the civic courage which has become visible in the revolutionary beginning. Then Berlin will play a new role like no other European city . . .'[85]

These were the words neither of an Arendtian Republican, nor of a Habermasian Federal Republican eager to emphasize the continuities with pre-1989 West Germany. It was Gerhard Schröder, the Chancellor himself, who seemed directly to take up two of the themes of the liberal-left analyzed in this chapter – and yet, in connection with the Walser–Bubis debate, he also adopted the rhetoric of normalization, even of a *Schlußstrich*, as he emphatically praised Walser.

---

[85] 'Eine offene Republik: Gunter Hofmann und Sigrid Löffler im Gespräch mit Bundeskanzler Gerhard Schröder', in *Die Zeit*, 4 February 1999.

Did this suggest that at least some left-liberal intellectuals were once again shaping the public discourse of a new Germany, just as much as they had eventually come to shape the parameters of public debate in the old Federal Republic? Or were Walser and his defenders the heralds of a different, 'renationalized' Germany, which so many on the Left feared?

Again, it is too early to tell. If the Berlin Republic officially began life with the move of the Federal government in 1999, and if one takes the developments in West Germany as a guide, the proper intellectual foundation of the 'new' Germany might still be a decade away. Everybody agrees that the 1990s were a period of rapid transition, but also that this transition is far from over, even if much change is couched in a relentless rhetoric of continuity. Nevertheless, the intellectual historian should at least offer some preliminary conclusions about the very recent past and the not-too-distant future.

Germany has changed in ways hardly imaginable ten years ago. And in some, but only some respects, so have its intellectuals. In the early 1990s, pacifism and anti-Americanism still reigned supreme on the Left, and an ostensibly conservative government was debating whether it should send a few pilots to Turkey in the Gulf War, which had been explicitly authorized by the UN Security Council. At the end of the decade, Germany went to War for the first time since 1945, sending soldiers to Kosovo, as part of a mission without any Security Council backing. Günter Grass and Jürgen Habermas (as well as most of the Left) opposed the Gulf War in 1991. Both supported the Kosovo intervention in 1999.

On the one hand, this suggested a change in the nature of German universalism and constitutional patriotism. Rather than deriving a form of German exceptionalism from a combination of selective univeralism and the German past, as Grass had done most prominently in 1990, German universalists now saw universalism as implying some form of strict uniformity — and especially of acting uniformly in concert with a West advancing a policy of human rights.

What did *not* change, however, was a strong tendency to debate policy issues such as military interventions using the grammar of the past — only the results from the equations with the past changed fundamentally. In 1991, for Enzensberger, Saddam Hussein simply equaled Hitler, while the Left, with a truly warped imagination, identified with Iraqi civilian victims, as if they were German civilian victims of the Second World War, all united in innocence as victims of Anglo-American bombs. Baghdad became Dresden. Both interpretations, needless to say, obscured actual developments — and arguably depleted the moral authority of anyone appealing to the past in such an unreflective way.[86]

---

[86] This is not even to speak of the problems associated with analogical reasoning, especially in foreign policy. See Yuen Foong Khong, *Analogies at War: Korea, Dien Bien Phu, and the Vietnam Decisions of 1965* (Princeton: Princeton University Press, 1992).

In 1999, the Left claimed to have learnt its lesson not so much in *Realpolitik*, as in drawing the right moral-cum-political conclusions from the past. Rather than 'never again War', the *cri de coeur* became 'never again Auschwitz'. Both claims were morally incontestable. Yet, relatively few observers noticed that both, in their own way, were equally reductionist slogans, lending themselves to *simplifications terribles*. More importantly, few noted the apparent arbitrariness of basing one's moral and political legitimacy on the past, if the opposite conclusions could be drawn from it within a span of ten years. Of course, it does not follow from the fact that an event is open to multiple, contested interpretations that it holds no lessons at all – after all, every collective memory will be both internally conflicted and publicly contested. But such contestation was of course precisely what the purveyors of such slogans tried to avoid. Drawing on Auschwitz did little to illuminate the moral, let alone the political, stakes in Kosovo. If anything, the comparison had more to do with Germans comforting themselves about making the right moral choices, rather than any genuine empathy with past or present victims. This is not to say that there should be a political *cordon sanitaire* around the Holocaust – as if anybody had the authority to erect one and as if such a device could ever be effective. It is also not to say that the Holocaust is necessarily unrepresentable, unspeakable and incomparable – although it seems undeniable to me that aspects of it are indeed precisely that.[87] The point is that 'drawing lessons', as laudable as this might be in the abstract, can itself be a strategy of *consolation*, of extracting a comforting meaning from the past, rather than adopting a more painful strategy of *confrontation* with the past.[88] Any recourse to the Holocaust conditioned more by one's own *crise de conscience* than critical reflection was unlikely to lead to a more profound political and moral engagement with human reality.

At the same time, advocates of constitutional patriotism and proponents of 'national identity' still faced each other across what seemed like an unbridgeable divide. This was not because German universalism was 'rootless' and a theoretical construct to escape from Germanness, as its detractors always claimed. On the contrary, there still was very much a 'land' even in the universalist fatherland. German univeralism was rooted in a particular past and often referred to that past in rather unmediated ways, as when 'never again Auschwitz' became the explicit historical background for a policy in support of human rights. For such lessons it did not actually matter whether the Holocaust had been an entirely extraordinary event, a German specificity or part of larger historical developments – what mattered was that universally valid insights could be derived from it.

---

[87] 'Unspeakability', however, refers to the testimonies of Survivors, not to second-order observations on the Holocaust – a distinction intellectual observers wishing to identify with the victims often collapse more or less unwittingly.

[88] Lawrence L. Langer, *Admitting the Holocaust* (New York: Oxford University Press, 1995), 5.

But the reverse of this point did not follow – in other words, there was no reason why every universalism needed recourse to the Holocaust to be effective or even fully comprehended.[89] Yet, it remains politically and morally seductive to substitute analogy for argument.

On the other hand, the proponents of constitutional patriotism could not avoid recognizing that, generally, remembrance of the past necessarily involved some recourse to the national framework: it seemed that they could not have 'working through the past' without national identity – even if this national past became the basis of a more universalist position. This was the weak spot which Bohrer had identified. He had also understood that by making the Holocaust and a successful *Vergangenheitsbewältigung* the centre of their political position, the Left would always find it difficult to accept multiple, competing memories as legitimate.

On the other hand, it was Bohrer who had always demanded a conception of German nationhood which could be universalized. And, ironically, it was the Left which now offered such a conception: after all, the idea that patriotism – and present political legitimacy – could be based on having overcome the past was not necessarily a German one, even if the Germans might have had the most extreme and thorough experience in this regard. In the Left's view, then, *Vergangenheitsbewältigung was* national identity *and* German normality. But at the same time, the Left could recommend this model as a patriotism to be exported to other countries, as a *Modell Deutschland* for a culture of 'post-totalitarian legitimacy', in which the permanent responsibility of a collective subject, rather than the triumphal presentation of one's own past became the basis of national identity.[90] In such a model, public acknowledgements of past crimes, mutual suspicion and conflicts about the past could actually be presented as sources of personal autonomy as well as social integration, rather than threats to national stability, as conservatives feared. So the language of 'post-nationalism' and 'post-conventional identities' in one sense only obscured the fact that the Left could offer its own, positive version of national identity, even if it was based on a negative past and allowed for a more inclusive and civic form of identity. Thus, there was no such thing as a 'negative identity' or an 'anti-memory', after all – a fact not lost on postmodern critics who sought to further 'de-centre' constitutional patriotism, fearing that it would fail on account both of its strong universalist demands and its particularist demands to engage with a particular negative past. And as with any other conception of national identity, the memory serving this civic identity would have to be selective and, by definition, instrumental. While the

---

[89] Saul Friedlander, 'Introduction', in *Probing the Limits of Representation: Nazism and the 'Final Solution'* (Cambridge, Mass.: Harvard University Press, 1992), 1–21; here 19–20.

[90] Helmut Dubiel, *Niemand ist frei von der Geschichte: Die nationalsozialistische Herrschaft in den Debatten des Deutschen Bundestages* (Munich: Hanser, 1999), 291.

Left's version of national identity was certainly not 'triumphalist', it was propelled by pride in the overcoming of the past, and, sometimes, a rather too quick and too aggressive appropriation of the victims. After all, Germany, in a symbolic gesture fraught with contradictions, was now the first nation in which the perpetrators would build a monument for their victims.

More importantly, the claim that the political system of the Federal Republic had only developed a democratic culture to the extent that it had opened itself to the memory of the past was both less obvious and less universalizable than the Left imagined. There certainly had been the theoretical and practical connection which Jaspers, Sternberger and Habermas had drawn between debating the past and an open, democratic public sphere, as well as the idea of democratic accountability. But there were also significant examples of transitions of dictatorship to democracy where this link had not proven crucial and where citizens had moved on from dealing with the past to basing legitimacy on quite different issues. In particular – and I can only gesture towards these scenarios – it might be that institutional or essentially Hobbesian strategies of necessity have to come before a 'permanent working through the past', and that advocating cultural strategies in certain fragile contexts might be politically irresponsible.

While the Left sought to export its idea of 'post-totalitarian legitimacy', the opponents of constitutional patriotism and univeralism never failed to demand a more positive German self-image, and a more concrete notion of national identity. But they found it difficult to specify such a 'positive self-image'. What else, if not the success story of the Federal Republic, could be the basis of such an image? And was this story not in turn one about a turn to the West, liberal democracy, and, yes, universalist values?

Moreover, the universalists had one distinct advantage in the debate on German identity: at least to some extent, they were debating institutions, rather than 'collective psychology', although they also often drifted into the discourse of 'self-consciousness', 'self-confidence' and 'weak egos'. Such debates, by definition, i.e. by their defining terms, could have no conclusion. Which is why so often German intellectuals (and even policy-makers) were eager for an outside opinion from another country to break the inner-German stalemate and announce a verdict on collective German psychology.

But how then could some of the false dichotomies and structural incompatibilities which characterized so much of the endless debates on German identity be overcome? It seemed that German universalists would have to find a political language which did not directly filter every political question through the past. The victims of Auschwitz did not die for the purpose of helping the formulation of present-day foreign policy. And sooner or later, the reproach of instrumentalization would be uttered more subtly and more convincingly by somebody less obstinate, less defensive than Martin Walser. Advocates of a German national identity, on the other hand, would have to find a language of talking about Germany which did not seek to obliterate the German past either through relativization or a false monumentalization, which did not reverse the liberalization of German political thought and which offered more than collective comfort in the image of some final national reconciliation – or else, they would founder just as much as the New Right had foundered.

What seemed to emerge *de facto* at the end of the 1990s was a rather paradoxical development, which neither Right nor Left had intended. There had been no obvious 'renationalization', as the Left feared and the New Right had wished for, and neither had there been a *Schlußstrich* or the exclusion of the critical intellectual from the public sphere, for which some on the Right seemed to have hoped. Instead, commemoration and 'normalization' under the auspices of a left-wing government seemed to go hand in hand. Contrary to the fear that, after 1989, there would be collective amnesia and therefore collective amnesty, there was an unprecedented amount of commemoration and remembrance in the 1990s. This suggests that perhaps Bohrer and his allies might have been somewhat right in thinking that only a united Germany could take on the task of mourning properly. On the other hand, the dialecticians operating from inside the culture of suspicion claimed that this unprecedented commemoration was in itself a subtle form of forgetting – or the preparation for such a final act of forgetting. There can indeed be little doubt that, as Geoffrey Hartman has pointed out, 'collective forgetting can itself assume the guise of memory' – especially through the unreflective monumentalization and sacralization of memory, even a memory of the victims.[91] In fact, one of the perverse lessons of the Right's recurring failure to draw a 'thick line under the past' might be that, rather than trying to awaken the Germans from the nightmare of history, making them sleepwalk through it might be the most effective strategy for systematic forgetting. After all, as Robert Musil claimed, 'there is nothing in the world as invisible as monuments'.[92] And for many observers, there was something all-too-visible and unsettling about the fact that the Germans, with their 'monument-mania' seemed to have appropriated the Jewish insight that 'the secret of memory is redemption' – and their own redemption in particular.[93] And yet, for all

[91] Geoffrey H. Hartman, 'Introduction: Darkness Visible', in Geoffrey H. Hartman (ed.), *Holocaust Remembrance: The Shapes of Memory* (Oxford: Blackwell, 1994), 1–20; here 15.

[92] Musil quoted by Huyssen, *Twilight Memories*, 250.

[93] Andreas Huyssen, 'Monumental Seduction', in Mieke Bal *et al.* (eds), *Acts of Memory: Cultural Recall in the Present* (Hanover: University Press of New England, 1999), 191–207; here 192.

the justified concerns about the need for 'counter-monuments', rather than monumentalization, there could also be an exaggerated suspicion of symbolism and formalism, which many on the Left, clinging to the '68 aversion to formality, curiously seemed to share with Walser. Rather than rejecting symbolism *tout court*, symbols and the conflicts over the collective memories to which they refer could themselves be sites of not just of mourning, but of reflective memory and in particular continued reflection through disagreements within agreed rules of debate.

In the end, the only safe prediction seems to be that what will continue is the rhetoric of continuity itself, as far as German governments are concerned. The other safe prediction is that a new generation – whether termed 'Berlin Generation' or something else – has an incentive to define itself against its predecessors, including the intellectuals who dominated life in the Federal Republic. Otherwise, they might feel like Max Weber's generation haunted by a successful unification and the accomplishments of their forebears. As Weber famously put it, 'at our cradle stood the most frightful curse history can give any generation as a baptismal-gift: the hard fate of the political *epigone*'.[94] In a sense, then, the idea of a 'Berlin Republic' seemed to become a self-fulfilling prediction – if only for those who anxiously made it.

Another Lease on Public Life?

Where does all this leave German intellectuals? Despite the frequent claims throughout the 1990s about 'silence' and the end of the traditional role of the intellectual, it was far from obvious that an era had come to an end yet. In fact, rather than unification discrediting the intellectuals of the sceptical generation, it arguably gave them another lease on public life. Grass, Habermas, Enzensberger and Walser, now with more firmly established and predictable roles than ever before, still dominated debates in the 1990s, whether on the Gulf War, asylum policies, the character of commemoration or the Western intervention in Kosovo. While they might have made spectacular misjudgements in 1990, because they saw too much of a parallel with the 1950s, this comparison was of course not entirely unreasonable in the sense that, yet again, a new state had to face questions about continuities, identity and institutions – questions which intellectuals had made it their special task to answer. Had the division continued, perhaps the sceptical generation might have quietly retired. But instead they once again, for better or for worse, entered the public sphere, in particular 'instructing' a new Germany in conserving its democratic legacies from the old Federal Republic.

---

[94] Max Weber, 'The Nation State and Economic Policy', in *Weber: Political Writings*, 1–28; here 24.

Claims that the intellectuals had been 'sidelined' or had 'failed to foresee' major developments in 1990, suggests that there once had been a glorious time when they had enjoyed unmediated political influence and not been 'too late' in their political commentaries. The only time when this might have been even remotely true were the *dix glorieuses* from the early 1960s to the early 1970s. But even then, they had hardly had as much influence as hindsight seemed to suggest, nor had they necessarily been 'ahead of the times', as so much mythmaking led younger generations to believe. The *Gruppe 47* with its 'permanent crisis' (Böll), the hastily put together paperbacks of the 1960s, whose content ranged from timid support for the SPD, laced with open mandarin contempt for party politics, to thinly disguised anti-Americanism, which equated Hiroshima and the Holocaust with great and insouciant world-historical judgements – they probably did contribute to the liberalization of the Federal Republic.[95] But they were no grounds for a retrospective heroization of the intellectuals. If anything, the history of intellectuals in the Federal Republic suggests that intellectuals are at their most effective when they react against ossified structures of authority – although it seems that even in such cases, they often come too late and seem to be articulating a consensus of dissent at the very eve of its disintegration. Few intellectuals can rise to the occasion of 'providing meaning' during times of rapid historical change. But this in itself should not detract from their more important long-term role.

Arguably, the only intellectuals truly discredited by the unification debates were some of the intellectuals of the generation of 1968. Their critics, however, had a tendency to lump *all* intellectuals together, caricaturing the positions of members of the sceptical generation to delegitimate the role of the intellectual as democratic citizen alongside the role of the intellectual as advocate of socialist utopias. The intellectuals of the generation of 1968 themselves either adopted a new strenuous scepticism and self-consciously hard-headed realism, adhered to inflexibly with the fervour of the convert, or retreated into defensiveness. The former in particular exhibited the paradox of a forced pragmatism which had something curiously unpragmatic about it. As with right-wing intellectuals after 1945, cold conduct seemed to be an appealing, self-protective attitude after a 'world-historical' defeat.

What, then, explained the continuing influence of the sceptical generation? In retrospect, it seems that its enduring prominence had something to do with the fact that, at least in some respects, its members had been curiously privileged. They had the moral authority which came with personal experience of the Nazi regime – and yet they were not in any obvious way as guilty as their elders. They also had the ability to differentiate between different roles in National Socialism, and were less prone to the

---

[95] Heinrich Böll, 'Angst vor der Gruppe 47?', in *Merkur*, Vol. 19 (1965), 775–83.

totalizing suspicion characteristic of the generation of 1968. Moreover, their model of the 'democratic citizen' did not only prove more lasting than models of the 'party intellectual', the mandarin or the Marxist partisan, the Federal Republic, with its ingrained 'protest culture', also became *their* state, as much as they criticized it. They themselves eventually turned into state representatives, defining the very polity against which they had first defined themselves. In retrospect, it even seems that Kohl and Habermas were both Adenauer's grandchildren, although neither would have been pleased with this family resemblance.[96] And, paradoxically, not least through the very culture of protest, Germany had become a trusted country abroad. Rather than the cliché which claims that a people cultivating a climate of suspicion is itself suspicious, the insight held that questioning and debate had made Germany a more liberal-democratic country, which after all, depended on suspicious citizens — especially when these citizens had learnt to suspect institutions, rather than personal conscience, as the intellectuals were often prone to do. When Günter Grass, Germany's premier suspicious citizen, appeared in his first ever tails at the Nobel Prize ceremony in Stockholm, the paradoxical outcome of this process of achieving trust through suspicion was revealed to the world.

The intellectuals of the sceptical generation, then, were always present at the creation — or rather, multiple creations: the seeming 'restoration' of the early 1950s, which they had good reason to criticize and which in many ways seemed to have shocked them even more than the total collapse of 1945, the intellectual foundations of the Federal Republic in the late 1950s and early 1960s, when politicians and intellectuals seemed to take each other more seriously than ever before or after, and finally, they were once again the central figures at the creation of the unified country — even if they often misinterpreted this creation in the ways I have discussed in previous chapters.

And yet, profound unease remained. Part of the reason was that, irrespective of whether intellectuals can legitimately claim any representativeness at all, the question was increasingly raised whether figures like Grass and Habermas could speak for East Germans. Impressionistic evidence suggests that they could not. After all, already in 1990, Habermas had essentially dismissed East Germans, whereas Grass had a fateful tendency to idealize their oppression — and not much changed thereafter. In the same vein, as I have argued in the previous section, it was not clear that the past still spoke to the present in the same way it might have in the 1950s and 1960s. Whether the Germans were able openly to deal with

---

[96] Habermas, however, also recognized in Kohl a fellow member of his generation by virtue of his resistance to any aestheticization of the state. See 'Es gibt doch Alternativen: Jürgen Habermas antwortet auf Fragen nach den Chancen von Rot-Grün, der Ära Kohl und der Zukunft des Nationalstaats', in *Die Zeit*, 8 October 1998.

their past had once been the clear standard applied by left-liberal intellectuals (but also, for instance, by the American occupiers) as to whether Germany had yet become another, democratic country. But given the challenges of the post-Cold War world, it was not clear whether this standard was still appropriate – and whether, as I have suggested, making the past into a source of direct guidelines for policies in the present did not do a disservice both to the past and the present. Moreover, it was by now highly unlikely that commemoration would somehow disappear from the public sphere, if it was not suspiciously guarded by 'democratic elites'. Remembrance had become a much more nuanced, diverse and decentralized process, especially among the young, and at the same time remained constitutive for the 'self-understanding' of the new Germany.[97]

More importantly, every generational experience inevitably comes with certain blind spots. The intellectuals of the sceptical generation cannot be an exception and it was likely that with time, some of their own claims to legitimacy would be eroded. One early indication of this was the revelation that many of the teachers of the historians among the sceptical generation had been much closer to the National Socialists than previously suspected, and that, more importantly, their pupils had either not questioned them or kept this knowledge to themselves.[98] This quiescence probably had less to do with direct moral failings, than with the peculiar German university system, in which quasi-feudal dependencies are cultivated over decades, and which has not fundamentally changed to this day – despite '1968'. Power, and patronage in particular, in conjunction with personal memories, probably warped more than one dispute, which will become more transparent as various debates recede in time and new aspects are revealed. One other area, where numerous observers have seen particular blind spots, is an artistic engagement with the Holocaust itself and its consequences, in particular the representation of absence, and dealing with German suffering during the War in a way that is not relativizing and sentimental.[99]

What this also suggests is that intellectuals might want to turn their

---

[97] Michael Kohlstruck, *Zwischen Erinnerung und Geschichte: Der Nationalsozialismus und die jungen Deutschen* (Berlin: Metropol, 1997).

[98] Wulf Kansteiner, 'Mandarins in the Public Sphere: *Vergangenheitsbewältigung* and the Paradigm of Social History in the Federal Republic of Germany', in *German Politics and Society*, Vol. 17, No. 3 (1999), 84–120.

[99] Ernestine Schlant, *The Language of Silence: West German Literature and the Holocaust* (New York: Routledge, 1999). The most important exception with regard to both subjects is probably W. G. Sebald, who has not only provided what one might call an anatomy of German melancholy, but, indirectly, an anatomy of Jewish absences, while confronting both Jewish and German victimhood, without moral or historical relativization of the former. See in particular *The Emigrants*, trans. Michael Hulse (New York: New Directions, 1997) and *Luftkrieg und Literatur* (Munich: Hanser, 1999).

moral searchlights on issues which have less to do with 'high politics', let alone 'the political', and instead question some of the institutions of German social life – with their hierarchies, their immobility, their peculiar mixture of rule-bound formality and personal '68-inspired informality, their often illiberal practices and even corruption. Intellectuals, one might say, have too often been fixated on the state as such, a fixation stemming from the polarization of the early 1960s, when intellectuals and politicians took each other so seriously. In other words, while politics has undoubtedly become more liberal and democratic, other areas and institutions of social life have remained thoroughly illiberal. Rather than escaping into global-cum-world-historical questions, such as the generation of 1968 was wont to do in the 1980s, and as members of the sceptical generation like Grass often did, it might be time to offer a more precise and localized critique – which is not to resurrect the false dichotomy between Sartre's 'general' and Foucault's 'specific intellectual'. Such a critique might be advantageous not least because intellectuals have undoubtedly lost any larger framework with which to interpret globalization, to pick the most obvious example. Democratic socialism, as an ill-defined background consensus for the intellectuals of the sceptical generation, has evaporated, and attempts at redefining the political have mostly remained theoretically impotent. The idea of 'the West', i.e. the liberal democratic states of Western Europe, which was their implicit model of the good polity, does not seem to offer much in the way of normative prescriptions, as 'the West' itself remains confused by new political and, above all, socioeconomic challenges.

There also remain questions about the character of German intellectual exchange itself. Curiously, a general culture of consensus, even of immobilism, in the country as a whole, continues sharply to contrast with the polemical culture of suspicion characterizing intellectual exchange. The problem is not that German debates are too polemical – in fact, they are still constrained, and the New Right, for all its moral faults, was probably right in pointing to some of these constraints. The real problem is that these debates are too personal. And this is not a question of the passing of generations who had lived through the Third Reich, as some commentators argued, implying more or less bluntly that the problem would die with the protagonists. After all, the '68ers had also not consciously lived through the Third Reich – and yet, they took the culture of suspicion to an extreme. The issue is rather a certain intellectual style and the logic of mutual unmasking, which could never find enough certainty to end suspicion and the probing of individual conscience. Of course, the dialectical twists in some of the theories underlying the culture of suspicion further exacerbated this problem.

Moreover, there remains the 'structured decisionism', which, according to Charles Maier's perceptive observation, characterizes not only intellectual exchange, but German political and economic life more generally.[100] This refers to a tendency rationally and bureaucratically to limit choice as much as possible, so that in the narrow space remaining for choice, a seemingly irrational decision has to be made. Choice is then a matter of conflicting wills and seemingly irrational, innermost personal beliefs. In the same vein, when the shared search for consensus fails, the ensuing conflict tends to be particularly sharp and couched in the language of innermost convictions. In this sense, shared ritualistic assertion in public commemoration and highly personalized conflict exist side by side. The point is not necessarily to decrease conflict – after all, democracy itself is a form of contained conflict – but to widen and deepen conflict, while at the same time making it less deep qua less personal. In short, civility and a capacity to 'make a coherent politics possible among those who differ' might be as important for a productive intellectual culture as the intellectuals' talents for subversion and suspicion.[101] Hans Werner Richter's dream of 'Anglo-Saxon debate' has yet to be redeemed – and rather than such debate leading to a loss of German peculiarity as nationalists on the Right and opponents of globalization on the Left both feared, such debate could lead to a clearer, more contested and ultimately more productive expression of such peculiarities – even an expression of the German language's 'metaphysical excess', which Adorno once talked about and which so frequently lent itself to a 'self-righteous' pseudo-depth.[102]

In addition, debates often tend to shift immediately from the most personal to the most impersonal and historical. Grass and Walser would debate issues of deep sincerity one moment, and then, seemingly effortlessly, shift to German 'drives', the course of national history and even the apocalypse. What was missing, arguably, was precisely the political – but not in a strictly Arendtian or Schmittian sense, nor as a placeholder for 'the cultural' or 'the historical', but rather in the sense of a recognition of individual and collective agency which did not depend on one's conscience and which was not always necessarily thwarted by impersonal forces. But how, then, could the country arrive at a more civilized discourse in which the intellectuals stir up debate, inform discussions and offer alternatives without personal suspicions and even injuries, caused, ironically, by a search for an impossible consensus?

One factor which might support the movement towards a more civilized and open discourse is the end of the Cold War itself, which so often distorted intellectual argument. In half a nation, there was a constant temptation to tell half-truths, and to blur the boundaries between internal as

---

[100] Maier, *The Unmasterable Past*, 156–9.

[101] Goldfarb, *Civility and Subversion*, 220.

[102] Theodor W. Adorno, 'Auf die Frage: Was ist deutsch', in *Gesammelte Schriften*, 691–701; here 701.

well as external enemies, and between legitimate critique and irreconcilable political enmity. Now, there is no other country either to delegitimate critique, or to sustain any utopian hopes which could then feed an irresponsible culture of suspicion, in which complacency and critique could go hand in hand. Clichés about the intellectual as traitor and the fear that any anti-totalitarianism merely supports the powers-that-be might at last safely be retired.

Furthermore, the culture of suspicion might lose some of its more dialectical moments. Suggestions that anti-Nazis were the real Nazis could flourish in a situation where, for one thing, some self-declared anti-Nazis really had been Nazis, and, also where, once again, not concrete institutional expressions, but secret personal motivations, became the ultimate proof of political reliability. The culture of suspicion will itself remain suspect, as long as suspicion can so easily be turned into insinuation and insult. At the same time, German intellectuals have to be careful to resist not only the consensus of the powerful, but also the consensus of fellow intellectuals, and to make the persistent, painful effort to think beyond the intellectual *juste milieu* in a highly differentiated and complex society. The experience of the generation of 1968 during the unification debates suggests that sometimes unthinking and constrained dissent can be worse than no dissent at all. What is needed, above all, however, is an engagement with the wider world that was less self-referential, less quick in connecting all political issues to the past and, above all, less quick in invoking 'Auschwitz'. As has often been remarked not only by advocates of German Romanticism, the 'post-national' West Germany was in many ways thoroughly provincial, even illiberal. Rather than mourning the loss of the old Republic and limiting their interventions to defensively preserving continuities with pre-1989 West Germany, intellectuals might want actively to engage with an age in which the challenges to liberal democracy come from new and unsuspected quarters. Germans certainly have an interest in their intellectuals doing so.

Conclusions

Having analyzed the responses of West German intellectuals to unification, the anatomy of New Right thinking, and, finally, the potential normative foundations for the Berlin Republic, it is time to take stock of the parameters and central concepts of German debates on national identity. Where do the views examined leave these concepts, and how do intellectuals position themselves with regard to them? The following concepts and themes have been 'distilled' from the debates and amount to a shared – but also sharply disputed – language of talking about Germany. I shall start with the central – and essentially contested – concept of the nation, before discussing a number of adjacent key concepts such as normality and constitutional patriotism. The way intellectuals position themselves vis-à-vis these concepts then also effectively yields a distinction between left and right. Finally, I shall offer some reflections on the characteristics of German political culture which can be inferred from the unification debate.

The Nation

Nowhere was the nation as much in question as in Germany after 1945, as Hitler seemed to have destroyed nationhood and the idea of the nation-state alongside nationalism. Nevertheless, even the Left had at certain points before 1989 attempted to link democratic socialism, pacifism and nationalism, most notably in the early 1980s. But during and after 1989, the Left remained fundamentally opposed to unification, since they assumed that a larger state would necessarily entail the return (and a vindication) of the traditional nineteenth-century nation-state and of nationalism. Such a return, they thought, would amount to a historical regression, given that West Germany was already safely on its way to becoming a genuinely post-national, post-materialist democracy. In accordance with what had become an orthodoxy during the 1980s, the only adequate form of social cohesion in a post-fascist polity remained post-nationalism.

For many on the Left, unification seemed to entail an automatic forgetting of the past. Especially if left-wing intellectuals viewed the division as punishment, unity would amount to an amnesty and necessarily be followed by amnesia. They held that since nationhood had been so inextricably linked with National Socialism, any return of national sentiments and pre-1945 collective memories would mean a diminished remembrance of the Holocaust. In this sense, memory amounted to a zero-sum game for the Left.

In 1990, the fear of a return of nationalism also depended on two – often implicit – historical analogies. One was the 'first unification' of 1871, which intellectuals thought showed some disconcerting parallels to developments in 1990. In both cases, the process seemed to be centred on the executive, and, so intellectuals assumed, subsequently would have to rely on nationalism in order to compensate for the missing republican foundations. The other parallel was the 1950s: given West Germany's post-fascist democratic deficit, intellectuals had then warned of a return of nationalism and authoritarianism, but also criticized what they saw as hypocritical reunification policies. With Adenauer's self-declared grandson in power in 1990, Kohl's policies – which ostensibly relied more on a desire for economic prosperity than political freedom – and, most fundamentally, the addition of 17 million East Germans seemingly wedded to authoritarian attitudes, intellectuals thought they had to re-enact previous roles. Apart from such a conventional reliance on historical analogies, there was for some intellectuals of the sceptical generation a real sense of synchronicity. Grass's *Vergegenkunft* and Habermas's 'anamnestic solidarity' often seemed like complex theoretical elaborations of Koselleck's insight that for his generation the War – and guilt – had never quite ended.[1] In the case of the '68ers, Aron's diagnosis of a 'psychodrama' held true long after the 1960s – and in 1990 such 'psychodrama' was combined with a fateful sense of being caught in a time warp. The post-national vanguard of the Left suddenly found itself as the historical rearguard, and was confronted with a situation in which, paradoxically, the post-national country was catching up with the outdated model of the nation-state by uniting with what seemed like another, particularly 'belated' country.

What conception of the nation did left-wing intellectuals actually oppose or propose in their interventions? Surprisingly, they often did not differentiate the concept at all, but used it merely as shorthand for a return of the nationalist past, or implied that it was a form of belonging morally inferior to more universalist forms of allegiance. They remained caught in dichotomies like national unity *or* political freedom, nationalism *or* republicanism, statehood *or* *Kulturnation*. Where the Right relied on a *socially* exclusionary concept of the nation by stressing its ethnic elements, the Left often saw the nation as an exclusive political *concept* which could not be thought together with principles such as freedom and democracy. In this sense, as much as 'the nation' was the prime target of the Left's critique, the concept remained ill-defined, and, fundamentally, stood either

---

[1] Koselleck, 'Glühende Lava'.

for a regression to an authoritarian past, or even for a specific German 'national character' which would automatically reassert itself in a larger state. The latter was Grass's position which assumed what can only be described as a negative mythical German essence.

Liberal thinkers, on the other hand, were by and large more accepting of the nation-state and attempted to fuse nationhood with the democratic achievements of the Federal Republic. Different liberals assigned different weights to these elements. All were eager to point out, however, that, for the first time, national unity and freedom were possible at the same time. They – and the old liberal institutionalists among them in particular – also assumed that institutional safeguards and the long-term transformations in political culture were sufficient to guard against the danger of a return of authoritarianism; hence, their basic distrust, both of leading politicians and the people at large, was much less pronounced than among left-wing intellectuals.

Conservative thinkers, in turn, openly appealed to national solidarity as a resource to provide social cohesion. They actually shared the Left's assumption (even if they reversed its judgement) that a larger state automatically meant the vindication of nationalism and the return of a genuinely German culture. However, a profound paradox remained for conservatives whose definition of nationality was cultural, against the political one centred on constitutional patriotism advocated by the Left. After all, if they advocated the *Kulturnation*, they would have to accept its prominent representatives, including Günter Grass, Christa Wolf and Heiner Müller, since, after all, the German *Kulturnation* was defined by writers and artists attempting to formulate their version of national identity. One, it seemed, could not be had without the other.

Given that the opposition to nationhood was such a defining feature of the Left's stance, it was not surprising that the New Right adopted the nation as the conceptual core of its political programme: here the intellectual field clearly structured orthodoxies and heterodoxies. The New Right, drawing on the theory of 'ethno-pluralism', saw the nation as an ethnic community of fate. This led them to advocate a position of closing the borders around what they essentially perceived as a large German family, and to recommend the assertive pursuit of national interests. The failure of the New Right was partly explained by the fact that the nation – after 1989 – was simply insufficient as a conceptual core. What was noticeable, above all, however, was how ill-defined 'the nation' remained – for both left and right. In the end, only liberals situated the concept of the nation in a new conceptual context, arguing that, for the first time, freedom, democracy and a unified nation could exist at the same time, and that *Verfassungspatriotismus* and a 'heterogeneous nation-state' might go together.

Sonderweg versus Normality

Sonderweg and Normality are conceptually and logically linked, but they mean radically different things when applied to the past and to the future. The picture is further complicated if one takes *Sonderweg* to refer to matters of foreign policy on the one hand, and to cultural critique on the other. Logically, this yields a four-by-four matrix of positions on the *Sonderweg*, all of which were filled by at least one intellectual.

For left-wing intellectuals, insisting on the *Sonderweg* thesis with reference to the time prior to 1945 was as important as presenting the old Federal Republic as having finally left the special path to join 'the West', in both a cultural and a political sense. Mirroring this position, the New Right attempted to refute the historical *Sonderweg* thesis, at the same time declaring the old Federal Republic as a historical exception and warning of a future *Sonderweg*, if the government did not assert national interests. Only the New Right, however, called for a significant loosening of foreign policy ties to the West, and the defence of a peculiar German culture at the same time.

The picture on the Left was not clear-cut as far as the future of the *Sonderweg* was concerned. Left-wing intellectuals in one sense always insisted that Germany was 'special' by virtue of its 'Holocaust identity'. Grass was explicitly prepared to embark on a new German *Sonderweg* with a confederation – and even to continue a German 'pariah' existence in the image of the *Kulturnation*. He and many other intellectuals, following the arguments Karl Jaspers had advanced in the 1960s, affirmed that Germany might be exceptional in having learnt lessons from its peculiar history which pointed to repudiating the nation-state altogether.

In general, the Left accused the Right of being 'normalizers', and the Right, by and large, accepted the charge, holding up 'normality' as a desirable way of dealing with the past as well as the future. Increasingly, however, the Left came to appropriate the term 'normality' itself, but insisted, somewhat paradoxically, that the 'normality' of the Berlin Republic would have to be a different one than that of other countries. In particular, a 'normal' Germany would have to be an especially European Germany. But whether such a 'European Germany', still highly conscious of its 'Holocaust identity', was in fact the European norm, was of course itself questionable.

Arguably, *Sonderweg* and normality remain the two most powerful concepts in the debate about German identity and will continue to structure any discussion about future policies, despite the fact that some of the very historians who had initially proposed the *Sonderweg* thesis have become considerably more sceptical about it. Even those who view the conceptual pair as epistemologically, historically and ideologically flawed seem unable to stop using it. In one sense, this is hardly surprising, as long as the relational concept of identity remains central to German debates. Moreover, in one sense every democratic state defines for itself a kind of 'political normality', and, if appropriately rephrased, every political issue can be treated in terms of exceptionalism. The 'normal', it seems, is simply a central part of a normal German political language to debate the normative.

Or is it? Whether the specific categories of *Sonderweg* and normality are the most appropriate for thinking about German history and the future is questionable for at least four reasons. To the extent that German questions should now be social questions, rather than national ones, i.e. institutional ones, rather than identitarian ones – as Ralf Dahrendorf first insisted in the mid-1960s – does the conceptual pair *Sonderweg* and Normality not present a particularly poor way of even addressing these issues, and actually divert attention from them? In one way, almost all intellectuals were 'nationalists' in the basic sense that national questions took precedence over institutional ones. And in retrospect it might even seem that the acrimoniousness of many debates was due to a narcissism of minor differences on national questions, rather than basic institutional ones. My point is not that national questions do not matter, or that inner democratic attitudes and political culture are always less important than formal, institutional ones. Globalization in particular, however, poses great challenges to, above all, the institutional imagination, for which the preoccupation with national questions has left many intellectuals unprepared. Especially if the Left is to find a new critical language, it will have to be one that combines moral with institutional issues in a novel way.

Second, while 'normality' has become a norm (and a polemical weapon) for the Right, the question what precisely this 'normality' actually consists in is hardly ever addressed. What is 'European normality' or 'nation-state normality' at the beginning of the twenty-first century, beyond the psychosocial language of 'self-confidence' and 'insecurity'? Deeper probing might lead to uncomfortable questions about diverging European state traditions, in which the different 'normalities' of diverse political cultures could prove incompatible, and even more fundamental normative questions about the survival of democracy and legitimacy in nation-states enfeebled by globalization.

Third, the conceptual pair *Sonderweg*–Normality is adjacent to the dangerous conceptual pair of Pathology–Health of the body politic.[2] Not surprisingly, the *Sonderweg* is frequently associated with national 'neurosis' and all kinds of diseases quickly projected onto society. Of course, this is not a German peculiarity; there have been 'British', 'French' and 'European diseases' – just as the 'politics of identity' and the 'surfeit of memory'

---

[2] Thanks to Giuliana Lund on this point.

have been larger Western phenomena in the last two decades.[3] And the search for peculiarities is not in itself a German peculiarity either, just as there have been other post-war attempts to formulate 'antinationalism as a national paradigm', for instance in Scandinavia and Switzerland.[4] Nevertheless, it is the combination of languages of the past, of pathology and of collective psychology which seems unique, and which contributes to both the acrimoniousness and the vacuity of German debates – since there cannot be an even remotely objective or at least intersubjective standard for judging the state of the supposed 'affliction'.

Fourth, whatever one's political persuasion, the fact remains that *Sonderweg*–Normality is a thoroughly historicist and relativistic tool of analysis, or at least a political weapon of 'moralizing historicism' (Reinhart Koselleck). And at least in the logic of the Right, only those who have no self-confidence need constantly to compare themselves to others. Arguably, however, the very fact of an on-going debate on 'normality' continues to point to an anomaly, thereby making every right-wing claim about normality self-subverting. Normal countries, it seems, do not debate their normality.

Self-Confidence

The use of a simplistic and homogenizing 'national psychology', or what Dahrendorf once called 'a psycho-social analysis of identity searches and identity crises', remains a common currency in German public discourse.[5] Germany is variously described as 'neurotic' and 'insecure', a claim inevitably followed by the call for a new 'self-confidence', which even became the leitmotiv of the New Right. Usually the demand for self-confidence is linked with an imperative to realize national interests. Moreover, many observers relate self-confidence to self-consciousness, playing on the double meaning of the German *Selbstbewußtsein*, which signifies both. The self the Germans are supposed to be conscious of is naturally the national self – which in turn is contained in the national past, rather than some common future destiny.

However, the call for self-confidence is neither new nor is it now confined to the Right. It has been sounded by conservatives for a long time, but the concept has also increasingly been used in a positive manner by

[3] Charles S. Maier, 'A Surfeit of Memory? Reflections on History, Melancholy and Denial', in *History and Memory*, Vol. 5, No. 2 (1993), 136–52.

[4] Arne Ruth, 'Postwar Europe: The Capriciousness of Universal Values', in *Daedalus*, Vol. 126, No. 3 (1997), 241–76.

[5] Dahrendorf, ' "Eine deutsche Identität" '.

Habermas and other left-wing intellectuals. Often self-confidence has been identified as the state of mind of a strong *Bürgertum*. This partly builds on the *Sonderweg* thesis, one of its contentions being that Germany lacked a strong *Bürgertum* and therefore self-confidence, particularly in Wilhelmine Germany. As with 'normality', the Left increasingly came to accept what seemed like a plausible claim about the new Germany, but also attempted to appropriate the concept and endow it with new meanings.

'Self-confidence', then, remains an elusive, though widely shared goal for intellectuals. Moreover, this psycho-social claim about the state of 'the national mind' is one that can be interpreted as in line with or against 'the West', thereby remaining open to various uses in ideological battle. However, as I have already argued, the debates on collective psychology contain no discernible standards for political judgement, and only add to the fruitlessness and seeming futility of many German debates. They also encourage the self-serving illusion that somehow intellectuals, rather than supplying arguments in the public sphere, a task already difficult enough if it is to be exercised effectively and responsibly, can infuse the people with 'self-confidence'. Finally, the focus on the national and individual self and its true state of self-confidence and convictions perpetuates an unfortunate tendency in political discourse to privilege interiority and sincerity.

Auschwitz

'Auschwitz', as shorthand for both the moral catastrophe of the Holocaust and German guilt, remains a central symbol, a metaphor as well as an argument on the intellectual field, which even representatives of the New Right who viewed *Vergangenheitsbewältigung* as a totalitarian ploy to eradicate German identity, could not quite circumvent. Instead they tried to seize it and present themselves as the true defenders of the authenticity of 'Auschwitz'. 'Auschwitz', in other words, remained open to instrumentalization and moral claim-making from all sides: Grass deduced a moral prohibition on unification from it, Bohrer did the opposite. Grass chose the most extreme interpretation possible of Jaspers's original notion of the German as pariah, while Bohrer equated political responsibility with a national responsibility which could only be assumed in a unified state. However, the very fact that directly opposite conclusions could be drawn from Auschwitz in itself suggested that at least this particular past might have stopped shining light on the particular political present in the form of any clear 'lessons learnt'.

There remains a fine line between a democratic remembrance capable of doing justice to the victims and strengthening the sense of republican liberal achievements in Germany on the one hand, and instrumentalizing the victims on the other. Certainly, there are rhetorically and morally inappropriate ways of invoking the notion of the Holocaust. But beyond a core of blatant abuses – and Grass's claims were sometimes among them – it becomes very contestable what is an illegitimate instrumentalization and what is not. It seems that there is simply no way of absolutely transcending the charge of instrumentalization, to the extent that even the charge of instrumentalization might in itself be an instrumentalization. To put it differently: partly because of the intellectuals' public insistence on a 'Holocaust identity', there has been a long-lasting and contested discourse on Auschwitz. But every meta-comment, every second-order observation on this discourse inevitably and immediately becomes part of it. Beyond the core of obvious abuses, there is no neutrality, only contestation.[6] This would apply as much to Habermas's linkage between post-nationalism and the Holocaust, which was in danger of becoming a civil religion instrumentalizing Auschwitz, as to Walser and his call for mnemonic privatization. However, as long as competing memories and meanings of the Holocaust are articulated in the public sphere, Jaspers's injunction – albeit inadvertently – is still heeded and might actually strengthen a liberal public sphere. It will not do so, however, if contestation is intimately linked with the culture of suspicion which intellectuals fostered in the Federal Republic. The culture of suspicion had its uses in detecting continuities, but could also lead to an excessive personalization of political debates.

In any event, it is not up to the Germans alone whether Auschwitz can be made a matter of individual conscience. Others will remind them of it, as for other countries, just as for the German Left, Germany might never be just another country. The fact that accepting the imperative to remember willingly – without instrumental considerations – in the past, has brought the country clear benefits should be an encouragement to continue doing so – although, paradoxically, avoiding this instrumental logic is the only way of making it hold true. This, after all, was the 'dialectic of normalization'.

Foundation versus Continuity

Ironically, the intellectual most in favour of continuing the liberal tradition of the old Federal Republic, was most vocal in his call for a democratic 're-founding': Jürgen Habermas conceived of a national referendum as an act of foundation precisely in the interest of continuity and as a reaffirmation of constitutional patriotism. Implicit was the assumption that East Germans had to be given a swift introduction to republican values, and that, unlike in 1945, a proper founding through democratic procedures

---

[6] Jörg Lau, 'Der normale Verdacht', in *Die Zeit*, 19 November 1998.

should be carried out this time. In this sense, as much as Habermas saw the East German revolution as merely 'catching-up', his own Rousseauean act of foundation had an element of 'catching up' in the West German context. Other left-wing intellectuals, arguing in an even more explicitly republican vein, also claimed that a foundation, even a founding myth grounded in the East German revolution, was crucial for ensuring the stability of what they saw – unlike Habermas – as a genuinely new polity.

But it was the Right which mostly called for change or even a 'new beginning without taboos'. In fact, the usual positions of left and right frequently seemed reversed. The Left, which had taken a highly critical stance towards continuities between nineteenth century Germany, the Nazi period and Adenauer's 'restoration', now tried to salvage as much as possible of the post-national, post-materialist promise of the Federal Republic across the historical divide of 1989 – which contributed to the Left's defensiveness and its unfortunate emphasis on security and past certainties, rather than the new liberties and life chances which 1989 promised. Conservatives, on the other hand, were eager to reclaim some of the continuities which the Left had criticized, while advocating a clear break with some of the thought patterns they associated with West Germany. While it still made sense to speak of left and right in Germany, their association with change and conservatism increasingly came to be reversed. At the same time, Left and Right often shared the view that a foundation myth was in fact not just desirable but necessary for the larger Germany to provide social cohesion and a new political ethos, which could take the form of republicanism and nationalism respectively. Consequently, the meaning of 1989, as a 'year zero', remains fiercely contested.

Politics and Aesthetics

Bohrer and his followers in the *Literaturstreit* called for a strict separation between literature and politics, lest literature become subject to *Gesinnung* and fail to achieve the hermetic self-referentiality suggested by High Modernism. However, Bohrer was himself not able to sustain the strict distinctions he advocated, since the state in turn was to be subject to aesthetic standards. Even in Bohrer's case, however, the concrete form of a renegotiation of the relationship between the state and its aesthetic representation remained unclear. So far, the supposed 'return of the nation' has hardly led to the retrieval of specifically German 'irrational traditions', even if Strauß and others adopted a very self consciously 'conservative revolutionary' vocabulary refracted through postmodernism.

While many prominent intellectuals made interventions after 1989, there was also ample evidence that younger writers became increasingly suspicious of a *littérature engagée* and the role of the writer in politics.[7] The sceptical generation continued to dominate most debates, even if direct political advocacy became rarer. Arguably, this was not just a matter of wider 'postmodern' predilections and individual choice. A fundamental dilemma was the lack of any easily identifiable 'general interest' which intellectuals could responsibly advocate. The democratization of West Germany after 1945 was such a clear interest, and the intellectuals, by performing the role of 'democratic citizens' could directly contribute to it. More importantly, there is a significant theoretical and practical link between democracy and what intellectuals tend to do best – deliberation. The effectiveness of the sceptical generation was not least due to the fact that they could actually promote a goal to which intellectuals – as *intellectuals* – could make a genuine contribution. The reverse side of the paradox of the democratic intellectual who speaks for, rather than to the people, was that, like democrats more generally, the democratic intellectual did not need any particular expertise. There are no 'experts' in democracy, and the intellectuals' lack of expertise only proved the point that citizens needed the right attitudes, rather than particular knowledge. Arguably, all of this is much less true with issues – and I can only gesture at the most obvious ones – such as ecology, moral disagreements about bioethics and technology, or instances of international conflict that are less moralized and ideologized than the Cold War.

The Constitution

West German intellectuals of the sceptical generation, conscious of the failures of their Weimar predecessors, all more or less explicitly subscribed to the values embodied in the Constitution – at least in theory, as their critiques of the political order were always declared as immanent. This allegiance had several reasons: the very distrust of the intellectuals vis-à-vis the population seemed to be enshrined in a Constitution built around the idea of a 'militant democracy'. But there was also the fact that many intellectuals thought the Constitution was actually as democratic as possible, but as yet insufficiently realized. In either case, however, West German intellectuals' allegiance was grounded in their basic attitudes of distrust and a disposition to be discriminating in their political judgements, and their self-conception as remedying the post-fascist democratic deficit.

When a new democratic deficit seemed to open up after 1989, intellectuals like Habermas and Grass once more relied on the Constitution as a

[7] Uwe Wittstock, 'Wieviel Literatur im Leben, wieviel Politik in der Poesie? Eine Umfrage unter deutschsprachigen Schriftstellern der Jahrgänge 1950 bis 1960', in *Neue Rundschau*, Vol. 103, No. 2 (1992), 95–130.

powerful argumentative weapon, just as they had done in the 1960s and after. But as they charged the government with having violated the Constitution and ever more fervently pointed to the basic illegitimacy of unification, arguably distrust came to override their disposition to be discriminating in their political judgements to such an extent that they themselves lost some of their intellectual legitimacy. For almost all sides in the debate, however, the Constitution had an enormous symbolic value and was widely seen as capable of – and even crucial in – achieving social integration. The only significant exception were some members of the generation of 1968. Already in the 1960s, they had attacked West Germany as a thinly veiled fascist state and a number of them repeated the charge in the early 1990s. For them, West Germany had in fact never quite become post-fascist, but remained in a state of 'latent fascism'. The Constitution was a mere façade.

On the other hand, there were many on the Left who came to change their views, often through long and bitter ideological battle, and to share in the 'legalization' and 'liberalization' of the Left which Habermas's later work exemplified. While there was a tendency to idealize such paths as a public, dialectical 'learning process', in which, with benevolent and self-serving hindsight, even the most absurd extremes played a vital part, this newly found confidence in the 'only formal' qualities of political life was a significant development.

The importance of one fact should not be lost sight of, however. It remains a novelty that all major intellectuals in a German state subscribe to the values of a liberal democratic Constitution, and resist the temptation to interpret social complexity and conflict in terms of a 'cultural crisis' which in turn could only be overcome by a fundamental political self-transformation. This temptation was, after all, the one to which both Left and Right, each in their own way, gave in during the Weimar Republic. The fact that a self-declared Marxist like Habermas would make the Constitution central to his conception of political identity, and that the New Right was at pains to emphasize its devotion to the Constitution might seem unremarkable in itself – but is extraordinary in the *longue durée* of German history.

Constitutional Patriotism

There had always been at least three visions of constitutional patriotism: Sternberger's original concept, centred mainly on the state and his curious mixture of Aristotelianism and an emphatic German notion of *Burgerlichkeit*, all of which did not exclude national solidarity with the East Germans; Bracher's post-nationalism, which was mainly grounded in the historical lessons from Weimar's failure; and finally Habermas's version based on 'post-conventional identities', which became dominant towards the late 1980s. However, even Habermas's *Verfassungspatriotismus*, as much as it was designed to be a 'thin identity', remained ethically and historically anchored in a particular historical identity, namely the 'Holocaust identity' of the West Germans. Without the moral catastrophe of National Socialism, according to Habermas, there would have been no democratic German political culture – and no post-nationalism.

In most discussions of constitutional patriotism, there remains a fundamental tension between advocating *Verfassungspatriotismus* as a critical standard for existing practices on the one hand, and, on the other hand, seeing constitutional patriotism itself as a model of identity, and therefore of 'normality' and even 'conformity'. In many instances, the Left was trying to have both, i.e. constitutional patriotism as an anti-nationalist national identity, but without is exclusionary implications.

Moreover, there remains the question of the proper relationship between constitutional patriotism and economic life. Would there have to be a chasm, as in Habermas's Kantian vision, where the political sphere was cleansed of private interests, and where the Constitution enabled a diverse 'life-world', but was cut off from the economic sphere as a site of pure instrumental reason? This division between pure politics and sordid self-interest, between utopia and ideology, so to speak, would have to be addressed in future formulations of the concept.

Finally, constitutional patriotism, it seems, would be all the more successful the more it argued for argument, rather than for any particular argument about the past. Otherwise, it was in danger of becoming a civil religion. And a German civil religion would in all likelihood be coupled with a strong emphasis on personal belief and conscience – precisely contrary to the emphasis which Habermas himself had always placed on formalism and proceduralism. An expression of such a strong emphasis on personal belief would, for instance, be the intense questioning of prospective citizens on whether they subscribed to the Constitution. Also, the more constitutional patriotism was focused on the experience of the Holocaust as a negative foundation and filter through which all traditions had to pass, rather than a multiplicity of events and traditions, the less inclusive it might turn out to be.

Part of the difficulty for the Left in accepting argument, rather than privileging a particular argument, was an ambiguity between advocating a free public sphere in which participants had equal access and were free to test out propositions, and closing that public sphere to particular right-wing arguments. Very often the mere articulation of disreputable opinions was seen by the Left as dangerous and even as defeat. For instance, the Left never came to terms with the fact that it had – *horribile dictu* – won the *Historikerstreit*. Instead of admitting this fact, a narrative of an ever-present threat of rising nationalism, which seemed essential for preserving the Left's own cohesion, had to be kept intact by claiming that the fact that 'right-wing opinions' which had previously been confined to extremists had been aired in the public sphere in itself constituted a setback for the Left. Ultimately, both Left and Right found it difficult to accept a more robust notion of free speech, just as they found it difficult to be faithful to their disagreements in a civil manner.

The Political

The return of the political, along with 'the return of the nation' and 'the return of history' became a central claim, even a cliché, in post-unification Germany. However, unlike the return of nation and history, claims which were clearly advanced by the Right, the 'return of the political' was marshalled by a whole range of intellectuals, most of whom situated themselves vis-à-vis Carl Schmitt and Hannah Arendt. In conservative contributions, Schmitt was present in major arguments criticizing the 'self-organizing society' overburdening the state, a foreign policy which supposedly failed to take account of conflict, and any position which denied that politics was fundamentally about the identification of friends and enemies. On the other hand, in order to remedy the republican deficit remaining after unification, a number of left-wing intellectuals tried to recover Arendt's republicanism, which was seen as a possible antidote to the new wave of nationalism and to the supposed 'erosion' of the political, i.e. the disappearance of public spaces in which citizens could deliberate and act freely. But ultimately, it also promised new political perspectives in the wake of the 'exhaustion of utopian energies'.

Thus, German intellectuals laid out two visions of the future Berlin Republic: an étatiste one, indebted to Schmitt, that took the regaining of sovereignty in 1990 as foundational and envisioned the Berlin Republic as more political in the sense of a sovereign pursuit of national interests outside and a state confronting a clearly delineated society within; the other a republican one, in which the memories of 1989 were kept alive, civil society valorized and foreign policy increasingly dealt with through European federated structures. In a sense, both visions presumed that new spaces for political action were opening up. Consequently, both visions could be seen as countering a public discourse that primarily focused on technocratic necessities and neo-liberal economics. In this sense, they set the power of politics against what Musil called *Herrschaft der Sachzusammenhänge* [the domination of objective relations]. On a more pessimistic reading, however, the Arendtian moment was a fleeting one, and Beck and the Arendtians merely projected the developments leading up to 1989 onto 1999 and beyond. Nevertheless, given that the debate on the political was in many ways a coded debate on 'normality', it at least signified a more direct – and, indeed, more political – engagement with institutional questions and Germany's future than the debate on normality and self-confidence.

Left and Right

A frequent claim after 1989 was the supposed dissolution of the distinction between left and right. Such a claim was not surprising in itself after a major historical caesura. The distinction had also been prominently questioned in the aftermath of 1945, but, more surprisingly, came under suspicion even at the height of the Cold War.[8] After 1989, the argument that it had dissolved was made almost exclusively by left-wing intellectuals. The Right, and particular the New Right, knew exactly who they were, even if they did not always know what they wanted beyond cultural hegemony. Unlike 1920s Conservative Revolutionaries, members of the New Right never claimed that they were simply 'beyond left and right', even if they insisted that they were 'young' and an 'avant-garde'.

Once again, it was the ideologically weaker party, or at least the side which was facing an 'ideological identity crisis' which had an interest in denying the distinction between left and right. In particular, some of the intellectuals who adopted what seemed *prima facie* like much more right-wing positions, had a stake in blurring the distinction. In particular, disillusioned left-wingers and New Right intellectuals sometimes came to share an anti-modern and, in particular, anti-liberal cultural pessimism. On the other hand, attempts at vigorously debating what remained at the heart of left and right positions quickly exhausted themselves in self-recrimination, reproaches and empty rituals of re-enacting previous positions – in short, a renewed *Lagerdenken*.

Nevertheless, despite all the supposed 'discursive disorder' which numerous intellectuals thought they discerned after 1989, many concepts clearly remained associated with left or right. Claims about 'the return of history' were advanced by the Right and played off against the supposed ahistorical rationalism of the Left, and in particular, the Left's historiographical approaches indebted to the social sciences. In the same vein, the concept of nation remained by and large on the Right, while republicanism served as the main left-wing counterclaim to nationalism. Nationalist particularism versus forms of universalism still mapped onto right and left, with the exception of the nationalist and anti-American Left which joined the New Right. Other concepts, however, including 'the political' itself,

[8] Walter Dirks, 'Rechts und Links', in *Frankfurter Hefte*, Vol. 1, No. 6 (1946), 24–37, and Manfred Delling, 'Links und rechts – gibt es das noch?', in *Sonntagsblatt*, 13 May 1963.

remained fiercely contested and marked the open discursive space which still existed — and will persist — between left and right.

The Intellectual Field: Rules and Rigidities

The concepts surveyed above amount to a shared language of talking about Germany. Even the implacable opponents of some of these concepts cannot avoid positioning themselves vis-à-vis them in one way or other, as long as they have not managed to change their meaning radically by repositioning them in new conceptual contexts, or to push them out of public discourse altogether.

Debates on the German intellectual field tend to be self-conscious, self-referential and self-contained. Despite the comparative dimension of the central conceptual pair *Sonderweg* and Normality, German intellectuals remain inward-looking as well as backward-looking, and caught in the terms of a 'national psychology'. True, concepts on any intellectual field will need to be vague to be politically useful. However, in the German case, the debate is often not even so much about concepts, as about clichés. Intellectuals try to pin clichés on their opponents, such as 'Protestant inwardness', 'extremism' and 'followers of the *Sonderweg*'. Images of the past, in particular the Nazi past, are plundered in a politics of memory to shift the perceptions of the present through changing perceptions of the past. All intellectuals remain faithful to the lesson from the *Historikerstreit* that German identity can be redefined only through a reinterpretation of the past. That identity is constituted mostly through history and memory remains an unquestioned assumption.

Frequently, debates serve the purpose of moral demarcation, rather than exchanging arguments. In particular, putting feelings on public display constitutes a command for position-taking, rather than the start of a conversation. Intellectual groups, whether on the Left or Right, regularly portray themselves as victims of a media hegemony exercised by the opposite 'camp'. Writers like Walser went even further in denouncing the public sphere altogether as a realm of shallow opinions. Strauß argued in a similar vein, thereby returning to the prejudices against 'the media' and a chaotic, as well as commodified (but also democratic) public sphere, which had been prevalent among the Weimar mandarins with their suspicion of the *Man*. Another common feature was the appropriation of the intellectual opponent's central concepts, which became a favourite tactic of the New Right, whereas the rather defensive positioning of 'contraphobia' remained a central move for the anti-fascist (and therefore anti-nationalist) generation of 1968. Finally, *Lagerdenken*, the Manichean thinking for which the Left was criticized after 1989, is as common on the intellectual field now as it was during the Cold War. It has led not only to particularly vituperative and personal debates, but also to thinking *ex negativo*, 'contraphobic' political self-definitions and excessive attention to 'positionality' on the part of both the old Left and the New Right.

The Past in the Present: Exorcism, Expatriation and Escapism

Throughout the history of the Federal Republic, instances of major political and intellectual conflict were couched in the language of the past and German continuities. The '68ers accused their country of fascism, and were themselves subject to the suspicion of 'left-wing fascism'; the terrorists radicalized the reproach of fascism, and were themselves portrayed as 'Hitler's children'; and in 1990, the Left saw a reincarnation of the aggressive nation-state of the past, just as much as the Right saw the Left continuing the fateful German *Sonderweg*. In the same vein, intellectuals have conceived ingenious conceptions of time to come to terms with the fact that 'the past will not – and should not – pass away', from *Vergegenkunft* to 'anamnestic solidarity', which, above all, put the pastness of the past in doubt. Only those who either dissolved the recent past into a *longue durée*, as the New Right tried to, or who sought to defend the pastness of the past against the present, as in the case of Walser's 'defence of childhood', explicitly denied a strong sense of synchronicity – but the very fact that they felt it necessary to put up such strong historiographical or literary defences showed how acutely aware they in fact were of precisely such synchronicity.

So the past has been returning as political rhetoric and personal trauma for more than half a century now. And the rhetoric could be found on both the Right and the Left. Apart from its obvious polemical value as the ultimate rhetorical weapon, it would frequently – though not always – serve to set the speakers up as *ex post facto* resisters, just as a strong self-incrimination might in fact often have been exculpatory. '*Qui's-accuse, s'excuse*', as Enzensberger put it in 1964. If only the past could be imported into the present, then winning the present political struggle could also, or so this logic would imply, make a difference to the past. Consequently, for both left and right, political conflict could take on the quality of a collective exorcism. And it seemed that especially in the 'belated nation', intellectuals had a tendency to come too late and make up for it through ex-post facto action.

Moreover, the past came to be bound up with the contorted politics of anti-communism, anti-totalitarianism and anti-fascism. As I have argued above, anti-totalitarianism and anti-fascism came to be competing, even structurally incompatible principles in the Federal Republic. This incompatibility often led to the mutual expatriation of Left and Right in the name of a bitter narcissism of minor differences over what should in

theory have been a common ground of negating the Nazi past.[9] The Right
made the Left into fellow-travellers and properly part of the other, still
totalitarian Germany, i.e. the GDR, while for the Left, clinging to the logic
of anti-fascism, conservatives, capitalists and nationalists did not belong in
an anti-fascist Germany at all. In addition to this mutual expatriation
prompted by the logic of the Cold War, there was then a diachronic expatriation whereby one's political opponent was transported into the past and
tarnished in some way with National Socialism. In that sense, Left and
Right would expatriate each other from their common country, but also
exculpate themselves from a common past. In short, exorcism and expatriation went hand in hand – which, above all, resulted in the sense of a
contemporary quality of the non-contemporary, or, as the Germans put it,
die Gleichzeitigkeit des Ungleichzeitigen.

While it was a crucial and valuable part of the task of left-liberal intellectuals after 1945 to detect and denounce continuities, the mere rhetoric
of continuity could be – and often was – politically irresponsible. Such a
rhetoric about a return of the past could in retrospect be justified as a
matter of self-refuting prophecies – but more often than not, it was not
the prophecies which refuted themselves, but the fact that even at the time
they were made, the prophecies were absurd.

Invoking the past frequently furnished the participants of debates with
a moral certainty which otherwise could hardly be had in pluralist democratic societies. Invoking the past for the justification of foreign and military policies, as in the Kosovo War in 1999, was also designed to lend these
policies a self-evident character and moral legitimacy which they might
or might not have had, had there been a proper debate about their meaning
for the present. In short, invoking the past could often function as a way
to avoid politics – or at least avoid finding a language for the political
present, which relied on arguments instead of analogies, and prepared the
participants to live with the moral uncertainty and the precariousness of
even the most careful political judgements in complex and morally
ambiguous situations. In the same vein, political language could be avoided
in favour of an economic language of populist anti-capitalism, to which
Grass and Habermas resorted in 1990 and which also furnished a false
moral certainty.

Jaspers and his followers after 1945 were right to assert that acknowledging guilt was the first step in the direction of political freedom and
maturity, and that public communication about the past would ultimately
contribute to the Germans' capacity for political judgement. But the
claim that there remains as direct a link between politics and remembrance needs itself to be subject to continuous public communication. And
it would seem that in a pluralist, democratic country with multiple competing memories, the link should become less direct to avoid the dangers

---

[9] Dubiel, *Niemand ist frei.*

of an anti-nationalist national 'civil religion' centred on the Holocaust. This is not to assent to the conservative view that any engagement with the past would lead to present instability, as traditions, memories and 'self-confidence' were called into question. On the contrary, this conservative anxiety which held that individuals were anthropologically incapable of critically engaging with their personal past and their country's history without endangering 'national identity', had been empirically false at least since the late 1950s.

After 1989, there is at last the chance to chart a new course in which the past can be responsibly invoked, and where the false dichotomy of instrumentalization and privatization is resisted. The post-unification period also affords the opportunity to forge an anti-totalitarian consensus to which both Right and Left can subscribe in a common country which, after all, has experienced both forms of totalitarianism in the twentieth century. Habermas explicitly endorsed this possibility, when he claimed in 1994 that 'now for the first time an antiauthoritarian consensus – one deserving of that name because it is not selective – can be formed among us. This ought to be a common basis on which Right and Left can then differentiate themselves from each other'.[10] In the same vein, with the dis-appearance of the division, there is no longer always 'another Germany' on which the past and the worst traits of the present can be projected. And conversely, the tendency for witch hunts of 'internal enemies', which was an expression of the Cold War as much as the uncertainty of the Germans about their own democracy, could be overcome in favour of a genuine acceptance of conflict within liberal-democratic rules. For this idea, Germans have the unique concept of *Streitkultur* – a culture of civilized dispute – but the very fact that it is necessary to invoke such a highly nor-mative concept seems evidence for the absence of the thing itself. Such an acceptance of conflict might also further a 'sense of reality' which observers from Arendt onwards found missing – and which is of course not the same as a 'realist' approach to politics and foreign policy in particular. After 1989, then, there was the chance finally to come to terms with both the past *and* the present, and to resist the temptation to think and feel in other times, and other countries. It might be worth remembering that Hannah Arendt prefaced her flawed masterpiece, *The Origins of Totali-tarianism*, with a quotation from Karl Jaspers in German: *'Weder dem Vergangenen anheimfallen noch dem Zukünftigen. Es kommt darauf an, ganz gegenwärtig zu sein'.*[11] This coming to terms with the present, then, could also mean creating a genuinely political language – which is not to

---

[10] Habermas, *A Berlin Republic*, 47. Habermas still resisted the supposed Cold War vocabulary of totalitarianism – but surely Nazism was more than 'authoritarianism'.

[11] Hannah Arendt, *The Origins of Totalitarianism*, new ed. with added prefaces (New York: Harcourt Brace, 1976), vii: 'To fall victim neither to the past nor the future. It is crucial to be completely present'.

say that such a language cannot also be a moral language – but one which stops contaminating the past and being contaminated by the past in turn. The art of separation, after all, is a liberal one.

So, for all the socio-economic (and moral) difficulties in the wake of unification, 1989 should still be seen as a liberation – from the moral-cum-intellectual confines of the Cold War, from the compensatory functions of literature in the absence of political structures, from the obsession with mutual unmasking, from the compulsion to create cohesion through forgetting on the Right, and the compulsion to suspect on the Left.

German Intellectuals, Unification and National Identity

After 1945, young German intellectuals sought a decisive break with Weimar intellectual mandarin traditions. Time and again, they insisted that they had learnt the lessons of Weimar – and, in particular, its tragic left-wing intellectuals who had hastened the demise of the Republic. Instead, beginning in the late 1950s, they sought to advocate a cultural consolidation of democratic institutions in the face of a post-fascist democratic deficit. Against what they saw as Adenauer's hypocritical reunification policies, they also called for national solidarity (without nationalism) vis-à-vis the Germans in the GDR. Not least because of their generational experience, one of their most basic political dispositions was a distrust of nationalism, but also, to some extent, of the Germans as a people as such. They were, however, also willing to be more discriminating in their political judgements than their Weimar predecessors, and therefore to acknowledge and further the liberal democratic achievements of the Federal Republic.

As the democratic deficit and the appeal of nationalism diminished over time, these intellectuals retreated somewhat from the public sphere. However, with the sudden prospect of unification in 1990, many intellectuals re-entered the public sphere, where they often re-enacted roles – and re-articulated positions – which they had already formulated as early as the 1960s. They feared that with the addition of 17 million undemocratic East Germans calling for *ein Volk*, and the 'return of the nation-state', Germany might yet again suffer from a democratic deficit and see renewed nationalism. Given that Adenauer's grandson so clearly appealed to a pan-German economic miracle identity and centred the unification process on the executive, thereby reinforcing the perception of a new 'Chancellor democracy', intellectuals saw ominous parallels with the 1950s and feared the establishment of continuities with pre-1945 Germany. In response, they advanced concepts such as the *Kulturnation* and constitutional patriotism. In most cases, their conceptual frameworks showed a marked consistency with their views in the past.

As events passed them by, as they were subjected to often vicious attacks from right-wing journalists, and as they turned in on themselves in an acrimonious debate on 'what was left', space opened up on the intellectual field potentially to be filled by New Right intellectuals. These intellectuals, however, remained excessively fixated on their primary political opponents, the generation of '68, and generally at the level of cultural criticism, rather than concrete policy proposals. In the face of the New Right onslaught, the centre held. There was a considerable loosening and readjusting of conceptual constraints after 1989, but, contrary to what many observers predicted, there was no overall shift to the right. Neither did the 'return of history' or the nation-state translate into a classical pursuit of national interests or a return of popular nationalism. Partly, this can be explained by the party-political and personal continuities at the top. A Chancellor deeply committed to European political and monetary union, with a somewhat autocratic leadership style solidly built on what we now know was a quasi-feudal system of personal dependencies, could not be expected to be swayed by the warnings of 'the new Punks of the right' (Peter Pulzer). But ultimately, it was the fact that West German political culture remained by and large robustly liberal and democratic – even in the face of considerable social anomie and economic dislocation in the wake of unification. At least to some extent, this was due to the interventions of West German intellectuals in the past fifty years, overly distrustful of their own people as they might often have been.

Bibliography

Adorno, Theodor W. 'Auferstehung der Kultur in Deutschland?', in *Frankfurter Hefte*, Vol. 5 (1950), 469–77.

Adorno, Theodor W. *Minima Moralia: Reflexionen aus dem beschädigten Leben* (Frankfurt/Main: Suhrkamp, 1951).

Adorno, Theodor W. 'Was bedeutet: Aufarbeitung der Vergangenheit?', in *Gesammelte Schriften*, ed. Rolf Tiedemann, Vol. 10 (Frankfurt/Main: Suhrkamp, 1977), 555–72.

Adorno, Theodor W. 'Auf die Frage: Was ist deutsch?', in *Gesammelte Schriften*, ed. Rolf Tiedemann, Vol. 10 (Frankfurt/Main: Suhrkamp, 1977), 691–701.

Adorno, Theodor W. *Negative Dialektik* (1966; Frankfurt/Main: Suhrkamp, 1994).

Adorno, Theodor W. 'Kulturkritik und Gesellschaft', in Petra Kiedaisch (ed.), *Lyrik nach Auschwitz? Adorno und die Dichter* (Stuttgart: Reclam, 1995), 27–49.

Albrecht, Clemens *et al. Die intellektuelle Gründung der Bundesrepublik: Eine Wirkungsgeschichte der Frankfurter Schule* (Frankfurt/Main: Campus, 1999).

Altmann, Rüdiger. 'Die formierte Gesellschaft (1965)', in *Abschied vom Staat: Politische Essays* (Frankfurt/Main: Campus, 1998), 61–70.

Améry, Jean. 'Jargon der Dialektik', in *Merkur*, Vol. 21 (1967), 1041–59.

Andersch, Alfred. 'Das junge Europa formt sein Gesicht', in Hans Schwab-Felisch (ed.), *Der Ruf: Eine deutsche Nachkriegszeitschrift* (Munich: Deutscher Taschenbuch Verlag, 1962), 21–6.

Anter, Andreas. *Max Webers Theorie des modernen Staates: Herkunft, Struktur und Bedeutung* (Berlin: Duncker & Humblot, 1995).

Anz, Thomas (ed.). *'Es geht nicht um Christa Wolf': Der Literaturstreit im vereinten Deutschland* (Munich: Sprangenberg, 1991).

Apel, Karl Otto. 'Zurück zur Normalität? Oder können wir aus der nationalen Katastrophe etwas Besonderes gelernt haben? Das Problem des (welt-)geschichtlichen Übergangs zur postkonventionellen Moral aus spezifisch deutscher Sicht', in Forum der Philosophie Bad Homburg (ed.), *Zerstörung des moralischen Selbstbewußtseins: Chance oder Gefährdung?* (Frankfurt/Main: Suhrkamp, 1988), 91–142.

Arendt, Hannah. *On Violence* (New York: Harcourt Brace, 1970).

Arendt, Hannah. *The Origins of Totalitarianism*, new ed. with added prefaces (New York: Harcourt Brace, 1976).

Arendt, Hannah. 'Besuch in Deutschland', in Hannah Arendt, *Zur Zeit: Politische Essays*, ed. Marie Luise Knott (Munich: Deutscher Taschenbuch Verlag, 1989), 43–70.

Arendt, Hannah. *The Human Condition* (1958; Chicago: University of Chicago Press, 1989).

Arendt, Hannah. *On Revolution* (1963; New York: Penguin, 1990).

Arndt, Hans-Joachim. *Die Besiegten von 1945: Versuch einer Politologie für Deutsche samt Würdigung der Politischen Wissenschaft in der Bundesrepublik Deutschland* (Berlin: Duncker & Humblot, 1978).

Assmann, Aleida and Frevert, Ute. *Geschichtsvergessenheit/Geschichtsversessenheit: Vom Umgang mit deutschen Vergangenheiten nach 1945* (Stuttgart: Deutsche Verlags-Anstalt, 1999).

Assmann, Jan. *Das kulturelle Gedächtnis: Schrift, Erinnerung und politische Identität in frühen Hochkulturen* (Munich: C. H. Beck, 1997).

Backes, Uwe *et al.* (eds). *Die Schatten der Vergangenheit. Impulse zur Historisierung des Nationalsozialismus* (Berlin: Propyläen, 1990).

Baier, Lothar. *Volk ohne Zeit: Essay über das eilige Vaterland* (Berlin: Wagenbach, 1990).

Baring, Arnulf. *Deutschland, was nun? Ein Gespräch mit Dirk Rumberg and Wolf Jobst Siedler* (Berlin: Siedler, 1991).

Barnouw, Dagmar. *Weimar Intellectuals and the Threat of Modernity* (Bloomington: Indiana University Press, 1988).

Barnouw, Dagmar. *Germany 1945: Views of War and Destruction* (Bloomington: Indiana University Press, 1996).

Bathrick, David. *The Powers of Speech: The Politics of Culture in the GDR* (Lincoln: University of Nebraska Press, 1995).

Baukle, Bernward (ed.). *Hannah Arendt und die Berliner Republik: Fragen an das vereinigte Deutschland* (Berlin: Aufbau, 1996).

Baumgart, Reinhard. 'Das Einhorn brüllt, der Löwe tanzt', in *Der Spiegel*, 20 August 1979.

Beck, Ulrich. 'Die unvollendete Revolution', in *Der Spiegel*, 18 December 1989.

Beck, Ulrich. *Risk Society: Towards a New Modernity*, trans. Mark Ritter (1986; London: Sage, 1992).

Beck, Ulrich. *Die Erfindung des Politischen: Zu einer Theorie reflexiver Modernisierung* (Frankfurt/Main: Suhrkamp, 1993).

Beck, Ulrich. 'Vom Veralten sozialwissenschaftlicher Begriffe: Grundzüge einer Theorie reflexiver Modernisierung', in Christoph Görg (ed.), *Gesellschaft im Übergang: Perspektiven kritischer Soziologie* (Darmstadt: Wissenschaftliche Buchgesellschaft, 1994), 21–43.

Beck, Ulrich. 'World Risk Society as Cosmopolitan Society? Ecological Questions in a Framework of Manufactured Uncertainties', in *Theory, Culture & Society*, No. 4 (1996), 1–32.

Becker, Jurek. 'Gedächtnis verloren – Verstand verloren', in *Die Zeit*, 18 November 1988.

Becker, Jurek. 'Über die letzten Tage: Ein kleiner Einspruch gegen die deutsche Euphorie', in *Neue Rundschau*, Vol. 101, No. 1 (1990), 90.

Behrmann, Günter C. 'Kulturrevolution: Zwei Monate im Sommer 1967', in Clemens Albrecht et al., *Die intellektuelle Gründung der Bundesrepublik: Eine Wirkungsgeschichte der Frankfurter Schule* (Frankfurt/Main: Campus, 1999), 312–78.

Benhabib, Seyla. *Critique, Norm, and Utopia: A Study of the Foundations of Critical Theory* (New York: Columbia University Press, 1986).

Benhabib, Seyla. *The Reluctant Modernism of Hannah Arendt* (Thousand Oaks, CA: Sage, 1996).

Benjamin, Walter. *Illuminations*, ed. Hannah Arendt, trans. Harry Zohn (London: Fontana, 1992).

Benz, Wolfgang. 'Sorgen im freudigen Augenblick', in Wilhelm von Sternburg (ed.), *Geteilte Ansichten über eine vereinigte Nation: Ein Buch über Deutschland* (Frankfurt/Main: Anton Hain, 1990), 53–9.

Benz, Wolfgang. *Zwischen Hitler und Adenauer: Studien zur deutschen Nachkriegsgesellschaft* (Frankfurt/Main: Fischer, 1991).

Bergfleth, Gerd. *Zur Kritik der palavernden Aufklärung* (Munich: Matthes & Seitz, 1984).

Berglar, Peter et al. *Deutsche Identität heute* (Stuttgart: von Hase & Koehler, 1983).

Bering, Dietz. *Die Intellektuellen: Geschichte eines Schimpfwortes* (Stuttgart: Klett-Cotta, 1978).

Betz, Wolfgang. 'Deutschlandpolitik on the Margins: On the Evolution of Contemporary New Right Nationalism in the Federal Republic', in *New German Critique*, No. 44 (1988), 127–57.

Bialas, Wolfgang. *Vom unfreien Schweben zum freien Fall: Ostdeutsche Intellektuelle im gesellschaftlichen Umbruch* (Frankfurt/Main: Fischer, 1996).

Bielefeldt, Heiner. *Kampf und Entscheidung: Politischer Existentialismus bei Carl Schmitt, Helmuth Plessner und Karl Jaspers* (Würzburg: Königshausen & Neumann, 1994).

Bleek, Wilhelm and Maull, Hanns (eds). *Ein ganz normaler Staat? Perspektiven nach 40 Jahren Bundesrepublik* (Munich: Piper, 1989).

Blücher, Viggo Graf. *Die Generation der Unbefangenen* (Düsseldorf: Diederich, 1967).

Bobbio, Norberto. *Left and Right: The Significance of a Political Distinction* (Cambridge: Polity, 1996).

Böckenförde, Ernst-Wolfgang. 'Der verdrängte Ausnahmezustand: Zum Handeln der Staatsgewalt in außergewöhnlichen Lagen: Carl Schmitt zum 90. Geburtstag gewidmet', in *Neue Juristische Wochenschrift*, Vol. 31 (1978), 1881–90.

Bohrer, Karl Heinz. 'Die linke Minderheit: Theorie und Praxis der Rebellen von Berlin', in *Frankfurter Allgemeine Zeitung*, 23 June 1967.

Bohrer, Karl Heinz. 'Die mißverstandene Rebellion', in *Merkur*, Vol. 22 (1968), 33–44.

Bohrer, Karl Heinz. *Die gefährdete Phantasie, oder Surrealismus und Terror* (Munich: Hanser, 1970).

Bohrer, Karl Heinz. 'Staatsräson und Moral: Am Beispiel Bölls', in *Frankfurter Allgemeine Zeitung*, 2 February 1972.

Bohrer, Karl Heinz. 'Was heißt hier "Verantwortlichkeit der Intellektuellen"?', in *Frankfurter Allgemeine Zeitung*, 26 September 1972.

Bohrer, Karl Heinz. *Die Ästhetik des Schreckens: Die pessimistische Romantik und Ernst Jüngers Frühwerk* (Munich: Hanser, 1978).

Bohrer, Karl Heinz. 'Deutschland – noch eine geistige Möglichkeit: Bemerkungen zu einem nationalen Tabu', in *Frankfurter Allgemeine Zeitung*, 28 April 1979.

Bohrer, Karl Heinz. *Ein bißchen Lust am Untergang: Englische Ansichten* (Munich: Hanser, 1979).

Bohrer, Karl Heinz (ed.). *Mythos und Moderne: Begriff und Bild einer Rekonstruktion* (Frankfurt/Main: Suhrkamp, 1983).

Bohrer, Karl Heinz. 'Die Ästhetik des Staates', in *Merkur*, Vol. 38 (1984), 1–15.

Bohrer, Karl Heinz. *Die Kritik der Romantik: Der Verdacht der Philosophie gegen die literarische Moderne* (Frankfurt/Main: Suhrkamp, 1989).

Bohrer, Karl Heinz. 'Und die Erinnerung der beiden Halbnationen?', in *Merkur*, Vol. 44 (1990), 183–8.

Bohrer, Karl Heinz. 'Widerspruch zu Hermann Lübbe', in *Merkur*, Vol. 44 (1990), 530–3.

Bohrer, Karl Heinz. 'Provinzialismus (III). Das Vakuum', in *Merkur*, Vol. 45 (1991), 348–56.

Bohrer, Karl Heinz. 'Why We are Not a Nation – And Why We Should Become One', in Harold James and Marla Stone (eds), *When the Wall came down: Reactions to German Unification* (New York: Routledge, 1992), 60–70.

Bohrer, Karl Heinz. 'Gibt es eine deutsche Nation?', in Siegfried Unseld (ed.), *Politik ohne Projekt? Nachdenken über Deutschland* (Frankfurt/Main: Suhrkamp, 1993), 225–35.

Bohrer, Karl Heinz. *Suddenness: On the Moment of Aesthetic Appearance* (New York: Columbia University Press, 1994).

Bohrer, Karl Heinz. 'Schuldkultur oder Schamkultur und der Verlust an historischem Gedächtnis', in *Neue Zürcher Zeitung*, 12 December 1998.

Böll, Heinrich. 'Polemik eines Verärgerten', in Horst Krüger (ed.), *Was ist heute links? Thesen und Theorien zu einer politischen Position* (Reinbek: Rowohlt, 1962), 43–6.

Böll, Heinrich. 'Angst vor der Gruppe 47?', in *Merkur*, Vol. 19 (1965), 775–83.

Borchert, Konstanze et al. (eds). *Für unser Land: Eine Aufrufaktion im letzten Jahr der DDR* (Frankfurt/Main: IKO, 1994).

Bourdieu, Pierre. *The Field of Cultural Production* (Cambridge: Polity, 1993).

Bourdieu, Pierre. *In Other Words: Towards a Reflexive Sociology* (Cambridge: Polity, 1994).

Boveri, Margret. 'Variationen des Selbstverständlichen', in *Merkur*, Vol. 22 (1968), 765–71.

Bracher, Karl Dieter. 'Leserbrief an die "Frankfurter Allgemeine Zeitung", 6 September 1986', in *'Historikerstreit': Die Dokumentation der Kontroverse um die Einzigartigkeit der nationalsozialistischen Judenvernichtung* (Munich: Piper, 1987), 113–14.

Bracher, Karl Dieter. 'Kein Anlaß zu Teuto-Pessimismus', in *Süddeutsche Zeitung*, 24 May 1989.

Bracher, Karl Dieter. 'Der deutsche Einheitsstaat – Ein Imperativ der Geschichte?', in *Basler Zeitung*, 17 February 1990.

Braese, Stephan et al. (eds). *Deutsche Nachkriegsliteratur und der Holocaust* (Frankfurt/Main: Campus, 1998).

Brandt, Peter and Ammon, Herbert (eds). *Die Linke und die nationale Frage: Dokumente zur deutschen Einheit seit 1945* (Reinbek: Rowohlt, 1981).

Brenner, Michael. *After the Holocaust: Rebuilding Jewish Lives in Postwar Germany*, trans. Barbara Harshav (Princeton: Princeton University Press, 1997).

Breuer, Stefan. *Anatomie der Konservativen Revolution* (Darmstadt: Wissenschaftliche Buchgesellschaft, 1993).

Breuer, Stefan. *Ästhetischer Fundamentalismus: Stefan George und der deutsche Antimodernismus* (Darmstadt: Wissenschaftliche Buchgesellschaft, 1995).

Brill, Heinz. *Geopolitik heute: Deutschlands Chance?* (Berlin: Ullstein, 1994).

Brockmann, Stephen. *Literature and German Reunification* (Cambridge: Cambridge University Press, 1999).

Broder, Henryk M. 'Verostung', in Jörg-DieterVogel et al. (eds). *Neues Deutschland: Innenansichten einer wiedervereinigten Nation* (Frankfurt/Main: Fischer, 1993), 38–41.

Broszat, Martin/Friedländer, Saul. 'A Controversy about the Historicization of National Socialism', in *New German Critique*, No. 44 (1988), 85–126.

Brubaker, Rogers. *Citizenship and Nationhood in France and Germany* (Cambridge, Mass.: Harvard University Press, 1992).

Brumlik, Micha. 'Birth of a Nation? Gedankensplitter zur Einheit', in Arthur Heinrich and Klaus Naumann (eds), *Alles Banane: Ausblicke auf das endgültige Deutschland* (Cologne: PapyRossa, 1990), 151–62.

Brumlik, Micha. 'Basic Aspects of an Imaginary Debate', in *New German Critique*, No. 52 (1991), 102–8.

Brunner, Otto et al. (eds). *Geschichtliche Grundbegriffe*, Vol. 7 (Stuttgart: Klett-Cotta, 1992).

Bubik, Roland. 'Herrschaft und Medien. Über den Kampf gegen die linke Meinungsdominanz', in Heimo Schwilk and Ulrich Schacht (eds), *Die Selbstbewußte Nation: 'Anschwellender Bocksgesang' und weitere Beiträge zu einer deutschen Debatte* (Berlin: Ullstein, 1994), 182–94.

Bubik, Roland. *Wir 89er: Wer wir sind – was wir wollen* (Berlin: Ullstein, 1995).

Bubis, Ignatz. 'Wer von der Schande spricht', in *Frankfurter Allgemeine Zeitung*, 10 November 1998.

Bude, Heinz. *Deutsche Karrieren: Lebenskonstruktionen sozialer Aufsteiger aus der Flakhelfer-Generation* (Frankfurt/Main: Suhrkamp, 1987).

Bude, Heinz. 'Die Soziologen der Bundesrepublik', in *Merkur*, Vol. 46 (1992), 569–80.

Bude, Heinz. *Bilanz der Nachfolge: Die Bundesrepublik und der Nationalsozialismus* (Frankfurt/Main: Suhrkamp, 1992).

Bußmann, Walter. *Treitschke: Sein Welt- und Geschichtsbild* (Göttingen: Muster-Schmidt-Verlag, 1981).

Caldwell, Peter C. 'Ernst Forsthoff and the Legacy of Radical State Theory in the Federal Republic of Germany', in *History of Political Thought*, Vol. 5 (1994), 615–41.

Caldwell, Peter C. *Popular Sovereignty and the Crisis of German Constitutional Law: The Theory & Practice of Weimar Constitutionalism* (Durham: Duke University Press, 1997).

Chotjewitz-Häfner, Renate and Gansel, Carsten (eds). *Verfeindete Einzelgänger: Schriftsteller streiten über Moral und Politik* (Berlin: Aufbau, 1997).

Dahrendorf, Ralf. *Reisen nach innen und außen: Aspekte der Zeit* (Munich: Deutscher Taschenbuch Verlag, 1986).

Dahrendorf, Ralf. 'Zeitgenosse Habermas. Jürgen Habermas zum sechzigsten Geburtstag', in *Merkur*, Vol. 43 (1989), 478–87.

Dahrendorf, Ralf. ' "Eine deutsche Identität" ', in *Merkur*, Vol. 44 (1990), 231–5.

Dahrendorf, Ralf. 'Die Sache mit der Nation', in *Merkur*, Vol. 44 (1990), 823–34.

Dahrendorf, Ralf. 'Die Zukunft des Nationalstaates', in *Merkur*, Vol. 48 (1994), 751–61.

Delling, Manfred. 'Links und rechts – gibt es das noch?', in *Sonntagsblatt*, 13 May 1963.

Devigne, Robert. *Recasting Conservatism: Oakshott, Strauss, and the Response to Postmodernism* (New Haven: Yale University Press, 1994).

Dieckmann, Friedrich. 'Die Linke und die Nation', in *Merkur*, Vol. 48 (1994), 762–70.

Diederichsen, Diederich. 'Der Anarch, der Solitär und die Revolte: Rechte Poststrukturalismus-Rezeption in der BRD', in Richard

Faber *et al.* (eds), *Rechtsextremismus: Ideologie und Gewalt* (Berlin: Edition Hentrich, 1995), 241–58.

Diner, Dan (ed.). *Zivilisationsbruch: Denken nach Auschwitz* (Frankfurt/Main: Fischer, 1988).

Diner, Dan. *Kreisläufe: Nationalsozialismus und Gedächtnis* (Berlin: Berlin, 1995).

Dirks, Walter. 'Rechts und Links', in *Frankfurter Hefte*, Vol. 1, No. 6 (1946), 24–37.

Dirks, Walter, 'Der restaurative Charakter der Epoche', in *Frankfurter Hefte*, Vol. 5 (1950), 942–54.

Diwald, Hellmut. *Geschichte der Deutschen* (Berlin: Propyläen, 1978).

Dohnanyi, Klaus von. 'Eine Friedensrede', in *Frankfurter Allgemeine Zeitung*, 14 November 1998.

Dohse, Rainer. *Der Dritte Weg: Neutralitätsbestrebungen in Westdeutschland zwischen 1945 und 1955* (Hamburg: Holsten, 1974).

Dubiel, Helmut. 'Linke Trauerarbeit', in *Merkur*, Vol. 44 (1990), 482–91.

Dubiel, Helmut. 'Über moralische Souveränität, Erinnerung und Nation', in *Merkur*, Vol. 48 (1994), 884–97.

Dubiel, Helmut. *Niemand ist frei von der Geschichte: Die nationalsozialistische Herrschaft in den Debatten des Deutschen Bundestages* (Munich: Hanser, 1999).

Dutschke, Gretchen. *Wir hatten ein barbarisches, schönes Leben* (Cologne: Kiepenheuer & Witsch, 1996).

Dutschke, Rudi *et al. Mein langer Marsch: Reden, Schriften und Tagebücher aus zwanzig Jahren* (Reinbek: Rowohlt, 1980).

Duve, Freimut. *Vom Krieg in der Seele: Rücksichten eines Deutschen* (Frankfurt/Main: Eichborn, 1994).

Ebermann, Thomas and Trampert, Rainer. *Die Offenbarung der Propheten: Über die Sanierung des Kapitalismus, die Verwandlung linker Theorie in Esoterik, Bocksgesänge und Zivilgesellschaft* (Hamburg: Konkret Literatur, 1996).

Eichberg, Henning. *Nationale Identität: Entfremdung und nationale Frage in der Industriegesellschaft* (Munich: Langen Müller, 1978).

Eley, Geoff and Blackbourn, David. *The Peculiarities of German History* (Oxford: Oxford University Press, 1985).

Ely, John D. 'The "Black-Brown Hazelnut" in a Bigger Germany: The Rise of a Radical Right as a Structural Feature', in Michael G. Huelshoff *et al.* (eds), *From Bundesrepublik to Deutschland: German Politics after Unification* (Ann Arbor: University of Michigan Press, 1993), 235–68.

Enzensberger, Hans Magnus. 'Am I a German?', in *Encounter*, No. 4 (1964), 16–18.

Enzensberger, Hans Magnus. *Deutschland, Deutschland unter anderm: Äußerungen zur Politik* (Frankfurt/Main: Suhrkamp, 1967).

Enzensberger, Hans Magnus. 'The Writer and Politics', in *Times Literary Supplement*, 28 September 1967.

Enzensberger, Hans Magnus. 'On leaving America', in *New York Review of Books*, 28 February 1968.

Enzensberger, Hans Magnus. *Die Furie des Verschwindens* (Frankfurt/Main: Suhrkamp, 1980).

Enzensberger, Hans Magnus. 'Gangarten – Ein Nachtrag zur Utopie: Wenn ein Alltag anbricht, der ohne Propheten auskommt', in *Frankfurter Allgemeine Zeitung*, 19 May 1990.

Enzensberger, Hans Magnus. 'Ausblicke auf den Bürgerkrieg', in *Der Spiegel*, 21 June 1993.

Eppler, Erhard. *Die Wiederkehr der Politik* (Frankfurt/Main: Insel, 1998).

Esslin, Martin. 'A German Correspondent Reports from London', in *Encounter*, No. 5 (1980), 72–7.

Faulenbach, Bernd. 'Historische Tradition und politische Neuorientierung: Zur Geschichtswissenschaft nach der "deutschen Katastrophe" ', in Walter H. Pehle and Peter Sillem (eds), *Wissenschaft im geteilten Deutschland: Restauration oder Neubeginn nach 1945?* (Frankfurt/Main: Fischer, 1992), 191–201.

Fest, Joachim. 'Schweigende Wortführer', in *Frankfurter Allgemeine Zeitung*, 30 December 1989.

Fichter, Tilman. *Die SPD und die Nation. Vier sozialdemokratische Generationen zwischen nationaler Selbstbestimmung und Zweistaatlichkeit* (Berlin: Ullstein, 1993).

Fischer, Fritz. *Griff nach der Weltmacht: Die Kriegszielpolitik des kaiserlichen Deutschland* (Düsseldorf: Droste, 1961). English translation: *Germany's Aims in the First World War* (London: Chatto & Windus, 1967).

Fisher, Marc. *After the Wall: Germany, Germans and the Burdens of History* (New York: Simon and Schuster, 1995).

Forsthoff, Ernst. 'Verfassung und Verfassungswirklichkeit der Bundesrepublik', in *Merkur*, Vol. 22 (1968), 401–14.

Forsthoff, Ernst. *Rechtsstaatlichkeit und Sozialstaatlichkeit* (Darmstadt: Wissenschaftliche Buchgesellschaft, 1968).

Freeden, Michael. *Ideologies and Political Theory: A Conceptual Approach* (Oxford: Oxford University Press, 1996).

Freeden, Michael. 'Is Nationalism a Distinct Ideology?', in *Political Studies*, Vol. 46 (1998), 748–65.

Friedlander, Saul. 'Introduction', in Saul Friedlander (ed.), *Probing the Limits of Representation: Nazism and the 'Final Solution'* (Cambridge, Mass.: Harvard University Press, 1992), 1–21.

Freyer, Hans. *Theorie des gegenwärtigen Zeitalters* (Stuttgart: Deutsche Verlags–Anstalt, 1955).

Fühlberth, Georg. *Eröffnungsbilanz des gesamtdeutschen Kapitalismus: Vom Spätsozialismus zur nationalen Restauration* (Hamburg: Konkret Literatur, 1993).

Fuhr, Eckhard. 'Deprimierend', in *Frankfurter Allgemeine Zeitung*, 10 November 1998.

Fulbrook, Mary. *Anatomy of a Dictatorship: Inside the GDR 1949–1989* (Oxford: Oxford University Press, 1995).

Garton Ash, Timothy. *In Europe's Name: Germany and the Divided Continent* (London: Jonathan Cape, 1993).

Gaus, Günter. *Wo Deutschland liegt: Eine Ortsbestimmung* (Hamburg: Hoffmann und Campe, 1983).

Gehlen, Arnold. *Über kulturelle Kristallisation* (Bremen: Angelsachsen, 1961).

Gehlen, Arnold. 'Das Engagement der Intellektuellen gegenüber dem Staat', in *Merkur*, Vol. 18 (1964), 401–13.

Gehlen, Arnold. *Moral und Hypermoral: Eine pluralistische Ethik* (Frankfurt/Main: Athenäum, 1969).

Gehlen, Arnold. *Man: His Nature and Place in the World*, trans. Clare McMillan and Karl Pillemer (New York: Columbia University Press, 1988).

Gessenharter, Wolfgang. *Kippt die Republik? Die Neue Rechte und ihre Unterstützung durch Politik und Medien* (Munich: Knaur, 1995).

Geulen, Eva. 'Nationalism: Old, New and German', in *Telos*, No. 105 (1995), 2–20.

Geuss, Raymond. *The Idea of a Critical Theory: Habermas and the Frankfurt School* (Cambridge: Cambridge University Press, 1981).

Giesen, Bernhard. *Intellectuals and the German Nation: Collective Identity in an Axial Age*, trans. Nicholas Levis and Amos Weisz (Cambridge: Cambridge University Press, 1998).

Gildea, Robert. *The Past in French History* (New Haven: Yale University Press, 1994).

Giordano, Ralph. *Die zweite Schuld oder von der Last Deutscher zu sein* (Hamburg: Rasch und Röhring, 1987).

Girard, René. *Violence and the Sacred*, trans. Patrick Gregory (Baltimore: Johns Hopkins University Press, 1977).

Glotz, Peter C. 'Rechtsfiguren für den Konflikt', in *die tageszeitung*, 21 June 1989.

Glotz, Peter. 'Der Ulrich der Deutschen', in *Die Zeit*, 18 May 1990.

Glotz, Peter. *Der Irrweg des Nationalstaats* (Stuttgart: Deutsche Verlags-Anstalt, 1990).

Glotz, Peter. *Die falsche Normalisierung: Die unmerkliche Verwandlung der Deutschen 1989 bis 1994* (Frankfurt/Main: Suhrkamp, 1994).

Göbel, Andreas *et al.* (eds). *Metamorphosen des Politischen: Grundfragen politischer Einheitsbildung seit den 20er Jahren* (Berlin: Akademie, 1995).

Goldfarb, Jeffrey. *Civility and Subversion: The Intellectual in Democratic Society* (Cambridge: Cambridge University Press, 1998).

Goldhagen, Daniel Jonah. *Hitler's Willing Exe-cutioners: Ordinary Germans and the Holo-caust* (New York: Knopf, 1996).

Goldmann, Harvey. *Politics, Death and the Devil: Self and Power in Max Weber and Thomas Mann* (Berkeley: University of California Press, 1992).

Grass, Günter. *Essays, Reden, Briefe, Kom-mentare [Werkausgabe in zehn Bänden*, Vol. 9], ed. Daniela Hermes (Neuwied: Luchterhand, 1987).

Grass, Günter. *Kopfgeburten oder die Deutschen sterben aus*, in *Werkausgabe in zehn Bänden*, Vol. 4, ed. Christoph Sieger (Neuwied: Luchterhand, 1987), 139–270.

Grass, Günter. *Gegen die verstreichende Zeit* (Hamburg: Lucherhand, 1991).

Grass, Günter. *Ein weites Feld* (Göttingen: Steidl, 1995).

Grass, Günter. *Der Schriftsteller als Zeitgenosse* (Munich: Deutscher Taschenbuch Verlag, 1996).

Grass, Günter. *Der Autor als fragwürdiger Zeuge* (Munich: Deutscher Taschenbuch Verlag, 1997).

Grass, Günter. 'Zwischen den Stühlen. Was heißt heute Engagement? Dankesrede zum Fritz-Bauer-Preis', in *Die Zeit*, 29 April 1998.

Greffrath, Matthias. 'Freunde, hört die Signale! Kleine Predigt zum Ende des linke Trauerjahres', in *Die Zeit*, 9 November 1990.

Greiffenhagen, Martin. *Das Dilemma des Kon-servatismus in Deutschland* (Munich: Piper, 1971).

Greiffenhagen, Martin. *Jahrgang 1928: Aus einem unruhigen Leben* (Munich: Piper, 1988).

Greiffenhagen, Martin and Sylvia. *Ein schwieriges Vaterland: Zur politischen Kultur Deutschlands* (Munich: List, 1979).

Greiffenhagen, Martin and Sylvia. *Ein schwieriges Vaterland: Zur politischen Kultur im vereinigten Deutschland* (Munich: List, 1993).

Gremliza, Hermann L. *Krautland einig Vaterland* (Hamburg: Konkret Literatur, 1990).

Greven, Michael Th. 'Hannah Arendt – Plural-ität und Gründung der Freiheit', in Peter Kemper (ed.). *Die Zukunft des Politischen: Theoretische Ausblicke auf Hannah Arendt* (Frankfurt/Main: Fischer, 1993), 69–96.

Gross, Johannes. *Die Deutschen* (Stuttgart: Schef-fler, 1968).

Gross, Johannes. *Begründung der Berliner Repub-lik: Deutschland am Ende des 20. Jahrhunderts* (Stuttgart: Deutsche Verlags-Anstalt, 1995).

Grosser, Dieter. *Die Überwindung der Teilung: Der innerdeutsche Prozeß der Vereinigung* (Stuttgart: Deutsche Verlags-Anstalt, 1998).

Grosser, Dieter. *Das Wagnis der Währungs-, Wirtschafts- und Sozialunion: Politische Zwänge im Konflikt mit ökonomischen Regeln* (Stuttgart: Deutsche Verlags-Anstalt, 1998).

Grunenberg, Antonia. 'Macht kommt von möglich . . . ', in Antonia Grunenberg and Lothar Probst (eds), *Einschnitte: Hannah Arendts politisches Denken heute* (Bremen: Edition Temmen, 1995), 83–95.

Guggenberger, Bernd. 'Klammheimlicher The-menwechsel: Die Deutsche Verfassungsdis-kussion zwischen Wiedervereinigung und Maastricht', in Bernd Guggenberger and Andreas Maier (eds), *Der Souverän auf der Nebenbühne: Essays und Zwischenrufe zur deutschen Verfassungsdiskussion* (Opladen: Westdeutscher Verlag, 1994), 14–20.

Güntner, Joachim. 'Grass-Wirbel. Zum Erwachen des engagierten Intellektuellen. Eine Nachlese', in *Neue Zürcher Zeitung*, 29 October 1997.

Habermas, Jürgen. 'Mit Heidegger gegen Hei-degger denken: Zur Veröffentlichung von Vor-lesungen aus dem Jahre 1935', in *Frankfurter Allgemeine Zeitung*, 25 July 1953.

Habermas, Jürgen. 'Illusionen auf dem Heirats-markt', in *Merkur*, Vol. 10 (1956), 996–1004.

Habermas, Jürgen *et al. Student und Politik: Eine soziologische Untersuchung zum politischen Bewußtsein Frankfurter Studenten* (Neuwied: Luchterhand, 1961).

Habermas, Jürgen. *Protestbewegung und Hochschulreform* (Frankfurt/Main: Suhr-kamp, 1969).

Habermas, Jürgen. *Philosophisch-politische Profile* (Frankfurt/Main: Suhrkamp, 1973).

Habermas, Jürgen. 'Stumpf gewordene Waffen aus dem Arsenal der Gegenaufklärung: An Prof. Kurt Sontheimer', in Freimut Duve *et al.* (eds), *Briefe zur Verteidigung der Republik* (Reinbek: Rowohlt, 1977), 54–72.

Habermas, Jürgen (ed.), *Observations on 'The Spiritual Situation of the Age': Contemporary German Perspectives*, trans. Andrew Buchwalter (1979; Cambridge, Mass.: MIT Press, 1984).

Habermas, Jürgen. *Die neue Unübersichtlichkeit* (Frankfurt/Main: Suhrkamp, 1985).

Habermas, Jürgen. 'Eine Art Schadensabwicklung: Die apologetischen Tendenzen in der deutschen Geschichtsschreibung', in *'Historikerstreit': Die Dokumentation der Kontroverse um die Einzigartigkeit der nationalsozialistischen Judenvernichtung* (Munich: Piper, 1987), 62–76.

Habermas, Jürgen. *The Philosophical Discourse of Modernity: Twelve Lectures*, trans. Frederick Lawrence (1985; Cambridge, Mass.: MIT Press, 1987).

Habermas, Jürgen. 'Walter Benjamin: Consciousness-Raising or Rescuing Critique', in Gary Smith (ed.), *On Walter Benjamin: Critical Essays and Recollections* (Cambridge, Mass.: MIT Press, 1988), 90–128.

Habermas, Jürgen. *The New Conservatism: Cultural Criticism and the Historians' Debate*, ed. and trans. Shierry Weber Nicholsen (Cambridge, Mass.: MIT Press, 1989).

Habermas, Jürgen. 'Volkssouveränität als Verfahren', in *Merkur*, Vol. 43 (1989), 465–77.

Habermas, Jürgen. *The Structural Transformation of the Public Sphere: An Inquiry into a Category of Bourgeois Society*, trans. Thomas Burger and Frederick Lawrence (1962; Cambridge: MIT Press, 1989).

Habermas, Jürgen. *Strukturwandel der Öffentlichkeit: Untersuchungen zu einer Kategorie der bürgerlichen Öffentlichkeit* (1962; Frankfurt/Main: Suhrkamp, 1990).

Habermas, Jürgen. 'Modernity – An Incomplete Project', in Hal Foster (ed.), *Postmodern Culture* (London: Pluto Press, 1990), 3–15.

Habermas, Jürgen. *Die nachholende Revolution* (Frankfurt/Main: Suhrkamp, 1990).

Habermas, Jürgen. 'Yet Again: German Identity', in *New German Critique*, No. 52 (1991), 84–101.

Habermas, Jürgen. 'Zur Entwicklung der Sozial- und Geisteswissenschaften in der Bundesrepublik', in *Texte und Kontexte* (Frankfurt/Main: Suhrkamp, 1991), 207–15.

Habermas, Jürgen. 'Die zweite Lebenslüge der Bundesrepublik', in *Die Zeit*, 11 December 1992.

Habermas, Jürgen. *The Past as Future*, trans. Max Pensky (1991; Lincoln: University of Nebraska Press, 1994).

Habermas, Jürgen. 'Ein politisch zivilisiertes Land', in *Focus*, 28 August 1995.

Habermas, Jürgen. *Between Facts and Norms: Contributions to a Discourse Theory of Law and Democracy*, trans. William Rehg (1992; Cambridge, Mass.: MIT Press, 1996).

Habermas, Jürgen. 'National Unification and Popular Sovereignty', in *New Left Review*, No. 219 (1996), 3–13.

Habermas, Jürgen. 'Unruhe erste Bürgerpflicht', reprinted in Wolfgang Kraushaar (ed.), *Die Protestchronik 1949–1959*, Vol. 3 (Hamburg: Rogner and Bernhard, 1996), 1899.

Habermas, Jürgen. *A Berlin Republic: Writings on Germany*, trans. Steven Randall (1995; Lincoln: University of Nebraska Press, 1997).

Habermas, Jürgen. *Die postnationale Konstellation* (Frankfurt/Main: Suhrkamp, 1998).

Habermas, Jürgen. *The Inclusion of the Other: Studies in Political Theory*, eds. Ciaran Cronin and Pablo De Greiff (1996; Cambridge, Mass.: MIT Press, 1998).

Hacke, Christian. *Weltmacht wider Willen: Die Außenpolitik der Bundesrepublik Deutschland* (Berlin: Ullstein, 1993).

Hallberg, Robert von. *Literary Intellectuals and the Dissolution of the State: Professionalism and Conformity in the GDR*, trans. Kenneth J. Northcott (Chicago: University of Chicago Press, 1996).

Hartman, Geoffrey H. 'Introduction: Darkness Visible', in Geoffrey H. Hartman (ed.),

294 • Bibliography

Holocaust Remembrance: The Shapes of Memory (Oxford: Blackwell, 1994), 1–22.

Haug, Wolfgang Fritz. *Der hilflose Antifaschismus: Zur Kritik der Vorlesungsreihen über Wissenschaft und NS an deutschen Universitäten* (Frankfurt/Main: Suhrkamp, 1967).

Heer, Hannes and Naumann, Klaus (eds). *War of Extermination: The German Military in World War II 1941–1944* (1995; Oxford: Berghahn, 1999).

Heidegger, Martin. 'Brief über den "Humanismus"', in *Wegmarken* [*Gesamtausgabe*, Vol. 9] (Frankfurt/Main: Vittorio Klostermann, 1976), 313–64.

Heinrich, Arthur. 'Alles eins?', in Arthur Heinrich and Klaus Naumann (eds). *Alles Banane: Ausblicke auf das endgültige Deutschland* (Cologne: PapyRossa, 1990), 7–18.

Heilbrunn, Jacob. 'Germany's New Right', in *Foreign Affairs*, Vol. 76, No. 6 (1996), 80–98.

Hellmann, Gunther. 'Goodbye Bismarck? The Foreign Policy of Contemporary Germany', in *Mershon International Review*, No. 40 (1996), 1–39.

Henrich, Dieter. *Eine Republik Deutschland: Reflexionen auf dem Weg aus der deutschen Teilung* (Frankfurt/Main: Suhrkamp, 1990).

Henrich, Dieter. *Nach dem Ende der Teilung: Über Identitäten und Intellektualität in Deutschland* (Frankfurt/Main: Suhrkamp, 1991).

Herbert, Ulrich. *Best: Biographische Studien über Radikalismus, Weltanschauung und Vernunft, 1903–1989* (Bonn: J. H. W. Dietz, 1996).

Herbert, Ulrich. 'Academic and Public Discourses on the Holocaust: The Goldhagen Debate in Germany', in *German Politics and Society*, Vol. 17, No. 3 (1999), 35–53.

Herf, Jeffrey. *Divided Memory: The Nazi Past in the Two Germanys* (Cambridge, Mass.: Harvard University Press, 1997).

Herles, Wolfgang. *Nationalrausch* (Munich: Kindler, 1990).

Hermand, Jost. *Kultur im Wiederaufbau: Die Bundesrepublik 1945–1965* (Munich: Nymphenburger, 1986).

Herzinger, Richard and Stein, Hannes. *Endzeit-Propheten oder Die Offensive der Antiwestler* (Reinbek: Rowohlt, 1995).

Heym, Stefan. 'Ash Wednesday in the GDR', in *New German Critique*, No. 52 (1991), 31–5.

Hieber, Jochen. 'Gegen den Abstieg gespielt und gewonnen', in *Frankfurter Allgeneine Zeitung*, 24 March 1997.

Hillgruber, Andreas. *Zweierlei Untergang: Die Zerschlagung des Deutschen Reiches und das Ende des europäischen Judentums* (Berlin: Siedler, 1986).

Hoeges, Dirk. *Kontroverse am Abgrund: Ernst Robert Curtius und Karl Mannheim: Intellektuelle und 'freischwebende Intelligenz' in der Weimarer Republik* (Frankfurt/Main: Fischer, 1994).

Holub, Robert C. *Jürgen Habermas: Critic in the Public Sphere* (London: Routledge, 1991).

Horkheimer, Max and Adorno, Theodor W. *Dialektik der Aufklärung: Philosophische Fragmente* (1944; Frankfurt/Main: Fischer, 1988). English translation: *Dialectic of Enlightenment*, trans. John Cummings (New York: Continuum, 1976).

Horster, Detlef and van Reijen, Willem van. 'Interview mit Jürgen Habermas', in Detlef Horster, *Habermas zur Einführung* (Hamburg: Junius, 1992), 97–126.

Hughes, H. Stuart. *Sophisticated Rebels: The Political Culture of European Dissent 1968–1987* (Cambridge, Mass.: Harvard University Press, 1990).

Huyssen, Andreas. 'After the Wall: The Failure of German intellectuals', in *New German Critique*, No. 52 (1991), 109–43.

Huyssen, Andreas. *Twilight Memories: Marking Time in a Culture of Amnesia* (London: Routledge, 1995).

Huyssen, Andreas. 'Monumental Seduction', in Mieke Bal *et al.* (eds), *Acts of Memory: Cultural Recall in the Present* (Hanover: University Press of New England, 1999), 191–207.

Ignatieff, Michael. 'Unheimliche linke Träume. Warum tun deutsche Intellektuelle sich so schwer mit der Einheit?', in *Die Zeit*, 19 October 1990.

Inacker, Michael J. 'Macht und Moralität. Über eine neue deutsche Sicherheitspolitik', in Heimo Schwilk and Ulrich Schacht (eds), *Die Selbstbewußte Nation: 'Anschwellender Bocks-*

gesang' und weitere Beiträge zu einer deutschen Debatte (Berlin: Ullstein, 1994), 346–89.

Jäger, Wolfgang and Villinger, Ingeborg. Die Intellektuellen und die deutsche Einheit (Freiburg: Rombach, 1997).

James, Harold. A German Identity: 1770 to the Present Day (London: Phoenix, 1994).

Jarausch, Konrad. The Rush to German Unity (New York: Oxford University Press, 1994).

Jaspers, Karl. Die Schuldfrage (Zürich: Artemis, 1946). English translation: The Question of German Guilt, trans. E. B. Ashton (New York: Dial Press, 1947).

Jaspers, Karl. Freiheit und Wiedervereinigung: Über Aufgaben deutscher Politik (Munich: Piper, 1960).

Jaspers, Karl. Lebensfragen der deutschen Politik (Munich: Deutscher Taschenbuch Verlag, 1963).

Jeismann, Michael. Mahnmal Mitte: Eine Kontroverse (Cologne: DuMont, 1999).

Jens, Walter, 'Nachdenken über Deutschland: Warnung vor dem Winken aus dem Zuschauerraum', in Neue Rundschau, Vol. 101, No. 1 (1990), 91–3.

Jones, William David. The Lost Debate: German Socialist Intellectuals and Totalitarianism (Urbana: University of Illinois Press, 1999).

Jungk, Robert. 'Veränderung ist möglich', in Frank Blohm and Wolfgang Herzberg (eds), 'Nichts wird mehr so sein, wie es war': Zur Zukunft der beiden deutschen Republiken (Frankfurt/Main: Luchterhand, 1990), 126–32.

Kaes, Anton. From Hitler to Heimat: The Return of History as Film (Cambridge, Mass.: Harvard University Press, 1989).

Kallscheuer, Otto. 'Die Linke, Deutschland und Europa: Versuch, einige Widersprüche zur Sprache zu bringen', in Frank Blohm and Wolfgang Herzberg (eds), 'Nichts wird mehr so sein, wie es war': Zur Zukunft der beiden deutschen Republiken (Frankfurt/Main: Luchterhand, 1990), 133–49.

Kaltenbrunner, Gerd-Klaus (ed.). Sprache und Herrschaft: Die umfunktionierten Wörter (Munich: Herder, 1975).

Kansteiner, Wulf. 'Mandarins in the Public Sphere: Vergangenheitsbewältigung and the Paradigm of Social History in the Federal Republic of Germany', in German Politics and Society, Vol. 17, No. 3 (1999), 84–120.

Kemper, Peter (ed.). Die Zukunft des Politischen: Theoretische Ausblicke auf Hannah Arendt (Frankfurt/Main: Fischer, 1993).

Kesting, Marianne. 'Revolutionäre Geste als Kunst: Karl Heinz Bohrers Auseinanderstzung mit der "Kursbuch-Linken"', in Die Zeit, 3 July 1970.

Khilnani, Sunil. Arguing Revolution: The Intellectual Left in Postwar France (New Haven: Yale University Press, 1993).

Khong, Yuen Foong. Analogies at War: Korea, Dien Bien Phu, and the Vietnam Decisions of 1965 (Princeton: Princeton University Press, 1992).

Kielmannsegg, Peter Graf. 'Grundgesetz über alles', in Die Zeit, 23 February 1990.

Kielmannsegg, Peter Graf. 'Vereinigung ohne Legitimität?', in Merkur, Vol. 47 (1992), 561–75.

Kittel, Manfred. Die Legende von der 'Zweiten Schuld': Vergangenheitsbewältigung in der Ära Adenauer (Berlin: Ullstein, 1993).

Kleinert, Hubert and Mosdorf, Siegfried. Die Renaissance der Politik: Wege ins 21. Jahrhundert (Berlin: Siedler, 1998).

Klemperer, Victor. I Shall Bear Witness: The Diaries of Victor Klemperer 1933–41, trans. Martin Chalmers (London: Weidenfeld and Nicolson, 1998).

Klemperer, Victor. The Diaries of Victor Klemperer 1942–45, trans. Martin Chalmers (London: Weidenfeld and Nicolsen, 1999).

Knabe, Hubertus. Die unterwanderte Republik: Stasi im Westen (Berlin: Propyläen, 1999).

Kniesche, Thomas. '"Das wird nicht aufhören, gegenwärtig zu bleiben." Günter Grass und das Problem der deutschen Schuld', in Hans Adler and Jost Hermand (eds), Günter Grass: Ästhetik des Engagements (Bern: Peter Lang, 1996), 169–97.

Knütter, Hans-Helmuth. Die Faschismus-Keule: Das letzte Aufgebot der Linken (Berlin: Ullstein, 1993).

Kocka, Jürgen. 'Nur keine neuen Sonderwege: Jedes Stück Entwestlichung wäre als Preis für die deutsche Einheit zu hoch', in *Die Zeit*, 19 October 1990.

Kohl, Helmut. 'Für einen produktiven Konflikt', in *Die Zeit*, 4 May 1973.

Kohlstruck, Michael. *Zwischen Erinnerung und Geschichte: Der Nationalsozialismus und die jungen Deutschen* (Berlin: Metropol, 1997).

Koselleck, Reinhart. 'Glühende Lava, zur Erinnerung geronnen', in *Frankfurter Allgemeine Zeitung*, 6 May 1995.

Kracauer, Siegfried. *Die Angestellten: Aus dem neuesten Deutschland* (Frankfurt/Main: Societats, 1930).

Kraushaar, Wolfgang. 'Von der Totalitarismus-zur Faschismustheorie: Zu einem Paradigmenwechsel in der Theoriepolitik der bundesdeutschen Studenetenbewegung', in Claudia Keller (ed.), *Die Nacht hat zwölf Stunden, dann kommt schon der Tag: Antifaschismus – Geschichte und Neubewertung* (Berlin: Aufbau, 1996), 234–51.

Kraushaar, Wolfgang. 'Autoritärer Staat und Antiautoritäre Bewegung: Zum Organisationsreferat von Rudi Dutschke und Hans-Jürgen Krahl auf der 22. Delegiertenkonferenz des SDS in Frankfurt (4.–8. Sept. 1967)', in Wolfgang Kraushaar (ed.), *Frankfurter Schule und Studentenbewegung: Von der Flaschenpost zum Molotowcocktail 1946–1995*, Vol. 3 (Hamburg: Rogner and Bernhard, 1998), 15–33.

Krockow, Christian Graf von. *Die Entscheidung: Eine Untersuchung über Ernst Jünger, Carl Schmitt, Martin Heidegger* (Stuttgart: F. Enke, 1958).

Krockow, Christian Graf von. 'Staatsideologie oder demokratisches Bewußtsein: Die deutsche Alternative', in: *Politische Vierteljahresschrift*, Vol. 9 (1965), 118–31.

Kuby, Erich. *Der Preis der Einheit: Ein deutsches Europe formt sein Gesicht* (Hamburg: Konkret Literatur, 1990).

Kunz, Norbert W. 'Auf der Suche nach eine neuen Utopie des Sozialismus', in Martin Gorholt and Norbert W. Kunz (eds.), *Deutsche Einheit – Deutsche Linke: Reflexionen der politischen und gesellschaftlichen Entwicklung* (Bonn: Bund, 1991), 147–68.

Laak, Dirk van. 'Nicht West, nicht Ost oder Zaungäste auf Bindungssuche', in Hans-Martin Lohmann (ed.), *Extremismus der Mitte: Vom rechten Verständnis deutscher Nation* (Frankfurt/Main: Fischer, 1994), 88–104.

Laak, Dirk van. *Gespräche in der Sicherheit des Schweigens: Carl Schmitt in der Geistesgeschichte der frühen Bundesrepublik* (Berlin: Akademie, 1993).

Laak, Dirk van. 'Trotz und Nachurteil: Rechtsintellektuelle im Anschluß an das "Dritte Reich"', in Wilfried Loth and Bernd-A. Rusinek (eds.), *Verwandlungspolitik: NS-Eliten in der westdeutschen Nachkriegsgesellschaft* (Frankfurt/Main: Campus, 1998), 55–77.

Lamers, Karl (ed.). *Suche nach Deutschland: Deutsche Identität und die Deutschlandpolitik* (Bonn: Europa Union, 1983).

Langbein, Hermann. *Der Auschwitz-Prozeß: Eine Dokumentation*, 2 Vols. (1965; Frankfurt/Main: Büchergilde Gutenberg, 1995).

Langer, Lawrence L. *Admitting the Holocaust* (New York: Oxford University Press, 1995).

Larmore, Charles. *The Morals of Modernity* (Cambridge: Cambridge University Press, 1996).

Lassman, Peter and Speirs, Ronald (eds.). *Weber: Political Writings* (Cambridge: Cambridge University Press, 1994).

Lattmann, Dieter. 'Wie heimatlos ist die Linke heute?', in *Stuttgarter Zeitung*, 8 April 1972.

Lau, Jörg. 'Der normale Verdacht', in *Die Zeit*, 19 November 1998.

Lau, Jörg. *Hans Magnus Enzensberger: Ein öffentliches Leben* (Berlin: Fest, 1999).

Leavis, F. R. (ed.), *Mill on Bentham and Coleridge* (London: Chatto & Windus, 1962).

Leggewie, Claus. *Druck von rechts: Wohin treibt die Bundesrepublik?* (Munich: C. H. Beck, 1993).

Leicht, Robert. 'Einheit durch Beitritt: Warum am Grundgesetz rühren?', in *Die Zeit*, 23 February 1990.

Lepsius, M. Rainer. 'Das Erbe des Nationalsozialismus und die politischen Kulturen der Nachfolgestaaten des "Großdeutschen

Reiches"', in Michael Haller *et al.* (eds), *Kultur und Gesellschaft: Verhandlungen des 24. Deutschen Soziologentages* (Frankfurt/Main: Campus), 247–64.

Lethen, Helmut. *Verhaltenslehren der Kälte: Lebensversuche zwischen den Kriegen* (Frankfurt/Main: Suhrkamp, 1994).

Lettau, Reinhard. 'Täglicher Faschismus: Evidenz aus fünf Monaten', in *Kursbuch*, No. 22 (1970), 1–44.

Lietzmann, Hans. ' "Verfassungspatriotismus" und "Civil Society": Eine Grundlage für Politik in Deutschland?', in Rüdiger Voigt (ed.), *Abschied vom Staat – Rückkehr zum Staat?* (Baden-Baden: Nomos, 1993), 205–27.

Lilla, Mark. 'The Other Velvet Revolution: Continental Liberalism and its Discontents', in *Daedalus*, Vol. 123, No. 2 (1994), 129–57.

Linz, Juan J. 'Some Notes Towards a Comparative Study of Fascism in Sociological Perspective', in Walter Laqueur (ed.), *Fascism: A Reader's Guide* (Aldershot: Scolar, 1991), 3–121.

Litt, Theodor. *Von der Sendung der Philosohie* (Wiesbaden: Dieterich'sche Verlagsbuchhandlung, 1946).

Lohmann, Hans-Martin (ed.). *Extremismus der Mitte: Vom rechten Verständnis deutscher Nation* (Frankfurt/Main: Fischer, 1994).

Lübbe, Hermann. 'Es ist nichts vergessen, aber einiges ausgeheilt: Der Nationalsozialismus im Bewußtsein der deutschen Gegenwart', in *Frankfurter Allgemeine Zeitung*, 24 January 1983.

Lübbe, Hermann. 'Carl Schmitt liberal rezipiert', in Helmut Quaritsch (ed.), *Complexio Oppositorum: Über Carl Schmitt: Vorträge und Diskussionsbeiträge des 28. Sonderseminars 1986 der Hochschule für Verwaltungswissenschaften Speyer* (Berlin: Duncker & Humblot, 1988), 427–40.

Luhmann, Niklas. 'Immer noch Bundesrepublik? Das Erbe und die Zukunft', in Otthein Rammstedt and Gert Schmidt (eds.), *BRD Ade! Vierzig Jahre in Rück-Ansichten* (Frankfurt/Main: Suhrkamp, 1992), 95–100.

Luhmann, Niklas. *Social Systems*, trans. John Bednarz, Jr., with Dirk Baecker (1984; Stanford: Stanford University Press, 1995).

Maclean, Ian *et al.* (eds), *The Political Responsibility of Intellectuals* (Cambridge: Cambridge University Press, 1990).

Maier, Charles S. *The Unmasterable Past: History, Holocaust, and German National Identity* (Cambridge, Mass.: Harvard University Press, 1988).

Maier, Charles S. 'A Surfeit of Memory? Reflections on History, Melancholy and Denial', in *History and Memory*, Vol. 5, No. 2 (1993), 136–52.

Maier, Charles S. *Dissolution: The Crisis of Communism and the End of East Germany* (Princeton: Princeton University Press, 1997).

Major, Patrick. *The Death of the KPD: Communism and Anti-communism in West Germany, 1945–1956* (Oxford: Oxford University Press, 1997).

Mann, Thomas. 'Ansprache im Goethejahr 1949', in *Gesammelte Werke*, Vol. 11 (Frankfurt/Main: S. Fischer, 1960), 481–97.

Mannheim, Karl. 'The Problem of Generations', in *From Karl Mannheim*, ed. Kurt H. Wolff (New Brunswick: Transaction, 1993), 351–98.

Markovits, Andrei and Gorski, Phillip S. *The German Left: Red Green and Beyond* (Cambridge: Polity, 1993).

Marquard, Odo. *Abschied vom Prinzipiellen* (Stuttgart: Reclam, 1981).

Marquard, Odo. *Skepsis und Zustimmung: Philosophische Studien* (Stuttgart: Reclam, 1994).

Märtesheimer, Peter and Frenzel, Ivo (eds.). *Im Kreuzfeuer: Der Fernsehfilm Holocaust: Eine Nation ist betroffen* (Frankfurt/Main: Fischer, 1979).

Mayer-Iswandy, Claudia. 'Ästhetik und Macht: Zur diskursiven Unordnung im vereinten Deutschland', in *German Studies Review*, Vol. 19 (1996), 501–23.

McCole, John. *Walter Benjamin and the Antinomies of Tradition* (Ithaca: Cornell University Press, 1993).

Mehring, Reinhard. *Carl Schmitt zur Einführung* (Hamburg: Junius, 1992).

Meier, Christian. *Deutsche Einheit als Herausforderung: Welche Fundamente für welche Republik?* (Munich: Hanser, 1990).

Meier, Christian. 'Die Republik denken', in *Frankfurter Allgemeine Zeitung*, 29 April 1994.

Meier, Heinrich. *Carl Schmitt & Leo Strauss: The Hidden Dialogue*, trans. J. Harvey Lomax (1988; Chicago: University of Chicago Press, 1995).

Meier-Bergfeld, Peter. 'Über das Hissen der schwarz-rot-goldenen Flagge in Wien', in Heimo Schwilk and Ulrich Schacht (eds.), *Die Selbstbewußte Nation: 'Anschwellender Bocksgesang' und weitere Beiträge zu einer deutschen Debatte* (Berlin: Ullstein, 1994),195–226.

Meinecke, Friedrich. *Die deutsche Katastrophe* (Zurich: Aero, 1946).

Meinecke, Friedrich. *Cosmopolitanism and the National State*, trans. Robert B. Kimber (Princeton: Princeton University Press, 1970).

Meyer, Thomas. *Die Transformation des Politischen* (Frankfurt/Main: Suhrkamp, 1994).

Mitscherlich, Alexander and Margarete. *Die Unfähigkeit zu trauern: Grundlagen kollektiven Verhaltens* (Munich: Piper, 1967). English translation: *The Inability to Mourn: Principles of Collective Behavior*, trans. Beverley R. Placzek (New York: Grove Press, 1975).

Mitscherlich, Alexander. 'Vaterlose Gesellen: Alexander Mitscherlich über den Frankfurter SDS-Kongreß und die Studentenrebellion', in *Der Spiegel*, 8 April 1968.

Mohler, Armin. *Die Konservative Revolution in Deutschland 1918–1932: Grundriss ihrer Weltanschauungen* (Stuttgart: F. Vorwerk, 1950).

Mohler, Armin. *Die Fünfte Republik: Was steht hinter de Gaulle?* (Munich: Piper, 1963).

Mohler, Armin. *Was die Deutschen fürchten: Angst vor der Politik – Angst vor der Geschichte – Angst vor der Macht* (Stuttgart: Seewald, 1966).

Mohler, Armin. *Tendenzwende für Fortgeschrittene* (Munich: Criticón, 1978).

Mohler, Armin (ed.). *Wirklichkeit als Tabu: Anmerkungen zur Lage* (Munich: R. Oldenbourg, 1986).

Mohler, Armin. *Liberalenbeschimpfung: Drei politische Traktate* (Essen: Heitz & Höffkes, 1990).

Mohler, Armin. 'Gleichheit und Differenz', in: *Criticón*, No. 129 (1992), 22–3.

Mohr, Reinhard. *Zaungäste: Die Generation, die nach der Revolte kam* (Frankfurt/Main: Fischer, 1992).

Mommsen, Hans. 'Von Weimar nach Bonn: Zum Demokratieverständnis der Deutschen', in: Axel Schildt and Arnold Sywottek (eds.), *Modernisierung im Wiederaufbau: Die westdeutsche Gesellschaft der 50er Jahre* (Bonn: Dietz, 1993), 745–58.

Mommsen, Wolfgang J. *Nation und Geschichte* (Munich: Piper, 1990).

Moses, A. D. 'The Forty-Fivers: A Generation Between Fascism and Democracy', in *German Politics and Society*, Vol. 17 (1999), 94–126.

Müller, Heiner. *Zur Lage der Nation* (Berlin: Rotbuch, 1990).

Muller, Jerry Z. *The Other God That Failed: Hans Freyer and the Deradicalization of German Conservatism* (Princeton: Princeton University Press, 1987).

Naumann, Klaus. *Der Krieg als Text: Das Jahr 1945 im kulturellen Gedächtnis der Presse* (Hamburg: Hamburger Edition, 1998).

Neaman, Elliot. 'A New Conservative Revolution? Neo-Nationalism, Collective Memory, and the New Right in Germany since Unification', in Hermann Kurthen *et al.* (eds). *Antisemitism and Xenophobia in Germany after Unification* (New York: Oxford University Press, 1997), 190–208.

Neaman, Elliot Y. *A Dubious Past: Ernst Jünger and the Politics of Literature after Nazism* (Berkeley: University of California Press, 1999).

Negt, Oskar. 'Der gebrochene Anfang', in Frank Blohm and Wolfgang Herzberg (eds), *'Nichts wird mehr so sein, wie es war': Zur Zukunft der beiden deutschen Republiken* (Frankfurt/Main: Luchterhand, 1990), 19–44.

Negt, Oskar and Kluge, Alexander. *Maßverhältnisse des Politischen: 15 Vorschläge zum Unterscheidungsvermögen* (Frankfurt/Main: S. Fischer, 1992).

Negt, Oskar (ed.). *Der Fall Fonty: 'Ein weites Feld' von Günter Grass im Spiegel der Kritik* (Göttingen: Steidl, 1996).

Neuhaus, Volker. *Schreiben gegen die verstreichende Zeit: Zu Leben und Werk von Günter Grass* (Munich: Deutscher Taschenbuch Verlag, 1997).

Niethammer, Lutz. *Posthistoire: Has History Come to an End?*, trans. Patrick Camiller (London: Verso, 1992).

Niethammer, Lutz. 'Geht der deutsche Sonderweg weiter?', in Antonia Grunenberg (ed.), *Welche Geschichte wählen wir?* (Hamburg: Junius, 1992), 23–54.

Noack, Paul. *Deutschland, deine Intellektuellen: Die Kunst, sich ins Abseits zu stellen* (Berlin: Ullstein, 1991).

Noelle-Neumann, Elisabeth and Köcher, Renate. *Die verletzte Nation: Über den Versuch der Deutschen, ihren Charakter zu ändern* (Stuttgart, Deutsche Verlags-Anstalt, 1987).

Nolte, Ernst. *Der Faschismus in seiner Epoche: Die Action française, der italienische Faschismus, der Nationalsozialismus* (Munich: Piper, 1963). English translation: *Three Faces of Fascism*, trans. Leila Vennewitz (London: Weidenfeld and Nicolson, 1965).

Nolte, Ernst. 'Vergangenheit, die nicht vergehen ist: Eine Rede, die geschrieben, aber nicht gehalten werden konnte', in *'Historikerstreit': Die Dokumentation der Kontroverse um die Einzigartigkeit der nationalsozialistischen Judenvernichtung* (Munich: Piper, 1987), 39–47.

Nolte, Ernst. 'Untergang der Bundesrepublik? Zur Frage der Kontinuität in der Nachkriegsgeschichte', in *Frankfurter Allgemeine Zeitung*, 5 September 1990.

Nolte, Ernst. 'Die unvollständige Revolution', in *Frankfurter Allgemeine Zeitung*, 24 January 1991.

Nolte, Ernst. 'Links und Rechts. Über Geschichte und Aktualität einer politischen Alternative', in Heimo Schwilk and Ulrich Schacht (eds), *Die Selbstbewußte Nation: 'Anschwellender Bocksgesang' und weitere Beiträge zu einer deutschen Debatte* (Berlin: Ullstein, 1994), 145–62.

Oevermann, Ulrich. 'Zwei Staaten oder Einheit? Der "dritte Weg" als Fortsetzung des deutschen Sonderweges', in *Merkur*, Vol. 44 (1990), 91–100.

Osborne, Peter. 'Times (Modern), Modernity (Conservative)? Notes on the Persistence of a Temporal Motif', in *New Formations*, No. 28 (1996), 132–41.

Palonen, Kari. *Politik als Handlungsbegriff: Horizontwandel des Politikbegriff in Deutschland 1890–1933* (Helsinki: The Finnish Society of Sciences and Letters, 1985).

Pannier, Jörg. *Das Vexierbild des Politischen: Dolf Sternberger als politischer Aristoteliker* (Berlin: Akademie, 1996).

Parkes, K. Stuart. *Writers and Politics in West Germany* (Beckenham: Croom Helm, 1986).

Parkes, Stuart. 'Introduction', in Arthur Williams *et al.* (eds), *German Literature at a Time of Change 1989–1990: German Unity and German Identity in Literary Perspective* (Bern: Peter Lang, 1991), 1–20.

Parkhurst Clark, Priscilla. *Literary France: The Making of a Culture* (Berkeley: University of California Press, 1987).

Peitsch, Helmut. 'West German Reflections on the Role of the Writer in the Light of Reactions to 9 November 1989', in Arthur Williams *et al.* (eds), *German Literature at a Time of Change 1989–1991: German Unity and German Identity in Literary Perspective* (Bern: Peter Lang, 1991), 155–86.

Pensky, Max. 'On the use and abuse of memory: Habermas, anamnestic solidarity, and the *Historikerstreit*', in *Philosophy and Social Criticism*, Vol. 15 (1989), 351–80.

Pensky, Max. 'Jürgen Habermas and the antinomies of the intellectual', in Peter Dews (ed.), *Habermas: A Critical Reader* (Oxford: Blackwell, 1999), 211–37.

Peukert, Detlev J. K. *The Weimar Republic: The Crisis of Classical Modernity*, trans. Richard Daveson (1987; London: Penguin, 1991).

Peukert, Detlev J. K. 'The Genesis of the "Final Solution" from the Spirit of Science', in Thomas Childers and Jane Caplan (eds), *Reevaluating the Third Reich* (New York: Holmes & Meier, 1993), 234–52.

Plessner, Helmuth. *Die verspätete Nation* (1935; Stuttgart: W. Kohlhammer, 1959).

Plessner, Helmuth, 'Wie muß der deutsche Nation-Begriff heute aussehen?', in *Merkur*, Vol. 21 (1967), 211–23.

Plessner, Helmuth. 'Grenzen der Gemeinschaft: Eine Kritik des sozialen Radikalismus', in *Gesammelte Werke*, Vol. 5, eds Günter Dux et al. (Frankfurt/Main: Suhrkamp, 1985), 7–133.

Preuß, Ulrich K. *Revolution, Fortschritt und Verfassung: Zu einem neuen Verfassungsverständnis* (Frankfurt/Main: Fischer, 1994).

Prinz, Michael and Zitelmann, Rainer (eds), *Nationalsozialismus und Modernisierung* (Darmstadt: Wissenschaftliche Buchgesellschaft, 1994).

Prokop, Siegfried (ed.), *Die kurze Zeit der Utopie: Die 'zweite' DDR im vergessenen Jahr 1989/90* (Berlin: Elefanten Press, 1994).

Quint, Peter E. *The Imperfect Union: Constitutional Structures of German Unification* (Princeton: Princeton University Press, 1997).

Rabinbach, Anson and Zipes, Jack. (eds). *Germans and Jews since the Holocaust: The Changing Situation in West Germany* (New York: Holmes & Meier, 1986).

Rabinbach, Anson. 'Editor's Introduction', in *New German Critique*, No. 44 (1988), 3–4.

Rabinbach, Anson. 'The Jewish Question in the German Question', in *New German Critique*, No. 44 (1988), 159–92.

Rabinbach, Anson. *In the Shadow of Catastrophe: German Intellectuals between Apocalypse and Enlightenment* (Berkeley: University of California Press, 1997).

Raddatz, Fritz J. 'Die linke Krücke Hoffnung', in *Die Zeit*, 14 September 1990.

Rammstedt, Otto and Schmidt, Gert (eds). *BRD ade! Vierzig Jahre in Rück-Ansichten* (Frankfurt/Main: Suhrkamp, 1992).

Raulff, Ulrich. 'Das geteilte Gedächtnis', in *Frankfurter Allgemeine Zeitung*, 10 November 1998.

Richter, Hans Werner. 'Fünfzehn Jahre', in *Almanach der Gruppe 47 1947–1962* (Reinbek: Rowohlt, 1962), 7–16.

Richter, Hans Werner. 'In einem zweigeteilten Land', in Horst Krüger (ed.), *Was ist heute links? Thesen und Theorien zu einer politischen Position* (Munich: Paul List, 1963), 94–100.

Richter, Hans Werner. *Briefe*, ed. Sabine Cofalla (Munich: Hanser, 1997).

Ringer, Fritz K. *The German Mandarins: The German Academic Community 1890–1933* (Cambridge, Mass.: Harvard University Press, 1969).

Ritter, Gerhard. *Europa und die deutsche Frage* (Munich: Bruckmann, 1948).

Ritter, Henning. 'Translatio rei publicae: Der Umzug von Regierung und Parlament als Gründungsakt der Berliner Republik', in *Frankfurter Allgemeine Zeitung*, 18 December 1996.

Rödel, Ulrich et al. *Die demokratische Frage* (Frankfurt/Main: Suhrkamp, 1989).

Röhl, Karl Rainer. *Linke Lebenslügen: Eine überfällige Abrechnung* (Berlin: Ullstein, 1994).

Röpke, Wilhelm. *Die deutsche Frage* (Erlenbach-Zurich: Eugen-Rentsch, 1945).

Rorty, Richard. *Contingency, Irony and Solidarity* (Cambridge: Cambridge University Press, 1989).

Rorty, Richard. *Objectivism, Relativism, and Truth* (Cambridge: Cambridge University Press, 1991).

Ross, Jan. 'Staatsfeindschaft: Anmerkungen zum neuen Vulgärliberalismus', in *Merkur*, Vol. 51 (1997), 93–194.

Rousso, Henry. *The Vichy Syndrome: History and Memory in France since 1944*, trans. Arthur Goldhammer (Cambridge, Mass.: Harvard University Press, 1991).

Rühmkorf, Peter. *Tabu I: Tagebücher 1989–1991* (Reinbek: Rowohlt, 1995).

Rühmkorf, Peter. *Die Jahre, die Ihr kennt: Anfälle und Erinnerungen* (1972; Reinbek: Rowohlt, 1999).

Ruth, Arne. 'Postwar Europe: The Capriciousness of Universal Values', in *Daedalus*, Vol. 126, No. 3 (1997), 241–76.

Sa'adah, Anne. *Germany's Second Chance: Trust, Justice, and Democratization* (Cambridge, Mass.: Harvard University Press, 1998).

Safranski, Rüdiger. 'Destruktion und Lust. Über die Wiederkehr des Bösen', in Heimo Schwilk and Ulrich Schacht (eds), *Die Selbstbewußte Nation: 'Anschwellender Bocksgesang' und weitere Beiträge zu einer deutschen Debatte* (Berlin: Ullstein, 1994), 237–48.

Salamun, Kurt. *Karl Jaspers* (Munich: C. H. Beck, 1985).

Schacht, Ulrich,. 'Stigma und Sorge. Über deutsche Identität nach Auschwitz', in Heimo Schwilk and Ulrich Schacht (eds). *Die Selbstbewußte Nation: 'Anschwellender Bocksgesang' und weitere Beiträge zu einer deutschen Debatte* (Berlin: Ullstein, 1994), 57–68.

Schäuble, Wolfgang. 'Der Platz in der Mitte: Sonderwege und Staatsräson', in *Frankfurter Allgemeine Zeitung*, 6 July 1994.

Schelsky, Helmut. *Die skeptische Generation: Eine Soziologie der deutschen Jugend* (Düsseldorf: Eugen Diederich, 1957).

Schelsky, Helmut. *Die Arbeit tun die anderen: Klassenkampf und Priesterherrschaft der Intellektuellen* (Opladen: Westdeutscher Verlag, 1975).

Schelsky, Helmut. 'Über das Staatsbewußtsein', in *Die politische Meinung*, No. 185 (1979), 30–5.

Schildt, Axel. *Moderne Zeiten: Freizeit, Massenmedien und 'Zeitgeist' in den 50er Jahren* (Hamburg: Christians, 1995).

Schildt, Axel. 'Der Umgang mit der NS-Vergangenheit in der Öffentlichkeit der Nachkriegszeit', in Wilfried Loth and Bernd-A. Rusinek (eds), *Verwandlungspolitik: NS-Eliten in der westdeutschen Nachkriegsgesellschaft* (Frankfurt/Main: Campus, 1998), 19–54.

Schildt, Axel. *Konservatismus in Deutschland: Von den Anfängen im 18. Jahrhundert bis zur Gegenwart* (Munich: C. H. Beck, 1998).

Schildt, Axel. *Ankunft im Westen: Ein Essay zur Erfolgsgeschichte der Bundesrepublik* (Frankfurt/Main: S. Fischer, 1999).

Schildt, Axel. *Zwischen Abendland und Amerika: Studien zur westdeutschen Ideenlandschaft der 50er Jahre* (Munich: R. Oldenbourg, 1999).

Schirrmacher, Frank. 'Walser: Friedenspreisträger 1998', in *Frankfurter Allgemeine Zeitung*, 5 June 1998.

Schlant, Ernestine. *The Language of Silence: West German Literature and the Holocaust* (New York: Routledge, 1999).

Schmid, Wilhelm. *Was geht uns Deutschland an?* (Frankfurt/Main: Suhrkamp, 1993).

Schmidt, Dieter. 'Wird die "Gruppe 47" überschätzt? WdA-Interview mit dem Schriftsteller Martin Walser', in *Welt der Arbeit*, 10 May 1963.

Schmitt, Carl. *Verfassungslehre* (1928; Berlin: Duncker & Humblot, 1970).

Schmitt, Carl. *The Concept of the Political*, trans. George Schwab (1934; New Brunswick, NJ: Rutgers University Press, 1976).

Schmitt, Carl. *The Crisis of Parliamentary Democracy*, trans. Ellen Kennedy (1926; Cambridge, Mass.: MIT Press, 1985).

Schmitt, Carl. *Political Romanticism*, trans. Guy Oakes (1925; Cambridge, Mass.: MIT Press, 1985).

Schmitt, Carl. *Political Theology: Four Chapters on the Concept of Sovereignty*, trans. George Schwab (1934; Cambridge, Mass.: MIT Press, 1985).

Schmitt, Carl. 'Das Zeitalter der Neutralisierungen und Entpolitisierungen', in *Positionen und Begriffe im Kampf mit Weimar – Genf – Versailles 1923–1939* (1940; Berlin: Duncker & Humblot, 1988), 120–32.

Schmitt, Carl. *Glossarium: Aufzeichnungen der Jahre 1947–1951* (Berlin: Duncker & Humblot, 1991).

Schneider, Peter. *Lenz* (Berlin: Rotbuch, 1973).

Schneider, Peter. 'Man kann sogar ein Erdbeben verpassen', in *Die Zeit*, 27 April 1990.

Schneider, Peter. 'Die Angst der Deutschen vor den Idealen', in *Frankfurter Allgemeine Zeitung*, 13 May 1991.

Schneider, Peter. 'Gefangen in der Geschichte', in *Der Spiegel*, 18 January 1993.

Schoch, Bruno. 'Renaissance der Mitte – Ein fragwürdiger Bestandteil deutscher Ideologie kehrt wieder', in *Deutschlands Einheit und Europas Zukunft*, ed. Bruno Schoch (Frankfurt/Main: Suhrkamp, 1992), 120–49.

Schoenbaum, David and Pond, Elizabeth. *The German Question and other German Questions* (London: Macmillan, 1996).

Schöllgen, Gregor. *Angst vor der Macht. Die Deutschen und ihre Außenpolitik* (Berlin: Ullstein, 1993).

Schörken, Rolf. *Jugend 1945: Politisches Denken und Lebensgeschichte* (Frankfurt/Main: Fischer, 1994).

Schröder, Richard. 'Es ist doch nicht alles schlecht', in *Die Zeit*, 31 May 1991.

Schrenck-Notzing. Caspar von. *Charakterwäsche: Die amerikanische Besatzung in Deutschland und ihre Folgen* (Stuttgart: Seewald, 1965).

Schuh, Franz. 'Der letzte Ästhet', in *Die Zeit*, 2 April 1998.

Schulze, Hagen. 'In der Mitte Europas: Ein normaler Nationalstaat', in Josef Becker (ed.), *Wiedervereinigung in Mitteleuropa: Außen- und Innenansichten zur staatlichen Einheit Deutschlands* (Munich: Ernst Vögel, 1992), 159–73.

Schulze, Hagen. *Staat und Nation in der europäischen Geschichte* (Munich: C. H. Beck, 1995).

Schwarz, Hans-Peter. 'Das Ende der Identitätsneurose', in *Rheinischer Merkur*, 7 September 1990.

Schwarz, Hans-Peter. *Die Zentralmacht Europas: Deutschlands Rückkehr auf die Weltbühne* (Berlin: Siedler, 1994).

Schwilk, Heimo and Schacht, Ulrich (eds). *Die Selbstbewußte Nation: 'Anschwellender Bocksgesang' und weitere Beiträge zu einer deutschen Debatte* (Berlin: Ullstein, 1994).

Sebald, W. G. *The Emigrants*, trans. Michael Hulse (New York: New Directions, 1997).

Sebald, W. G. *Luftkrieg und Literatur* (Munich: Hanser, 1999).

Seebacher-Brandt, Brigitte. 'Ein Linker träumt vom Überleben der DDR', in *Rheinischer Merkur*, 14 September 1989.

Seebacher-Brandt, Brigitte. *Politik im Rücken, Zeitgeist im Sinn* (Berlin: Ullstein, 1995).

Seel, Martin. *Die Kunst der Entzweiung: Zum Begriff der ästhetischen Rationalität* (Frankfurt/Main: Suhrkamp, 1985).

Seibt, Gustav. 'Gespräch als Gesetz', in *Frankfurter Allgemeine Zeitung*, 16 June 1989.

Semler, Christian. 'Der Weg ins Freie: Verrat und Identität der Linken', in *Kursbuch*, No. 116 (1994), 25–36.

Serres, Michael. 'Das Sakrament des Büffels: Zum Umgang mit dem Nationalsozialismus

im Frühwerk Heinrich Bölls', in Stephan Braese *et al.* (eds), *Deutsche Nachkriegsliteratur und der Holocaust* (Frankfurt/Main: Campus, 1998), 213–27.

Simon, Dieter. 'Die Einheit des Rechts in der Vielheit der Systeme', in *Frankfurter Allgemeine Zeitung*, 8 December 1992.

Sloterdijk, Peter. *Critique of Cynical Reason*, trans. Michael Eldred (1983; Minneapolis: University of Minnesota Press, 1987).

Smelser, Roland and Zitelmann, Rainer (eds). *Die braune Elite: 22 biographische Skizzen* (Darmstadt: Wissenschaftliche Buchgesellschaft, 1990).

Smoltczyck, Alexander. 'Ein Butt und drei Bücklinge', in *Der Spiegel*, 13 December 1999.

Söllner, Alfons. *Deutsche Politikwissenschaftler in der Emigration: Studien zu ihrer Akkulturation und Wirkungsgeschichte* (Opladen: Westdeutscher Verlag, 1996).

Sommer, Theo (ed.). *Denken an Deutschland: Zum Problem der Wiedervereinigung* (Hamburg: Nannen, 1966).

Sontheimer, Kurt. *Antidemokratisches Denken in der Weimarer Republik: Die politischen Ideen des deutschen Nationalismus zwischen 1918 und 1933* (Munich: Nymphenburger, 1962).

Sontheimer, Kurt. *Das Elend unserer Intellektuellen: Linke Theorie in der Bundesrepublik Deutschland* (Hamburg: Hoffmann und Campe, 1976).

Sontheimer, Kurt. *Von Deutschlands Republik* (Stuttgart: Deutsche Verlags-Anstalt, 1991).

Speicher, Stephan. 'Totentänze für die zivile Republik: Über Günter Grass, den Repräsentanten und Dichter des Nachkriegs-Deutschland, und die Beschwörung der Vergangenheit', in *Berliner Zeitung*, 16 October 1997.

Sperber, Manès. 'Vom Mißgeschick deutscher Intellektueller in der Politik: Erwägungen eines aufmerksamen Zeitgenossen', in *Süddeutsche Zeitung*, 31 December 1977.

Stein, Dieter. 'Niederwertung der Konservativen', in *Junge Freiheit*, No. 4 (1992), 2.

Stein, Dieter. 'Der metapolitische Holzweg der Rechten', in *Junge Freiheit*, 14 February 1997.

Stern, Frank. *The Whitewashing of the Yellow Badge: Antisemitism and Philosemitism in Postwar Germany* (Oxford: Pergamon, 1992).

Stern, Fritz. *The Politics of Cultural Despair: A Study in the Rise of the Germanic Ideology* (Berkeley: University of California Press, 1961).

Sternberger, Dolf. 'Jaspers und der Staat', in Klaus Piper (ed.), *Karl Jaspers: Werk und Wirkung* (Munich: Piper, 1963), 133–41.

Sternberger, Dolf. 'Böll, der Staat und die Gnade', in *Frankfurter Allgemeine Zeitung*, 2 February 1972.

Sternberger, Dolf, 'Verfassungspatriotismus', in *Frankfurter Allgemeine Zeitung*, 23 May 1979.

Sternberger, Dolf. *Staatsfreundschaft* [*Schriften*, Vol. 4] (Frankfurt/Main: Suhrkamp, 1980).

Sternberger, Dolf. *Die Politik und der Friede* (Frankfurt/Main: Suhrkamp, 1986).

Sternhell, Zeev. *Neither Right nor Left: Fascist Ideology in France*, trans. David Maisel (Princeton: Princeton University Press, 1996).

Strauß, Botho. *Die Erinnerung an einen, der nur einen Tag zu Gast war* (Munich: Hanser, 1985).

Strauß, Botho. 'Anschwellender Bocksgesang', in *Der Spiegel*, 8 February 1993.

Stürmer, Michael. 'Geschichte in geschichtslosem Land', in *Frankfurter Allgemeine Zeitung*, 25 April 1986.

Süskind, Patrick. 'Deutschland, eine Midlife-Crisis', in *Der Spiegel*, 17 September 1990.

Swartz, David. *Culture and Power: The Sociology of Pierre Bourdieu* (Chicago: University of Chicago Press, 1997).

Syberberg, Hans Jürgen. *Vom Unglück und Glück der Kunst in Deutschland nach dem letzten Kriege* (Munich: Matthes & Seitz, 1990).

Taguieff, Pierre-André. *La République menacée* (Paris: textuel, 1996).

Templin, Wolfgang. 'Die Emanzipation der DDR und die hilflose wetsdeutsche Linke', in: Helga Grebing *et al.* (eds.). *Sozialismus in Europa: Festschrift für Willy Brandt* (Essen: Klartext, 1989).

Thierse, Wolfgang. 'Überlegungen zur Zukunft der Linken in Deutschland', in: Michael Müller and Wolfgang Thierse (eds), *Deutsche Ansichten: Die Republik im Übergang* (Bonn: J. H. W. Dietz Nachf., 1992), 85–104.

Torpey, John. *Intellectuals, Socialism and Dissent: The East German Opposition and its Legacy* (Minneapolis: University of Minnesota Press, 1995).

Trauberg, Ursula. *Vorleben* (Frankfurt/Main: Suhrkamp, 1968).

Treitschke, Heinrich von. 'Bundesstaat und Einheitsstaat', in *Politische Schriften* (Leipzig: Verlag von S. Hirzel, 1903), 77–242.

Trommler, Frank. 'Die nachgeholte Résistance: Politik und Gruppenethos im historischen Zusammenhang', in Justus Fetscher *et al.* (eds), *Die Gruppe 47 in der Geschichte der Bundesrepublik* (Würzburg: Königshausen & Neumann, 1991), 9–22.

Vad, Erich. *Strategie und Sicherheitspolitik: Perspektiven im Werk von Carl Schmitt* (Opalden: Westdeutscher Verlag, 1996).

Van der Will, Wilfried. 'From the 1940s to the 1990s: the critical intelligentsia's changing role in the Federal Republic', in *Debatte*, Vol. 5 (1997), 25–48.

Venohr, Wolfgang (ed.). *Ohne Deutschland geht es nicht* (Krefeld: Sinus, 1985).

Venohr, Wolfgang. *Die deutsche Einheit kommt bestimmt* (Bergisch-Gladbach: Gustav Lübbe, 1982).

Villa, Dana R. *Arendt and Heidegger: The Fate of the Political* (Princeton: Princeton University Press, 1996).

Viroli, Maurizio. *For Love of Country: An Essay on Patriotism* (Oxford: Oxford University Press, 1995).

Vollmer, Antje. 'Tips für David: Plädoyer für eine ökologische Konföderation', in Frank Blohm and Wolfgang Herzberg (eds), *'Nichts wird mehr so sein, wie es war': Zur Zukunft der beiden deutschen Republiken* (Frankfurt/Main: Luchterhand, 1990), 117–25.

Vollmer, Antje. *Die schöne Macht der Vernunft: Auskünfte über eine Generation* (Berlin: Verlag der Nation, 1991).

Vollmer, Antje. 'Woher kommt diese Wut?', in *Der Spiegel*, 15 November 1993.

Vollrath, Ernst. 'Wie ist Carl Schmitt an seinen Begriff des Politischengekommen?', in *Zeitschrift für Politik*, Vol. 36, No. 2 (1989), 151–66.

Vollrath, Ernst. 'Hannah Arendt bei den Linken', in Antonia Grunenberg and Lothar Probst (eds), *Einschnitte: Hannah Arendts politisches Denken heute* (Bremen: Edition Temmen, 1995), 9–22.

Wagenbach, Klaus. 'Intellektuelle an der Wahlfront', in *Die Weltwoche*, 17 September 1965.

Wagenbach, Klaus et al. (eds). *Vaterland, Muttersprache: Offene Briefe, Reden, Aufsätze, Gedichte, Manifeste, Polemiken* (Berlin: Wagenbach, 1995).

Wagner, Richard. 'Für eine Linke ohne Sozialismus', in *Kursbuch*, No. 104 (1991), 55–64.

Waine, Anthony. *Martin Walser* (Munich: C. H. Beck, 1980).

Walser, Martin (ed.). *Die Alternative oder Brauchen wir eine neue Regierung?* (Reinbek: Rowohlt, 1961).

Walser, Martin. *Erfahrungen und Leseerfahrungen* (Frankfurt/Main: Suhrkamp, 1966).

Walser, Martin. *Fiction* (Frankfurt/Main: Suhrkamp, 1970).

Walser, Martin. *Die Gallistl'sche Krankheit* (Frankfurt/Main: Suhrkamp, 1972).

Walser, Martin. *Wie und wovon handelt Literatur: Aufsätze und Reden* (Frankfurt/Main: Suhrkamp, 1973).

Walser, Martin (ed.). *Die Würde am Werktag* (Frankfurt/Main: Fischer, 1980).

Walser, Martin. *Dorle und Wolf* (Frankfurt/Main: Suhrkamp, 1987).

Walser, Martin. *Über Deutschland reden* (Frankfurt: Suhrkamp, 1989).

Walser, Martin. *Auskunft: 22 Gespräche aus 28 Jahren*, ed. Klaus Siblewski (Frankfurt/Main: Suhrkamp, 1991).

Walser, Martin. *Zauber und Gegenzauber: Aufsätze und Gedichte* (Eggingen: Edition Isele, 1995).

Walser, Martin. *Deutsche Sorgen* (Frankfurt/Main: Suhrkamp, 1997).

Walser, Martin. *Ein Springender Brunnen* (Frankfurt/Main: Suhrkamp, 1998).

Walser, Martin. 'Die Banalität des Guten: Erfahrungen beim Verfassen einer Sonntagsrede aus Anlaß der Verleihung des Friedenspreis des Deutschen Buchhandels', in *Frankfurter Allgemeine Zeitung*, 12 October 1998.

Wehler, Hans-Ulrich. 'Aufforderung zum Irrweg', in *Der Spiegel*, 24 September 1990.

Wehler, Hans-Ulrich. 'Von der Herrschaft zum Habitus', in *Die Zeit*, 25 October 1996.

Weiss, Reinhard (ed.). 'Ich habe ein Wunschpotential': Gespräche mit Martin Walser* (Frankfurt/Main: Suhrkamp, 1998).

Weißmann, Karlheinz. *Rückruf in die Geschichte: Die deutsche Herausforderung: Alte Gefahren – neue Chancen* (Berlin: Ullstein, 1993).

Weißmann, Karlheinz. 'Arnold Gehlen: Von der Aktualität eines zu Unrecht Vergessenen', in *Criticón*, No. 153 (1997), 31–6.

Weizsäcker, Richard von. 'Der Streit wird gefährlich', in *Frankfurter Allgemeine Zeitung*, 20 November 1998.

Westphalen, Joseph von. 'Das große Fressen. Letzte Polemik gegen die deutsche Einheit', in *Die Zeit*, 18 March 1990.

Weyrauch, Wolfgang (ed.). *Ich lebe in der Bundesrepublik: Fünfzehn Deutsche über Deutschland* (Munich: List, 1961).

Wiesel, Elie. *Die Nacht zu begraben, Elischa* (Munich: Bechtle, 1963).

Wiggershaus, Rolf. *The Frankfurt School: Its History, Theories and Political Significance*, trans. Michael Robertson (1988; Cambridge: Polity, 1990).

Willke, Helmut. *Ironie des Staates: Grundlinien einer Staatstheorie polyzentrischer Gesellschaft* (Frankfurt/Main: Suhrkamp, 1992).

Willms, Bernard. *Kritik und Politik: Jürgen Habermas oder das politische Defizit der 'Kritischen Theorie'* (Frankfurt/Main: Suhrkamp, 1973).

Willms, Bernard (ed.). *Handbuch zur deutschen Nation*, 4 Vols. (Tübingen: Hohenrain, 1988).

Wittstock, Uwe. 'Wieviel Literatur im Leben, wieviel Politik in der Poesie? Eine Umfrage unter deutschsprachigen Schriftstellern der Jahrgänge 1950 bis 1960', in *Neue Rundschau*, Vol. 103, No. 2 (1992), 95–130.

Wolf, Christa. *Auf dem Weg nach Tabou* (Cologne: Kiepenheuer & Witsch, 1994).

Woodstock Road Editorial, *Interview with Lord Dahrendorf*, November 1994 [unpublished].

Young, James E. *The Texture of Memory: Holocaust Memorials and Meaning* (New Haven: Yale University Press, 1993).

Zagajewski, Adam. 'Lobrede auf einen strengen Deutschlehrer: Was wir Günter Grass verdanken, habt ihr nie begriffen', in *Frankfurter Allgemeine Zeitung*, 30 November 1999.

Zelikow, Philip and Rice, Condoleezza. *Germany Unified and Europe Transformed: A Study in Statecraft* (Cambridge, Mass.: Harvard University Press, 1997).

Zens, Maria. 'Vergangenheit verlegen: Zur Wiederherstellung nationaler Größe im Hause Ullstein', in *Blätter für deutsche und internationale Politik*, Vol. 38 (1993), 1364–75.

Zimmer, Mattias. 'Return of the Mittellage? The Discourse of the Centre in German Foreign Policy', in *German Politics*, Vol. 6 (1997), 23–38.

Zitelmann, Rainer. *Hitler: Selbstverständnis eines Revolutionärs* (Darmstadt: Wissenschaftliche Buchgesellschaft, 1990).

Zitelmann, Rainer. *Adenauers Gegner: Streiter für die Einheit* (Erlangen: Straube, 1991).

Zitelmann, Rainer. 'Uncomfortable Questions', in Harold James and Marla Stone (eds). *When the Wall came down: Reactions to German Unification* (London: Routledge, 1992), 106–7.

Zitelmann, Rainer et al. (eds). *Westbindung? Chancen und Risiken für Deutschland* (Berlin: Propyläen, 1993).

Zitelmann, Rainer. *Wohin treibt unsere Republik?* (Berlin: Ullstein, 1994).

Index